For Bobbi,
with many congratulations,
John

THE GRUPPE 47 FIFTY YEARS ON
A RE-APPRAISAL OF ITS LITERARY
AND POLITICAL SIGNIFICANCE

GERMAN MONITOR No. 45
General Editor: Ian Wallace

THE GRUPPE 47 FIFTY YEARS ON
A RE-APPRAISAL OF ITS LITERARY
AND POLITICAL SIGNIFICANCE

Edited by

Stuart Parkes
and John J. White

Amsterdam - Atlanta, GA 1999

∞ The paper on which this book is printed meets the requirements of "ISO 9706:1994, Information and documentation - Paper for documents - Requirements for permanence".

ISBN: 90-420-0687-0 (bound)
©Editions Rodopi B.V., Amsterdam - Atlanta, GA 1999
Printed in The Netherlands

Table of Contents

ACKNOWLEDGEMENTS

The editors gratefully acknowledge the support and financial assistance given by the following people and institutions. All helped to make possible either the original conference or this publication:

- the Austrian Cultural Institute, London, in particular the director Dr Emil Brix
- the German Academic Exchange Service, London, in particular the then director Dr Christiane Gabriel
- the Goethe Institute, London, in particular the director Herr Albert Wassener and Frau Wilderotter-Ikonomou
- the Institute of Germanic Studies, University of London, in particular the then director E. M. Batley, the deputy director Prof. John Flood, the Institute Librarian William Abbey and Karin Hellmer and Jane Lewin of the administrative staff
- Department of German, King's College London
- Centre for European Studies, University of Sunderland
- Mrs Ann C. Weaver for editorial assistance
- the Rowohlt Verlag for permission to reproduce poems by Peter Rühmkorf.

Stuart Parkes, Sunderland; John White, London;
April 1999

STUART PARKES, JOHN J. WHITE

Introduction

The contributions in this volume are based on papers delivered at a three-day symposium entitled 'Die Gruppe 47 in der deutschen und österreichischen Literatur und Gesellschaft' which was hosted jointly by the Goethe Institute, London and the University of London's Institute of Germanic Studies in September 1997. Contributors were invited to investigate aspects of the pre-history and evolution of the Gruppe 47, the political and cultural context of the enterprise's early years, its significance within Austrian and German literary life (both West and East German), as well as to assess the stimulus which the Group's meetings and ethos gave to the work of individual writers.

The first day's proceedings, which took place at the Goethe Institute, were rounded off by a panel discussion dedicated to the role played by writers' associations such as the Gruppe 47 within the literary life of the German-speaking countries. The panel comprised the guest of honour, the writer Jürgen Becker, winner of the 1967 Preis der Gruppe 47 for his prose work *Ränder*, the critic and broadcaster Martin Lüdke of the Südwestfunk, together with four academic specialists in the literature of the period: Keith Bullivant (University of Miami), Katrin Kohl (Jesus College, Oxford), Timm Menke (Portland State University) and Rhys Williams (University of Wales, Swansea). Whilst the evening's discussion ranged over possible analogues to the Gruppe 47 and the role groups had played in German cultural life, and the importance of the Gruppe 47 (as an economic, intellectual and political focal point) in the Western zones of occupation and the subsequent Federal Republic, what emerged was the extent to which the Group should be seen as *sui generis*, owing its influence principally to the eminent guiding role played by its founder Hans Werner Richter.

By a happy but unplanned coincidence, the second day of the London symposium saw the German publication of what has already been acclaimed as one of the most important sources of information on the history of the Gruppe 47: Sabine Cofalla's meticulously annotated

scholarly edition of Hans Werner Richter's correspondence.[1] The
conference organisers, mindful of the difficulties faced by those
attending early meetings of the Gruppe 47 when wartime damage to the
transport infrastucture had not been fully repaired, were relieved that
Dr Cofalla was able to fly out from London in mid-symposium to be
present at the Carl Hanser Verlag's Munich launch of her work and yet
be back at the Germanic Institute the following day to give her own
stimulating paper on the Gruppe 47 as a generational phenomenon.
There can hardly have been any contributors to the symposium who
were not sent back to reconsider parts of their papers in the light of the
correspondence's mine of new first-hand information about the various
phases of the Group's history and Hans Werner Richter's importance
for a whole range of German writers.

At a time when an appreciation of the Group's considerable
contribution to the rebuilding and consolidating of post-war German-
language literature, not to mention its role in encouraging it to assume a
sense of social responsibility, risks becoming lost among the less
edifying memories of the various feuds and squabbles that marked the
years immediately before its demise and as a result of the changed
agenda of post-unification Germany, it was salutary to be so forcefully
reminded by Jürgen Becker of just how formative and supportive a
factor contact with the Gruppe 47 could be for a young writer. Besides
taking part in the panel discussion, Herr Becker also made a welcome
contribution to the symposium by giving a reading from his latest novel
Der fehlende Rest.[2]

*   *   *

In July 1969, almost two years after student demonstrators had
interrupted the last regular meeting of the Gruppe 47, a resigned Hans
Werner Richter wrote to Wolfgang Hildesheimer: 'Unsere Zeit läuft
langsam aus. Die letzten zwei Jahrzehnte haben uns gehört. Die
kommenden gehören uns nicht mehr. So habe ich jetzt auch die
»Gruppe 47« beerdigt, in meiner eigenen Brust, ein seltsames Stück
schöner Erinnerungen. Die »Hochzeit« der Literatur läuft nicht mehr
aus. Sie ist schon zuende.' (*HWRB*, p.695). While many around him in
Germany were talking of the 'death of literature', Richter still felt
confidently able to identify his life's main project — stretching from his

early cultural work in various US PoW camps via his involvement with *Der Ruf* to the various high-profile meetings of the Gruppe 47 in the late 1950s and early 1960s (rivalled in importance in the eyes of many only by the annual Frankfurt Book Fair) — with what he chose to think of as 'Die Hochzeit der [westdeutschen] Literatur'.

To many it must have seemed as if the final nail had been driven into the Group's coffin at the Princeton meeting in the spring of 1966. The wisdom of taking the Group to the United States at a time when the war in Vietnam was visibly escalating month by month and of making what had hitherto remained largely a West German literary event (the previous exceptions having been the meetings in Cap Circeo, Italy in 1954 and Sigtuna, Sweden in 1964) into a transatlantic media circus appeared as symptomatic of what Dieter E. Zimmer diagnosed as the 'Anpassungskrise, in der sich die Gruppe befindet'.3 Moreover, the reluctance of many of the old guard to take part in either the Sigtuna or the Princeton meetings led to more confrontational splits and factional clashes than the Group had previously experienced. Richter may have tried to derive a modicum of consolation from the idea that it was he, rather then his adversaries, who dissolved the Group, but it had in any case been falling apart, as he himself conceded in his 1967 comment: 'Die Gruppe zerfällt in ein Dutzend kleine Gruppen' (*HWRB*, p.640).

Over the years the Group had become something of an anachronism and was losing the loyalty of too many former stalwarts. A number of those in Richter's inner circle began suggesting that it might be time to call a halt. The pages of Richter's correspondence which document his attempts to ensure that a strong enough contingent drawn from the Group's leading lights attended the Sigtuna meeting make depressing reading, his disappointment showing through in such phrases as 'angesichts dieser Misére [sic] im letzten Augenblick' (*HWRB*, p.540). Charges of betrayal, diminishing esprit de corps or hiding behind transparent excuses, such as the pressing claims of the latest work-in-progress or the pleading of family circumstances, are levelled at almost every writer failing to accept an invitation to Sweden. Indeed, many of the respondents, despite declarations of fidelity to the Group, were scarcely able to conceal the view that the golden years were over and that the Group had lost both its raison d'être and its aura.

Nevertheless, Richter was not being immodest when he claimed: 'Die letzten zwei Jahrzehnte haben [der Gruppe 47] gehört'. The Group had always had to contend with adversity — socio-economic difficulties facing both writers and publishers alike in the early period, the hostility of the restorative CDU regime and of the reactionary wing of post-1945 German literature, the problems of being too successful and experiencing the unwelcome glare of media publicity, as well as having to face suspicions of cultural dirigisme and elitism — but until the late 1960s it had managed to weather all adversities. Whether it ended because it had accomplished too well what it had set out to achieve or whether it had outlived its purpose is likely to remain a matter of debate for a long time to come. What was clear by the late 1960s was that the Group had changed beyond all recognition from what it had been in the 'heroic' early period. One only has to compare the, as Raddatz put it, relative 'Abgeschlossenheit' (Lettau, p.276) of the early venues with the glare of publicity surrounding the Berlin and Princeton meetings ('literarisches Gladiatorenspiel' and 'Schau-Debatte' are among the pejorative terms used by journalists at the time) or the 'Schriftsteller unter sich' ambience of the early criticism with the part played later by 'Großkritiker' and publishers to appreciate the changes that had taken place.

In July 1947 Richter wrote to Wolfgang Lohmeyer, himself like Richter a former PoW held in the United States and a contributor to *Der Ruf*:

> Ohne das Wiedererwachen einer scharfen, echten und gesunden Kritik ist jeder neue Anfang sinnlos. Es sind einfach zuviel Schlacken da, die vorerst beseitigt werden müssen. Das können Sie nur mit einem scharfen Seziermesser. Es muss geschnitten werden, grausam, schonungslos und ohne jede Rücksicht. Der Schrei nach dem Positiven ist sinnlos solange nicht die Erkenntnis des Negativen ihm vorausgeht. Was ich unter echter Kritik verstehe, brauche ich Ihnen nicht auseinanderzusetzen. Sie muss wieder von dem unbedingten Fanatismus zur Wahrheit getragen werden. Ich lehne jede Manier des sogenannten gepflegten Stils, jeden Versuch vor einem müden und versuchten Publikum mit akademischen Bildungsfloskeln zu brillieren, als den Krebsschaden unserer Zeit ab. Wir müssen wieder lernen einfach, echt, wahr und, wenn es not tut, gegen uns selbst grausam zu sein. Sind wir durch einen Abgrund gegangen, um uns nun mit einer hohlen Welt des müden Scheins über den seelischen und geistigen Abgrund, in dem wir noch immer leben, hinweg zu retten? [...] Das Wort muss wieder lebendig werden. Es

> muss in seiner Unmittelbarkeit den Gegenstand treffen, es muss aussagen und
> aufrütteln [...]. Das wird unsere Aufgabe sein. Eine harte Aufgabe, der wir
> vielleicht nicht gewachsen sind. Aber wir wollen es versuchen, weil man
> heute gezwungen ist, immer wieder mit dem Versuch zu beginnen, wenn man
> noch existieren will. (*HWRB*, p.13)

If one discounts the melodramatic metaphors and a rhetoric of
ruthlessness, which even includes the favoured term of the Nazis
'Fanatismus' but which is unypical of the Richter of the next two
decades, what one has here in essence is the rationale behind both *Der
Ruf* and the early meetings of the fledgling Gruppe 47. The salient role
of *Der Ruf* — and in particular the removal of Alfred Andersch and
Hans Werner Richter as the journal's editors — in preparing for the
founding of the Group is well documented, with the contributions of
van der Will and Flanagan in the present volume casting further light on
this aspect of the Group's complex pre-history.

In some respects contrasting with the more blatantly
programmatic nature of *Der Ruf*, Richter's accounts of what made the
Gruppe 47's meetings unique invariably emphasise the informality,
collegiality and practical workshop dimension of the gatherings. He
speaks of 'eine Gemeinschaft von Freunden [...] ein Kreis', aware of its
founding goals: 'Bis jetzt geht die Kritik [...] lediglich von zwei
Gesichtspunkten aus und zwar zuerst von dem rein formalen,
handwerklichen Können und dann von der Echtheit des Gelesenen'
(*HWRB*, p.77). A Group meeting is, he explains to a somewhat diffident
Ernst Kreuder, already enjoying fame as the author of *Die Gesellschaft
vom Dachboden*:

> keine Tagung [...], wir kommen lediglich zusammen, um uns zu unterhalten
> und einiges aus unseren unveröffentlichten Arbeiten vorzulesen. Es gibt
> weder eine Tagesordnung noch ein Programm, noch sonst ein Reglement.
> [...] Ich möchte noch einmal betonen, dass das ganze Zusammentreffen rein
> privater Natur ist und einen unterhaltenden Charakter trägt. (*HWRB*, p.52)

In 1948 Günter Groll (himself a member) had published a keynote
article explaining the Group's deliberately informal identity. The piece,
programmatically entitled 'Die Gruppe, die keine Gruppe ist', speaks of
'ein Kreis von privaten Freunden und literarischen Bekannten'. He
stresses:

> Niemand hat ihn einberufen, beauftragt oder gar lizensiert. Niemand dachte
> oder denkt daran, ihn zu organisieren. Die Gruppe, die eigentlich keine
> Gruppe ist und 1947 bemerkte, daß sie existierte, ist ein freier

Zusammenschluß von jungen Schriftstellern, von Publizisten und Journalisten, verstärkt durch einige Maler und Zeichner. Sie hat keine Statuten und Mitgliedslisten. Sie hat keineswegs (wie die meisten Gruppen nach dem zweiten Weltkrieg) ihre ideologische Konzeption. Sie ist ein Arbeitskreis: man kommt zuweilen zusammen, tauscht Erfahrungen aus, liest und kritisiert neue Arbeiten, und hält menschlichen Kontakt [...].[4]

Kröll sees the early phase of the Group as 'gesichert durch die tragenden Mentalitäts-Säulen tiefsitzender Ideologie- und Organisationsfeindlichkeit'.[5] Certainly, Richter's belief that 'kollektive Kunst' was impossible, 'daß ein Dichter nur in der Einsamkeit seines Wesens, in der Abgeschiedenheit seines Studierzimmers arbeiten kann' (*HWRB*, p.77) was also an influential factor in determining how the Gruppe 47 was presented.

The myth of the group that was to all intents and purposes not a group was zealously nurtured over the coming years. Even as late as 1964, Hans Magnus Enzensberger felt called upon to remind outsiders that: 'An 362 Tagen des Jahres ist die Gruppe 47 nur virtuell vorhanden, als ein Gespenst'.[6] Nevertheless, Richter was at times, especially during the founding phase, not averse to thinking of 'his' Gruppe 47 as a circumscribed group with a finite number of members. In this spirit he reports to Nicolas Sombart that he has just sent a letter 'an alle Mitglieder der Gruppe 47', adding 'Auch Ernst Kreuder und Günter Eich haben sich jetzt unserer Gruppe angeschlossen' (*HWRB*, p.54). In another to all intents and purposes internal memo, dated 22 October 1949, he writes: 'Als Angehörige der Gruppe betrachten wir' and sets out 34 names in alphabetical order, before appending a second list of people considered to be 'Gäste der Gruppe' (*HWRB*, p.93). However, three weeks later he has had second thoughts. Attributing his earlier remarks to an uncharacteristic 'Anfall von Organisationswut', he retreats to the familiar myth: 'Was ich Dir da geschrieben habe über die sogenannte Zugehörigkeit zur Gruppe 47 ist natürlich Quatsch. Niemand gehört dazu und alle gehören dazu. [...] Wer sich dazugehörig fühlt, gehört dazu' (*HWRB*, p.94). And from this point on, the mystification of the Gruppe 47's peculiar constitution becomes part of a skilfully orchestrated public image. Even after the Group's demise, Richter can console himself, thanks to what Friedhelm Kröll calls his 'mythisierende Gruppendefinition',[7] with the almost biblical thought that 'wenn drei oder vier von uns sich in einer Kneipe treffen, dann ist das eben schon die Gruppe 47' (*HWRB*, p.711).

The deliberate fluidity and informality of Richter's group-concept enjoyed a number of distinct advantages. Instead of looking like a closed in-group, the Gruppe 47 could present itself as having in principle an open-door policy towards virtually all literary newcomers. This is the way in which Alfred Andersch presented it to a reclusive Arno Schmidt:

> Ich möchte Sie im Namen der Gruppe sehr herzlich [...] einladen. Ich könnte mir denken, daß es auch für Sie ganz interessant ist, einmal ein paar Kollegen kennenzulernen; in größeren Zeitabständen läßt sich so etwas ertragen. [...] Sie können sich am ersten Tag den Laden einmal ansehen, und dann selbst entscheiden, ob Sie [vorlesen] wollen oder nicht. [8]

Militant solidarity (the Group's beginnings were both anti-fascist and anti-authoritarian (cf. *HWRB*, p.423)) could go hand in hand with the image of a writer's workshop and review of work-in-progress. 'Die Tagungen der Gruppe 47 waren immer Arbeitstagungen', Richter recalls.[9] Words like 'Arbeitsgemeinschaft', 'Werkkreis' or Hans Magnus Enzensberger's metaphor of the 'Zentralcafé einer Literatur ohne Hauptstadt'[10] were calculated to make the Group seem anti-elitist, pragmatic and at the same time supportive when it came to the matter of publishing outlets. It is evident that this spirit of constructive collegiality owed much to the bonhomie of Richter himself, 'Gruppenführer, Diskussionsleiter und *maître de plaisir* in einer Person', as one observer remarked (Lettau, p.52).

Jürgen Schutte points to two important house rules which also greatly contributed to the maintenance of amicable, yet at the same time uncompromising criticism: 'Ich denke, es waren diese zwei Regeln: die Unzulässigkeit von Grundsatzdebatten und das Verbot der Gegenrede des kritisierten Autors, durch die die spontane Kritik über zwanzig Jahre hinweg [...] für die Autoren produktiv wirkte.'[11] No doubt, the informality of meetings was also ritually stressed in order to blunt suspicions of a clandestine literary mafia or media manipulation, although the occurrence of such terms as 'Totalitätsanspruch', 'Umschlagplatz Literatur' or even comparisons with the Nazi *Reichsschrifttumskammer* (see especially Hahn in this volume) suggest that the strategy did not convince everybody. Yet Richter astutely combined the image of a relaxed series of poetic workshops with the maintenance of strong contacts with the media (radio stations, reviewers — many of whom were Group members writing *pro domo* — and academe). *Die Zeit* soon came to be regarded as the Group's *Hausorgan*, although Richter also had good connections with the *Süddeutsche Zeitung* and a number of leading publishing houses. By 1967 almost two hundred writers had sat in the 'Elektrischer Stuhl' (or as Horst Bienek preferred to call it: the 'Ehren-Fauteuil') and more than a hundred critics and guests had been invited to attend the Group's various meetings. In a recent discussion F.C. Delius recalled: 'es war der literarische Himmel. Wir wollten alle in den Himmel kommen.' This prompted the reply from Jürgen Schutte that this was 'ein schöner Ausdruck, besonders wenn man diesen Himmel nicht allzuweit vom literarischen Markt ansiedelt' ('Gespräch', p.196). In terms of literary prestige, publishing and publicity, the first two decades after 1947 really did seem to have belonged to the Gruppe 47, although clouds were gathering on the horizon.

In the twentieth year of the Group's existence, Richter was invited by a certain Hans Dollinger to write a foreword to his forthcoming anthology *außerdem. Deutsche Literatur minus Gruppe 47 = wieviel?* After initially agreeing, he decided to pull out although the anthology did eventually contain a 'Grußwort' from him. In a letter to Hildesheimer he explains his decision as follows: 'ich schreibe kein Vorwort [...]. Es war nur ein Scherz, aber ich kann schon keinen Scherz mehr machen, ohne dass es nicht ausgenützt wird' (*HWRB*, p.643). Dollinger's anthology may well have struck Richter as too frivolous for the increasingly polemical climate of the mid-1960s. By allowing his 'Brief an den Herausgeber' to be published, however, he was deflecting the charge (implicit in the whole *außerdem* project) that the Gruppe 47 had set its sights on literary hegemony in Germany. According to Richter, 'der Anspruch, die Gruppe 47 umfasse die ganze deutsche Gegenwartsliteratur ist nie erhoben worden, weder von mir noch von anderen'.[12] Indeed, there were many writers who kept their distance from the Group, some remaining distinctly aloof, others observing its activities from a benevolent distance. Within West Germany, the names of such prominent writers as Wolfgang Koeppen, Ernst Kreuder, Hans Erich Nossack and Arno Schmidt, from the older generation, and Rolf Hochhuth and Max von der Grün, who was instrumental in founding the alternative Gruppe 61, spring to mind. The Austrian writers associated with the Wiener Gruppe and the Residenz Verlag also remained outside. Quite clearly there are enough names to give the lie to any claim that the 'außerdem' element amounted to 'nicht viel'. One reason for reluctance to be involved with the Group was aversion to the inevitable 'Vereinsmeierei' that accompanied its meetings; the media circus quality that afflicted the events in later years was another. Hildesheimer was not alone in wishing to avoid 'den Trieb (und damit auch die Betriebsamkeit der jüngeren Kollegen)' (*HWRB*, p.424), as schisms and disputes became more evident in the 1960s. Others stayed away, either permanently or progressively, because they were artistic 'Einzelgänger'. Koeppen — who once did set off for a meeting — on one occasion mockingly thanks Richter for an invitation to the first international 'Paralytikertreffen' (*HWRB*, p.199), while others found collective support in other groupings.[13]

Nevertheless, six years after Dollinger's anthology, Heinrich Vormweg felt able to identify 'die "junge deutsche Literatur der Moderne"' as 'weitgehend identisch mit der Gruppe 47',[14] and Marcel Reich-Ranicki, doubtless with his eye more on provocative effect, declared the Group to be 'so verschwommen, daß man heute alle Schreibenden unter fünfzig Jahren als Gruppe 47 bezeichnen muß' (cf. *HWRB*, p.430). There are various reasons why Dollinger's tendentious equation is too crude to operate with; it discounts all attempts to define the Gruppe 47 as a fluid, informal set of gatherings and works with a rigid in-group/outsider model. It also takes no account of many individual writers' fluctuating relations with the Group (on this, see Finlay, Waine and Williams in the present volume). Moreover, Dollinger's anthology had been assembled with a deliberate polemical purpose, not to encourage a non-partisan assessment of how representative the Group was within West German literature. Nevertheless, the equation in its title did sum up a controversial issue which had repeatedly haunted Richter, not only because of hostile charges from various quarters concerning the Group's alleged bid for cultural monopoly, but also on occasions when its achievements were in need of public commemoration.

At the time when Andersch was planning his 'Bibliographie der Gruppe 47' intended to give readers of *Texte und Zeichen* some sense of the 'Umfang des der "Gruppe 47" angehörenden Autoren-Kreises und der Qualität (oder Nicht-Qualität) der Werke dieser Autoren',[15] Richter began to have distinct misgivings:

> Über die Bibliographie der Gruppe 47 habe ich mich zuerst sehr gefreut, aber
> dann doch Bedenken bekommen, wenn auch geringfügige. Jetzt haben wir

> also, plötzlich doch Mitglieder oder nicht? Das wollte ich verhindern, andererseits ist es für viele Leute wichtig, endlich einmal zu wissen, was gehört eigentlich dazu. (*HWRB*, p.197)

This latter argument seems to have prevailed (rather than the cautious solution represented by Andersch's reference to a *circle* of writers *belonging to the Gruppe 47*). And not for the only time. For in February 1961 Richter responds to Walter Mannzen's list of members of the Gruppe 47 needed for the *Almanach* they were jointly preparing by suggesting corrections to it:

> Die Leute mit Kreuz möchte ich zur Gruppe zählen, alle anderen nicht. [...] Hier in der Festlegung liegt für mich der Haken der ganzen Angelegenheit. Gerade das Nichtfestgelegte, nicht Vereinsmässige war ja das Wesen der Gruppe 47. Wenn man es jetzt so genau fixiert, geht es von dieser Atmosphäre der ››geheimnisvollen Loge‹‹ verloren. Ich weiß deshalb nicht recht, ob wir uns mit diesem Buch nicht selbst einen schlechten Dienst erweisen. (*HWRB*, p.338)

Richter had for once become the victim of his own presentational strategy.

'Auch Celan kam durch die Gruppe 47 nach oben', Richter wrote to Fritz J. Raddatz at a point when the question of his inclusion in the *Almanach* arose (*HWRB*, p.405). The response to his reading may have been largely negative, but Celan still came away from the 1952 Niendorf meeting with a contract from the Deutsche Verlags-Anstalt. Obviously, winning the Group's prize (a prize usually funded by one of the Federal Republic's major publishing houses and not awarded in every year) was the most coveted endorsement a young up-and-coming writer could receive. But it would give a false image of the Group's activities to focus exclusively on its *Prominenz*, its top twenty writers, and ignore the fact that lesser-known participants such as Herbert Eisenreich, Gisela Elsner, Ludwig Harig, Jakov Lind, Helga M. Novak, Günter Seuren and Ruth Rehmann were probably more dependent on the stimulus and contacts afforded by the Group than those who had already 'arrived'.

'Die Leute von der Gruppe 47 sind doch mutig: sie scheuen sich nicht, einem noch unvollendeten, riesigen Roman, aus dem man zwei Kapitel gehört hatte, den Preis zu geben', Marcel Reich-Ranicki noted in 1958 in response to the award of the Prize to Günter Grass for his readings from *Die Blechtrommel* at that year's Großholzleute meeting (Lettau, p.141). Indeed a certain lack of clarity existed over whether it was the writer, the work (be it a completed manuscript or a work-in-progress) or the extract that was being judged and in some cases rewarded. If one examines the list of prize-winners between 1950 and 1967, the prize's function is open to various interpretations. In the early years, major figures were awarded the prize for major achievements: Eich, Aichinger and Bachmann for new unpublished work that was read to the Group. In these cases, something finite, a selection of single complete poems or a short story, was being judged. But the stipulation that writers read from unpublished material had its drawbacks. That Heinrich Böll, who had already published *Der Zug war pünktlich* and had most of the stories for *Wanderer, kommst du nach Spa...* ready in manuscript form, should decide, after gauging the mood of the Group, to read his in the event prize-winning story *Die schwarzen Schafe* (then published as a single story by the Middelhauve Verlag) tells us a lot about how writers were already tailoring their offerings to suit the needs of the occasion. Equally revealing is the way in which Böll's performance is characterised: 'er hatte mit seiner Geschichte von den schwarzen Schafen bewiesen, daß er nicht nur über eine breite menschliche Substanz und einen feinen Humor verfügt, sondern auch brillant und mit scharfer Pointierung zu erzählen versteht' (Lettau, p.60). As Schutte has pointed out:

> es kam im Laufe der Zeit dazu, daß die Autoren für ihre Lesungen Texte auswählten, von denen sie annehmen konnten, daß sie bei einer solchen Spontankritik gut wegkommen. Es empfahl sich, die Lesung nicht nur vergleichsweise kurz zu machen, sondern auch kurzweilig. Den Vorteil hatten also eher witzige, skurrile oder eingängige, nicht zu schwer verständliche Texte. ('Gespräch', p.191)

This is an issue considered by Katrin Kohl in the present volume in her account of Peter Rühmkorf's fluctuating reception at the hands of the Group and one which has a bearing on the disappointing response to Celan as well as to the way that, whereas Grass's reading from his poems and of *Onkel, Onkel* had not been well received, the two well-chosen chapters from *Die Blechtrommel*, as seen above, gained him the prize. That Walser should receive the prize for his 'Geschichte eines älteren Herren' (later published as 'Templones Ende') can be read as encouragement to move out of Kafka's shadow (see Waine's contribution to the present volume). Nevertheless that he should have been singled out for one of the stories from what was to become *Ein*

Flugzeug über dem Haus, a collection usually dismissed as derivatively kafkaesque, rather than for any of the later, more substantial social satires, suggests that at times the Preis der Gruppe 47 was a matter of detecting signs of promise rather than rewarding real achievement. The list of prizewinners may well resemble some hall of fame of post-1945 German literature, but if one recalls which specific works gained the prizes for such writers as Böll, Walser, Morriën and Bichsel and simultaneously bears in mind who had read at the same meeting without emerging as that year's *victor ludorum*, then the vagaries of the prize-awarding mechanism become obvious. Also, it is as well to bear in mind that while wit, listener-friendliness, the knack of epitomising the fashion of the moment (be it 'Kahlschlag', 'Magischer Realismus', a specifically socially satirical form of *littérature engagée* or the more experimental prose of Becker's *Ränder*) were being institutionalised as requisite literary virtues, certain forms of writing were fated seldom to find acceptance among the Group.

Helmut Heißenbüttel was warned in advance by fellow-poet Wolfgang Weyrauch that the Group was not accustomed to experimental poetry. Hence, not surprisingly, his reading from *Topographien* met with incomprehension: 'reine Assoziationslyrik [...] zu großen Teilen esoterischer Selbstausdruck' (Raddatz); 'keine Poesie, nichts Lyrisches' (F.-J. Schneider); 'ich kann mit solchen Gedichten sehr wenig anfangen, aber poetisch sind sie auf alle Fälle'.[16] If Arno Schmidt had overcome his aversion to literary gatherings and had read from one of his major novels of the 1950s, say *Das steinerne Herz* or *KAFF*, it is not difficult to imagine the resistance his work would have encountered. Such prose was too visual and densely innovative to lend itself to public reading. Likewise, many of the most important radio plays of the late fifties and early sixties, particularly the work of the 'Neues Hörspiel' writers, were too dependent on technical realisation for their acoustic value to have been appreciated at a reading.

The privileging of the 'Kleinform' or the extract over the whole was conceivably a price worth paying, if creative writers were freed from arid academic criticism and spontaneity was able to return to the domain of literary response. However, the increasing role that a small group of prominent critics (Walter Höllerer, Walter Jens, Joachim Kaiser and Marcel Reich-Ranicki[17]) played at the Group's meetings did much to destroy the previous 'Arbeitskreis' ambience. The problem was not one of theoreticians versus practising authors (after all, both Jens and Höllerer were also creative writers), but of the nature and insistence of the opinions voiced. At the Princeton gathering, an American academic used to the rigours of New Criticism found the level of theoretical debate embarrassingly unsatisfactory. A rather jejeune impressionistic criticism was contributing to the problems of 'Stegreifkritik' already endemic to the reading ritual.

This was a key factor contributing to the Group's demise. At the same time many others have been suggested, which makes the story of the end of the Gruppe 47 as a literary circle less clear than that of its beginnings. Its alleged debilitating pluralism (Rolf Schroers noted 'ein literarisches Profil hat die Gruppe nicht, sie ist literarisch immun' (Lettau, p.382)), its seemingly narrow focus on literature, which was said to mask 'soziale Indifferenz'[18] at a time when the era of culinary *belles-lettres* and/or affirmative 'Anpassungsliteratur' was past, the need for a new more democratic organisational structure:[19] all these were issues that led to the view that in a changing political and literary world the Group was now becoming something of a white elephant. Writing to thank Andersch for his support in 1966, Richter confesses:

> mich haben diese vielen Beschimpfungen getroffen, zum ersten Mal in dieser Nachkriegszeit [...]. Es haben, abgesehen von Höllerer und Grass, nur ein paar junge Leute zu mir gehalten: Lettau, Roehler, Herburger, Hey. Von der Generation, die mit uns angefangen hat, niemand: kein Eich, kein Schnurre, kein Böll, kein Hildesheimer, nur Schnabel und du. (*HWRB*, p.631f.)

That Andersch, despite his problems with the Group, was still willing to identify with it, as was Böll on occasion, as Finlay points out in this volume, suggests that it remained important to them.

It is of course tempting to indulge in speculation about the role played by the Gruppe 47 in the literary life of the German-speaking countries: whether *Die Blechtrommel* had been written or achieved immediate international recognition because of, or despite, the Group; whether the politicisation of West German literature in the late 1960s occurred so late because of the Group's affirmative tendencies (as early as 1951 Louis Clappier had seen in the preferences expressed at the Dürkheim meeting evidence of a 'Literatur der Flucht' (Lettau, p.67)); how many writers were discouraged after reading at a meeting or disadvantaged by not seeming to belong. Nevertheless, for twenty years German literature did belong to the Group, in the sense that it helped writers to profit from an informal forum, it encouraged productive criticism, it discovered and promoted some of the major luminaries of post-war German-language writing and played a vital part in facilitating the publication of important new work.

As well as being a major factor of the literary life of the German-speaking countries in the post-war era, the Gruppe 47 also sought to contribute to political developments, especially in the Federal Republic. This is not surprising, since its origins lie in the largely political journal *Der Ruf*, the subject of the first two contributions in this volume. Indeed, if *Der Ruf* had not been proscribed by the American occupation authorities, there would presumably have been no Gruppe 47 — at least not in the form in which it developed.

As the essays by van der Will and Flanagan in this volume show, there are a number of political issues to be considered in relation to *Der Ruf*. They concern both the political situation in which it was produced and the nature of what was written. There can be no doubt that the authors of *Der Ruf*, in particular its co-editors Hans Werner Richter and Alfred Andersch, totally misread the political situation, in particular the ability of Germans to influence events following the unconditional surrender of 1945. As another intellectual, Alfred Kantorowicz, who shared the ambition of Richter and Andersch to maintain German unity and founded the journal *Ost und West* with this specific aim, noted in its first edition in 1947, Germany was destined to be an 'object' rather than a 'subject' in political affairs.[20]

Linked with this issue is the question of legitimacy. Despite their own participation in a war that had been unleashed by Germany, Richter and Andersch exonerated not only themselves, but also the whole of their generation, from any responsibility for Nazi war crimes. The mystique they attached to this 'young' generation is discussed at length in this volume by Cofalla. Others took a different view, not least the philosopher Karl Jaspers, one of the first to wrestle with the problem of guilt in the aftermath of war and defeat. In the introduction to *Die Schuldfrage*, which first appeared in 1946, he states:

> Seien wir uns klar: Daß wir leben und überleben, verdanken wir nicht uns selbst: daß wir neue Zustände mit neuen Chancen in der furchtbaren Zerstörung haben, haben wir nicht durch eigene Kraft erreicht. Geben wir uns keine Legitimität, die uns nicht zukommt.[21]

Whereas the authors of *Der Ruf* tended to see only the new opportunities referred to by Jaspers, he fully accepted German political liability, and therefore guilt, for what had happened. The stance adopted in *Der Ruf* amounts in essence to an espousal of the largely discredited claim that 1945 was somehow 'year zero', a wiping clean of the slate at the start of a new era. The reluctance to confront the past is exemplified by comments made by Richter in 1956: 'Wir wollen keine Wiederauferstehung des unseligen Entnazifizierungsgesetzes, wir sind vielmehr der Ansicht, daß die Vergangenheit vergessen und vergeben werden soll'.[22] In effect, this amounts to an exoneration of genocide.

The reluctance of Andersch and Richter to engage with questions raised by the German past can be linked with the topic of Flanagan's contribution: the question of whether the authors of *Der Ruf* were in fact German nationalists. She rejects this claim, pointing out that any apparently nationalistic ideas expressed in the journal were far removed from traditional German nationalism. In fact, it is possible to posit a link with the ideas of the first post-war SPD leader Kurt Schumacher, who was critical of the western Allies and upheld the ideal of German unity, but, given his experiences at the hands of the Nazis, can hardly be linked with their abhorrent views. Nevertheless, both he and *Der Ruf* were out of step with an era when thinking in national terms increasingly gave way to what has been called 'post-nationalism', a term that has frequently been applied to the Federal Republic, at least prior to unification in 1990.

The political role of the Gruppe 47 after the banning of *Der Ruf* is equally controversial. At one extreme stands Frank Trommler's extremely disparaging characterisation of the Group's political stance as 'nachgeholte Résistance',[23] which suggests that it was seeking to compensate for the earlier failure of intellectuals during the Weimar Republic to resist Nazism by adopting an oppositional stance towards the Federal Republic. At the other extreme one finds Günter Grass's recent statement about his own political activity in the 1960s, which, given his closeness to Richter at the time, can be taken, some thirty years later, as a continuing endorsement of the activities of the Group as a whole. He refers specifically to the failures of writers during the Weimar Republic as the legitimation of his own involvement in politics in the 1960s:

> es gab [...] viele, die begriffen, daß der Schriftsteller zugleich Bürger seines
> Landes ist und daß er [...] nicht hohepriesterlich über der Gesellschaft

> schwebt, sondern ihr verantwortlich zugehört. Es galt, eine Lehre aus den
> Versäumnissen der Weimarer Republik zu ziehen [...], und ich bin immer
> noch stolz, zum Sieg der Sozialdemokraten beigetragen zu haben.[24]

This is a very much an echo of Richter's own views when he looked
back to the origins of the Group. Writing to Raddatz in August 1966, he
says that the need to avoid the mistakes of the past was the reason for its
foundation:

> Meine Überlegung war, auf keinen Fall dürfen die Fehler wiederholt werden.
> Das war die eigentliche Ursache für die Entstehung der Gruppe 47. Deshalb
> versuchte ich eine Art Corpsgeist unter den linken Literaten zu züchten [...]
> deswegen die Methoden der Gruppe 47 mit der Förderung einer Polemik, die
> der angelsächsischen sehr nahe kommt. (*HWRB*, p.623)

Reactions to Trommler's criticism of the Group may conceivably
vary according to how the fledgling democracy of the Federal Republic
in the 1950s and 1960s is regarded. Clearly it bore no similarity to the
dictatorship of the Third Reich. At the same time, there are reasons to
criticise it, in particular for its lax attitude to the Nazi past which
allowed many former high-ranking servants of the Nazis to continue
their careers unscathed and the authoritarian methods of the Federal
Republic's first chancellor, Konrad Adenauer.[25] Reluctance to confront
the past was, however, as already seen, the Achilles heel of the founders
of the Gruppe 47. Moreover, as Sonnleitner shows in the present
volume in the context of the relationship between Richter and Ilse
Aichinger, the Group's convenor preferred to keep silent when faced
with reminders of Nazi anti-Semitism. Sonnleitner, as well as van der
Will and Williams, quote Richter's 1949 novel *Die Geschlagenen*, in
which the author appears to stand by his main character's reluctance, on
the basis of an ideology of military comradeship, to help the Americans
when taken prisoner despite his declared opposition to the Nazis.

Before one can finally seek to pass judgement on the political role
of the Gruppe 47, it is first necessary to determine which political
activities can safely be associated with it, no easy task given its loose
structures and lack of 'membership' in the normal sense of the word.
The various resolutions that originated at Group meetings, if one
accepts Enzensberger's claim referred to above about the only times the
Group existed, must clearly be taken into consideration, although these
were not always signed by all those present. For example, Günter Grass,
did not sign the resolution on the 1962 *Spiegel*-Affair, which surfaced
whilst the Group was meeting in Berlin. This created such a stir by its

reference to 'so-called military secrets' that Richter felt obliged to issue a supplementary explanatory statement to the Deutsche Presseagentur (see Lettau, pp.458f.). Nevertheless, given the undemocratic nature of this attack on the freedom of the press by the Adenauer government and the Defence Minister Franz Josef Strauß in particular, this was one occasion when the Group could be claimed to have been entirely on the side of right. Moreover, the subsequent wave of protest did contribute to political change. Strauß was forced to resign and Adenauer subsequently to name the day of his retirement. The same positive view can be taken of the Group's opposition to the plans by the Adenauer government to take control of the proposed new second television channel. This provoked a letter of protest in the autumn of 1960, which was vindicated by the rejection of Adenauer's plans by the Federal Constitutional Court. A third resolution in this area dating from 1967 was directed against the Springer Press, which the 106 signatories, who spoke of themselves as '[d]ie Schriftsteller der Gruppe 47', saw as endangering press freedom.[27] In this case it is less easy to speak of short-term success; nevertheless the Group can be said to have played a valuable part in defending and enhancing freedom of expression in the Federal Republic.

In total there were eleven such resolutions. The first, objecting to the Soviet intervention in Hungary, shows that the Group could be close to the political consensus of the day. By contrast, one of the most controversial was undoubtedly the 1965 protest against the Vietnam War (Lettau, pp.459-62). It spoke of the Vietcong as a 'nationale und soziale Befreiungsbewegung', whilst criticising the destructive consequences of the Americans' use of modern military hardware. This resolution too failed to attract universal support, an undoubted sign of the increasing strains that were to lead to the disintegration of the Group two years later. Among the non-signatories were Richter and Grass, who considered it too radical (*HWRB*, p.580). The row rumbled on and led to an open confrontation between Richter and Peter Weiss in Princeton. The Vietnam War was to become a leading issue for the student movement of the late 1960s; that the protest of radical students at the 1967 Pulvermühle meeting of the Group hastened its demise underlines how it was unable to survive in a more radical political climate, a point made by Cofalla in this volume.

In addition to the various resolutions, there are a number of political publications which can be linked to the Gruppe 47, all dating from the 1960s. In the intervening years, after the banning of *Der Ruf* Richter had always maintained his interest in politics; for example, he was behind the Grünwalder Kreis, a forum for intellectuals and politicians to discuss issues of the day with the aim of strengthening democracy. This forum was, however, kept largely separate from the Group, with Richter himself speaking of transferring the Group's methods to the new body.[27] The greater involvement of the Group with politics in the 1960s can be explained by the change of paradigm from 'non-conformism' to 'commitment', as analysed in this volume by Peitsch, the emergence of a new generation of arguably more 'political' writers such as Grass and Walser and the increased fame of the Group which meant that political activity by those associated with it attracted wider attention. Finally, as we have already seen, Richter, despite his vision of the Group as a loosely organised body, did embark on a process of institutionalisation in the 1960s with the publication in 1962 of the *Almanach der Gruppe 47*.

In the 1960s the Group became associated with the Social Democratic Party, although it should be stressed that support for that party was not universal, with Böll and Andersch, for example, far from happy with the centrist policies it had increasingly adopted. In its 1959 Godesberg Programme, the SPD had abandoned all vestiges of Marxism, as well as accepting the position of the Federal Republic within the system of western alliances. It ceased, for example, to support the anti-nuclear movement in which Richter had been involved. At the same time, it sought to make itself more attractive to all sections of society, not merely the traditional working class, a step that allowed greater co-operation with writers.

In 1961 and 1965 two volumes were produced in which writers advocated voting for the SPD in the federal elections of those years. Both can be associated with the Gruppe 47. The first, *Die Alternative oder Brauchen wir eine neue Regierung?*, was edited by Martin Walser and contained twenty contributions, almost three quarters of which were by writers who can be associated with the Group. Names include Richter himself, Grass, Enzensberger and Lenz. In general, the support given to the Social Democrats was lukewarm, given the party's perceived swing to the right, as epitomised by Enzensberger's comment about it: 'Sie biedert sich bei ihren Feinden an, sie ist zahm, sie apportiert und macht Männchen'.[28] Four years later there appears to have been an attempt to be more 'professional'. The volume *Plädoyer für eine neue Regierung*, edited this time by Richter himself, devotes a great deal of space to personalities. The inclusion of twelve essays about SPD politicians or their close allies suggests a non-ideological conception of politics in which names matter more than issues. Hence, it is no wonder that more radical writers such as Heinrich Böll felt alienated from the Group at this time. Apart from Rolf Hochhuth and the editor of *Der Spiegel* Rudolf Augstein, all the contributors to Richter's volume can be associated with the Gruppe 47. They include Reinhard Lettau, the editor of the Group's *Handbuch* and Hans Schwab-Felisch, who edited the first published collection of contributions from *Der Ruf*.[29] In addition to these publications occasioned by the two elections, Richter edited a volume immediately following the erection of the Berlin Wall, *Die Mauer oder Der 13. August*, and a year later a collection of essays with the significant title *Bestandsaufnahme. Eine deutsche Bilanz*.[30] These are all works that show how the Gruppe 47 and its convenor came to be increasingly associated with politics.

Evaluations of the political stance adopted by Richter and the majority of the Gruppe 47 vary. Both Sonnleitner and Schneider-Handschin cite in their essays Ingeborg Bachmann's disparaging view that what were supposedly radical views would have counted as no such thing in other European countries. Finlay shows how Böll mocked the idea that anyone should be frightened of the Group's politics. Cofalla speaks of 'komplementäre Opposition', suggesting that it remained within the consensus of the Federal Republic.[31] By contrast, the Berlin academic Hans Dieter Zimmermann dedicates his critique of radical intellectuals, published shortly after the end of European communism, *Der Wahnsinn des Jahrhunderts* to Richter and the Gruppe 47, seeing them as models of political commitment.[32] That the Group was not entirely a toothless tiger is suggested by some of the reactions of its opponents. The clash with Hermann Josef Dufhues is chronicled here particularly by Hahn, whilst Preece recalls the celebrated 'Pinscher' insult delivered by Adenauer's successor Ludwig Erhard. Events in the first two decades of the Federal Republic, such as the *Spiegel*-Affair, show that the kind of exchanges that occurred between the Group and its opponents were not simply political theatre. Just as Grass's first novel

Die Blechtrommel provoked howls of rage in conservative literary circles who saw it as blasphemous, similarly his direct political intervention in the 1965 election for the SPD when he toured areas where the party was weak was regarded by some in the CDU as a provocation.[33]

Equally, a case can be made for the support given to the SPD by many associated with the Group, however uninspiring and pusillanimous that party might have appeared after Godesberg. What the new democracy of the Federal Republic required by the 1960s was a peaceful change of government of the kind that finally came about in 1969 and to which, despite the impossibility of quantifying the influence exercised by it, the Gruppe 47 by its earlier political activities can be said to have contributed. Such a change could only be achieved by the SPD, whatever its flaws. Grass's evocation of political progress through the symbol of a snail in his account of his political activities in the 1972 work *Aus dem Tagebuch einer Schnecke* can be claimed to have been appropriate in a country where, following defeat and destruction, caution was the watchword. Moreover, the late 1960s were not only a time of political change, however limited. The student movement of 1967/1968 changed German society, making it more open and less hierarchical. Although the Gruppe 47 may have foundered on the emerging student movement, it contributed to the change of mood that accompanied the era of radical protest. Its protests over the Vietnam War, for instance, pre-dated the first major student demonstration over this issue by a year.

Since German unification, both the literature of the early decades of the Federal Republic and the kind of politics associated with it have attracted strong criticism, not least by Frank Schirrmacher, the cultural editor of the *Frankfurter Allgemeine Zeitung*, who has stressed the dominant role of the Gruppe 47.[34] Some of this criticism appears contradictory in that it links the Group with a discredited left-wing agenda, such as the détente policies of the 1960s and 1970s, as practised by Willy Brandt, that are claimed to have prolonged the existence of communism, whilst criticising a lack of true radicalism. It is hoped that this volume, which is far from uncritical, will help readers to a deeper knowledge of a phenomenon the influence of which cannot be disputed and which, whatever its flaws, made in the eyes of many a positive contribution to the development of literature and politics in the

German-speaking countries. The praise for the Group expressed by two post-war European politicians with undoubted moral stature Willy Brandt and Václav Havel, the latter also a highly talented writer, speaks volumes in itself.[35]

Footnotes

[1] Hans Werner Richter, *Briefe*, ed. Sabine Cofalla (Munich: Hanser, 1997). Further references to this edition are to be found in the text under *HWRB*.

[2] Jürgen Becker, *Der fehlende Rest* (Frankfurt a. M.: Suhrkamp, 1997).

[3] Reinhard Lettau (ed.), *Die Gruppe 47. Bericht, Kritik, Polemik. Ein Handbuch* (Neuwied and Berlin: Luchterhand, 1967), p.229. Further references to this volume are to be found in the text under Lettau.

[4] *Süddeutsche Zeitung* (10 April 1948), reprinted in Lettau, p.31.

[5] Friedhelm Kröll, *Gruppe 47* (Stuttgart: Metzler, 1979), p.27.

[6] Hans Magnus Enzensberger, 'Die Clique', in: Hans Werner Richter (ed.), *Almanach der Gruppe 47* (Reinbek bei Hamburg, Rowohlt, 1962), p.23.

[7] Kröll, *Gruppe 47*, p.3. The mechanics of such mythicizing is explored systematically in Kröll's *Die "Gruppe 47". Soziale Lage und gesellschaftliches Bewußtsein literarischer Intelligenz in der Bundesrepublik* (Stuttgart: Metzler, 1977).

[8] Arno Schmidt, *Der Briefwechsel mit Alfred Andersch*, ed. Bernd Rauschenbach (Zurich: Arno Schmidt Stiftung im Haffmanns Verlag, 1985), p.16.

[9] Hans Werner Richter, 'Fünfzehn Jahre', in: Richter, *Almanach*, p.13.

[10] Enzensberger, 'Die Clique', in: Richter, *Almanach*, p.27.

[11] Sabine Cofalla, Friedrich Christian Delius, Jürgen Schutte, 'Ein Gespräch über die Gruppe 47', in: Toni Richter, *Die Gruppe 47 in Bildern und Texten* (Cologne: Kiepenheuer & Witsch, 1997), p.192. Further references to this volume are to be found in the text under 'Gespräch'.

[12] Hans Dollinger, *außerdem. Deutsche Literatur minus Gruppe 47 = wieviel?* (Munich: Scherz Verlag, 1967), p.5.

[13] See Ralf Schnell, 'Literarische Opposition zur Gruppe 47 am Beispiel Erich Nossack', in: Justus Fechter, Eberhard Lämmert, Jürgen Schutte (eds), *Die Gruppe 47 in der Geschichte der Bundesrepublik* (Würzburg: Königshausen & Neumann, 1991), pp.152-65.

[14] Heinrich Vormweg, 'Geschichte der Prosa in der Bundesrepublik' in: Dieter Lattmann (ed.), *Kindlers Literaturgeschichte der Gegenwart in Einzelbänden* (Munich: Kindler, 1973), p.263.

[15] *Texte und Zeichen*, 1: 1 (1955), 140.

[16] Fritz J. Raddatz, 'Wiedersehen mit der Gruppe 47', in: Lettau, p.111. See also Charlotte Stephan, 'Junge Autoren unter sich' (Lettau, pp.106f.), especially the verdict on Heißenbüttel's reading: 'nicht jedermanns Sache. Vorzüge, Gefahren und Faszination der 'additiven" lyrischen und prosaischen Dichtung waren oft Gegenstand heftiger Diskussionen' (p.107).

[17] As his correspondence shows, Richter was well aware of the problems and took note of the fact that moves were afoot to ostracise Reich-Ranicki. His motives for not acting decisively in this matter are unclear. Reich-Ranicki was certainly an important opinion-moulder and has remained so, as his role in the TV programme *Literarisches Quartett*, the controversies following his savaging of Günter Grass's *Ein weites Feld* and Martin Walser's *Ein springender Brunnen* in 1995 and 1998 respectively show. The 'Großkritiker' are also the principal target of Walser's satire on the Gruppe 47 in his parody of Rilke's letter to a young author: Martin Walser, 'Brief an einen ganz jungen Autor', in: Walser, *Erfahrungen und Leseerfahrungen* (Frankfurt a. M.: Suhrkamp, 1965), pp.155-62.

[18] Hans Mayer (ed.), *Deutsche Literaturkritik* vol.4: *Vom Dritten Reich bis zur Gegenwart (1933-1969)* (Frankfurt. a. M.: Fischer, 1972), p.53.

[19] Walser created a stir and certainly annoyed Richter with his plea for 'social ownership' of the Gruppe 47: Martin Walser, 'Sozialisieren wir die Gruppe 47', *Die Zeit*, (3July 1964).

[20] See K. Stuart Parkes, *Writers and Politics in West Germany* (Beckenham: Croom Helm, 1986), p.26.

[21] Karl Jaspers, *Die Schuldfrage* (Munich: Piper, 2nd ed. 1996), p.9.

[22] Richter quoted in: Sabine Cofalla, *Der "soziale Sinn" Hans Werner Richters* (Berlin: Weidler, 1997), p.111f.

[23] Frank Trommler, 'Die nachgeholte Résistance. Politik und Gruppenethos im historischen Zusammenhang' in: Fetscher, *Die Gruppe 47*, pp.9-22.

[24] Günter Grass et al., *Rotgrüne Reden* (Göttingen: Steidl, 1998), pp.15f.

[25] The most controversial figure with a previous involvement with National Socialism was undoubtedly Hans Globke, the civil servant with a leading position in the Bundeskanzleramt. During the Third Reich he had co-authored the commentary to the Nuremberg Race Laws. It can, however, be argued that the incorporation of people with a Nazi past into the structures of the Federal Republic helped to stabilise the new democratic state. The leading positions occupied by former Nazis in the Federal Republic was also a focus of GDR propaganda, although that state too did not make a fully clean sweep.

[26] See Klaus Wagenbach (ed.), *Vaterland Muttersprache* (Berlin: Wagenbach, 1979), p.251.

[27] See Cofalla, *Der "soziale Sinn"*, p.98

[28] Hans Magnus Enzensberger, 'Ich wünsche nicht gefährlich zu leben', in: Martin Walser: *Die Alternative oder Brauchen wir eine neue Regierung?* (Reinbek bei Hamburg: Rowohlt, 1961), p.66.

[29] Hans Schwab-Felisch (ed.), *Der Ruf. Eine deutsche Nachkriegszeitschrift* (Munich: dtv, 1962).

[30] Hans Werner Richter (ed.), *Die Mauer oder Der 13. August* (Reinbek bei Hamburg: Rowohlt, 1961). Hans Werner Richter (ed.), *Bestandsaufnahme. Eine deutsche Bilanz* (Munich, Vienna, Basle: Kurt Desch, 1962).

[31] See Cofalla, *Der soziale Sinn*, pp.114-16.

[32] Hans Dieter Zimmermann, *Der Wahnsinn des Jahrhunderts* (Stuttgart: Kohlhammer, 1992). The 'blurb' on the back cover speaks of Richter's 'demokratische Arbeit innerhalb und außerhalb der Gruppe 47 [als] Vorbild'.

[33] See Parkes, *Writers and Politics*, p.136.

[34] Frank Schirrmacher, 'Abschied von der Literatur der Bundesrepublik', *Frankfurter Allgemeine Zeitung*, 2 October 1990.

[35] In the 1960s Richter harboured the ambition of holding a meeting of the Group in Prague, something that was rendered impossible by the Soviet-led invasion of 1968. However, following the end of communism, this was remedied when writers asociated with the Group were able to take part in a gathering at Schloss Dobris in Czechoslovakia at which Havel, in his new political role as President of Czechoslovakia (and later the Czech Republic), accepted the 'Das Politische Buch' prize of the Friedrich-Ebert-Stiftung for his book *Fernverhör*. (See Toni Richter, *Die Gruppe 47 in Bildern und Texten*, p.172).

WILFRIED VAN DER WILL

The Agenda of Re-education and the Contributors of *Der Ruf* 1946-47

Efforts to re-educate the German people politically began among prisoners of war and continued after the war in the various zones of occupation. The co-editor of the post-war journal *Der Ruf* , Hans Werner Richter, had himself been part of this programme as a PoW in the USA, having been involved in a journal of the same name in this period. This did not mean that either journal accepted the American approach. The post-war *Ruf* rejected the concept of re-education, with the contributors regarding their own 'young' generation as untainted by the evils of Nazism. Although the idea that Germany should forge its own destiny was unrealistic at this time, *Der Ruf* can nevertheless be seen as one of the first manifestations of democratic debate in post-war Germany.

Systematic studies based on the literary documents left by the writers who took part in the earliest meetings of the Gruppe 47 have only just begun.[1] They will enable us to determine in more specific historiographical and analytical detail the writers' understanding of themselves in a situation of fundamental normative uncertainty in the aftermath of the wartime Allies' victory over Nazi Germany. This essay will attempt an assessment of that situation in terms of the tensions between writers and politics and the long-term effects of that strained relationship on the shaping of political culture in the Federal Republic. Before the creation of the Group, *Der Ruf* had opened up and captured important spaces within critical public opinion immediately after the Second World War. This short-lived journal initially defined much of the argumentative terrain in which the minority intellectual culture developed and thus set a pattern characterised by a continuing struggle for influence on the formation of public opinion. The contributors to *Der Ruf* were essentially engaged in a contest for moral-political supremacy against other elites and gave a lead which the Gruppe 47 was to follow. We shall consider here the initial motivations of a group of intellectuals who, despite and because of their being sidelined by the unfolding political and economic agenda of the post-war period, must be recognised for the long-term effects of their politics of protest. Over five decades they dramatised and eventually helped to obviate the long-standing irreconcilability between *Geist* and *Macht* in German cultural and political history. The considerations that follow, though fragmentary, will attempt to gather support for these assertions.[2]

The reason for the occupation of Germany after the Second World War was to prevent that country from ever again unleashing military hostilities in Europe. In order to achieve this goal various schemes were conceived by the different Allies, from the dismantling of Germany's industrial base to endowing the Germans with a less militaristic mentality. Such a fundamental departure from what was widely perceived as their ingrained, though hopefully not unalterable, national character was to be contained within a political structure which would make Germans disinclined to generate aggressive designs.

At the end of hostilities in 1945, the Soviet Union wanted restitution for its enormous material losses, if not revenge for the millions of its citizens killed by the war. It also wanted to make sure of a secure western border. The Americans intended to exploit whatever German know-how in terms of people and patents they could lay their hands on. The French wished to see German power permanently curtailed by political division. In contrast, the British had pored over German textbooks and plumped for re-education or, as Nicholas Pronay has classically put it: 'The British alternative in fact was to go for the mind instead of the body'.[3] The diverse Allied wishes were not necessarily irreconcilable at this stage, because each of these powers had subsidiary designs which might fuse with the major interests of the other powers. For example, Britain thought it essential to dissolve Prussia as a mainspring of German militarism and imperial nationalism. Hence in this respect it could go some way to meeting French demands. The Soviet Union, far from wanting to sever its Eastern Zone from the rest of the nation, was hoping for reparations from the whole of Germany and therefore initially cooperated with the Western Allies. As we now know, it was the British policy of re-education which, however differently interpreted, won general acceptance in the Allied Control Commission. Despite the deep-seated anti-German feelings of the victors this policy was remarkably free of any spirit of revenge. The commanders of the occupation forces tried to make this quite clear. In explaining to the American troops the decree on non-fraternisation the leadership of the U.S. 21st Army Group insisted that it did not mean revenge. The guilty were to be punished as the first stage of re-education. The Germans had to be guided back to the values of decency and self-respect. This way the peace was to be won.[4] For good measure, it was German party politicians and officials who were put in charge of carrying out school and local government reforms and the bulk of denazification early in 1946.

The young journalists and writers striving for position in the media at that time also thought that Germany had to be transformed from an agent of aggression to one of integration and reconciliation in the heart of Europe. *Die Wandlung* was a key-word in the deliberations of the post-fascist intelligentsia and the title of one of their influential journals.[5] Considering the similarities of purpose between the Allies and the aspiring young German writers, notably those of *Der Ruf*, the literary historian is faced with a number of questions. If there was such an overlap of interests between the benevolent aims of the Allies and those of the German critical elites, why could they not work in tandem or at the very least form a tacit alliance? Why was there such an ostensible gulf between the contributors to *Der Ruf* and the policies for Germany of the Western democracies? Why did the Munich *Ruf* so insistently repeat the divisions of opinion which particularly Richter and Mannzen had developed in relation to the American officers on the editorial board of the eponymous PoW-camp journal issuing from Fort Kearney (notably between 15 October 1945 and 1 April 1946)? Why were the German writers marginalised from the mainstream of politics even before they found themselves alienated by what they perceived to be the encrusted structures of capitalist restoration in the formative period of the Federal Republic?

The answer is, in a sense, short and simple: these intellectuals, both as former PoWs or as returned émigrés, had become irritated by the presuppositions of the programme of re-education even before the actual end of the Second World War. The reason for this lay in their perception of the Germans during the Nazi period and above all during the war. Crucially, they did not consider all their compatriots as incorrigibly infested with Nazism and hence found it difficult to accept the notion of collective guilt which appeared to inform the fundamental attitude of the Western Allied officers. From the start the contributors to *Der Ruf* thought that this concept was much too crude, implicitly fell prey to the Hitlerite identification of the Nazi movement with the essence of Germanness, and was only apt to block the individual German's detailed and sensitive reflection on Nazism. As a result these post-fascist intellectuals, themselves not entirely free from the relics of the National Socialist mindset,[6] reverted to the well-worn cliché of the opposition between *Geist* and *Macht*, culture and politics, with most of its contradictions and absurdities. However, over the years they came to set an example for the independent citizen of participating in public discourse. They were able to find spaces in the development of critical public opinion, not only because they posed fundamental challenges first to the Allies and then to sections of the German political class, but also because they acted in conformity with the Western interpretation of human freedom. *Der Ruf*, like the Gruppe 47 which arose from the journal's early extinction as a result of the censorship of the U.S. Military Government, acted as a substitute for the absent metropolitan coffee houses of the dispersed cultural intelligentsia.[7]

In order to illustrate the self-positioning of these 'politisch engagierte Publizisten mit literarischen Ambitionen'[8] let us look more closely at how their paternalistic organiser, Hans Werner Richter, expressed his existential and political attitudes from the penultimate year of the war to the point when the Gruppe 47 came into being. In the process of re-analysing Richter's own reflections, in *Der Ruf* in 1946-47, in his retrospective novel *Die Geschlagenen*[9] of 1949 and in his subsequent reminiscences,[10] it will become opportune also to refer to literary figures who participated in the public discourse that characterised the situation before the foundation of the Federal Republic.

Re-education was one of the policy options which began to be discussed in academic and political circles in Britain and the USA well before the end of the war. Even at the end of the First World War there had been voices in Britain which suggested such a policy. It was after a parliamentary debate in 1917 about 'how to change the heart of Germany' that the highly secretive Political Intelligence Department was founded. With the help of re-education, if not with the policy as it was actually executed, the Allies meant to tackle the problem at its most deep-rooted level. It involved an attempt at changing fundamentally the attitudes, the values and the civic character not only of the elites but also of ordinary Germans. Rather than wreaking revenge it was thought essential that Germany should be given the political and legal framework of democracy as well as the mentality to go with it. Western foreign policy staffs were clear that all this could not be achieved in the form of an institutional and ideological implant into Germany from outside. Even as early as 1943 there was no doubt that re-education had to be a collaborative enterprise, basically carried out by democratically minded Germans of conservative, liberal or socialist persuasion. A policy paper now in the British Public Record Office warns against any overzealous attitudes on the part of the occupying forces: 'the days of St Boniface are past and any hortatory efforts from without to "convert" the Germans will harden their unrepentant hearts. Germans alone can re-educate their fellow countrymen.'[11] While the British approach, for all the contradictory elements embedded in it, was fundamentally political, the American one was moral. The Americans' overriding aim was to expunge Nazism. Amongst other measures this entailed confronting the Germans with the atrocities committed in the concentration camps and suggesting to them that they bore some collective guilt for what had happened. Although this charge was never formally levied against German soldiers or civilians, it was conveyed by the way American officers treated them, or at least this was how many Germans believed they were being treated. Needless to say, it offended the anti-fascists among them, particularly those who could not point to a documented record of overt opposition, but nevertheless had felt no sympathies for Nazism. Not being able to prove their oppositional mentality, they found themselves classed amongst the many opportunists who lied about their involvement with the Third Reich and its ideology.

The case of Hans Werner Richter looked just like this. As a Trotskyite he had agitated against National Socialism before Hitler seized power in 1933. Then he disappeared to Paris for some time but, finding it difficult to live there, returned and even applied to be received into the *Reichsschrifttumskammer*. He was conscripted in 1940 and taken prisoner in 1943 at Nettuno in the battle at Monte Cassino. Richter appears never to have grasped the absurdity of his position in fighting for a cause that he did not consider to be his own and against people who, politically, were far closer to his ideas than his fellow soldiers. It has always been assumed, and Richter never contradicted it, that the figure of the protagonist in *Die Geschlagenen*, Obergefreiter Gühler, absorbed many of his author's own experiences. The disjuncture between Gühler and the American officer who interrogates him after his capture in Italy is most instructive, not least because it foreshadows the competition for the legitimacy of moral leadership between the German critical intelligentsia post-1945 and the Western Allies and prepares the argument for an alternative, autonomously German, political vision which, as it turned out, never had any chance in post-war reality.

Once it is established that Gühler is against Hitler he is trapped by the American officer's chiaroscuro logic. The battle still rages and the officer wants to know the exact positions of Gühler's batallion, but Gühler refuses to give this information, deviously saying that he is, after all, no artillery man. The American officer then goes back to basics and the following dialogue ensues:

> "Sie sind doch ein Gegner der Nazis?"
>
> "Da oben liegen keine Nazis, sondern Kameraden von mir."
>
> "Sie helfen den Krieg abkürzen."
>
> "Nein", sagte Gühler und stand dabei auf, "der Krieg hat seine eigenen Gesetze. Jede Stellung, die ich Ihnen sage, bedeutet dreißig bis vierzig Volltreffer für die Kameraden, die jetzt noch eine Chance haben, mit dem Leben davonzukommen."
>
> [...]
>
> "Ich verstehe Sie nicht",[...]"wenn Sie gegen Hitler sind, müßten Sie auf unserer Seite gegen Deutschland kämpfen."
>
> Gühler nahm eine Zigarette.
>
> Wieder beugte sich der Dolmetscher über den Tisch und gab ihm Feuer. Gühler sah ihm dabei voll ins Gesicht. Dann sagte er langsam:
>
> "Ich bin Sozialist und ein Deutscher. Es gibt für mich nur eine Möglichkeit. In meinem Land meine Idee durchzusetzen. Aber nicht gegen mein Land. Nicht für fremde Interessen." (*Die Geschlagenen*, pp.124f.)

These answers by a German PoW are obviously presented with the full force of conviction, although they are riddled with contradictions. One might have some sympathy with Gühler for not wanting to shorten the odds of survival for the comrades he had been fighting with. However, his unhesitating answer seems to suggest that he is entrapped by the sheer mystique of comradeship, if not the unquestioned feeling of warmth provided by the *völkisch* community which he feels honour bound to protect, irrespective of his comrades' manifest Nazi sympathies. Gühler's last answer is fundamentally flawed because it allows for no recognition of the Allies having to sacrifice the lives of their soldiers in order to create the freedom of opinion in Germany which would permit an open advocacy of socialist views in the first place. Gühler assumes that Nazi rule in Germany is based mainly on terror and chooses to ignore the fact that it was also widely supported by the fanaticism of conviction. In his political simple-mindedness he assumes that the Allies' role can be limited to removing the Nazis from power in order then to leave Germany to the Germans. It becomes clear in the course of the novel that Gühler cannot understand why the Americans do not welcome him unreservedly as an ally and treat him as an equal. He is therefore greatly disappointed by the realisation that, in the eyes of the Americans, all Germans are amongst the defeated: '"Ja", sagte Gühler, "für die haben wir alle den Krieg verloren, du und ich und die Nazis, die in den Baracken liegen und uns an den Galgen wünschen. Sie sehen keinen Unterschied"'(p.248). In real life, Richter also took a little while to understand that he could not just conceive of himself as a victor. Only after having been commandeered to work on *Der Ruf — Blätter für deutsche Kriegsgefangene* in Fort Kearney does he finally comprehend his status as one of the vanquished. The paper's constant assertions of German collective guilt changed Richter's mood abruptly from 'Ich fühle mich als Sieger' to 'In jenen Tagen [i.e. four months after the war] wurde mir endgültig bewußt, daß auch ich zu den Verlierern gehörte.'[12]

The author of *Die Geschlagenen* is, of course, quite aware of the fanatical Nazi convictions held by some his comrades and he describes in vivid detail the regime of terror that they create under the noses of their captors in the American PoW-camps. However, rather than this being recognised as disrupting Gühler's cosy notion of military comradeship, it is used in criticism of the Americans. There is more than one suggestion in the book that the American army personnel, far from protecting the anti-Nazis, are actually driving them into the arms of the Nazi fanatics. Similarly, there is the suggestion that the American occupation of Germany would only mean a change of dictatorial master, not liberation at all, but at best victory and defeat at the same time.

These views are strikingly similar to those promoted by Richter, Andersch and others in 1946-47 in *Der Ruf. Unabhängige Blätter der jungen Generation* From the start scepticism about re-education, which turns to criticism and finally to rejection, is relentlessly maintained. True, there is some praise by Andersch for the British work with German PoWs at Wilton Park. But this is an absolute exception. Translated not as 'Umerziehung' or 'Erziehung zur Demokratie' but rather mischievously as 'Rückerziehung', the policy of re-education is thought to be doomed to failure, both because the cream of the Anglo-American writers, artists and educators is not involved and because the young generation in Germany is not deemed to need any re-education. That the generational divide is some kind of absolution from Nazism appears to be a sacrosanct conviction amongst the contributors to *Der Ruf*. It is initially expressed by Andersch in his essay 'Das junge Europa formt sein Gesicht':

> Denn die junge deutsche Generation, die Männer und Frauen zwischen 18 und
> 35 Jahren, getrennt von den Älteren durch die Nicht-Verantwortlichkeit für
> Hitler, von den jüngeren durch das Front- und Gefangenschaftserlebnis, durch
> das 'eingesetzte' Leben also, — sie vollziehen die Hinwendung zum neuen
> Europa mit leidenschaftlicher Schnelligkeit.[13]

Andersch seems loath to state the obvious, namely that this generation of
Germans thought in European terms mainly because of its double
conditioning. The Third Reich as the hegemon of Europe had taught it to do
so and the excesses of nationalism, having made Germany into an
international pariah, left it little option but to abhor all nationalism and
project itself as European.

The second reason for refusing to acknowledge re-education as a
necessary option was the *Ruf*-contributors' preference for the paradoxes of
existentialism. Having learnt from across the Rhine that 'l'existence précède
l'essence', they argued that the image of the human itself had been sullied not
just by National Socialism, but by anonymous economic-bureaucratic
machines and by the dubious turn taken by technology in the development
of the nuclear bomb. The existence of human beings, irrespective of
ideology, race and class had to be put centre stage again, argued Richter. His
notion of the 'lost' generation is therefore conceived not in national but in
global terms and serves to relativise the agonies of the German young
generation by absorbing it into young humankind's need for renewal. In
other words, re-education could have meaning only in assisting youth
worldwide to regain its anthropological poise by rebuilding an ethos of
solidarity in order to overcome the mountainous moral and intellectual ruins
left by the hell of the war.

The third reason was that there was allegedly nothing to learn that the
young generation had not already learned. According to the journalist Walter
Heist in his contribution 'Das deutsche Volk und die Demokratie', young
Germans proudly remember the republican, democratic and socialist impetus
of the German working class which established democracy in the Weimar
Republic, although that class was to be eventually betrayed by its leaders.
For him re-education is 'Rückerziehung' in the sense of making the German
people acquiesce in the imperialist designs of the Western powers. Having
been dragged into the abyss by the 'faulen Geschäfte des deutschen
Kapitalismus' it is now being utilised for those of foreign capital:

> Man spricht von Demokratie und meint dabei die Ausschaltung mißliebiger
> Konkurrenten. Man spricht von der Befreiung der Völker und spannt sie in die

> eigenen imperialistischen Pläne ein. Das sieht das deutsche Volk, das ein
> empfindliches demokratisches Gewissen hat, und wird mißtrauisch. [...]
>
> Unter dem Vorwand der Demokratisierung hat man bis jetzt nur die
> demokratischen Kräfte im Volk gelähmt.[14]

Quite apart from the preposterous claim that the German people at the end of
the war had a 'sensitive democratic conscience', it is through the mobilisation
of simplistic communist interpretations of fascism from the 1930s that the
author here unthinkingly equates re-education with a mendacious regime's
attempts at thought control to ensure the democratic paralysis of the German
people as a political subject. A further variant of this argument was that the
suggestion that the policy of re-education was a contradiction in terms in that
it was carried out under the aegis of a military dictatorship.

But there was a fourth, more legitimate and more realistic, reason why
re-education was believed to be not only a devious, contradictory and
unethical enterprise by the Allies, but one that was politically imprudent, for
it heralded the permanent division of Germany. In his famous essay
'Deutschland — Brücke zwischen Ost und West' Hans Werner Richter
argued what he had already suspected at the time of the Fort Kearney *Ruf*,
namely that 'Rückerziehung' destroyed the unity of the German nation:

> Indem man ein Volk zu trennen versucht, indem man versucht, diese Trennung
> im geistigen Sein dieses Volkes zu vertiefen, reißt man nicht nur die Kluft
> zwischen dem östlichen und dem westlichen Teil dieses Landes auf, sondern
> läßt diese Kluft zu jenem Abgrund zwischen dem westlichen und dem östlichen
> Teil Europas werden, der nicht mehr überbrückbar ist.[15]

The intellectuals of *Der Ruf* ardently desired a socialist humanism in ethics
and a democratic socialism in politics that would be able to reconcile
individual freedom and social cohesion with economic planning. They
tirelessly declared that the hour for such a new social order had come. Yet
they were realistic enough to perceive what they called the 'cold revolution'
in the Soviet Zone, which was being forced through without any democratic
consent. At the same time they were haunted by the capitalist restoration in
the West, which, though recognised as being 'eine Wiederherstellung
rechtsstaatlicher Verhältnisse, wie sie vor 1933 gegeben waren', was feared
to be pregnant with the same disasters that befell the world thereafter.
Richter's report on a tour of the Eastern Zone, which appeared in *Der Ruf* in
August and September 1946, is very eloquent in voicing concern over the
ominous developments which inaugurated what came to be known as the
'Cold War': 'Drüben das proletarische Deutschland, hier die Reste des

bürgerlichen. Die Zonengrenze ist der Kaiserschnitt durch Deutschlands
Mitte. Er kann tödlich sein.'[16] Winston Churchill, perhaps unconsciously
borrowing a phrase first used by Joseph Goebbels, had spoken of an 'Iron
Curtain'[17] in March that year, but, of course, the implications here were
quite different. Churchill's main concern was the advance of Soviet power
into the heart of Europe which prompted the US Secretary of State, James
Francis Byrnes, to call for its containment in his famous speech in Stuttgart
on 6 September 1946. Churchill's Zurich speech, calling for a European
Union, followed on 19 September 1946. The inescapable Cold-War division
was manifest and the outlines of a political partnership between Western
Germany and the Western Allies, however unequal to start with, were
conceivable. This was, of course, what the contributors of *Der Ruf* had
feared. It would mean that the independent intelligentsia, which aspired to be
the voice of the young generation in Germany, was relegated to the sidelines
of history. In the spring of 1947 Andersch, aware of speaking against the
trend of public opinion in the Western Zones, warns of the consequences that
any intensification of East-West tension must have for Germany and the
world, namely the endangering of peace and the consignment of Germany to
the status of battleground of the great powers.

> Nur wenn Deutschland als geschlossenes Gebilde, als strategisch zwar
> kontrollierter, aber in sich autonomer Raum erhalten bleibt, wird es aus seinem
> Herzen und aus seiner Kraft heraus an jener europäischen Lösung mitarbeiten
> können, die allein den Frieden der Welt zu sichern vermag. Ein geteiltes
> Deutschland hingegen würde nicht anderes sein als das Aufmarsch-Glacis der
> großen Mächte.[18]

At this stage, Andersch had become pessimistic about the possibility
of an alternative post-war politics in which the victors, having completed
what he and Richter considered their main task, namely the military defeat of
Nazism, would withdraw from Germany and leave it to the young generation
to sort things out. The idolisation of the young generation by the *Ruf*
contributors is astonishing. They were blind to its enmeshment with Nazi
ideology and saw the distinction of that generation in its proven capability to
form community and practise solidarity under conditions of enormous
hardship. This is why Richter and his protagonist Gühler feel it would have
been treachery to deliver fellow soldiers into the hands of the Allies. Without
any sense of betrayal or apology Rüdiger Proske described this central
experience of solidarity in Hitler's war machine in an essay on the young
generation in *Frankfurter Hefte*:

> Und dann waren da die Gemeinschaften, innerhalb derer wir nicht mehr einsam waren. Kleine, unübersehbare Gemeinschaften, die Besatzung eines Schiffes, eines Flugzeuges, die Bedienungsmannschaft eines Gerätes, eine Infanteriegruppe, eine Staffel, eine Schnellbootflottille. Wissen jene, die von uns reden, was es heißt, rechts und links neben sich auf der Ebene Kameraden in den Schützenlöchern liegen zu sehen oder schräg hinter sich in den Flugzeugen Freunde zu wissen, oder such mitten im Atlantik zum Rudel mit anderen zu treffen?[19]

Sure enough Proske considered the bellicose aims of such martial communities wrong, but judged their feelings of internal cohesion to be genuine.

Der Ruf interpreted democracy as meaning that the young generation had to be given its head. It would furnish an elite to guide the mass of the population onto the path of conscious political citizenship. Echoes of Heinrich Mann's seminal essay 'Geist und Tat' of 1910 are detectable here. The *Ruf*-authors argued that the self-determination of the Germans was a prerequisite not only of peace but also of the necessary ideological synthesis between East and West. Germany, instead of becoming an 'Aufmarsch-Glacis' of opposing ideological systems, would instead become their round table for compromise:

> Deutschland wäre nicht mehr Berührungs- und Reibungsfläche zweier Machtsphären, sondern neutrale Experimentierfläche zweier Ideen-Räume, auf der die Deutschen selbst gehalten wären, eine Synthese zu finden und vorzuleben, die der ganzen Welt zum Vorbild dienen könnte.[20]

Such utopias of a paradigmatic, neutral, European and rehabilitated Germany proved illusory in the post-war situation, but kept feeding the peace and protest movements for the decades of the Cold War to come. The critique of individual politicians and ideological tendencies by increasingly prominent writers and journalists became a feature of the Federal Republic's political culture. It helped bolster its scarce resources of democratic tolerance. In their enthusiasm for political reflection the contributors of *Der Ruf* set an example for the creation of public debate about matters of fundamental democratic concern. To this extent they challenged the moral legitimacy first of the Allied elites and later of German politicians. In other words, they took on board the core of re-education and lived up perfectly to its ideal-type criterion, helping to transform a society from the passive authoritarianism of dictatorship to the active citizenship of democracy.

Footnotes

[1] See Sabine Cofalla, *Der "soziale Sinn" Hans Werner Richters. Zur Korrespondenz des Leiters der Gruppe 47* (Berlin: Weidler, 1997).

[2] See also Wilfried van der Will, 'From the 1940s to the 1990s. The critical intelligentsia's changing role in the political culture of the Federal Republic', *Debatte. Review of Contemporary German Affairs*, 5: 1 (1997), 25-48. For an earlier study see K. Stuart Parkes, *Writers and Politics in West Germany* (London and Sydney: Croom Helm, 1986).

[3] Nicholas Pronay, 'Introduction', in Nicholas Pronay and Keith Wilson (eds), *The Political Re-Education of Germany and her Allies after World War II* (London and Sydney: Croom Helm, 1985), p.1.

[4] Quoted in Hermann Glaser, *Die Kulturgeschichte der Bundesrepublik Deutschland*, vol. 1: *Zwischen Kapitulation und Währungsreform 1945-1948* (Frankfurt a. M.: Fischer, 1990), p.124.

[5] *Die Wandlung. Eine Monatszeitschrift*, unter Mitwirkung von Karl Jaspers, Werner Krauss und Alfred Weber, hrsg. von Dolf Sternberger, verlegt von Lambert Schneider in Heidelberg bei Carl Winter, Universitätsverlag, 1946ff.; Auflage 30 000.

[6] See Urs Widmer, *1945 oder die 'Neue Sprache'. Studien zur Prosa der 'Jungen Generation'* (Düsseldorf: Schwann, 1966), pp.32ff.

[7] It was Hans Magnus Enzensberger, who in his essay 'Die Clique' famously called the meetings of the Gruppe 47 'das Zentralcafé einer Literatur ohne Hauptstadt', in: Hans Werner Richter (ed.), *Almanach der Gruppe 47* (Reinbek bei Hamburg: Rowohlt, 1962), p.27.

[8] Hans Werner Richter, in: *Almanach*, p. 8.

[9] Hans Werner Richter, *Die Geschlagenen* (Munich: dtv, 1969). Further references to this work are to be found in the text under *Die Geschlagenen*.

[10] Hans Werner Richter, 'Wie entstand und was war die Gruppe 47?', in: Hans Werner Richter, *Von Erfahrungen und Utopien. Briefe an einen jungen Sozialisten* (Frankfurt a. M.: Eichborn, 1981), particularly pp.71-110.

[11] 'The future of Germany', PS (43) 2, 8 August 1943, Public Record Office (London), FO 371/34459/C14087.

[12] Hans Werner Richter, in: Heinz Ludwig Arnold (ed.), *Die Gruppe 47. Ein kritischer Grundriß*, 2nd. edn. (Munich: text + kritik, 1987), pp.44f.

[13] Alfred Andersch, 'Das junge Europa formt sein Gesicht', in: Hans Schwab-Felisch (ed.), *Der Ruf. Eine deutsche Nachkriegszeitschrift* (Munich: dtv, 1962), pp. 21-26, here p.25.

[14] Walter Heist, 'Das deutsche Volk und die Demokratie', in: Schwab-Felisch, *Der Ruf*, pp.174-80, here pp.178f.

[15] Hans Werner Richter, 'Deutschland — Brücke zwischen Ost und West', in: Schwab-Felisch, *Der Ruf*, pp. 46-49, here p. 48.

[16] Hans Werner Richter, '"Wo sollen wir landen, wo treiben wir hin...?"', in: Schwab-Felisch, *Der Ruf*, pp. 237-52, here p.252.

[17] This image borrowed from the theatre was first used in relation to the policy of the USSR by Joseph Goebbels in a leading article in *Das Reich*, 25 February 1945: 'Wenn das deutsche Volk die Waffen niederlegte, würden die Sowjets, auch nach den Abmachungen zwischen Roosevelt, Churchill und Stalin, ganz Ost- und Südosteuropa zuzüglich des größten Teils des Reiches besetzen. Vor diesem einschließlich der Sowjetunion riesigen Territorium würde sich sofort ein eiserner Vorhang heruntersenken, hinter dem die Massenabschlachtung der Völker begänne.' In a radio broadcast on 2 May 1945 the image was subsequently used by Count Schwerin von Krosigk, briefly Grand Admiral Dönitz's Foreign Secretary: 'Im Osten wird der eiserne Vorhang immer weiter vorgerückt, hinter dem, den Augen der Welt entzogen, das Werk der Vernichtung der in der Gewalt der Bolschewisten gefallenen Menschen vor sich geht.' See Walter Lüdde-Neurath, *Regierung Dönitz* (Göttingen; Musterschmidt, 1964), pp.135f.

[18] Alfred Andersch, 'Jahrhundert der Furcht', in: Schwab-Felisch, *Der Ruf*, pp.180-83, here p.182.

[19] Rüdiger Proske und Werner Weymann-Weyhe, 'Wir aus dem Kriege. Der Weg der jüngeren Generation', *Frankfurter Hefte*, 3 (1948), 796.

[20] Alfred Andersch, 'Die Zonen und der Weltfriede', in: Schwab-Felisch, *Der Ruf*, pp.79-83, here p.82.

CLARE FLANAGAN

Der Ruf and the Charge of Nationalism

It still remains difficult to determine the exact reason for the banning of *Der Ruf* by the American authorities in 1947. One factor suggested is that the journal was tainted by the ideology of German nationalism, an accusation also advanced by some German commentators at the time. While it is true that the journal fought against the division of Germany and sought a German voice in international affairs, it at the same time demonstrably attacked atavistic nationalism. If it did display certain nationalistic tendencies, then this was nationalism in a much modified form. It must also be remembered that *Der Ruf* favoured democracy, something which was anathema to traditional German nationalists.

The recent fiftieth anniversary of the founding of the Gruppe 47 provoked renewed interest in questions of the reception and mythology of the Group. These particular questions apply equally to the journal edited by Andersch and Richter in the immediately preceding years — *Der Ruf*. The designation of 'myth' is particularly apt in the case of the journal since there is continuing fascination with its reputation as both traitor and national martyr, and with the mystery which still surrounds its demise. Originally created by the American Psychological Warfare Division to re-educate German prisoners-of-war in Van Etten, New York, in March 1945, and promoted to the headquarters of post-war planning at Fort Kearney, Rhode Island, it rapidly changed from protégé to rebel on its transfer to Germany where it continued publication under licence from the American occupation authorities.[1] It was suppressed by the Americans in April 1947 after a mere fourteen home editions. Prominent among the reasons suggested for the controversial withdrawal of the licence held by editors Andersch and Richter is the charge of nationalism. This charge, like the others, may have been mainly directed at the two men since the journal itself continued in publication under new editorship.

A symbol both of American investment in Western Germany but also of Allied censorship, *Der Ruf* exposes particularly well the tensions which existed and the vibrancy of German political inquiry during its brief (and unique) existence. It features frequently in histories of the occupation, of post-1945 West German culture, German-American relations, and the early Cold War in Germany. The reasons for its disappearance, however, are rarely explored.

There is little firm evidence from official sources relating to the facts behind the licence withdrawal. The American Military archives have been until recently incompletely catalogued, making research of the exact procedures difficult. What is known is that although Allied policies of denazification were not uniform, provision had been made for firm action in response to undesirable behaviour. One Control Council Directive permitted the 'removal from office and from positions of responsibility' 'of persons hostile to Allied purposes'.[2] A particular area of concern cited was the press (p.103, para.2). Given the existence of such rulings, there was, unsurprisingly, no requirement for the Allies to justify any actions taken.

Nor were Andersch and Richter clear about why action had been taken against them. Their publisher, Curt Vinz, was keen to stress that there had been disagreements between the publishing house and the two editors.[3] But Andersch and Richter were puzzled about why this would not have remained a matter for the two parties. They had also heard a rumour that the Americans only wished to remove Richter and that officers of the American Counter Intelligence Corps had proof that he was an agent of the SED.[4] Later, Richter suggested that it might have been the Russians who were responsible.[5] Andersch, it is claimed, saw the journal as a victim of the outbreak of the Cold War. Andersch and Richter also noted that Hans Wallenberg, an officer of American Military Government and editor of the official daily of the American zone, the *Neue Zeitung*, had identified two offending articles: one, 'Das patriotische Trinkwasser', identified a water-pump with signs that deceived thirsty non-Germans as a possible Werwolf monument; the other was a cynical piece claiming essentially that the occupation was endangering German culture — it predicted a brain-drain and advised any émigrés thinking of returning to Germany to be sure to arrange delivery of Care packages.[6] While these two articles may have raised eyebrows, it has been generally accepted that they are too trivial to account alone for the suppression. And in fact both do pale rather when compared to some other opinions published.

Concern on the part of the Americans seems to have been more general. There is evidence to suggest that there were, in American circles, objections to a new version of nationalism corresponding to, as they wrote, the 'good old stab-in-the-back legend'.7 Although the Americans were the ones who took action, criticism of the journal came from more than one quarter. Both the Russians and the French were said to have been displeased by opinions expressed in the journal — in this context it is usual to cite an article accusing a French communist leader of obsessive prejudice against the Germans, a piece incurring, it was rumoured, not only French, but also Soviet disapproval.8

The most overt criticism at the time, however, came from German sources, and the most specific accusations of nationalism from fellow journalists. The debate commenced in the last few issues under Andersch and Richter when charges from two former contributors were addressed. Erich Kuby, who was to be the next editor, had accused *Der Ruf* of using nationalistic jargon.9 In his attack in the *Süddeutsche Zeitung* in February 1947, he wrote that the journal had revealed weakness and displayed an inability to write objectively. It was easy, Kuby argued, to use such language — 'Der Nationalist hierzulande genießt mit Recht eine Art Narrenfreiheit' (Vaillant, p.205). C.H. Ebbinghaus, writing in the *Neue Zeitung*, made the same allegation, but recognised the language as tactical and inclusive (ibid.).

Richter, described by Walter Maria Guggenheimer as 'der politischste Kopf unter ihnen', dismissed Kuby's attack as absurd and scoffed at his poor use of political vocabulary.10 The journal treated more seriously Ebbinghaus's article, acknowledging Ebbinghaus's defence of the journal against accusations that they were exploiting the young and his warning that the journal might encourage 'Beifall von der falschen Seite'.11 While acknowledging this risk, it seems that they felt the onus lay on the reader not to misinterpret the journal. There was justification for this approach; one American contemporary praised the language they used as 'the only one apt to divert the young generation [...] from dangerous demagogues' (Richter-Archiv, 72/86/501).

In another response to obviously more general criticism, Richter rejected the accusation that they were 'verkappte Militaristen' by poking fun at *Der Ruf*'s critics; he wrote that, when the office was quiet, the journal's staff put on their monocles and played with tin soldiers.12 In the penultimate issue, the journal warned against the threat it perceived to the freedom of the press. This was Nazi practice, not yet erased, it argued — 'gelernt ist gelernt' — redirecting the same charge back to its critics.[13] Accompanying the article was a cartoon with a caption reading 'er sucht die nationalen Phrasen'. A man is pictured using a powerful magnifying-glass to examine copies of *Der Ruf*. Thus the journal strenuously rejected charges of nationalism and responded to threats of censorship with contempt.

It must have seemed ironic to the journalists that all this followed accusations by fellow prisoners-of-war in America of betrayal of their nation and compatriots.[14] In a further extraordinary development, this accusation was to be repeated in the sixties when revisionists condemned the holding of a post-war licence as amounting to collaboration with the Allied occupiers.[15] With this wealth of at times seemingly conflicting examples of criticism and praise, the debate surrounding *Der Ruf* can immediately be seen as one of national identity and reputation.

To what extent such accusations were justified is only clear on closer examination of the journal. There is opinion that might be viewed as nationalistic. American concern about a 'stab-in-the-back' theory is to a certain extent justified. The journal certainly demanded that the ordinary German be set apart from generals, politicians and top industrialists, who had betrayed their people.[16] After 1945, the betrayal from above was seen as much more significant, and *Der Ruf*'s opposition to the theory of collective guilt was forceful and unapologetic. Although far from alone in attributing particular blame to these groups, the journal was inevitably linked, because of the historical precedent, with the rise of nationalist politics.

One analysis of nationalism points to the 'strongest form of political nationalism' as being simply the desire for independence, and opposition to the occupation is easily traced within the journal's pages.[17] Objections were raised to censorship — there was the plea for freedom of the press, and one column was entitled 'Bücher, die wir nicht lesen dürfen'. The journal strenuously objected to the division of Germany, which it regarded as a consequence of Allied politics.[18] It repeatedly raised questions about reparations, an issue connected with both occupation politics and independent German representation. Another definition of nationalism mentions the desire for equal standing with others, and certainly the journal objected to the fact that Germany was not represented at the negotiating table for the discussions about the

Polish border and the fate of Pomerania and Silesia.[19] It wanted German involvement in world affairs and equal partnership in Europe. It argued vigorously for the repatriation of German prisoners-of-war held abroad — in the face of priority being given by the Allies at this point to the repatriation or resettlement of displaced persons (former *Zwangsarbeiter*)[20] — and, in this context, accused the British government of putting British economic welfare before Germany's moral well-being.[21] Perhaps most famously, there was the continuing passionate commitment to German-led re-education.[22] There is then clearly a range of ideals, all of which could be used to support an argument of nationalism as an editorial attitude.

It can be argued, however, that the defence against the charge of nationalism is equally strong. If nationalism is the exploitation of national awareness by 'political leaders', *Der Ruf* does not qualify. The editors were not political leaders and they refused to react to calls for a '*Ruf*-Partei'. Their aim was not to lead, but to question the status quo, to challenge authority, to educate others in matters of political freedom, and to defend those sections of the German people towards whom they felt affinity. *Der Ruf* criticised politicians, deplored the lack of clarity in political debate and attacked standards of political reporting.[23] It demanded that the press be responsible and bear its readership in mind. Above all, it wanted its readers to be critical. It saw its role as educating its readers in democracy and as part of this it had to demonstrate that occupation rule was not democratic government.[24] In all it strove always for a balanced analysis and praise was given where due. Positive attitudes to the Allies were voiced — the Americans were praised for their generosity, the British for their peace campaigns, the parliamentary system, the Labour government, and for promoting proper re-education by increasingly handing over responsibility to Germans.[25] One entire issue (Heft 5; 15 October 1946) was devoted to Franco-German rapprochement. There was then a reasonably balanced approach to analysis of contemporary affairs, one not in line with a narrow programme of national interest.

Indeed, *Der Ruf* condemned nationalism in others. It lamented the way that the blue-prints of the constitutions of Bavaria and Württemberg-Baden had exposed 'die deutsche Krankheit der autoritätssüchtigen Hörigkeit'.[26] As well as warning against this tendency, *Der Ruf* distinguished between two contemporary types of

German, the freedom fighters and the nationalists. The freedom fighters were those who sought synthesis between East and West. The nationalists on the other hand, whether unscrupulous members of the SED in the Eastern Zone or fanatical followers of Churchill in the West, were self-seeking and maintained the 'Un-Erziehbarkeit' of their own people.[27] The Allies, according to *Der Ruf*, were to blame for encouraging this nationalism, as they had failed to arrange a peace with Germany, and the only remedy was the establishment of a young German opposition. Readily admitting that this term 'opposition' might shock, *Der Ruf* insisted that the concept was fundamental to the process of democracy (ibid.).

Der Ruf nevertheless advocated a constructive and positive approach to the question of 'national belonging'. In his article 'Nationalismus und Nationalismus', Heinz Friedrich emphasised that while nationalism had proved its destructive potential, this did not mean 'daß wir nicht mehr vaterländisch denken dürfen'.[28] *Der Ruf* was, however, careful to specify the conditions necessary for the safe expression of such feelings. A sense of nationhood, defined in an editorial as 'die Liebe zu unserem Land und zu unserer Nation', was legitimate as long as it was placed within the framework of a stable parliamentary democracy.[29]

Clearly, we can distinguish between the aims of Andersch and Richter and their colleagues, and those of nationalists during the Third Reich. There was no messianism in *Der Ruf*, there was no pan-Germanism, no triumphalism. Nor did the journal advocate cultural purism. Far from fearing contamination by external influences, *Der Ruf* courted contemporary European figures and espoused current intellectual developments, particularly French ones, most crucially existentialism. So, rather than reinforcing the cultural exclusiveness of the German people, the journal promoted a broadening of culture and a widening of perspectives. 'Tolerance' and 'pluralism' were keywords, whereas ideology was rejected.[30] Democracy, civic responsibility and liberalism were likewise features of the journal's rhetoric. Its search for a 'Third Way', a synthesis of the good in each system, was in fact an ideal it shared with many others who also used the bridge metaphor. Proportional representation, it argued, would help protect Germany from repeating political mistakes. Internationalism as a significant post-war development was both mirrored and specifically celebrated as both means and end. This did not mean for *Der Ruf* international bloc movements, but international cooperation. It looked in particular to European partnership, a fundamental element of its programme.

Yet it is clear that, with definitions of nationalism varying so widely, much can be used or deemed to support the claim. Two significant examples which underline this are the themes of socialism and Europe. Even these, two of the central planks of *Der Ruf*'s programme, could have been regarded with suspicion. The journal's vulnerability is evident. Both Andersch's and Richter's commitment to socialism was clear in the journal and was rooted in their earlier involvement in German communist youth movements. Leaning too far to the left was another measure of undesirability in the Western zones and this might be deemed not only a counter-argument to the charge of nationalism, but another valid alternative in explaining the journal's suppression. But Hobsbawm in his analysis of the general decline of the nation as a central issue after 1945, has pointed to nationalist discourse re-entering the domain of left-wing politics: an 'alliance', as he put it, 'of nationalism with the Left which had seemed so natural before 1848'.[31] So the association of national emancipation and a left-wing agenda — and the marked evidence of this in the Eastern Zone — may have added to general mistrust of the journal in the West. Even the European perspective would have carried historical associations with nationalist thought, Max Weber, for instance, having influentially commented on the need for the 'preservation of the German Reich as a great power among the "European world powers"'.[32] Given such historical aspects of German thought, it would perhaps have been viewed as impudence to expect an equal place in Europe. Although primarily concerned with parallels with National Socialism, monitors of the new German situation often turned in this way to the more distant past for ammunition against or in defence of Germany's predominantly anti-Nazi intellectual representatitives.

Three conclusions emerge. First, the unstinting commitment of *Der Ruf* to the essence of democracy is the reverse of traditional notions of nationalism. Second, despite the commitment to democracy, the empathy established between *Der Ruf* and the German public could have been regarded as a threat. At a time of emotional vulnerability, the journal's very success in reaching the people could have triggered a sense of unity, of belonging, and what was a collective sense of loss might have become a celebration of togetherness. The journalists of *Der Ruf* above all voiced compassion, compassion for the maimed soldier (the 'legless uniformed'), and for the starving, for the young people unable to forget their fellow-soldiers who had died beside them in battle, as well as the mothers desperately trying to trace them.[33] They urged understanding for the voiceless, the stunned. They embraced all and in doing so evoked a sense of nationhood which was perhaps perceived to be dangerous. Third, the solidarity with fellow Germans conveyed by *Der Ruf* closely conforms to a new type of post-1945 nationalism, subsequently identified in political theory. This 'benevolent' form of nationalism was described by veteran analyst of German nationalism, Louis Snyder, as a very different political phenomenon from the nationalism previously encountered, marking a change in the course of German history. Its emphasis, he wrote, was on a free people functioning in a free society. 'Young Germans', he stated, 'have chosen the moderation of liberal nationalism.'[34] The young had forged a new path, rejecting authoritarianism, Romanticism and other traditions of the past and seeking a European context. It has been argued elsewhere that the debate in the Western Zones about the German nation was in any case limited by the primacy of economic considerations so that the drive for restoration and nationalist slogans found no resonance with the population.[35] It is interesting to note that the Americans themselves recognised *Der Ruf*'s version of nationalism as 'new' (Richter-Archiv, 72/86/501, Bl.174). Nevertheless, even after the establishment of the Federal Republic, historians expressed scepticism about the sincerity of the change to Western-style democracy, so it is unsurprising that at this early stage doubt prevailed. *Der Ruf*'s devoted adherence to the principles of democracy was overlooked on account of its spirit of commitment to the German people.

Footnotes

[1] See Volker Christian Wehdeking, *Der Nullpunkt. Über die Konstituierung der deutschen Nachkriegsliteratur (1945-1948) in den amerikanischen Kriegsgefangenenlagern* (Stuttgart: Metzler, 1971), pp.6-11, 17-20; and Kurt W. Böhme, *Geist und Kultur der deutschen Kriegsgefangenen im Westen* (Bielefeld: Gieseking, 1968), p 1.

[2] Extracts from Control Council Directive No.24 (12 January 1946), quoted in: Beate Ruhm von Oppen (ed.), *Documents on Germany under Occupation*, 1945-54, (Royal Institute of International Affairs) (London: OUP, 1995), pp.102-07.

3 Jérôme Vaillant, *Der Ruf. Unabhängige Blätter der jungen Generation (1945-1949): Eine Zeitschrift zwischen Illusion und Anpassung* (Munich, New York, Paris: Saur, 1978), p.107. Further references to this volume are to be found in the text under Vaillant.

4 'Stellungnahme A. Anderschs und H.W. Richters zu ihrem Ausscheiden aus der "Ruf"-Redaktion', in: Vaillant, *Der Ruf*, p.210.

5 Hans Werner Richter, 'Beim Wiedersehen des "Ruf"', in: Hans Schwab-Felisch (ed.), *Der Ruf. Eine deutsche Nachkriegszeitschrift* (Munich: dtv, 1962), pp.7-9, here p. 7.

6 See 'Stellungnahme A. Anderschs und H.W. Richters'; Gerd Klaass, 'Das patriotische Trinkwasser', *Der Ruf*, 1: 14 (1 March 1947), 8; Walter M. Guggenheimer, 'Unmassgebliche Vorschläge zu einem umfassenden Austauschplan zwecks Rettung der deutschen Kultur', *Der Ruf*, 1: 14.14 (1 March 1947), 10-11; also in: Schwab-Felisch, *Der Ruf*, pp.231-36.

7 Akademie der Künste (West), Hans-Werner-Richter-Archiv, 72/86/501, Bl.174.

8 'An Herrn Marcel Cachin', *Der Ruf*, 1: 13 (15 February 1947), 1-2; 'Politisches Notizbuch', *Der Ruf*, 1: 13 (15 February 1947), 4.

9 *Süddeutsche Zeitung* (8 February 1947), quoted in: Vaillant, *Der Ruf*, pp.204-05.

10 Walter Maria Guggenheimer, 'Keineswegs wie Donnerhall', *Frankfurter Hefte*, 18 (1963), 350; Hans Werner Richter, 'Der Bürokraten-Überhang', *Der Ruf*, 1: 14 (1 March 1947), 7-8.

11 (DR), 'Sorgen im Lager der erhobenen Zeigefinger', *Der Ruf*, 1: 13 (15 February 1947), 3.

12 Hans Werner Richter, 'Wir verkappten Militaristen', *Der Ruf*, 1: 13 (15 February 1947), 7-8, here 7.

13 Hans Werner Richter, 'Die Sprachregelung', *Der Ruf*, 1: 15 (15 March 1947), 7-8.

14 Author's interview with journalist Günter Caspar.

15 Peter J. Humphreys, *Media and Media Policy in West Germany: the Press and Broadcasting since 1945* (Oxford and New York: Berg, 1990), p.3.

16 See, for example, (DR), 'Notwendige Aussage zum Nürnberger Prozeß', *Der Ruf*, 1: 1 (15 August 1946), 2; also in: Schwab-Felisch, *Der Ruf*, pp.26-29.

17 James G. Kellas, *The Politics of Nationalism and Ethnicity* (London: Macmillan, 1991), p.25.

18 (DR), 'Die Zonen und der Weltfriede', *Der Ruf*, 1: 6 (1 November 1946), 3; also in: Schwab-Felisch, *Der Ruf*, pp.79-83.

19 (DR), 'Die östliche Grenzfrage', *Der Ruf*, 1: 8 (1 December 1946), 3; also in: Schwab-Felisch, *Der Ruf*, pp.99-103.

[20] See Wolfgang Jacobmeyer, 'Strandgut des Krieges — "Displaced Persons"', in: *Deutsche im Ausland — Fremde in Deutschland. Migration in Geschichte und Gegenwart*, ed. by Klaus J. Bade (1992), pp.367-73, reproduced in *Das Dritte Reich: Ein Lesebuch zur deutschen Geschichte 1933-1945* (Munich: C.H. Beck, 1995), pp.303-06.

[21] Walter Heist, 'Nur eine Notiz...', *Der Ruf*, 1: 14 (1 March 1947), 8.

[22] (DR), 'Das junge Europa formt sein Gesicht', *Der Ruf*, 1: 1 (15 August 1946), 1-2; also in: Schwab-Felisch, *Der Ruf*, pp.21-26.

[23] See particularly (DR), 'Zeitungen lesen...', *Der Ruf*, 1: 1 (15 August 1946), 8; and (DR), 'Die Vergessenen?', *Der Ruf*, 1: 3 (15 September 1946), 2-3.

[24] (DR), 'Der grüne Tisch', *Der Ruf*, 1: 3 (15 September 1946), 1-2; also in: Schwab-Felisch, *Der Ruf*, pp.42-46.

[25] See (DR), 'Sorgen im Lager der erhobenen Zeigefinger' (see note 11); Fritz Woelcken, 'Die deutsche Schuld', *Der Ruf*, 1: 6 (1 November 1946), 8; Alfred Andersch, 'Die sozialistische Situation', *Der Ruf*, 1: 15 (15 March 1947), 4-6.

[26] Friedrich Minssen, 'Verfassungen — kritisch betrachtet (II)', *Der Ruf*, 1: 7 (15 November 1946), 3-4, here 3.

[27] (DR), 'Grundlagen einer deutschen Opposition', *Der Ruf*, 1: 8 (1 December 1946), 1-2, here 1; also in: Schwab-Felisch, *Der Ruf*, pp.94-99.

[28] Heinz Friedrich, 'Nationalismus und Nationalismus', *Der Ruf*, 1: 14 (1 March 1947), 8.

[29] (DR), 'Notwendige Aussage' (see note 16).

[30] See, for example, (DR), 'Die Chance der SPD', *Der Ruf*, 1: 7 (15 November 1946), 3; and 'Parteipolitik und Weltanschauung', same issue, 1-2.

[31] Eric Hobsbawm, *Nations and Nationalism since 1780* (Cambridge: CUP, 1990), p.150. This assessment is echoed in Louis L. Snyder, *German Nationalism. The Tragedy of a People. Extremism contra Liberalism in Modern German History*, 2nd edn (Port Washington: Kennikat Press, 1969), p.288.

[32] Montserrat Guibernau, *Nationalisms: The Nation-state and Nationalism in the Twentieth Century* (Oxford: Polity, 1996), p.38.

[33] See, for example, 'Warum schweigt die junge Generation?', *Der Ruf*, 1: 2 (1 September 1946), 1-2; also in: Schwab-Felisch, *Der Ruf*, pp.29-33.

[34] Louis L. Snyder, *Roots of German Nationalism* (Bloomington and Indianapolis: Indiana U.P., 1978), p.284.

[35] Walter Schmidt, 'The Nation in German History'; and Heinrich August Winkler, 'Nationalism and Nation-State in Germany', both in: Mikulas Teich and Roy Porter (eds), *The National Question in Europe in Historical Context* (Cambridge: CUP, 1993), pp.148-80, here p.166, and pp.181-95, here p.190, respectively.

HELMUT PEITSCH

Die Gruppe 47 und das Konzept des Engagements

Es wird immer wieder behauptet, die Gruppe 47 habe sich für 'engagierte Literatur' eingesetzt. Dabei wird übersehen, daß das Wort 'Engagement' in den öffentlichen Auseinandersetzungen um die deutsche Literatur in den vierziger und fünfziger Jahren kaum eine Rolle gespielt hat. Man sprach eher von Nonkonformismus, wenn es um gesellschaftskritische Literatur ging. Eine Wende stellte sich erst in den sechziger Jahren ein, als Stimmen laut wurden, die eine aktive Teilnahme der Schriftsteller am gesellschaftlichen Leben der Bundesrepublik einklagten. Diese Entwicklung ist im Zusammenhang mit der zur gleichen Zeit einsetzenden Entspannungspolitik zu sehen; inzwischen war es möglich geworden, linke Positionen in der Literatur und in der Politik einzunehmen.

Wer heute ein Feuilleton aufschlägt, begegnet früher oder später nicht nur der Feststellung, daß die engagierte Literatur tot ist, sondern auch dem Hinweis, daß solcherart tote Literatur von der Gruppe 47 repräsentiert worden sei.[1] Diese Gleichsetzung von Engagement und Gruppe 47 datiert nicht erst seit den Nachrufen auf die Literatur der alten Bundesrepublik, mit denen Bohrer, Greiner und Schirrmacher 1990 den Streit um Christa Wolfs *Was bleibt* nach Westen hin ergänzten,[2] sondern findet sich schon in der seit den siebziger Jahren aufblühenden Forschung zur Gruppe 47. Abgesehen davon, daß die dortige Wertung meist der der heutigen Kritiker diametral widerspricht, fällt aber auch auf, daß von den großen Literaturgeschichten über die Sammelbände bis zu Monographien und Aufsätzen eine Einschätzung vorherrscht, die, in Heinz Ludwig Arnolds Formulierung, lautet: Das Konzept der engagierten Literatur war für die Entwicklung der Gruppe 47 zu der deutschen Nachkriegsliteratur 'mit entscheidend'.[3]

    In diesem Aufsatz möchte ich meine Zweifel am veröffentlichten Selbstverständnis von Autoren der Gruppe 47 begründen.[4] Dabei werde ich in drei Schritten vorgehen: erstens die Verweigerung der Rezeption von Sartres Konzept darstellen, zweitens die Einbürgerung und Verdeutschung des Begriffs, drittens mit einer Vermutung schließen, weshalb die europäische Debatte über das Engagement mit Verspätung in der Bundesrepublik ankam.

Was die ersten fünfzehn Jahre der Geschichte der Gruppe 47 betrifft, so läßt sich an den Instanzen der bundesrepublikanischen Literaturverhältnisse belegen, daß die Werke der AutorInnen der Gruppe, die damals entstanden, verbreitet und gelesen wurden, nicht als eine Literatur des Engagements verstanden wurden. Auf dem Gipfel öffentlicher Legitimation von Gegenwartsliteratur, bei den Verleihungen des Büchner-Preises, fiel der Begriff nur einmal, und das geschah in der Rede eines Schweizers. Max Frisch, der 1958 die Probleme des Engagements diskutierte, und vier Jahre später Wolfgang Koeppen, der kein Gruppenmitglied war, blieben sogar bis zum Ende der Gruppe 47 die einzigen, die ihr Schreiben in Darmstadt als engagiert präsentierten. Im Gebrauch des Begriffs markierte Frisch seine Abweichung vom Konsens: 'der Ton, der uns zur Zeit vertrauter ist, [ist] der Ton des Anti-Engagement'.[5] Die geringe Zahl von Mitgliedern der Gruppe 47 unter den Preisträgern ist etwas, was der Büchner-Preis gemeinsam hat mit den Anthologien und Interview-Sammelbänden, in denen die deutsche Literatur damals von ganz anderen repräsentiert wurde.[6] Waren 5 von 16 Büchner-Preisträgern zwischen 1951 und 1967 Mitglieder der Gruppe, so 6 von den 15 Autoren, die Weyrauch 1960 erklären ließ *Ich lebe in der Bundesrepublik*, und 4 von den 15, mit denen Bienek 1962 *Werkstattgespräche* führte.[7] Keiner von ihnen 'bekannte sich' zu einer 'engagierten Literatur', wie Gerhard Hay es als Merkmal der Gruppe seit 1947 behauptet.[8] In den ersten fünfzehn Jahren der Existenz der Gruppe erschien in keiner der ihr durch Herausgeber verbundenen literarischen Zeitschriften auch nur ein einziger Artikel mit Engagement im Titel, weder in der *Literatur* noch in *Texte und Zeichen* oder den *Akzenten*; dafür fand sich das Problem periodisch in den Berichten der Tagespresse über internationale Kongresse. Insbesondere anläßlich deutsch-französischer Dichtertreffen wurde beklagt, 'daß die Scheidung der Geister [...] immer noch [...] sich nach dem Gegensatz von Poesie pure und Poesie engagée vollzog'.[9] In der Berichterstattung wurde der französische Begriff 'littérature engagée' als Zitat verwendet, wobei stets der Gegenbegriff 'poésie pure' mitzitiert wurde. Seit dem Frankfurter Schriftstellerkongreß von 1948 vollzog sich die Verwendung der französischen Zitate in einem Modus der doppelten

Abgrenzung, die den Begriff Nonkonformismus als Alternative
profilierte. Es ist bezeichnend, daß das Gruppenmitglied Armin
Eichholz in einem Bericht über ein Treffen der in Cap Circeo tagenden
Gruppe 47 mit italienischen Schriftstellern dem alternativen Terminus
eine italienische Herkunft andichtete: So 'spürte man doch eine
gemeinsame Aversion gegen das Sich-Festlegen auf die angebotenen
Weltanschauungen, eine innere Aufgeschlossenheit, die in Italien am
besten mit 'Nonkonformismus' umschrieben wird'.[10] Daß es keines
Imports bedurfte, belegt aber gerade der Sprachgebrauch des
Gruppenmitglieds, das 1950 die deutsche Übersetzung von Sartres
Qu'est-ce que la littérature? herausbrachte; in Hans Georg Brenners
eigener kritischer Terminologie war 'Konformismus' (Lettau, S.72) der
schärfste negative Begriff.

Die doppelte Abgrenzung von 'pure' und 'engagée', die
Nonkonformismus zur Alternative von Verpflichtung macht,
kennzeichnete die Stellungnahmen der — was literarische und politische
Orientierung angeht — unterschiedlichsten Mitglieder der Gruppe in
den vierziger und fünfziger Jahren. Sie läßt sich unter Berücksichtigung
der sukzessiven Integration wie der Prominenz zeigen an Alfred
Andersch wie an Hans Werner Richter, an Walter Jens wie Heinrich
Böll, an Hans Magnus Enzensberger wie Helmut Heißenbüttel, und nicht
zuletzt an Günter Grass.

Anderschs Fall ist deshalb besonders interessant, weil er — bis in
die Titel von Monographien[11] — zum Repräsentanten des Engagements
gemacht worden ist. Dabei wurde, wie Margaret Littler 1991 gezeigt
hat, die grundlegende Abgrenzung Anderschs von Sartres Konzept der
Verpflichtung übersehen.[12] Die Gleichsetzung von Literatur als Kunst
und Nonkonformismus ließ Andersch folgerichtig nicht nur Holthusen
und Lukács als Prediger des Konformismus gleichsetzen,[13] sondern
auch Sartres Begriff des Engagements nicht übernehmen. Die
Rezeptionsverweigerung ist deutlich schon in der einleitenden
Vorstellung von Sartre in der Anthologie *Europäische Avantgarde*
1949;[14] in der Gegenüberstellung von Sartre und Camus unter den
Stichworten Verpflichtung und Rebellion griff er genau das Moment
auf, das in seiner Sartre-Rezeption keine Rolle spielen sollte.[15] Zum
abgedruckten Ausschnitt 'Der Schriftsteller und seine Zeit' heißt es ganz
klar bei Andersch: 'Fällt es nicht auf, daß der Vielumstrittene, dem
seine Gegner vorwerfen, er predige eine bodenlose Freiheit, fast

ausschließlich von der Verpflichtung spricht, von der Notwendigkeit des 'engagement'?'[16]

Der kontrastierende Rekurs auf Camus wurde obligatorisch auch für andere Autoren der Gruppe 47 wie Siegfried Lenz; er definierte den Autor — nicht nur im Hamburger Gespräch von DDR- und BRD-Autoren — als 'keinem verpflichtet[e]' 'Ein-Mann-Partei';[17] im Zentrum der Diskussion stand 1961, so ein Teilnehmer:

> das Problem der litterature engagee oder non-engagee, was man mit seinen
> mehrfachen Verzweigungen auch noch mit anderen Namen bezeichnen kann,
> etwa der zweckgebundenen und der zweckfreien Literatur oder auch des
> Konformismus und des Nonkonformismus oder, wie einige es auch
> ausdrücken, der Ja-Sager und der Nein-Sager. (Ebd., S.83)

Im selben Jahr berief sich Walter Jens auf Camus' Nobelpreisrede, um das zweckfreie Neinsagen zu profilieren, wobei er auf einen Zusammenhang zwischen politischer und literarischer Orientierung aufmerksam machte. Die Ablehnung des Engagements und der innerliterarische Pluralismus der Gruppe verknüpften sich, wenn Jens zum Zitat aus Camus' Rede[18] hinzufügte:

> wer den Zerfall der Welt verhindern will, hat nicht nur den totalitären Kräften
> in politicis Paroli zu bieten und alle Einseitigkeit zu verneinen, er muß sich
> auch — auf literarischem Feld — gegen jeden Versuch wehren, eine
> Kanonisierung des einen, auf Kosten des anderen zu erreichen.[19]

Was Gunter E. Grimm speziell Andersch als eine 'einigermaßen vage' bleibende 'Einsicht' vorwirft, war wohl eine Bedingung des Funktionierens der Gruppe, daß nämlich 'Kunst [...] als solche der Dichotomie Engagement versus l'art pour l'art enthoben' sein sollte.[20] Zur Bedeutung von Anderschs 'Vagheit', die eine klare Abweisung des Engagements war, muß hinzugefügt werden, daß — entgegen einer verbreiteten Legende vom Ausnahmecharakter der Lesung des Essays *Deutsche Literatur in der Entscheidung* von 1947 — auch 'Die Blindheit des Kunstwerks' vorgelesen wurde, nämlich 1955 in Bebenhausen, und daß der Preis der Gruppe 47 ausdrücklich auch für Essays gestiftet wurde.[21] Christian Ferbers Bericht über die Lesung von Anderschs 'Kunstwerk'-Essay benutzte eine treffende Metapher: 'das rechte Bassin für die schöpferischen Wogen' (Lettau, S.115) verweist darauf, daß Grenzen gezogen wurden.

Die von Andersch in der Gegenüberstellung von Sartre und Camus als 'soziale Funktion'[22] und ästhetische Rebellion 1949 vorgenommene Form der doppelten Abgrenzung von engagierter wie reiner Literatur findet sich auch beim Organisator Richter. Ausgerechnet in seiner Rede zur Eröffnung der ersten Tagung des Grünwalder Kreises, der ja als politische Organisation von der literarischen der Gruppe selbst strikt getrennt gehalten wurde, begann Richter mit der Versicherung, die Unterscheidung sei 'völlig gleichgültig': 'es geht nicht um Ihre Entscheidung zwischen Literatur engagee und Literatur pure' (Schutte, S.239). In diesem Punkt stimmten Richter sowohl Böll als auch Heißenbüttel zu: 'Littérature engagée' und 'littérature pure' schienen keine echten Gegensätze, meinte Heißenbüttel über die Literatur nach den 'Vorwährungsjahre[n]', in denen er 'eher die Ausgangsbasis für die literarische Situation in der DDR erkennen [wollte] als für die der Bundesrepublik'[23] und Böll wandte sich zur selben Zeit gegen jegliche 'Gesinnungsliteratur',[24] aber auch gegen 'ein Dogma des Nicht-Engagiertseins' (Bienek, S.181): 'Die Manifeste der Engagierten sind meistens so peinlich wie die Gegenerklärungen derer, die sich für nicht engagiert erklären' (Böll, Bd.1, S.136). In Grass' öffentlicher Selbstverständigung fehlten zwar die französischen Begriffe, aber keineswegs der Mechanismus der doppelten Abgrenzung, von 'inhaltsfeindlichen Künstlern' einerseits, vom 'sozialen Realismus'[25] als 'Ideologie' (Grass, Bd.9, S.21) anderseits: 'würde ich es nicht [...] teilen in hier politisch bezogene und nur engagierte Literatur und dort ästhetisch bewußte l'art-pou-l'art-Literatur, sondern ich sehe da eher ein Zusammenklappen beider Dinge.'[26]

Bei Richter zeigte sich allerdings sechs Jahre nach seiner zitierten doppelten Abgrenzung, 1962 also, eine Veränderung, auch wenn er immer noch distanzierend die französischen Termini benutzte, als er sich gegen die Todeserklärungen für den realistischen Zeitroman zur Wehr setzte, die er von Jens und Enzensberger im selben Jahr zugestellt erhielt:

> Sagt man ihnen aber, ihre Einstellung sei nichts anderes als die Wiederholung des uralten 'l'art pour l'art-Standpunktes', also Literatur pure statt Literatur engagee, [...] so sind sie entsetzt und versuchen zu beweisen, daß die moderne Literatur ganz andere Wege gehe und nichts mehr mit diesen Auseinandersetzungen und vermotteten Begriffen zu tun hätte. (Schutte, S.292)

Von 'marionettenhaften Diskussionenen' hatte in der Tat Enzensberger in der Einleitung zur Suhrkamp-Anthologie *Vorzeichen* geschrieben,

aber schon der Umstand, daß er das Substantiv benutzte war Indiz von
Veränderung. Indem er Gisela Elsner, Ror Wolf, Jürgen Becker u.a.
charakterisierte, lieferte er eine Kurzfassung seines im gleichen Jahr
erschienenen Essays 'Poesie und Politik', der im Austausch mit Theodor
W. Adorno, dessen 'Zur Dialektik des Engagements' gleichfalls 1962
herauskam, gegen den Begriff des Engagements die gesellschaftliche
Funktion der Autonomie oder die kritische, durch Form das
gesellschaftliche Ganze negierende und darin ein ganz Anderes
antizipierende Funktion der Kunst ausspielte:

> Diese Schriftsteller rufen zwar nirgends das aus, was man gemeinhin
> Engagement nennt [...]. Aber sie wissen genau, daß der gesellschaftliche
> Gehalt, auf den es ankommt, einem Werk nicht aufzupfropfen ist; er findet
> sich dort, wo beim Schreiben die größte Strenge herrscht, von selbst ein;
> nicht an der Peripherie der bloßen Meinungen, sondern im Zentrum des
> poetischen Prozesses.[27]

Enzensberger wie Adorno trugen wider Willen zur Terminologisierung
des Begriffs Engagement bei. Gerade weil sie noch einmal den Konsens
der fünfziger Jahre festzuhalten suchten, markierte der veränderte
Sprachgebrauch schon die Defensive. Stand bei ihnen das schroff vom
Autor getrennte nonkonforme Werk im Zentrum,[28] so ging es im
selben Jahr Walter Jens in seiner Zurückweisung des Begriffs
Engagement um den nonkonformistischen Autor.

Als 'Archetypus des Nonkonformisten'[29] zeichnete ihn die
Verweigerung, die Negation aller Bindungen und Verpflichtungen aus.
In *Literatur und Politik* beschrieb Walter Jens ihn als den 'aus allen
Bindungen Entlassenen' (Jens 1963, S.17) im Hinblick auf Klasse, (Ebd.,
S.8) Nation (Ebd., S.10-11) und Macht im allgemeinen (Ebd., S.13).
Mit der Absage an jede Möglichkeit, indirekt — im Werk — sich
'politisch Gehör zu verschaffen', ließ Jens 'keine andere Wahl', 'als sich
[...] unmittelbar, mit Hilfe von Manifesten und Pamphleten' zu Wort zu
melden (Ebd., S17/18). Jens' ausdrückliche Auseinandersetzung mit
Sartres Engagementbegriff war ein Vergleich zwischen Frankreich und
der Bundesrepublik: 'Der Unterschied ist eklatant: während Camus und
Sartre, vom Résistancemythos inspiriert, alle Hoffnungen auf die
proletarischen Einsichten setzten, konnte es in Deutschland [...] in
keinem Augenblick zu einer Begegnung zwischen der Intelligenz und
der Arbeiterschaft kommen' (Ebd., S.8). Aber es war nicht nur der
'eklatant[e]' Unterschied zwischen Frankreich und der Bundesrepublik,

sondern auch der zwischen den beiden Franzosen Sartre und Camus, auf
den es Jens ankam:

> der deutsche Schriftsteller unserer Tage [...], von keiner Klasse beauftragt,
> von keinem Vaterland beschützt, mit keiner Macht im Bunde, ist in der Tat ein
> dreifach einsamer Mann. Doch gerade diese Stellung inmitten der Pole, die
> Bindungslosigkeit eben läßt ihn — eine ungeheure, einzigartige Chance! —
> so frei sein wie niemals zuvor. Im Unterschied zu Sartre und im Einklang mit
> Camus [...] fürchtet er nicht, sich durch solche Janusposition realer
> Wirkungsmöglichkeiten zu begeben. (Ebd., S.15-16)

Vom Frankfurter Schriftstellerkongreß 1948, wo der aus der
SBZ übergesiedelte Theodor Plievier die schon in den zwanziger Jahren
gebräuchliche Metapher wiederauflegte, bis zu Jens' programmatischer
Beschreibung der 'jungen deutschen Literatur der Moderne' dominierte
das Bild des Schriftstellers 'zwischen den Stühlen'.[30] Es fehlte auch
nicht in der Büchner-Preisrede von Frisch, wo es den Zusammenhang
zwischen der Verweigerung des Engagement-Begriffs und dem
Nonkonformismus beleuchtet: 'Vor die Wahl gestellt, ein Engagement
auf die Dogmen des Ostens oder ein Engagement auf die Dogmen des
Westens einzugehen, entscheiden sich die meisten von uns (nach ihren
Werken zu schließen) für l'art pour l'art' (*Preisreden*, S.65). In
Äußerungen von Mitgliedern der Gruppe 47 wurde das Bild vom
'zwischen den Stühlen' sitzenden Autor nur selten so direkt auf den
Kalten Krieg bezogen: Wolfgang Bächler war eine solche Ausnahme,
wenn er sich auf Sartre berief, um sein Selbstverständnis als 'Sozialist
ohne Parteibuch, ein Deutscher ohne Deutschland' zu erläutern:
Angezogen von Brecht, Bloch und Lukács folgte er Einladungen
Huchels und Hermlins in die DDR als 'Wanderer zwischen zwei
Welten', dem 'beiderseitigen Prozeß mißtrauend'.[31]

Mitte der sechziger Jahre markierte die einhellig ablehnende
Reaktion auf Emil Staigers Angriff auf die engagierte Literatur den
neuen Konsens, der sich seit dem Ende der 50er Jahre herauszubilden
begonnen hatte. Dokumentiert wurde die Verteidigung des Engagements
in der von Walter Höllerer herausgegebenen Zeitschrift *Sprache im
technischen Zeitalter*.[32] Aber auch die Zurückweisung einer
Pauschalkritik an der Gegenwartsliteratur, die im Namen der
bindenden, verpflichtenden Tradition der nationalen Klassik geführt
wurde, bedeutete noch keineswegs Einhelligkeit darüber, was
Engagement in der Literatur sei. Allerdings verdient die Einmütigkeit,

mit der auch das konservative Feuilleton die engagierte Literatur — und damit gleichgesetzt: die Gruppe 47 — verteidigte,[33] festgehalten zu werden, ebenso wie der Umstand, daß aus der bundesrepubikanischen Universitätsgermanistik Apologien des Engagements kamen (vgl. ebd., S.109). Der umfassende Charakter des Umschwungs im Konsens wird deutlich an einer Polemik Marcel Reich-Ranickis gegen Höllerer — diesmal in dessen Eigenschaft als Herausgeber der *Akzente* und als Autor eines Artikels im *Monat*; in beiden Zeitschriften hatte Höllerer den Slogan 'Literatur der Veränderung' ausgegeben, was Reich-Ranicki als 'Umschreibung der engagierten Literatur' deutete.[34] Aber — so Reich-Ranicki — Höllerer, 'dem man nachsagt, er pflege, wenn es jemand gewagt hat, in seiner Gegenwart von engagierter Kunst zu sprechen, sofort das Zimmer zu lüften und in besonders schweren Fällen auch desinfizieren zu lassen' (Reich-Ranicki, S.163), spreche jetzt nicht nur von Realismus, sondern 'sogar — wer hätte das gedacht — von Engagement [...], ohne diesen Begriff in höhnische Anführungszeichen zu setzen' (Ebd., S.165). Bei aller Suffisanz bleibt festzuhalten, daß Reich-Ranicki einen Wandel des literarischen Konsenses zutreffend erfaßte. Auch andere Kritiker hielten diesen Umbruch in Sachen Engagement fest, so Joachim Kaiser (Lettau, S.178) und Hans Schwab-Felisch. (Ebd., S.167-68) Dieter E. Zimmer resümierte die Tagung von Princeton 1966 mit dem Ergebnis: 'das Thema Engagement, das doch noch lange nicht ausdiskutiert scheint, wie immer behauptet wird' (Ebd., S.234). Günter Grass, der in Princeton seine Ablehnung des Begriffs engagierter Schriftsteller als Entsprechung zu 'Hofkonditor oder katholischer Radfahrer' (Grass, Bd.9, S.155) formulierte, hat 1975 in einem Rückblick den Beginn der Einbürgerung auf das 'Ende der Fünfziger Jahre' datiert (Arnold, S.103). Und in einem etwas früheren Rückblick hat 1972 ein anderer, gleichfalls dem Terminus 'littérature engagée' ablehnend gegenüberstehender Gruppenautor, Helmut Heißenbüttel, auch den Zeitpunkt genannt, zu dem der deutsche Engagement-Begriff durchgesetzt war: 'Mitte der sechziger Jahre' zusammen mit der Frage nach der gesellschaftspraktischen Funktion von Literatur.[35]

Diese Periodisierung legt nahe, in den Aufsätzen von Jens, Enzensberger und Adorno von 1962 bereits Reaktionen auf einen Prozeß der Desintegration des Konsenses der fünfziger Jahre zu sehen. Er begann sich abzuzeichnen mit einer Problematisierung des Konzepts

Nonkonformismus, die die Beziehung zwischen Literatur und Politik einschneidend veränderte, insofern sie zu einer Frage der Praxis gemacht wurde. Die verschiedenen Antworten, die auf das Fragwürdigwerden des Nonkonformismus gefunden wurden, gingen ein in die nun häufig werdenden individuellen Definitionen von Engagement.[36] Einer der frühesten Belege für die Problematisierung des Nonkonformismus von innen — im Unterschied zur geläufigen Polemik des konservativen Feuilletons von außen — ist Walsers Beitrag zu Weyrauchs Anthologie von 1960 mit dem Titel 'Skizze zu einem Vorwurf'. Obwohl er von dem Kontext, in dem diese Infragestellung stattfand und der in anderen Beiträgen wesentlich markanter hervortrat, schwieg: nämlich von der Entlegitimierung des Antitotalitarismus zugunsten des Antifaschismus,[37] war Walsers Offenhalten verschiedener Varianten von Praxis eine Bedingung seiner Wirkung. Im Kreuzungspunkt von aktuell gewordener Vergangenheitsbewältigung einerseits und Übergang vom Kalten Krieg zur Entspannungspolitik andererseits stellte Walser den 'simplen Non-Konformismus' als 'Nicht-Beteiligung an der Gesellschaft' (Weyrauch, S.114) auf eine Weise in Frage, die doppelt gelesen werden konnte: als revolutionäre Kritik am Integriert-Sein und als reformerischer Appell zur Mitarbeit am demokratischen Staat. Hieß es einerseits: 'wir lassen alles geschehen. [...] Wir haben uns mit unserer Rolle als Lorbeerbäume neben den Rednerpulten abgefunden' (Ebd., S.112), so anderseits: 'In welche Verlegenheit brächten uns ein Staat, eine Gesellschaft, die uns zur Mitarbeit einlüden!' (Ebd., S.114) Aus dieser Frageweise erklärt es sich, daß sich Walser im PEN-Podiumsgespräch mit DDR-Autoren ein Jahr später beim Streit zwischen Mayer und Reich-Ranicki, ob den 'scharfen Gegensätzlichkeiten zweier deutscher Staaten' 'ganz verschiedene Auffassung[en] von [...] der Funktion der Literatur' entsprächen (Müller-Marein, S.124), tendenziell auf die Seite Mayers stellte, indem er die Frage bejahte; Walser zitierte — ohne es ausdrücklich zu sagen — Sartres Vorwurf an Camus, wenn er Reich-Ranicki, der u.a. nach der Veröffentlichungsmöglichkeit für Sartres Werke in der DDR gefragt hatte, vorhielt: 'Was würde passieren, wenn Ranicki selber diese Fragen beantworten müßte?' (Ebd., S.127). Walsers Stellungnahme räumte nicht nur die Möglichkeit unterschiedlicher gesellschaftlicher Funktionen von Literatur ein, wenn er Ranicki abwies: 'Ich glaube nicht, daß Ranicki einen solchen Katalog einem grundsätzlich anderen System so präsentieren kann' (Ebd., S.127), sondern gestand dem nicht auf Nein-, sondern auf Ja-Sagen setzenden DDR-Modell ein 'historische[s]' 'Recht' zu (Ebd., S.128). Als in der Folge der Hamburger Diskussion Grass zum V. Schriftstellerkongreß der DDR eingeladen wurde, benutzte er allerdings Walsers Bild kritisch gegen die DDR-Literatur, um die 'Freiheit des Wortes' (Grass, Bd.9, S.29) zu fordern: 'Wenn Walser sieht, daß der Schriftsteller degradiert worden ist in seiner Bedeutung zu einer Randfigur wie die Topfpflanzen hier am Podium, so ist der Schriftsteller nicht nur in Westdeutschland dazu degradiert, er ist es auch hier' (Ebd., S.28).

Grass zog aus der Fragwürdigkeit des Nonkonformismus die Konsequenz, als Bürger, nicht als Schriftsteller politisch aktiv zu werden; dabei zeigte sein, teilweise zusammen mit Wolfdietrich Schnurre unternommener, Protest gegen den Bau der Mauer, einerseits wie schwer es war, die Rollen zu unterscheiden, anderseits welches Gewicht bei allen Beteiligten die Aktualisierung des Antifaschismus hatte. In seinem Brief an Anna Seghers schrieb Grass sich selbst die Rolle von Klaus Mann, Seghers hingegen die von Gottfried Benn zu (Ebd., S.33-34); entscheidend aber war die im widersprüchlichen Kontext von Gefahr von rechts in der Bundesrepublik und Verhinderung von Entspannung durch die Mauer in der DDR aufgeworfene Titelfrage seines Offenen Briefes: 'Und was können die Schriftsteller tun?' (Ebd., S.33), auf die der gemeinsam mit Schnurre verfaßte Offene Brief die Antwort gab: 'Wer schweigt, wird schuldig' (Ebd., S.35).

Es war die kategorische Feststellung Grass' und Schnurres: 'Es gibt keine "Innere Emigration", auch zwischen 1933 und 1945 hat es keine gegeben' (Ebd., S.35-36), die das konservative Feuilleton so gegen die beiden Briefschreiber aufbrachte. Denn Joachim Günther oder W. E. Süskind sahen mit Recht nicht nur ihr Verhalten im Faschismus angegriffen,[38] sondern auch die Diskussion der unmittelbaren Nachkriegszeit wieder auf die Tagesordnung gesetzt. Friedrich Sieburg hatte schon in seinem Verriß von Weyrauchs Anthologie einen neuen 'Ton' als 'deutlich' festgehalten: 'das stille Bedauern darüber, daß die deutsche Intelligenz die große Gelegenheit zur Stunde Null versäumt hat'.[39] Und Hans Egon Holthusen hatte in der durch Weyrauchs Anthologie ausgelösten Debatte davor gewarnt, in einer 'Übernahme der östlichen Sicht' auf die Bundesrepublik als 'präfaschistisches Gebilde'

(Lettau, S.486) 'das Amt des Dichters auf aktiven Nonkonformismus festzulegen' (Ebd., S.490). Ostkontakt und Vergangenheitsbewältigung wurden von Holthusen verknüpft als Gefahr für den Dichter, von dem er nur verlangte, daß er 'ein stabiles und freiheitliches Gemeinwesen, in dem jeder nach Herzenslust auch Nonkonformist sein kann, in kritischer Sympathie als seine gegebene Heimat anerkennt' (Ebd., S.495).

Exakt diese Bejahung des bundesrepublikanischen status quo unterlief die publizistische Aktualisierung der Stunde Null, die explizit als versäumte Chance in den Jahren 1961-62 massiv in Erinnerung gebracht wurde. Richter machte Enzensberger auf die innere 'Zusammengehörigkeit' (Schutte, S.263) einiger Editionen dieser Jahre aufmerksam: des Neudrucks von Artikeln aus dem *Ruf* durch Schwab-Felisch[40] und Richters eigener Anthologien zur Gruppe selbst,[41] zur *Bestandsaufnahme* der Bundesrepublik[42] und zum Mauerbau. Es war die Wahrnehmung einer von der Innenpolitik der Bundesrepublik ausgehenden Gefahr eines Dritten Weltkriegs einerseits und der internationalen Chance von Entspannung anderseits, die in der Sicht des Organisators der Gruppe die 'nicht' 'erfüllt[en]' 'Hoffnungen' (Schutte, S.264) von 1947 aktualisierten.

In dieser Situation bezeichnete sich als erster Autor der Gruppe 47 Wolfdietrich Schnurre unumwunden als 'engagierte[n] Schriftsteller' (Lettau, S.173) — erstmals in einem extrem polemischen Bericht über die Berliner Tagung von 1962, wo der doppelte Bezug auf die DDR einerseits, auf die Nazi-Vergangenheit anderseits die früher auch von ihm geübte doppelte innerliterarische Abgrenzung ersetzte.[43] Schnurre war auch der erste, der literarisches Engagement als 'Literatur nach Auschwitz' definierte.[44] Die Pflicht zur Vergangenheitsbewältigung ließ ihn speziell für Deutschland die Untrennbarkeit von Werk und Person in einer ethisch inspirierten Literatur fordern — gegen eine Tradition, die er durch traditionalistischen und modernistischen Formalismus gekennzeichnet sah.[45] Schnurre postulierte ein demokratisches Engagement für das Leben und den Menschen sowohl in Gestalt eines parteinehmenden, aber nicht parteigebundenen Realismus (Ebd., S.289) als auch durch direkten Einspruch außerhalb der Grenzen der Literatur:

> In Deutschland heute engagierter Schriftsteller zu sein, ist etwas anderes, als engagiert in Frankreich oder Polen zu schreiben [...], hier hilft uns nur eine unchiffrierte [...] Bewußtwerdung des Geschehenen weiter und [...] ein [...] von Grund auf geändertes Leben, in dem die Toten und Ermordeten ihren

unbestrittenen Platz neben den Neugeborenen haben, in dem die
Vergangenheit die Zukunft belehrt, in dem die Menschlichkeit
nationalistischem Machtanspruch die Stimme verwehrt, und
Verständigungswille und Verhandlungsbereitschaft Verstocktheit und
Anmaßung nicht aufkommen lassen. (Ebd., S.242-44)

Andere Mitglieder der Gruppe gaben in der breit geführten
Debatte zwar ganz andere Bestimmungen der Aktualität des Begriffs
Engagement,[46] dabei erwiesen sich aber übereinstimmend zwei
Probleme als zentral, die aus der tradierten doppelten Abgrenzung
folgten: einmal der Gegensatz von Verweigerung und Verpflichtung,
dann das Verhältnis von Schriftsteller als Bürger und Werk, oder die
Frage nach dem direkten oder indirekten Bezug zur Praxis. Es ergaben
sich zwei Varianten der verspäteten, nachholenden Rezeption des
Engagements, in denen die Autonomie des eigentlich Literarischen
unangetastet blieb: einmal das Engagement des Schriftstellers als
Bürger, dann der Verzicht auf die Literatur zugunsten der Aktion.
Aufgegeben wurde die in den fünziger Jahren als nonkonformistisch
vertretene Autonomie des Schriftsteller als Schriftsteller nur von einer
Minderheit.

Alle drei Varianten des Engagements — als Bürger, als Negation
der Literatur und in der Literatur — hatten durchaus ihre Entsprechung
in der Polyvalenz von Sartres Konzept von 1947; dessen von vornherein
gegebene Vieldeutigkeit war überdies angereichert durch Sartres spätere
Entwicklung, was vielfache Berufung auf ihn ermöglichte.[47]
Polarisierend und letztlich den innerliterarischen Pluralismus der
Gruppe 47 sprengend wirkten letztlich alle drei Varianten, weil sie eine
übergreifende Dominante in der Funktionsbestimmung von Literatur
entwarfen: Das bei Schnurre mit dem Begriff Bewußtmachung
anklingende Schlagwort Aufklärung erwies sich durch seinen Bezug auf
politische Praxis als spaltend.

Unter den Gruppenmitgliedern, die zwar seit 1962 anfingen, das
Substantiv 'Engagement' zu benutzen, aber seine Anwendung auf das
ausdrücklich so genannte politische Engagement des Schriftstellers als
Bürger beschränkten, war die Bindung der Gruppe 47 an die SPD, die
sie von Richter betrieben sahen, umstritten. In der Trennung von
autonomem literarischem Werk und engagierter politischer Publizistik
stimmten z.B. Andersch, Hildesheimer und Böll durchaus mit Richter
überein. Andersch forderte im Schlußwort seines Interviews mit Bienek

1962, 'das Werk und die politischen Äußerungen eines Schriftstellers voneinander zu trennen' (Bienek, S.151). Seine Begründung formulierte noch einmal die vom Kalten Krieg gesetzten Bedingungen des Aufstiegs der Gruppe 47:

> Ein Schriftsteller mag eine politische Haltung einnehmen, die ich durchaus nicht schätze, so darf ich doch mein literarisches Urteil über ihn davon nicht beeinflussen lassen. Es gibt einen einzigen Grundverrat, der einem Schriftsteller niemals verziehen werden kann: wenn er sich zu politischen Entscheidungen bekennt, welche die Freiheit der Literatur einschränken. (Ebd., S.151)

Diese antitotalitär formulierte Grenze des politischen Engagements profilierte nochmals die Autonomie des Literaturbegriffs: 'Ich bin überzeugt, daß ein Schriftsteller, solange er sich im Zustand eines solchen Verrats befindet, auch kein Werk von Rang hervorbringt' (Ebd., S.151). Ganz ähnlich sah Böll im politischen, publizistischen Engagement[48] eine Gefahr für das literarische Werk; gerade indem er einräumte, daß 'sich der Schriftsteller und der Zeitgenosse manchmal trennen, und der letztere kann dann, isoliert vom ersteren — dem Schriftsteller — 'Scheiße' schreien und Ohrfeigen austeilen', bestand er darauf: 'je engagierter er sich glaubt, fühlt, weiß, desto mehr sollte er nach Ausdruck suchen' (Böll, Bd.2, S.218). In den *Akzenten* erlaubte Hildesheimer dem Dichter des Absurden, der mit Camus in der Frage verharre,[49] nur einen 'Einsatz' 'für die gute Sache' außerhalb des Werks, 'im Leben' (Ebd., S.553):

> Ich trete nicht für den Konzentrationslagerroman, nicht für den Roman über Kollektivschuld und Sühne ein, auch das wären Teil-Aspekte, sondern für das weite Panorama eines an allen Schrecken und Grauen, an aller Tragik und Komik des Lebens geschulten Bewußtseins.[50]

Gerade weil Andersch, Böll und Hildesheimer in der Ablehnung des Engagements in der Literatur übereinstimmten, und hierin den Konsens der fünfziger Jahre fortsetzen, fiel ihre Opposition gegen die Bindung des politischen Engagements an die SPD um so entschiedener aus. Böll griff öffentlich das 'Peinliche' der von der 'Mehrheit [...] vollzogenen Annäherung an die SPD' an (Böll, Bd.1, S.198), weil z.B. das Engagement als Reklame für einen 'NATO Mann' (Schutte, S.327) wie den SPD-Wehrexperten Fritz Erler dem Kampf gegen die Remilitarisierung der fünfziger Jahre widerspreche; die Gruppe verdiene 'das Kose- oder Schimpfwort "nonkonformistisch"' 'nicht

mehr' (Böll, Bd.1, S.197), seit sie sich an eine Partei binde, 'die aus
Opportunismus die erste und einzige Antiatombewegung in der
Bundesrepublik verraten hat' (Ebd., S.198). Andersch wurde von
Richter 1965 gar nicht erst zum zweiten Wahlkampftaschenbuch
eingeladen, denn bereits 1961 hatte sich Richter bei Jens beklagen
müssen: 'Andersch schreibt nur, wenn er für die Deutsche
Friedensunion schreiben darf, was wir nicht wollen' (Schutte, S.290).[51]
Hildesheimer schließlich zitierte Sartre, dessen Ablehnungsschreiben
zum Nobelpreis, als er SPD-Engagement und Auslandstagungen der
Gruppe als 'bedenkliche Zeichen einer Eingliederung' deutete: 'wie die
Opposition sich mäßigt' (Ebd., S.318). Andersch kommentierte
Hildesheimers brieflichen Vorwurf eines 'milden Konformismus', selbst
gleichfalls an Richter schreibend: Hildesheimer drücke 'in
bewunderungswürdiger weise das aus [...], was auch ich denke. ich hätte
nie gedacht, dass ausgerechnet er, der doch nie politisch hervorgetreten
ist, eine so saubere Analyse liefern würde' (Ebd., S.319).

Es ist kein Zufall, daß derjenige Autor, der sich als Bürger für
die SPD seit 1965 am entschiedensten einsetzte, die Benutzung des
Begriffs Engagement hierfür ablehnte.[52] Allerdings verfolgte nicht nur
Grass' damaliger Mentor Richter in seinen Briefen beifällig 'das
politische Engagement [von] Günter Grass' (Schutte, S.305), sondern
auch Willy Brandt fügte 1965 in einen Interviewtext, den ihm das von
Grass initiierte Wahlkontor Deutscher Schriftsteller geschrieben hatte,
von sich aus das Wort Engagement ein, das der ängstliche Schreiber,
Peter Härtling, ängstlich vermieden hatte: Hatte Härtling die Sache in
einer wortreichen Polemik — im Stil der doppelten Abgrenzung —
verkleidet, einerseits gegen das 'traditionelle Vorurteil gegenüber dem
Intellektuellen, er sei ein egozentrischer Nörgler im Elfenbeinturm',
andererseits gegen Intellektuelle, die 'die Politik als eine l'art pour l'art
interpretieren', so hieß es bei Grass' Vorbild Brandt unumwunden:

> Die Intellektuellen haben [...] eine besondere Pflicht zum Engagement, nicht
> unbedingt in einer Partei, aber in der Mitverantwortung für die öffentlichen
> Angelegenheiten. Ich erwarte und bitte um Anregung, schöpferische Unruhe,
> Denkhilfe. Das ist oft unbequem. Aber Intellektuelle sind nun einmal nicht nur
> bequem. [...] Die Intelligenz ist nicht immer gut behandelt worden in unserem
> Staat. Ich möchte dazu beitragen, daß das Klima besser wird. Aber wahr
> bleibt, was Emile Zola so gesagt hat: 'Das Genie des Schriftstellers ist sein
> Mut.' Ich meine, der Mut muß auch dem Engagement gelten.[53]

Der Grund für die — von Brandt nicht geteilte — Zurückhaltung gegenüber dem Engagementbegriff wurde ein Jahr später im Streit ums politische Gedicht bei Grass und Härtling offenkundig: Die Trennung von Werk des Schriftstellers und Publizistik des Bürgers wurde von Autoren der Gruppe 47, exemplarisch von Erich Fried, aufgehoben;[54] dagegen bekräftigte Härtling, 'daß Schreiben und Handeln sich meistens ausschließen' und deren Identifikation im Engagement nur 'rhetorischen Hochmut" erzeuge: 'Es fragt sich, ob Gerede Handlung sein kann, ob die rhetorische Ohnmacht etwas bewirkt.'[55] Doch nicht nur Autoren setzten jetzt Schreiben und Handeln gleich, sondern bei Kritikern kehrte sich auch das umstrittene Verhältnis von Leben und Werk geradezu um; Reich-Ranicki etwa erklärte das Engagement im Werk für obligatorisch und die publizistische Parteinahme für fakultativ: 'Ein Schriftsteller äußert sich zu den Fragen seiner Zeit vor allem in Romanen, Erzählungen, Dramen oder Gedichten, in seinem Werk also' (Reich-Ranicki, S.19). 'Ob er sich zu Tagesereignissen in der Presse oder im Rundfunk äußert, muß seine Sache bleiben' (Ebd., S.111). Unter den Leitbegriffen Wirklichkeit, Kritik, Aufklärung und gesellschaftliche Funktion der Literatur plädierte Reich-Ranicki in der *Zeit* für eine im Werk des Schriftstellers zu erfüllende 'Pflicht' (Ebd., S.115) und 'Verantwortung' (Ebd., S.15), erstmals übrigens in einem Artikel über Wolfgang Koeppen 1961. Seit 1963 benutzte er hierfür den Begriff des Engagements — seit seiner Polemik gegen Alain Robbe-Grillet, in der er aus Koeppens Büchner-Preisrede zitierte, in der es 1962 bündig hieß: 'Der Schriftsteller ist engagiert gegen die Macht' (*Preisreden*, S.118). In Reich-Ranickis Entgegnung auf Robbe-Grillet wurde daraus eine Alternative für den Schriftsteller: 'Er hat [...] die Möglichkeit, die Fragen des Landes, dessen Bürger er ist, und der Epoche, in der er lebt, zu behandeln. Und er kann ihnen ausweichen, sie ignorieren. Dies ist einer der Unterschiede zwischen dem Schriftsteller, den man als 'engagiert', und demjenigen, den man als 'nichtengagiert' zu bezeichnen pflegt' (Reich-Ranicki, S.65). In einem Kommentar zu Horst Krügers durch den Frankfurter Auschwitz-Prozeß angeregtem auto-biographischem Bericht 'Das zerbrochene Haus' machte Reich-Ranicki klar, welche Aufgabe die Kritik zu erfüllen habe:

> Was fühlen und denken eigentlich diejenigen, die damals kleine Kinder waren, wenn erzählt wird, wie ihre Eltern drei Millionen Menschen in Auschwitz ermordet haben. [...] es geht [...] nicht um einzelne Autoren.

> Keiner ist verpflichtet, sich dieser Frage anzunehmen. Aber die deutsche
> Literatur unserer Zeit ist es. (Ebd., S.112)

Die Kritik erhielt von Reich-Ranicki die Aufgabe zugeschrieben, die
Literatur als Ganzes an ihr Engagement zu erinnern.

Wenn Reich-Ranicki über die gesellschaftskritische Funktion das
Engagement im Werk verankerte, so zielte sein Kritikerkollege Jens,
der freilich auch Autor war, auf eine Einheit von literarischem Werk
und Publizistik im Zeichen eines rhetorischen Engagements. 1964
widerrief er ausdrücklich seinen Vortrag von 1962, um stattdessen
'kritisches Engagement' als 'Synthese': 'poetische Agitation' nämlich zu
fordern.[56] Seine Begründung war, daß 'in den letzten Jahren' 'kritisch-
didaktisches Geschäft, Pädagogik in litteris' 'immer wichtiger
geworden' sei (Ebd.). Die bei Jens nur angespielte Bedeutung des
Eichmann- und des Auschwitz-Prozesses wurde zum zentralen
Argument in Baumgarts Schilderung seines Wegs als Leser — von
Borchert über Thomas Mann zu Beckett und schließlich Sartre, die in
die Verpflichtung des heute Schreibenden mündete, 'sich ums
Gegenwärtige und Irdische zu kümmern' (Schultz, S.154). Bei beiden
Kritiker-Autoren verbanden sich die Begriffe der 'Aufklärung'
(Baumgart, S.68) und des 'Kontakt[s] mit der Wirklichkeit' (Koch,
S.98) im Engagement, ebenso bei Reinhard Lettau (Ebd., S.78) und bei
Peter Rühmkorf, der 'Aufklärung' (Ebd., S.71) als einen Wiedergewinn
der in den fünfziger Jahren, er datierte von recht genau: von 1952 bis
1958, verbotenen Begriffe Gegenstand und Publikum ansah' (Ebd.,
S.68).

Martin Walsers späte Übernahme des Begriffs literarisches
Engagement fiel, vielleicht deshalb, bemerkenswert reflektiert aus; auch
bei ihm konkretisierte sich die Rezeption des Konzepts von einem
Engagement in der literarischen Arbeit als Ausarbeitung einer
Vorstellung von Aufklärung, ja bei Walser ging die Bestimmung der
öffentlichen Aufgabe insbesondere des Theaters dem ausdrücklichen
Reden vom Engagement um Jahre voraus, 'daß öffentlich wird, was
geschehen ist; daß zur Sprache gebracht wird, was verschwiegen
wurde'.[57] Er betonte noch 1966 in der Auseinandersetzung mit Grass
und Enzensberger einerseits, Peter Weiss anderseits: 'Das, was man
Engagement nennt, läßt sich nicht fordern.'[58] Walser setzte seine
Variante von Engagement als Aufklärung durch die literarische Arbeit
und als deren gleichzeitige Demokratisierung in Kontrast zu vier

anderen, die sich in den sechziger Jahren zuvor ausgebildet hatten, sozusagen drei rechts, eine links von ihm: als 'Reizlärm' (Ebd., S.104) als 'Zeremonie' (Ebd., S.107) und als '[p]olitische Kosmetik' (Ebd., S.110) einerseits, 'am [...] Rand des [...] Betriebs', in 'Ostermärschen, Protestkundgebungen und Aufklärungsaktionen' anderseits (Ebd., S.115). Ihm ging es um das Engagement des Schriftstellers 'in seinen Arbeiten' (Ebd., S.109). Nicht nur das Stichwort 'Aufklärung' verband in Walsers Sicht beide, sondern auch der Umstand, daß das Engagement 'provoziert', notwendig sei (Ebd., S,115). Dementsprechend definierte er: 'Jedes Engagement, das nicht die Demokratisierung der Arbeit als Zielvorstellung enthält, ist Freizeitgestaltung und Showbusiness' (Ebd., S.119). Walsers Insistieren auf seinem eigenen Engagiert-Sein durch Kleinbürgererfahrung unterschied ihn bereits zu diesem Zeitpunkt von anderen Gruppenmitgliedern, die später zur DKP stießen; bei Gerd Fuchs und Günter Herburger wurden die Stichworte des Kontakts mit der Wirklichkeit und der Aufklärung, die der Literatur eine gesellschaftliche Funktion sichern sollten, zugespitzt auf die Arbeiterklasse bzw. Arbeiterbewegung, weniger als Adressat denn als Gegenstand. Der Leiter einer Diskussion u.a. mit Walser, Herburger und Fuchs stellte eine Gegenüberstellung von drei Typen der BRD-AutorInnen der sechziger Jahre voran: der erste verstehe sich als unabhängig, zeitlos, subjektiv; der zweite als engagiert; der dritte als parteilich. Über die Engagierten hieß es: Sie 'akzeptieren Parteilichkeit als unvermeidlich, weil sie für Humanität eintreten. [...] So verstanden sei jede große Literatur parteilich, weil große Literatur immer engagierte Literatur sei. Aber das bedeute doch noch lange nicht Parteilichkeit im strengen parteipolitischen Sinn.'[59] Fuchs kleidete das Bekenntnis zu einer solchen Parteilichkeit in eine Absage an die nur kritische Position des Nonkonformismus wie an die nur humanistische Parteilichkeit des Engagements: 'Erst die sich [...] neu belebende Arbeiterbewegung hat das moralische Vakuum, das Faschismus und Adenauer-Zeit hinterließen, mit etwas Neuem, Positivem gefüllt. Sie hat der Literatur einen großen, einen neuen Gegenstand geschenkt.'[60] Herburger betonte: 'Ich begann politisch zu werden nicht in der Praxis, sondern in meinem Beruf, der Literatur' (Konjetzky, S.151).

Gegen die Polarisierung der Diskussion innerhalb der Gruppe 47 um die Kernfrage SPD, in deren Ablehnung sich sowohl Gegner wie Anhänger der literarischen Engagements einig waren, suchte Richter in einem programmatischen Artikel in der *Neuen Rundschau* 1967 noch einmal zwischen dem 'politischen Engagement' — außerhalb der Gruppe — und der eigentlich literarischen Arbeit der Autoren — in der Gruppe — zu unterscheiden, um am Beispiel Grass vs. Weiss Gemeinsamkeit wiederherzustellen.[61]

Die gerade auch von Grass immer wieder herausgestellte Arbeitsteilung zwischen Bürger und Künstler hatte jedoch nicht verhindern können, daß der Terminus 'Engagement' in die Konzeption des Literarischen selbst eindrang, auch bei Autoren, die sich der Politisierung, ob für die SPD oder links von ihr, widersetzten.[62] Eine von der Konkreten Poesie und der Sprachkritik geprägte Variante der Literarisierung des Engagement-Begriffs vertrat 1966 Heißenbüttel; er sprach vom 'Engagement der Erkenntnis'[63], indem er zwar zugestand, daß die autonome Literaturauffassung der 50er Jahre ihren 'Sinn einer gegen die Gesellschaft gerichteten Distanzierung verloren' habe (Ebd., S.313), aber hinreichend klar machte, daß er weder der 'Aufwertung von realistischen Literaturauffassungen' — ob als Engagement wie bei Reich-Ranicki oder als 'Neuer Realismus' bei Dieter Wellershoff — sowie 'außerliterarischer' Dokumentarliteratur (Heißenbüttel 1972, S.5) noch der 'Ablehnung literarischer Betätigung' (Ebd., S.6) folgen wollte. Auch bei Heißenbüttel lag der Übernahme des Engagementbegriffs — in einer Variante, die internationale Vorläufer in Alain Robbe-Grillets 'Engagement in den und für die Formen'[64] und Umberto Ecos 'Form als Engagement'[65] hatte — eine Kritik am bundesrepublikanischen Nonkonformismus der fünfziger Jahre zugrunde. Heißenbüttel erhob 1963 Arno Schmidt zur Ausnahme von der Regel der westdeutschen Literatur, indem er nur ihn als Entsprechung zu Beckett und Sarraute gelten ließ (Heißenbüttel 1978: S.694), als Teil jener internationalen Literatur der Moderne, die endgültig alle Nationalliteraturen, vor allem die deutsche,[66] ersetzt habe: Er 'gehört [...] nicht [...] zu denen, die unter der Warenmarke des Nonkonformismus dem Publikum liefern, was es lesen will' (Heißenbüttel 1978, S.695). Auch bei ihm signalisierte das Festhalten am innerliterarischen Nonkonformismus, wenn auch anders als bei Andersch, Böll oder Hildesheimer, unter dem neuen Namen Engagement zugleich die Unwilligkeit zur Festlegung auf die SPD:

> In dem Moment, in dem mit dem von Mitgliedern der Gruppe ins Leben
> gerufenen Wahlbüro für die SPD 1965 die Bindung an eine der

bundesdeutschen Parteien eindeutig gemacht wurde (im November 1964 wurde zum erstenmal eine Delegation auf einen SPD-Parteitag eingeladen, hier begann die politische Karriere von Günter Graß [!]), [...] zerfiel der Zusammenhalt [...], spaltete sich nun auf in eine SPD-Linie und in eine neomarxistische. Dieser Gegensatz war nicht zu überbrücken, da er über das Politische hinaus Auswirkungen auf die Literaturauffassung zur Folge hatte.[67]

Ein Beispiel für das von Heißenbüttel konstatierte 'Eindringen' 'theoretisch-politische[r] Positionen in das Literaturgespräch' (Ebd.) lieferte Peter Weiss. Er stellte mit radikaleren Schlußfolgerungen zur gleichen Zeit die Künstler-Bürger-Arbeitsteilung wie den radikalisierten Nonkonformismus in Frage; in den 'Zehn Arbeitspunkten eines Autors in der geteilten Welt' warf er sich und allen Nonkonformisten des 'bequemen dritten Standpunkt[s]' vor, 'aus Mangel an Bindungen' 'den Eigenwert der Kunst höher [zu] schätzen als ihren Zweck'.[68] Um den kapitalistisch-demokratisch 'Machthabenden' nicht länger durch alibihafte Kritik 'nur den Beweis für ihre Freigebigkeit' zu 'erstelle[n]', forderte er den passiven Kontakt des immer schon politischen Wortes mit der Bevölkerung durch einen 'bewußten' zu ersetzen (Ebd., 243-44). Ohne den Begriff Engagement zu verwenden, kam er in der Bestimmung der 'Aufgabe' der Literatur Sartres *Qu'est-ce que la littérature?* sehr nahe: gerade im Werk durch Aufsuchen der Wahrheit unter ihren Entstellungen (Ebd., S.241) zu einem Sozialismus beizutragen, der durch ständige Offenheit der Selbstkritik gekennzeichnet wäre (Ebd., S.246). Dieses Festhalten an der kritischen Funktion des Engagements auch innerhalb der Arbeiterbewegung und im Sozialismus wurde von der bundesrepublikanischen Kritik geflissentlich übersehen, ob Holthusen (vgl. Jaeckle, S.51) ausdrücklich nur im Falle von Weiss Staigers Verdammung der *littérature engagée* zustimmen wollte oder Reich-Ranicki die Absage an Unabhängigkeit mit der Frage beantwortete: 'Doch abhängig wovon und von wem?' (Reich-Ranicki, S.176). In der zwischen Weiss und Enzensberger im *Kursbuch* ausgetragenen Kontroverse wurde übersehen, daß Enzensberger an der Künstler-Bürger-Trennung festhielt. Gerade die Rolle, die hierbei die Bezugnahme auf Sartre spielte, war geeignet, die Kontinuität von Enzensbergers Stellung zum literarischen Engagement zu verdecken.[69]

Auf eine italienische Kritik am *Kursbuch* antwortete Enzensberger mit dem Eingeständnis, daß 'mit der Linken anderer

europäischer Länder [...] die 'Linksintellektuellen' in Deutschland bis
vor kurzem kaum etwas gemein hatten';[70] der italienische Kritiker hatte
es als 'lokalen Usus' herausgestellt, 'sich für nichts Bestimmtes
"einzusetzen"' (Ebd., S.183). Hatte der Nonkonformismus erlaubt,
politisch Stellung zu nehmen, solange die Gruppe 47 als Gruppe den
Primat innerliterarischer Kriterien garantierte, so mußte Engagement
durch Verpflichtung auf außerliterarische, reale gesellschaftliche Kräfte
und politische Organisationen die Gruppe als solche zerfallen lassen.
Zugespitzt: Die Rezeption des Engagements, sowohl des publizistischen
wie des literarischen, hat die Gruppe enden lassen. Die Gruppe 47 holte
die Engagement-Debatte, wie Michel 1965 zu Recht im *Kursbuch*
schrieb, 'verspätet'[71] nach; die entscheidende Ursache für die
bundesrepublikanische Verspätung war wohl der Kalte Krieg. Im
Übergang zur Entspannung erst wurde es möglich, über das zu
diskutieren, was vorher tabu gewesen war: vom Antifaschismus über
das Engagement bis zum Realismus.[72]

Nach dem Sieg im Kalten Krieg scheint Anlaß, daran zu erinnern,
denn der Sieg sieht manchmal eher wie eine Neuauflage aus; Klaus
Harpprecht z.B. publizierte in der *Zeit* 1996 einen Angriff auf die
Intellektuellen der alten Bundesrepublik,[73] der sich kaum anders liest
als z.B. seine Attacke auf die Gruppe 47 von 1952; aus der bloßen
Bereitschaft von Richters und Brenners Zeitschrift *Die Literatur*, über
die Erhaltung des PEN als 'Brücke zwischen Ost und West', über Sartre
sowie Brecht und Seghers zu diskutieren, folgerte Harpprecht damals
'Der Dichtung Jammer' in der Gruppe 47 (Schutte, S.211). Denn im
Mangel an einem Antikommunismus, der jede Diskussionsbereitschaft
ausgeschlossen hätte, sah er das Ergebnis eines überholten
Antifaschismus. Harpprechts Unterstellung, die er 1952 nicht zu
explizieren brauchte, war letztlich, daß Stalin nütze, wer Hitler
kritisiere; sie basierte auf den Voraussetzungen, erstens, daß der
Faschismus das kleinere Übel darstellte, zweitens, daß gegenwärtig
ausschließlich eine kommunistische Gefahr existiere, während die
faschistische Gefahr ein für alle Mal beendet sei. Fritz J. Raddatz'
Entgegnung hat 1996 nicht nur auf der historisch gegebenen
Notwendigkeit einer Kritik am Nachleben des Faschismus bestanden,
sondern auch verglichen:

> In Frankreich waren auch die Kommunisten Aragon und Eluard zuerst einmal
> französische Schriftsteller, und selbst Gegner wie Sartre und Raymond Aron

diskutierten miteinander. Hierzulande waren Johannes R. Becher oder Arnold Zweig oder Seghers — der nichtgespielte Brecht ohnehin — kaum noch Deutsche; jedenfalls hier nicht gedruckte deutsche Schriftsteller.[74]

In Raddatz' Vergleich der fünfziger Jahre in Frankreich und der Bundesrepublik wird der entscheidende Grund für die verspätete Einbürgerung und Verdeutschung des Fremdworts 'engagement' erkennbar: Die Zweistaatlichkeit des Kalten Kriegs der fünfziger Jahre bedeutete in der Bundesrepublik, den linken Flügel der deutschen Literatur als etwas Äußeres in die DDR zu verdrängen; so machte es erst der Entspannungsdialog der sechziger Jahre möglich, das nachzuholen, was in anderen westeuropäischen Ländern im Rahmen einer Nationalliteratur debattiert worden war: antifaschistisches Engagement in der Literatur. 1967 benutzte Hans Werner Richter eine gewiß problematische Metapher, aber der Sache nach hatte er recht, wenn er konstatierte: 'erst die Entspannung gebar den Marxisten Peter Weiss [...], die Entspannung gebar den politischen Publizisten Günter Grass, dessen Position konträr zu der von Peter Weiss ist' (Richter, S.297). Die Entspannung 'gebar' das Engagement in der BRD-Literatur.

Fußnoten

1 Vgl. Michael Braun, 'Abschied vom Engagement', *Freitag*, 18.7.1997; Ulrich Greiner, 'Die Vorzüge des Elfenbeinturms. Über Literatur und Engagement heute', *Merkur*, 51 (1997), 1093-104.

2 Vgl. zur Kritik hieran die immer noch aktuelle vergleichende Analyse Klaus-Michael Bogdals: 'Wer darf sprechen? Schriftsteller als moralische Instanz. Überlegungen zu einem Ende und einem Anfang', *Weimarer Beiträge*, 37 (1991), 597-603.

3 Heinz Ludwig Arnold, *Die drei Sprünge der westdeutschen Literatur. Eine Erinnerung* (Göttingen: Wallstein, 1993), S.29. Vgl. ähnlich Wilhelm Heinrich Pott, 'Die Philosophien der Nachkriegsliteratur', in: Ludwig Fischer (Hrsg.): *Literatur der Bundesrepublik bis 1967* (München: dtv, 1986 =Hansers Sozialgeschichte der deutschen Literatur vom 16. Jahrhundert bis zur Gegenwart, Bd.10), S.263-87, hier S.273.

4 Zum Problem der Verallgemeinerung vgl. aber Friedhelm Kröll, *Gruppe 47* (Stuttgart: Metzler, 1979), S.66, 72.

5 *Büchner-Preis-Reden 1951-1971*, Vorw.v. Ernst Johann (Stuttgart: Reclam, 1972), S.57-72, hier S.63. Weitere Hinweise auf diesen Band befinden sich im Text unter *Preisreden*.

6 Vgl. zur Frage der Repräsentanz — in direkter Polemik mit 'Schirrmacher und anderen' — Hermann Kinder, *Der Mythos von der Gruppe 47* (Eggingen: Edition Igele, 1991), S.15-16.

[7] Vgl. Wolfgang Weyrauch (Hrsg.), *Ich lebe in der Bundesrepublik. Fünfzehn Deutsche über Deutschland* (München: List [1960]); Horst Bienek (Hrsg.), *Werkstattgespräche mit Schriftstellern* (München: dtv, 1965). Weitere Hinweise auf diese Bände befinden sich im Text unter Weyrauch bzw. Bienek.

[8] Gerhard Hay, 'Von der Herkunft engagierter Literatur in Westdeutschland', *Der Deutschunterricht*, 33: 3 (1981), 23-30, hier S27.

[9] 'Ein Dichtertreffen', *Die Tat*, 27.11.1952.

[10] Reinhard Lettau (Hrsg.), *Die Gruppe 47. Bericht, Kritik, Polemik. Ein Handbuch.* (Neuwied und Berlin: Luchterhand, 1967), S.102. Weitere Hinweise auf diesen Band befinden sich im Text unter Lettau.

[11] Vgl. Ursula Reinhold, *Alfred Andersch. Politisches Engagement und literarische Wirksamkeit* (Berlin: Akademie, 1988).

[12] Margaret Littler, *Alfred Andersch (1914-1980) and the Reception of French Thought in the Federal Republic of Germany* (Lewiston, Queenston, Lampeter: Mellen Press, 1991), S.15. Aus der Abgrenzung erklärt sich die bemerkenswerte Kontinuität im Literaturbegriff von *Deutsche Literatur in der Entscheidung* (1947) über 'Die Blindheit des Kunstwerks' (1956) bis zur 'Notiz über die Schriftsteller und den Staat' (1966); vgl. *Das Alfred Andersch Lesebuch*, hrsg. v. Gerd Haffmans (Zürich: Diogenes, 1979), S.114; Alfred Andersch, *Die Blindheit des Kunstwerks und andere Aufsätze.* (Frankfurt a. M.: Suhrkamp, 1965), S.33; Alfred Andersch, 'Notiz über die Schriftsteller und den Staat', *Merkur*, 20 (1966), 398-400.

[13] Andersch, *Blindheit*, S.63.

[14] Vgl. zu den vorangegangenen *Neue Zeitung*- und *Horizont*-Stellungnahmen zum Existentialismus Waltraud Wende-Hohenberger, *Ein neuer Anfang? Schriftstellerreden zwischen 1945 und 1949* (Stuttgart: Metzler, 1990), S.157.

[15] Vgl. hierzu Mechthild Rahner, *'Tout est neuf ici, tout est à recommencer...'. Die Rezeption des französischen Existentialismus im kulturellen Feld Westdeutschlands (1945-1949)* (Würzburg: Königshausen & Neumann, 1993), S.310.

[16] Alfred Andersch, *Europäische Avantgarde* (Frankfurt a. M.: Verlag der Frankfurter Hefte, 1949), S.8.

[17] Siegfried Lenz, 'Der Sitzplatz eines Autors' (1965), in: ders., *Beziehungen. Ansichten und Bekenntnisse zur Literatur* (München: dtv, 1972), S.26. Vgl. Josef Müller-Marein, Theo Sommer (Hrsg.), *Schriftsteller: Ja-Sager oder Nein-Sager? Das Hamburger Streitgespräch deutscher Autoren aus Ost und West. Das vollständige Tonbandprotokoll* (Hamburg: Rütten & Loening, 1961), S.34. Weitere Hinweise auf den zweiten Band befinden sich im Text unter Sommer.

[18] Camus bestimmte die 'Aufgabe' seiner 'Generation' dahingehend, 'einzig von ihrer Ablehnung [der Geschichte als des Zeitalters der Ideologien] aus[zu]gehen'; vgl. zur Bedeutung dieser Rede auch für Günter Grass, Dieter Arker, *Nichts ist vorbei, alles kommt wieder. Untersuchungen zu Günter Grass' "Blechtrommel"* (Heidelberg: Winter, 1989), S.515.

[19] Walter Jens, *Literatur und Politik* (Pfullingen: Neske, 1963), S.38. Weitere Hinweise auf diesen Band befinden sich im Text unter 'Jens 1963'.

[20] Gunter E. Grimm, '"Nichts als die Wahrheit". Zu Alfred Anderschs Realismus-Konzept', *literatur für leser* H.3 (1993), 108-18, hier 110-11.

[21] Jürgen Schutte (Hrsg.): *Dichter und Richter. Die Gruppe 47 und die deutsche Nachkriegsliteratur. Austellungskatalog* (Berlin: Akademie der Künste, 1988), S.196. Weitere Hinweise auf diesen Band befinden sich im Text unter 'Schutte'.

[22] Andersch, *Europäische Avantgarde*, S.75

[23] Helmut Heißenbüttel, 'Annäherung an Arno Schmidt', in: Hans Mayer (Hrsg.), *Deutsche Literaturkritik, Vom Dritten Reich bis zur Gegenwart (1933-1968)*, Bd.4 (Frankfurt a. M.: Fischer, 1978), S.678-95, hier S.681.

[24] Heinrich Böll, *Aufsätze-Kritiken-Reden*, Bd. 1 (München: dtv, 1969), S.137. Weitere Hinweise auf diese Bände befinden sich im Text unter Böll.

[25] Günter Grass, *Werkausgabe in zehn Bänden*, hrsg.v. Volker Neuhaus, Bd.9: *Essays Reden Briefe Kommentare* (Darmstadt, Neuwied: Luchterhand, 1987), S.16. Weitere Hinweise auf diese Ausgabe befinden sich im Text unter Grass.

[26] Heinz Ludwig Arnold, *Gespräche mit Schriftstellern* (München: Beck, 1975), S.107. Weitere Hinweise auf diesen Band befinden sich im Text unter Arnold.

[27] Hans Magnus Enzensberger (Hrsg.), *Vorzeichen. Fünf neue deutsche Autoren* (Frankfurt a. M.: Suhrkamp, 1962), S.21.

[28] Vgl. die Buchveröffentlichungen Theodor W. Adorno, 'Engagement', in: ders.: *Noten zur Literatur III* (Frankfurt a. M.: Suhrkamp, 1965), S.109-35; Hans Magnus Enzensberger, *Einzelheiten II. Poesie und Politik* (Frankfurt a. M.: Suhrkamp, 1964), S.113-37.

[29] Walter Jens, *Deutsche Literatur der Gegenwart* (München: dtv, 1964), S.34. Weitere Hinweise auf diesen Band befinden sich im Text unter Jens 1964.

[30] Jens, *Deutsche Literatur*, S.38; vgl. Theodor Plieviers Rede in: Heinrich Bechtoldt (Hrsg.), *Literatur und Politik. Sieben Vorträge zur heutigen Situation in Deutschland* (Konstanz: Asmus, 1948). Die Einführung des Herausgebers grenzt den Frankfurter Kongreß gegen den Berliner von 1947 dreifach ab: 'schablonenhafter Konformismus', 'doktrinäre Rückversicherung' und 'das Zuviel an "engagee"' (S.11-12).

[31] Wolfgang Bächler, 'Zwischen den Stühlen', in: Karl Ude (Hrsg.), *Besondere Kennzeichen. Selbstporträts zeitgenössischer Autoren* (München: List, 1964), S.127-31, hier S.129. Vgl. aber zur vorherrschenden Verwendungsweise des Bildes Lenz in: Müller-Marein/Sommer, *Schriftsteller*, S.34-36; Grass in: Arker, *Nichts ist vorbei*, S.411-12; Reinhard Baumgart, 'David im Schatten Goliaths', in: Horst Krüger (Hrsg.), *Was ist heute links? Thesen und Theorien zu einer politischen Position* (München: List, 1963), S.56-69, hier S.68. Weitere Hinweise auf den Aufsatz von Baumgart befinden sich im Text unter Baumgart.

[32] Vgl. 'Der Zürcher Literaturstreit. Eine Dokumentation', *Sprache im technischen Zeitalter* H.22 (1967), 83-206. Bemerkenswert — im Sinne von Kontinuität — ist die abweichende Stimme Karl Heinz Bohrers; er verallgemeinert den Fall Staiger zu dem aller Germanisten, die historisch statt ästhetisch lesen, daraus folge 'zwischen Germanistik und aktueller Literatur eine Kluft' (S.121), die es bei Friedrich Gundolf

und Max Kommerell nicht gegeben habe; den Begriff 'Engagement' spart er sich für die faschistische Germanistik auf (S.118).

[33] Vgl. zu Hans Egon Holthusen und Karl August Horst: Erwin Jaeckle, *Der Zürcher Literaturschock. Bericht* (München, Wien: Langen-Müller, 1968), S.51, 84.

[34] Marcel Reich-Ranicki, *Wer schreibt, provoziert. Kommentare und Pamphlete* (München: dtv, 1966), S.167. Weitere Hinweise auf diesen Band befinden sich im Text unter Reich-Ranicki.

[35] Helmut Heißenbüttel, 'Neue Linke und die bundesdeutsche Literatur nach 1945. Ein Abriß', in: Heinz Ludwig Arnold (Hrsg.), *Geschichte der deutschen Literatur aus Methoden. Westdeutsche Literatur von 1945-71* Bd.3 (Frankfurt a. M.: Athenäum Fischer, 1972), S.1-7, hier S.3, 5. Weitere Hinweise auf diesen Aufsatz befinden sich im Text unter Heißenbüttel 1972.

[36] Vgl. die ausnahmslos aus den sechziger Jahren stammenden Quellen in der ersten literarhistorischen Darstellung, Horst Albert Glaser, 'Formen des Engagements. Ein Beitrag zur gegenwärtigen Situation', in: Thomas Koebner (Hrsg.), *Tendenzen der deutschen Literatur seit 1945* (Stuttgart: Kröner, 1971), S.139-56.

[37] Vgl. dazu — und zur konservativen Defensive — meinen Aufsatz, 'Discovering a Taboo: The Nazi Past in Literary-Political Discourse 1958-67', in: David Jackson (Hrsg.), *Taboos in German Literature* (Providence, Oxford: Berg 1996), S.135-63.

[38] Vgl. den Briefwechsel in: Hans Werner Richter (Hrsg.), *Die Mauer oder Der 13. August* (Reinbek bei Hamburg: Rowohlt, 1961).

[39] Friedrich Sieburg, *Verloren ist kein Wort. Disputationen mit fortgeschrittenen Lesern* (München: dtv, 1969), S.138.

[40] Hans Schwab-Felisch (Hrsg.), *Der Ruf. Eine deutsche Nachkriegszeitschrift* (München: dtv, 1962).

[41] Hans Werner Richter (Hrsg.), *Almanach der Gruppe 47* (Reinbek bei Hamburg: Rowohlt, 1962).

[42] Hans Werner Richter (Hrsg.), *Bestandsaufnahme. Eine deutsche Bilanz 1962. Sechsunddreißig Beiträge deutscher Wissenschaftler, Schriftsteller und Publizisten* (München, Wien, Basel: Desch, 1962).

[43] Vgl. zu Schnurres Priorität im einzelnen Iris Bauer, *'Ein schuldloses Leben gibt es nicht'. Das Thema 'Schuld' im Werk Wolfdietrich Schnurres.* (Paderborn: Igel, 1996), S.134-56: Standortbestimmung in den frühen sechziger Jahren: Schnurre als 'engagierter Schriftsteller'; vgl. ebenfalls Annelen Kranefuss: 'Die Spiegel-Krise des Wolfdietrich Schnurre', in: Ilse-Rose Warg (Hrsg.), *Er bleibt dabei. Schnurre zum 75.* (Paderborn: Igel, 1995), S.68-87.

[44] Wolfdietrich Schnurre, 'Warum ich nicht wie Swift schreibe', in: Uwe Schultz (Hrsg.), *Fünfzehn Autoren suchen sich selbst. Modell und Provokation* (München: List, 1967), S.20-32, hier S.21; vgl. auch seinen späteren Aufsatz 'Dreizehn Thesen gegen die Behauptung, daß es barbarisch sei, nach Auschwitz ein Gedicht zu schreiben (1978)', in: Petra Kiedaisch (Hrsg.), *Lyrik nach Auschwitz? Adorno und die Dichter* (Stuttgart: Reclam, 1995), S.123-26. Weitere Hinweise auf den Band *Fünfzehn Autoren* befinden sich im Text unter Schultz.

[45] Wolfdietrich Schnurre, *Schreibtisch unter freiem Himmel. Polemik und Bekenntnis* (Olten, Freiburg i. Br.: Walter, 1964), S.241.

[46] Vgl. die zeitgenössische Zusammenfassung von Horst Krüger, 'Der Schriftsteller in der Opposition', in: ders. u.a., *Literatur zwischen links und rechts. Deutschland. Frankreich. USA* (München: Ehrenwirth, 1962), S.7-28, hier S.8: 'Die deutsche Nachkriegsliteratur [...] ist kritisch, aggressiv und engagiert.', S.23; 'die Erfahrung des neuen, eigenen Gesichts der Bundesrepublik hat die Schriftsteller von 1947 ganz auf jene linke Linie festgelegt, die man bei uns heute gern mit einem verbrauchten Schlagwort Nonkonformismus bezeichnet.'

[47] Vgl. dazu meinen Artikel 'Engagement', in: Wolfgang Fritz Haug (Hrsg.), *Historisch-kritisches Wörterbuch des Marxismus* Bd.3 (Berlin, Argument, 1997), S.372-84.

[48] Vgl. Werner Koch (Hrsg.), *Selbstanzeige. Schriftsteller im Gespräch* (Frankfurt a. M.: Fischer, 1971), S.46. Weitere Hinweise auf diesen Band befinden sich im Text unter Koch.

[49] Wolfgang Hildesheimer, 'Erlanger Rede über das absurde Theater', *Akzente*, 7 (1960), 543-56, hier 547.

[50] Wolfgang Hildesheimer: 'Die Wirklichkeit des Absurden' (1967), in: Kiedaisch (Hrsg.), *Lyrik*, S.98-102, hier S.99-100.

[51] Nach dem Verbot der KPD im Jahre 1956 nahm die Deutsche Friedensunion ungefähr den gleichen Platz im Parteienspektrum der Bundesrepublik ein.

[52] Vgl. aber jetzt die angemessene Titelgebung von Hans Adler, Jost Hermand (Hrsg.), *Günter Grass. Ästhetik des Engagements* (New York u.a.: Lang, 1996).

[53] Klaus Roehler, Rainer Nitsche (Hrsg.), *Das Wahlkontor deutscher Schriftsteller in Berlin 1965* (Berlin: Transit, 1990), S.87 (Härtlings Entwurf), S.88 (Brandts Text).

[54] Vgl. zu diesem spezifischen Aspekt Volker Kaukoreit, 'Politische Tabuverletzungen. Erich Fried im Spiegel öffentlicher Auseinandersetzungen', *Text und Kritik*, H.91 (1986), 70-82.

[55] Peter Härtling, 'Gegen rhetorische Ohnmacht. Kann man über Vietnam Gedichte schreiben?', in: Kiedaisch (Hrsg.), *Lyrik*, S.102-06, hier S.102-03.

[56] 'Walter Jens: Gelehrter — Schriftsteller — Rhetor', in: Ude (Hrsg.), *Besondere Kennzeichen*, S.117-19, hier S.119.

[57] Martin Walser, *Erfahrungen und Leseerfahrungen* (Frankfurt a. M.: Suhrkamp, 1965), S.58. Zu seiner Entwicklung vgl. meinen Aufsatz 'Martin Walser — eine exemplarische Biographie? Der Abschied von der "öffentlichsten Öffentlichkeit"', *TheaterZeitSchrift*, H.25 (1988), 75-85; H.26 (1988-89), 110-21.

[58] Martin Walser, *Heimatkunde* (Frankfurt a. M.: Suhrkamp, 1968), S.24.

[59] Klaus Konjetzky, *Was interessiert mich Goethes Geliebte? Tendenziöse Gedanken und Gespräche über Literatur und Wirklichkeit* (München: Bertelsmann, 1977), S.134. Weitere Hinweise auf diesen Band befinden sich im Text unter Konjetzky.

[60] Gerd Fuchs, 'Die Beute des Herakles', *Kontext* 1 (1976), 258-69, hier 268.

[61] Hans Werner Richter, 'Zum politischen Engagement deutscher Schriftsteller', *Neue Rundschau*, 78: 1 (1967), 290-98, hier 297-98. Weitere Hinweise auf diesen Aufsatz befinden sich im Text unter Richter.

[62] Hans Erich Nossack ist hierfür ein Beispiel, das zeigt, wie sich über die Gruppe 47 hinaus der Konsens wandelte. Der von Sartre in den Nachkriegsjahren in Frankreich propagierte Nossack erklärte: 'Durch [...] ihr selbstverständliches Engagement [...] wirkt Literatur auch politisch revolutionär' (*Die schwache Position der Literatur. Reden und Aufsätze* (Frankfurt a. M.: Suhrkamp, 1967), S.23). Als 'selbstverständlich' galt ihm ein subjektives, 'ahistorisch(es)' Engagement (S.14) für den Menschen (S.90) gegen Abstraktion, Funktionalisierung, Konformismus 'herkömmlicher Bindungen' (S.74) und 'Wahrheiten' (S.60). Nossacks Differenz zu Sartre wird nicht nur in der kategorischen Bannung von Geschichte als 'Tagesereignisse' (S.90) und 'Tagesgespräch' (S.142) deutlich, sondern vor allem in dem Insistieren auf Literatur als Monolog (S.60). Wenn er den Autor als 'Widerstandskämpfer aus Instinkt' (S.73) bezeichnet, bezieht er sich auf Camus als Modell für des Partisanen Ausbruch aus der Herde und für jene spezifisch literarische Absage, deren Kritik in der Negation zugleich Utopie sei.

[63] Helmut Heißenbüttel, 'Spekulation über eine Literatur von übermorgen', in: Heinz Ludwig Arnold (Hrsg.), *Geschichte der deutschen Literatur aus Methoden. Westdeutsche Literatur von 1945-71*, Bd.3 (Frankfurt a. M.: Athenäum Fischer, 1972), S.308-15, hier S.315.

[64] Vgl. hierzu im einzelnen Brigitte Burmeister, *Streit um den Nouveau Roman. Eine andere Literatur und ihre Leser* (Berlin: Akademie, 1983), S.69-74, das Zitat von Robbe-Grillet auf S.73.

[65] Umberto Eco, 'Form als Engagement', in: ders., *Das offene Kunstwerk* (Frankfurt a. M.: Suhrkamp, 1973; zuerst italienisch, 1963/1967), S.237-292.

[66] Helmut Heißenbüttel, 'Es gibt keine deutsche Literatur', *Der Monat*, 17: 200 (1965), 112-20.

[67] Helmut Heißenbüttel, 'Literarische Archäologie der fünfziger Jahre', in: Dieter Bänsch (Hrsg.), *Die fünfziger Jahre. Beiträge zu Politik und Kultur* (Tübingen: Niemeyer, 1985), S.306-25, hier S.314.

[68] Peter Weiss: 'Zehn Arbeitspunkte eines Autors in der geteilten Welt', in: Beate Pinkerneil u.a. (Hrsg.), *Literatur und Gesellschaft. Dokumentation zur Sozialgeschichte der deutschen Literatur seit der Jahrhundertwende* (Frankfurt a. M.: Athenäum Fischer, 1973), S.241-46, hier S.243.

[69] Vgl. hierzu im einzelnen meinen Aufsatz 'Publizistische Transformationen der Utopie bei Hans Magnus Enzensberger', in: Rolf Jucker (Hrsg.), *Zeitgenössische Utopieentwürfe in Literatur und Gesellschaft. Zur Kontroverse seit den achtziger Jahren* (Amsterdam, Atlanta GA.: Rodopi, 1997), S.239-72.

[70] Joachim Schickel (Hrsg.), *Über Hans Magnus Enzensberger* (Frankfurt a. M.: Suhrkamp, 1970), S.190.

[71] Karl Markus Michel, *Die sprachlose Intelligenz* (Frankfurt a. M.: Suhrkamp, 1968), S.78.

72 Vgl. meinen Nachweis am Beispiel Wellershoff '"Kleine Schritte" zum Neuen Realismus: Dieter Wellershof als Leser und Lektor', in: Keith Bullivant u.a. (Hrsg.), *Dieter Wellershoff. Studien zu seinem Werk* (Köln: Kiepenheuer und Witsch, 1990), S.57-87.

73 Klaus Harpprecht, 'Totgesagt und sehr lebendig. Bonn und die intellektuelle Verweigerung: Die Opposition gegen die zweite deutsche Demokratie begann mit einem grollenden Abmarsch aus der Wirklichkeit', *Die Zeit*, 21.6.1996; vgl. besonders über die 'Gefahr des nachgeholten Widerstandes' 'jene spezifisch deutsche Verlogenheit, die nach 1968, als im Westen der Antifaschismus mehr als zwei Jahrzehnte post festum so recht erst erfunden wurde, jeden Winkel des Daseins durchdrang'.

74 Fritz J. Raddatz, 'Adenauers Visagist. Eine Polemik aus gegebenem Anlaß', *Die Zeit*, 28.6.1996.

JÜRGEN SCHUTTE

Literarische Restauration — Literarische Opposition
Vom Spielraum realistischer Literatur am Anfang der 50er Jahre

Die frühen fünfziger Jahre werden oft als Wendepunkt in der Entwicklung der deutschen Literatur betrachtet. Es heißt, der Neorealismus der unmittelbaren Nachkriegszeit sei durch neue ästhetische Paradigmen abgelöst worden. Eine neue Form kritisch-realistischen Schreibens hätte sich aber vielleicht behaupten können, wenn es eine publizistische Basis gegeben hätte. Ein solcher Versuch war die von Hans Werner Richter herausgegebene Zeitung *Die Literatur*, die weniger als ein Jahr bestand. Das Ziel war die 'Bildung einer neuen literarischen Öffentlichkeit' und 'eine Verjüngung der Demokratie'. Ein solches Projekt hatte aber kaum Aussichten auf Erfolg in dem kulturellen und politischen Klima der fünfziger Jahre. Erst ein Jahrzehnt später wurden die Ansätze der *Literatur* wieder aufgenommen.

In seinem 1961 erschienenen Essay *Deutsche Literatur der Gegenwart* über die Entwicklung der westdeutschen Literatur konstatierte Walter Jens:

> Mit einem Wort: der Neorealismus ist tot, und kein Genius wird die Nachkriegsprogramme noch einmal zum Leben erwecken. 1952 schlug das Pendel, sehr weit und für lange, zur anderen Seite aus. Ich glaube, ich könnte die Sekunde des Umschlags bezeichnen: es war in Niendorf an der Ostsee, Frühjahr 1952, eine Tagung der Gruppe 47 fand statt. Die Veristen, handwerklich-gute Erzähler, lasen aus ihren Romanen. Dann plötzlich geschah es. Ein Mann namens Paul Celan (niemand hatte seinen Namen vorher gehört) begann, singend und weltentrückt, seine Gedichte zu sprechen; Ingeborg Bachmann, eine Debütantin, die aus Klagenfurt kam, flüsterte, stockend und heiser, einige Verse; Ilse Aichinger brachte, wienerisch-leise, die 'Spiegelgeschichte' zum Vortrag. Damals, sieben Jahre nach dem Ende des Krieges, entfaltete sich [...] die junge deutsche Literatur der Moderne.[1]

Die 'poetologische Wende', von der die Literaturgeschichten sprechen, wenn sie das Ende der 'Kahlschlag'-Periode um 1950 beschreiben, hat in den literarhistorischen Darstellungen zu unterschiedlichen Begriffsbildungen und Bewertungen geführt. Man spricht, im Zusammenhang mit dem *comeback* von Gottfried Benn, von

einem ästhetischen Stimmungswandel, von einer Wiedergewinnung des
Poetischen. Auf der anderen Seite beklagt man die Enthistorisierung und
Ästhetisierung von Gesellschaft und Geschichte. Die kritische, sozial
engagierte Literatur der unmittelbaren Nachkriegszeit werde zugunsten
einer ungeschichtlichen 'dichterischen Aussage' zurückgedrängt. Von
innen, im Kreis um Hans Werner Richter, sah man das ähnlich. Louis
Clappier schrieb über die Tagung 1951 in Bad Dürkheim:

> "Wir müssen aus dem Provinzialismus herauskommen", sagte Walter Jens.
> "Es wird schwierig sein. Wir haben keine Hauptstadt. Wir haben keine große
> literarische Zeitung. Das letzte große literarische Gespräch fand in
> Deutschland statt über das Thema Der Bürger und der Künstler, und wurde
> als *Tonio Kröger* veröffentlicht. Das war 1903. Ich habe vor fünf Jahren zum
> ersten Mal von Kafka gehört. Wollen Sie, daß wir fürs Ausland schreiben?
> Die meisten von uns schreiben nicht einmal für Deutschland, sondern für ihre
> bayerischen und hessischen Flecken. Und dann übrigens: möchte man uns
> wirklich hören?"

Clappier fährt fort mit einer unüberhörbaren Empfehlung für den
zeitkritischen Realismus:

> Wir haben dann über seinen [Jens'] Roman *Der Blinde* gesprochen. Der Blinde,
> der tastend versucht, die Realität einer für ihn verlorengegangenen Welt wieder
> aufzubauen. Wie soll man das Suchen des Blinden verstehen können, wenn er
> uns nichts sagt über seine Leiden und über den Zustand seiner inneren Welt? Die
> Schriftsteller der Gruppe 47 und alle Deutschen, die schreiben können, werden
> vielleicht bald einsehen, daß das beste Mittel, die deutsche Literatur in Kontakt
> mit der Außenwelt zu bringen, darin besteht, daß sie sich bereiterklären, als
> Deutsche vom heutigen Deutschland und seinen Einwohnern zu berichten.[2]

In dem seinerzeit häufig gebrauchten Begriff des Provinzialismus
kulminiert die Frage, ob die nach dem Krieg so hoffnungsvoll angetretene
'junge Literatur' die an sie gestellten Erwartungen erfülle. Eher skeptisch
bis negativ beantworten die Autoren selbst um 1952 diese Frage. So stellt
Hans Georg Brenner anläßlich der Tagung in Niendorf fest, es gebe eine
gewisse Diskrepanz zwischen Können und Wollen, 'die die Kritiker nicht
recht deutlich machen können'[3] — eine Unsicherheit, die mir sehr
symptomatisch zu sein scheint. Denn in der Tat wußte man im Kreis um
Hans Werner Richter 1952 nicht mehr genau, wohin die literarische
Entwicklung gehe und was man selbst dazu beitragen könne. Es gab ein
verbreitetes Unbehagen an den Gegenständen und Schreibweisen der
Nachkriegszeit, am, wie Wolfgang Weyrauch formulierte, 'Realismus des

Unmittelbaren'.[4] Das Abgeschnittensein von der Weltliteratur und von der Tradition der Moderne wurde scharf empfunden. Umso mehr begrüßte man das Auftreten von Ingeborg Bachmann und Ilse Aichinger, um so begieriger hörte man auf die neuen Töne in der Lyrik Günter Eichs. Das Verständnis von den eigenen gesellschaftlichen und literarischen Handlungsmöglichkeiten hatte sich seit 1947 grundlegend gewandelt. Vom Pathos des 'Kahlschlags' und des Aufbruchs ist nicht mehr viel zu spüren, wenn Ilse Aichinger in ihrem Aufsatz 'Über das Erzählen in dieser Zeit' feststellt:

> Der Vergleich mit dem Fluß ist noch immer richtig. Aber wer heute Erzählungen mit Flüssen vergleicht, muß an reißendere Flüsse denken mit steileren und steinigeren Ufern, an die keiner, der einmal den Sprung gewagt hat, so leicht wieder zurück kommt. Und vielleicht an Grenzflüsse. Die Ufer, die vielen bisher Sicherheit bedeutet haben, sind zur Bedrohung geworden, und es verlockt den Fluß nicht mehr, daran zu spielen, er drängt schneller zum Meer. So liegt auch heute für den Erzählenden die Gefahr nicht mehr darin, weitschweifig zu werden, sie liegt mehr darin, daß er angesichts der Bedrohung und unter dem Eindruck des Endes den Mund nicht mehr aufbringt.[5]

Ein Stimmungsbild, in dem das Gefühl der Ausweglosigkeit den wenige Jahre zuvor noch vorherrschenden Optimismus abgelöst hat. So berichtet Jürgen von Hollander, ganz im gleichen Bildfeld bleibend, von der Tagung in Niendorf:

> Die Dichter tasten sich von Eindruck zu Eindruck, greifen hier an, skizzieren dort ein Bild, lassen es fallen, um es nie wieder aufzugreifen [...]. Ein Bild sah ich immer vor mir, wenn solche Gedichte gelesen wurden: einen breiten dunklen Fluß, auf dem — hier Treibholz, dort ein entwurzelter Baum — die Begriffe und Tatsächlichkeiten eines ehemaligen festen, nun hinweggespülten Landes treiben.[6]

Das Gefühl, die Wirklichkeit sei ungreifbar geworden, man könne die Realitäten nicht mehr festhalten und müsse diese Erfahrung einer äußersten Verunsicherung in dunklen, vielleicht auch hermetischen Schreibweisen ausdrücken, scheint für viele Autoren und Autorinnen auch der Gruppe 47 mittlerweile unabweisbar geworden.

Ich erinnere demgegenüber noch einmal an Hans Werner Richters programmatische Sätze in der Probenummer des *Skorpion* im Herbst 1947, die ebenfalls eine Suchbewegung im literarischen Feld beschreiben — aber vollkommen anders:

> Wir stehen an den Grenzpfählen einer neuen Zeit. Der Blick in das Land jenseits der Grenzpfähle ist uns versperrt. Wir befinden uns zwischen Gestern und

Morgen. Unsere Zeit ist ein Niemandsland zwischen den Zeiten. Sie ist voller Dunkelheit. Sie lebt in einer seelischen und geistigen Verwirrung, die ohne Grenzen ist. In einer solchen Zeit wächst der Literatur eine neue Aufgabe zu. Sie muß klären und führen. Sie kann sich nicht zurückziehen. Sie muß auf die Straße gehen und mit der Straße leben. Schon taucht allerorten die Frage auf "Wo steckt unsere junge Literatur?" Nun, sie wird kommen. Sie steht schon diesseits der Grenzpfähle. Wir werden sie sammeln und fördern, wir werden sie zusammenhalten und vorwärtstragen, denn "es wäre an der Zeit, dem Gegenstand, welchen die Beobachter so lange nur seitwärts angeschielt haben, auch einmal von vorn gerade ins Auge zu schauen". Ja, es ist an der Zeit. Wir wollen dem Gegenstand gerade ins Auge schauen.[7]

Im Vergleich dieser Äußerungen läßt sich der fast epochenweite Abstand ermessen, der zwischen den 'jungen Autoren' von 1947 und den von 1952 zu bestehen scheint. Dieser Abstand ließe sich auch verdeutlichen an der Gegenüberstellung zweier Wirklichkeitsbegriffe, auf die sich die Autoren schreibend beziehen. Während die kritisch-realistische Literatur der unmittelbaren Nachkriegszeit von der Existenz einer objektiven Realität ausgeht, der man schreibend 'gerad ins Auge zu schauen' habe, gesteht etwa Günter Eich als prominenter Vertreter der 'jungen deutschen Literatur der Moderne', er wisse nicht, was Wirklichkeit sei, er habe ihr gegenüber 'etwa die Schwierigkeiten wie ein taubstumm Blinder'. Die Wirklichkeit ist nicht gegeben, sondern sie wird schreibend erst hergestellt: 'In jeder gelungenen Zeile höre ich den Stock des Blinden, der anzeigt: Ich bin auf festem Boden.'[8]

Natürlich ist damit — und deswegen sagte ich 'scheint' — eine Tendenz angezeigt und kein abrupter Wechsel im literarischen Feld. Es ist ja nicht so, daß alle Autorinnen und Autoren übers Jahr ihre Wirklichkeitsauffassung und ihre Schreibweise geändert haben. Es geht um die jeweils vorherrschende Stimmung, um die Vorstellungen, die die Autorinnen und Autoren selbst von den Bedingungen ihrer Arbeit und damit indirekt von den Erwartungen ihres Publikums haben. Und es geht — mindestens auch — um eine Auseinandersetzung mit den von der konservativen Kritik formulierten Ansprüchen an die Literatur. So ist es sicher kein Zufall, daß sich ein Autor wie Heinrich Böll zu Beginn der 50er Jahre herausgefordert fühlt, die 'Trümmerliteratur' zu verteidigen und in diesem Zusammenhang seinen Wirklichkeitsbegriff kritisch zu klären.[9]

Wenn man die eingangs zitierte Beschreibung von Walter Jens über die Tagung von Niendorf, den *kairos* der 'jungen deutschen Moderne', mit dem vergleicht, was er selbst 1952 über die zeitgemäße Entwicklung der realistischen Literatur schrieb, dann wird diese Differenz zweier literarischer Konzepte noch einmal ganz unübersehbar. In einem Aufsatz mit dem Titel 'Kleines literarisches Lexikon' konstatiert Jens, daß der Neorealismus für die deutsche Literatur gerade erst beginne. Der Neorealismus — Jens orientiert sich an der zeitgenössischen italienischen Literatur und Filmkunst — sei eine Literatur des *Ist*, ihm entspreche eine Poetik, in der 'die Darstellung endet, das Leben selbst offenbar wird'. Der neorealistische Autor beschwöre die Kategorie der Wirklichkeit und verleugne den ästhetischen Schein; er befördere dadurch 'die Ablösung des Darstellens durch das Sein, das Gewinnen einer neuen objektiven Basis'. Nicht viel anders hatte Wolfgang Weyrauch fünf Jahre vorher den 'Realismus des Unmittelbaren', die an der amerikanischen Zwischenkriegsperiode orientierte Kurzgeschichte der Nachkriegszeit, begründet. Dabei ist es symptomatisch für die Situation im Jahr 1952, daß Jens sich genötigt sieht, die auf der Hand liegende Parallele explizit abzuweisen: 'Neorealismus ist nicht gleich Kahlschlag und nicht gleich Reportage. Die große Literatur des *Ist* steht noch bevor. Wir glauben an sie.'[10] Die Legitimationsbasis für kritisch-realistische Schreibweisen hatte sich seither gründlich geändert.

Wenn derselbe Walter Jens neun Jahre später nachdrücklich konstatiert, der Neorealismus sei tot und dieser Tod sei eben im Jahr 1952 eingeläutet worden, dann wird daran sehr eindrucksvoll sichtbar, daß und wie literarische Entwicklungsprozesse von den Beteiligten in Bildern und metaphorischen Mustern gedacht werden. Es kann auch deutlich werden, wie diese Bilder nicht nur orientieren, sondern gleichzeitig auch täuschen können.

Es läßt sich aber noch etwas anderes an diesen Äußerungen zeigen — und darum geht es mir vor allem. Literaturentwicklung hat nicht nur zu tun mit den Intentionen und Erwartungen der Autorinnen und Autoren, sondern vor allem mit der Möglichkeit, Positionen in der Öffentlichkeit zu erobern, d.h. mit der Möglichkeit, die künstlerischen Absichten nicht nur zur Sprache zu bringen, sondern auch zu öffentlicher Wirkung. Damit richtet sich der Blick auf die institutionellen Gegebenheiten, die Kräfteverteilung und die Bewegungen im literarischen Feld der frühen 50er Jahre, in denen es wieder einmal, mit zunächst geringem Erfolg, um den Realismus ging. Die modifizierte Weiterentwicklung des

Nachkriegsrealismus, um die sich Jens und andere um 1950 intensiv bemühten, hing aufs engste zusammen mit der Gründung einer literarischen Zeitschrift der Gruppe 47, in der neben Ilse Aichingers Betrachtungen 'Über das Erzählen in dieser Zeit' und Heinrich Bölls 'Bekenntnis zur Trümmer-Literatur' auch der zitierte Artikel über den Neorealismus von Walter Jens zuerst veröffentlicht wurde. Die Aussicht auf eine neue Form des kritisch-realistischen Schreibens — so lautet meine These — wäre in den 50er Jahren nicht so rasch und so nachhaltig verstellt worden, wenn es diese publizistische Basis für die junge deutsche Literatur, als Medium der kritischen Selbstverständigung und der Gewinnung eines breiteren Publikums, über längere Zeit gegeben hätte. Sie existierte jedoch nur ganze acht Monate.

Die Literatur. Blätter für Literatur, Film, Funk und Bühne wurden im Herbst 1951 erdacht. Während der Tagung der Gruppe 47 auf Burg Berlepsch bei Tübingen kam es zu Gesprächen zwischen den Autoren über das geplante publizistische Unternehmen, vor allem mit den Lektoren der Deutschen Verlagsanstalt in Stuttgart, bei der das Blatt erscheinen sollte. Die Vorbereitungen ziehen sich über den Winter 1951/52 hin, und am 15. Februar 1952 erscheint die erste Nummer. Das Blatt, nach Hans Werner Richters Vorstellungen im Layout und Format einer Zeitung, erschien alle vierzehn Tage im Umfang von 8 Seiten zu einem Preis von 50 Pfennig. Bereits nach vier Monaten kündigt der Verlag die Übereinkunft mit den Herausgebern Hans Werner Richter und Hans Georg Brenner. Es kommt zu einem Rechtsstreit, dann zu einem Vergleich, der die Bemühungen um eine andere Finanzierung der *Literatur* ermöglichen soll. Im November ist es dann endgültig vorbei, nach sechzehn Nummern wird die Zeitschrift eingestellt; sie hat das Jahr ihrer Gründung nicht überlebt.

Die Zeitschrift wäre ein Brückenkopf der zeitkritischen, realistischen Literatur gewesen und war als ein solcher gedacht. Ihre Gründung wird als eine kulturpolitische Aktion erkennbar, als Initiative einer Gruppe von Intellektuellen, die nicht bereit waren, das Wiedererstarken militaristischer Tendenzen und Institutionen, das Weitermachen der im Faschismus schwer belasteten geistigen Elite — kurz: die kulturelle Restauration hinzunehmen. Ähnlich wie schon im Münchner *Ruf* traten die Autoren der *Literatur* an gegen Tendenzen der Verinnerlichung, gegen die literarischen Wegbereiter des Faschismus und gegen das von Hans Egon Holthusen propagierte konservative Projekt einer 'Überwindung des Nullpunkts'[11] durch die Wiederbelebung überzeitlicher Werte und Verhaltensnormen. Diese kulturpolitische Offensive ist im Jahr 1952 ohne größere Resonanz geblieben. *Die Literatur* ist achteinhalb Monate erschienen und heute nahezu vollständig vergessen; in den Literaturgeschichten und den Monographien über die Gruppe 47 wird sie zumeist nicht einmal erwähnt. Erst 1954 mit den von Walter Höllerer und Hans Bender gegründeten *Akzenten* und 1955 mit Alfred Anderschs *Texte und Zeichen*, die auch nur knapp zwei Jahre existierten, bekommt die junge deutsche Literatur auf ganz anderer, akademischer Ebene wieder Publikationsorgane, in denen sie die Aneignung der europäischen Moderne wie die theoretische Diskussion voranbringen konnte. An der Differenz dieser Zeitschriften zu Hans Werner Richters Projekt eines literarischen 'Boulevardblatts' läßt sich die Verengung des Handlungsspielraums ermessen, welche die kritisch-realistische Literatur in den 50er Jahren hinzunehmen hatte.

Die Literatur wird von Hans Werner Richter im Leitartikel der ersten Nummer als ein publizistisches Projekt der 'jungen Generation' vorgestellt, das in Inhalt und Form einen frontalen Angriff auf die kulturellen Elite der jungen Bundesrepublik bedeutet, mit Selbstkritik allerdings auch nicht spart. Unter der Überschrift 'Courage?' entwickelt Richter *seine* Perspektive einer 'Überwindung des Nullpunkts'; er geht dabei von der Situation des Jahres 1945 aus:

> Und was geschah? Auf dem leeren Feld wurden Fassaden aufgerichtet, eine Fassade neben der anderen, Kongresse, Clubs, Akademien. Aber die Fassaden blieben Fassaden. Eine neue, aus dem Krieg, aus Lagern und Gefängnissen heimkehrende Generation begann zu schreiben, unbeholfen ohne jede Tradition, karg und sparsam aus Furcht vor dem entseelten Wort von gestern. Die Sprache — ein lebendiger, nicht ein steriler Körper — hatte ein Alltagsleben aber kein literarisches Leben mehr. Und hier begann das Experiment der jungen Generation. Sie griff bewußt auf die *Alltagssprache* zurück. [...] Und jetzt? Noch immer stehen die Fassaden auf dem leeren Feld. Aber jedermann weiß, daß es Fassaden sind. Noch immer bemüht sich eine junge Generation — gegen alle Widerstände der Restauration — der Sprache ein neues Leben einzuhauchen, den Kontakt zur weltliterarischen Entwicklung wiederherzustellen und die verhängnisvolle Zerrissenheit der deutschen Literatur aufzuheben.[12]

Nicht weniger als die 'Bildung einer neuen literarischen Öffentlichkeit und eines neuen Publikums' und eine 'Verjüngung der deutschen Demokratie' setzt sich die neue Zeitschrift zum Ziel. Richter verspricht eine 'planmässige Arbeit' an der 'Gesundung des literarischen Lebens in Deutschland'. Das bedeutet in Kürze: die Überwindung des Provinzialismus durch gleichberechtigte Einbeziehung der ausländischen Literatur und der deutschsprachigen Exilliteratur; die Kenntnisnahme der Literatur in der DDR, etwa durch 'Auskunft über Brecht' schon in der ersten Nummer; und schließlich die Auseinandersetzung mit der Entwicklung mit den populären Medien Funk und Film.

Ich kann hier leider nicht diskutieren, wie wirklichkeitsnah und aussichtsreich die von Richter vorgetragene Lagebeurteilung und das daraus entwickelte kulturpolitische Programm waren.[13] Daß die Kritik der Restauration nicht mit einfachen Willenserklärungen abzutun war, sondern eine intensive Diskussion auch in den eigenen Reihen erforderte, war den Autoren des Blattes nur zu bewußt. Sie waren, wie die eingangs zitierten Äußerungen zeigen, durchaus nicht der Meinung, daß der Realismus der 'jungen Generation' über jeden Zweifel erhaben sei. Das hinderte sie jedoch nicht, der herrschenden 'Geistigkeit', die zu Beginn der 50er Jahre weithin mit der Inneren Emigration identisch war, den Kampf anzusagen. Anknüpfend an die Gründung der *Literarischen Welt* durch Willy Haas im Jahr 1928 stellt Richter in seinem Editorial fest, es gehöre 'damals wie heute Courage dazu, ein solches Blatt zu einem Blatt der *offenen Polemik*, der harten, aber *echten Kritik* und der *unmißverständlichen Diskussion* zu machen'. Den provokativen Charakter solcher Formulierungen müssen wir uns heute durch eine Historisierung verständlich machen: Erst in Relation gesetzt zum kulturellen Klima der Adenauerzeit wird die Herausforderung deutlich, die diese Ankündigungen bedeuten. Die bald einsetzende, wütende Polemik gegen das neue Blatt beweist es.

Es war, wie gesagt, genauere Orientierung gefordert, wenn die Kritik an der herrschenden Kultur und das Programm einer 'jungen deutschen Literatur der Moderne' Bestand haben sollten. Dieser Aufgabe widmen sich in den folgenden Nummern der *Literatur* zahlreiche Artikel.[14] Ich gebe zwei Beispiele: Unter dem Titel 'Literarische Restauration — literarische Opposition' schreibt Walter Mannzen, Opposition setze eine Kenntnis der gesellschaftlichen Frontenbildungen voraus. Das Insistieren darauf, daß man eine weltanschauliche Basis brauche, unterscheidet seine Argumentation auffällig von dem 'totalen Ideologieverdacht'[15] und dem abstrakten Nonkonformismus vieler Autoren der Gruppe 47, aber auch von der Unklarheit, mit der Hans Werner Richter in seinem zitierten Editorial die kulturpolitischen Fronten beschrieben hatte. Mannzen unternimmt es, die Kritik an der kulturellen Restauration auf die grundlegenden Kategorien der europäischen

Aufklärung zu gründen. Weltanschaulich und historisch konsequent identifiziert er als die 'eigentliche Gefahr' die ideologische und literarische Gegenaufklärung, deren antidemokratischer Zug sich von dem gegen die französische Revolution mobilisierten autoritären Staatsverständnis der Romantik in der Tradition von Edmund Burke herleite. Es fallen die Namen Stefan George, Ernst Jünger, Oswald Spengler, Othmar Spann, Hans Zehrer, Ludwig Klages und Gottfried Benn. Die derart genauer bezeichnete antidemokratische Linie sieht Mannzen auch durch T. S. Eliot vertreten, ihren 'durch den Nobelpreis inaugurierten Weltrepräsentanten'. Eliots Konzept eines religiös begründeten autoritären Obrigkeitsstaates, sein royalistisch-klassizistisches Weltverständnis stelle 'den klassischen Fall der eigentlichen Restauration dar, und zwar einer — im monarchistischen England — noch monarchistischen Form, die aber alle Elemente zu einem neuen Faschismus in sich trägt'.[16]

'In der Demokratie scheiden sich die Geister. An ihrer Sprache sind sie zu erkennen'. So endet ein Artikel von Arnold Bauer in der ersten Nummer der Zeitschrift. Bauer konturiert den 'restaurativen Stil' durch seine Entgegensetzung zur Tradition eines Realismus, der die gesellschaftlichen 'Zustände und Gegebenheiten' *deutlich* hinstelle. Das gelte für Balzac und Zola, Keller und Fontane, Dickens und Dostojewski, Stendhal und Proust, Dreiser und Hemingway, Thomas Mann und Kafka.

> Ja auch für Kafka! Der Vordergrund ist und bleibt die Gesellschaft. Gewiß lassen sich gesellschaftliche Zustände transzendieren, doch erst muß der Autor sie kennen und darstellen können. Sie zu verschleiern haben nur diejenigen ein durchsichtiges Interesse, die sie versöhnt wissen wollen, weil sie die Klarheit scheuen. Wer enthüllt, der kritisiert; wer verschleiert, der duldet und nimmt hin. Unsere Verschleierer, die mit unkontrollierbaren metaphysisch getarnten Erlebniswerten operieren, wollen jedoch nicht so sehr das Gegebene verhüllen als Vergangenes verklären. [...] Heute ist der Begriff des Realismus fast schon zum Schimpfwort geworden. Morgen werden seine Widersacher über den Rationalismus die Nase rümpfen.[17]

Im Heft 12 druckte die Redaktion der *Literatur* die 1928 in der *Einbahnstraße* zuerst publizierten Thesen über die Technik des Kritikers von Walter Benjamin. Vermutlich ist dies der erste in der Bundesrepublik gedruckte Text des marxistischen Kritikers überhaupt, dessen Schriften dann 1955 und 1966 in einer von Theodor W. Adorno veranstalteten Auswahl erschienen. Die erste dieser Thesen lautet: 'Der Kritiker ist Stratege im Literaturkampf'.[18] Ich halte es nicht für einen Zufall, daß Hans

Werner Richter diesen Text vierzehn Tage nach dem Versuch der DVA, die Zeitung einzustellen, in das Blatt setzt. Benjamin hat in seiner bekannten Rezension einer Literaturgeschichte von Emil Ermatinger von 1930 diese militärische Metaphorik des literarischen Kampfes weiter ausgeführt:

> Die ganze Unternehmung ruft für den, der in Dingen der Dichtung zu Hause ist, den unheimlichen Eindruck hervor, es käme in ihr schönes, festes Haus mit dem Vorgeben, seine Schätze und Herrlichkeiten bewundern zu wollen, mit schweren Schritten eine Kompanie von Söldnern hineinmarschiert, und im Augenblick wird es klar: die scheren sich den Teufel um die Ordnung und das Inventar des Hauses; sie sind hier eingerückt, weil es so günstig liegt, und sich von ihm aus ein Brückenkopf oder eine Eisenbahnlinie beschießen läßt, deren Verteidigung im Bürgerkrieg wichtig ist. So hat die Literaturgeschichte sich's hier im Haus der Dichtung eingerichtet, weil sich aus der Position des "Schönen", der 'Erlebniswerte", des "Ideellen" und ähnlicher Ochsenaugen in diesem Hause sich in der besten Deckung Feuer geben läßt.[19]

An solche Schlachtbeschreibungen fühlt man sich erinnert, wenn man die Kritiken liest, die alsbald nach der Gründung der *Literatur* von allen Seiten über das Blatt hereinbrechen. Daß diese Gründung eine kulturpolitische Provokation war, haben die Gegner vielleicht zum Teil besser begriffen als die Herausgeber und Autoren des Blattes.

Dafür sprechen der Tonfall und die Argumentationsmuster der Kritiken. Ich zitiere als ein Beispiel unter vielen einen Aufsatz von Klaus Harpprecht mit dem Titel 'Hilfe — Literatur! Der Dichtung Jammer ficht uns an!':

> Man ist also da und läßt von sich hören. Denn man ist die "neue Generation" — wieder einmal. Man zählt vierzig Jährchen, ein bißchen drunter oder ein bißchen drüber, macht nichts. Jugend nach vorn! Als neue Generation sucht man einen neuen Weg und zwar grundsätzlich, in Leitartikeln. Zunächst wird festgestellt, daß "nicht nur der Geschmack des Bürgertums verdorben wurde", sondern auch "die Arbeiterschaft nach den ersten großen Anfängen der zwanziger Jahre wieder in jene dumpfe Gleichgültigkeit zurücksank, die weit von jedem geistigen und literarischen Leben entfernt ist". Es liegt also, wie man vernimmt, am Publikum.
> Diese Behauptung ist, mit Verlaub gesagt, etwas dreist. [...] Selbst für Untersuchungen über die Verwandtschaft jenes Herrn [Jean Paul Sartre] mit dem Tollkopf Stirner, dürften sie [die Leser] nicht so viel übrig haben, daß sie die *Literatur* abonnieren.
> Im Zitat: "Wir können sagen, daß das Für-sich, als Selbst, das Sein des Anderen in sein Sein einschließt, insofern es in seinem Sein als Nicht-der-Andere-Sein in

Frage steht." Soweit Sartre. Dann schon lieber Kreuzworträtsel, denkt der Arbeiter und der Bürger auch. Wer will es ihnen übelnehmen?[20]

Vier Hauptargumente der Kritiker, die sich zum großen Teil nicht nur auf die neue Zeitschrift, sondern auch auf die 'junge Generation' überhaupt bzw. auf die Gruppe 47 einschießen, möchte ich vergegenwärtigen.

Erstens: Die junge Literatur ist aus der Gosse. Das alte, immer wiederkehrende Argumentationsmuster, daß die Literatur verantwortlich gemacht wird für das, was sie beschreibt, wird etwa gegen Ilse Aichingers 'Spiegelgeschichte' mobilisiert:

> Können Sie übrigens wohl erraten, woran das junge Mädchen in der Spiegelgeschichte gestorben ist? Nun, bedenken Sie bitte, daß die 47er, die es ständig mit der Wirklichkeit haben, daß sie eine neorealistische Literatur der "Ist" propagieren. Also, woran ist das junge Mädchen gestorben? Nun, an einer Abtreibung natürlich, wie könnte es anders sein. Andere Todesarten wären doch reine Restauration.[21]

Zweitens: die junge Literatur ist Reportage, daher von gestern. Zu dem Roman *Sie fielen aus Gottes Hand*, für den Hans Werner Richter im März 1952 den von Exilverlagen und -autoren gestifteten René-Schickele-Preis erhielt, findet Günter Blöcker die folgenden Worte:

> Was vor siebzig Jahren eine große Tat war: die Entdeckung der Wirklichkeit, der "gemeinen" Wirklichkeit, für die Literatur — das ist heute, da es keine Nippes mehr zu zerschlagen, keine Gipsdenkmäler mehr zu stürzen und keine Jasminlauben mehr zu entblättern gilt, weil sie alle schon zerschlagen, gestürzt und entblättert sind, kein Verdienst mehr. Seitdem auch die verborgensten Zipfel der Wirklichkeit ans Licht der Literatur gezerrt worden sind, kann es schlechterdings nicht länger als Verdienst gelten, die Rolle des literarischen Photographen ad infinitum weiterzuspielen. [...] Autoren wie Hans Werner Richter, die sich gewiß sehr fortschrittlich dünken, wenn sie das Banner des sogenannten Neorealismus entfalten, sind Avantgardisten mit einer Verspätung von rund einem halben Jahrhundert.[22]

Blöcker attestiert Richters Roman Kargheit und seelische Dürre; er sei nichts mehr als ein armseliges Stenogramm des Lebens, kümmerlich, weil er das wichtigste auslasse, nämlich das, was zwischen und hinter den historischen Fakten liege. Carlo Levis 1945 erschienenes süditalienisches Tagebuch *Christus kam nur bis Eboli* wird dem Roman Richters positiv entgegengehalten, weil 'darin das Erlebnis in sprachliche Konturen gebannt ist, die das Flüchtige zeitlos und das Vergängliche unantastbar machen'. Bei

Richter dagegen stellt Blöcker eine 'totale Kapitulation des Wortes vor dem Stoff' fest .

Drittens: *Die Literatur* wolle die literarischen Zwistigkeiten der 20er Jahre wieder beleben. Damit ist exakt auf die Sollbruchstelle der Auseinandersetzung verwiesen, deren Grundriß bereits in der 'großen Kontroverse' des Jahres 1946 um das Exil und die Innere Emigration gelegt worden war. Es geht um die Tradition, an der die 'Überwindung des Nullpunkts' sich orientiert: am Konservativismus der Zeit vor dem Ersten Weltkrieg, auf den sich die Innere Emigration bezog — oder an den Literaturdebatten der zwanziger Jahre, die Richter mit dem Namen Willy Haas aufgerufen hatte und in denen Autoren wie Piscator, Brecht, Döblin und Heinrich Mann eine tonangebende Rolle gespielt hatten. Ohne daß diese Anknüpfungen in der *Literatur* explizit propagiert worden wären, trifft die Kritik Heinz Beckmanns doch genau in diese Kerbe:

> Merken diese 47er gar nicht, daß sie ihrerseits eine ausgemachte Restauration betreiben? Eine Restauration jenes Literatenspuks ['Literaten': das war der Ausdruck für die Autoren, deren Bücher am 10. Mai 1933 brannten] der zwanziger Jahre, dem wir die verhängnisvollste Zertrennung und Parteiung der deutschen Literatur verdankten. Ein junges Literaturblatt will kämpfen, das läßt sich verstehen. Doch fehlt es mangels Literatur heute sogar an Gegnern. Und so kleistert man sich eine Pappscheibe an den Baum, schreibt mit roter Farbe das Wort "Restauration" drauf und schießt, schießt immerfort bloß auf das eine Wort ohne zu ahnen, was man eigentlich damit meint.[23]

Viertens schließlich, in der 'roten Farbe' bei Beckmann vermutlich schon mitgemeint: Die Autoren machen sich zu *fellow-travellers* der Kommunisten. Beinahe reflexhaft verbindet sich die Polemik gegen die sozialistische Literatur bei Klaus Harpprecht mit der Verharmlosung des Mitläufertums in der Zeit des Faschismus:

> Der Brecht, die Seghers — denen trägt man es nicht nach, daß sie sich vor den Schlachtenwagen des roten Totalitarismus spannten. Sie irrten ja nur und man sollte sie beim Straucheln noch auffangen, um sie dann desto inniger an die demokratische Brust zu drücken. Anders, ganz anders, wenn einmal jemand, und sei es nur für wenige Wochen, gemeint hat, daß sich der braune Moloch vielleicht doch zähmen ließe. *Da* gibt es keine Gnade. Und so wird denn, gleich in der ersten Nummer der *Literatur*, wieder einmal Hans Carossa seine Geburtstagsadresse an Hitler aufs Butterbrot geschmiert. Das kann gar nicht oft genug aus der Schublade geholt werden. Hitler ist ja schließlich tot. Und Väterchen [Stalin] lebt noch. Oder?[24]

In einem Aufsatz mit dem Titel 'Literarische Archäologie der 50er Jahre'[25] hat Helmut Heißenbüttel der Gruppe 47 rückblickend den Vorwurf gemacht, sie habe ihre Wirksamkeit und ihre literarische Praxis theoretisch und historisch nicht entschieden genug reflektiert, sie habe sich damit begnügt, pragmatisch aufzugreifen und zu verstärken, was die kulturelle Situation von sich aus bot. Dieser Pragmatismus, den Heißenbüttel auch in der *Literatur* am Werk sieht, sei eine wesentliche Ursache für die Begrenzung und die mangelnde Entwicklungsfähigkeit der Gruppe 47 gewesen.

Welcher andere Weg war gegeben? Als eine publizistische Plattform zur Klärung und Festigung dessen, was man damals die 'junge deutsche Literatur der Moderne' nannte, war *Die Literatur* von Hans Werner Richter und den Autoren der Gruppe 47 projektiert. Sie bot die Möglichkeit, die konzeptionellen und programmatischen Diskussionen öffentlich zu führen und die eigenen künstlerischen Vorstellungen und Produktionen einem breiteren Publikum nahezubringen — beides notwendige Ergänzungen der Tagungspraxis. Der Zusammenhalt der Gruppe 47 beruhte ja auf der Tatsache, daß sie *keine* öffentliche Veranstaltung war, daß Diskussionen konzeptioneller und programmatischer Art während der Lesungen von Hans Werner Richter unterbunden wurden. Die Gruppe konnte also in den frühen 50er Jahren ein Forum für die öffentliche Erörterung und die Verbreitung ihres Literaturverständnisses gut brauchen. Denn die gesellschaftliche und künstlerische Orientierung der Autorinnen und Autoren war, wie wir sahen, auch nach eigenem Verständnis keineswegs unanfechtbar. Zudem traf die konservative Polemik gegen die Gruppe 47 und ihre Zeitschrift, bei aller elitären Herablassung, durchaus auch Schwachpunkte, an denen die Selbstkritik der Autoren und Autorinnen sich abmühte. Es erscheint mir keineswegs als abwegig, sondern als sehr reizvoll, darüber nachzudenken, was eine stabile Zeitschrift der Gruppe 47 für das kulturelle Klima in den 50er Jahren hätte bedeuten können. Mit dem Ende des Projekts nach knapp acht Monaten sind Ansätze verschüttet worden, die dann erst zehn Jahre später, in historisch veränderter Form, für die kulturelle Entwicklung der Bundesrepublik bedeutsam wurden.

Fußnoten

[1] Walter Jens, *Deutsche Literatur der Gegenwart* (München: dtv, 1964), S.129f.

[2] In: *Documents*, Paris, Juli/August 1951; wieder in: Reinhard Lettau (Hrsg.), *Die Gruppe 47. Bericht, Kritik, Polemik. Ein Handbuch* (Neuwied und Berlin: Luchterhand, 1967), S.65-68, hier S.68.

[3] Hans Georg Brenner, 'Kritisches und Selbstkritisches. Zur Tagung der Gruppe 47', *Die Literatur*, 1: 6 (1.6.1952) 1; wieder in Lettau (Hrsg.), *Handbuch* , S.72-77; hier S.73.

[4] Wolfgang Weyrauch, 'Realismus des Unmittelbaren', *Aufbau*, 2 (1946), 701-06.

[5] Ilse Aichinger, 'Über das Erzählen in dieser Zeit', *Die Literatur*, 1: 6 (1.6.1952), 1.

[6] In: *Der Kulturspiegel* (Bayerischer Rundfunk), Freitag, 13.6.1952. (Typoskript im Hans-Werner-Richter-Archiv).

[7] Hans Werner Richter, (Editorial), *Der Skorpion*, 1: 1 (1948 Probenummer gedr. Herbst 1947), S.9. Zitiert nach dem Reprint: *Der SKORPION. Mit einer Dokumentation zur Geschichte des "Skorpions" und einem Nachwort zur Geschichte der Gruppe 47 von Heinz Ludwig Arnold* (Göttingen: Wallstein, 1991). Richter zitiert Friedrich Schlegel.

[8] Günter Eich, 'Der Schriftsteller vor der Realität', in: ders., *Gesammelte Werke in vier Bänden . Revidierte Ausgabe*, Bd.4 (Frankfurt a. M.: Suhrkamp, 1981), S.613f.

[9] Vgl. Heinrich Böll, 'Bekenntnis zur Trümmer-Literatur' *Die Literatur* 1: 5 (15.5.1952), 1f. Wieder in ders., *Werke* Bd.7:. *Essayistische Schriften und Reden I, 1952-1963*, hrsg. von Bernd Balzer (Köln: Kiepenheuer und Witsch, 1978), S.31-55. Vgl. auch: Heinrich Böll: 'Der Zeitgenosse und die Wirklichkeit' (1953), in: ebd., S.71-75.

[10] Walter Jens, 'Kleines Literarisches Lexikon. II. Neorealismus', *Die Literatur*, 1: 4 (1.5.1952), 7.

[11] Hans Egon Holthusen, 'Die Überwindung des Nullpunkts', in: ders., *Der unbehauste Mensch* (München: Piper, 1951), S.137-68.

[12] Hans Werner Richter, 'Courage?', *Die Literatur*, 1: 1 (15.2.1952), 1.

[13] So zeugt es von einer erheblichen Wirklichkeitsferne, wenn Richter zur Zeit der großen Kämpfe um die Montan-Mitbestimmung und das Betriebsverfassungsgesetz eine 'dumpfe Gleichgültigkeit' der Arbeiter diagnostiziert.

[14] Ich nenne einige weitere Titel, um die Richtungen der Diskussionen anzudeuten: 'Der Streit um den Elfenbeinturm' (Herbert Fischer); 'Literatur als Instrument und Waffe' (ders.); 'Literatur und Krisenbewußtsein' (Erich Köhler), 'Sinn und Aufgabe der nachfaschistischen Literatur' (Helmut Günter); 'Wider den moralpädagogischen Hochmut der Kulturkritik' (Jürgen Habermas); 'Gibt es eine sozialistische Literatur?' (Gerhard Szcezesny).

[15] Vgl. Hans Mayer, *Zur deutschen Literatur der Zeit. Zusammenhänge, Schriftsteller, Bücher* (Reinbek bei Hamburg: Rowohlt, 1967).

[16] Walter Mannzen, 'Literarische Restauration — Literarische Opposition', *Die Literatur*, 1: 5 (15.5.1952), S.6.

[17] Arnold Bauer, 'Der restaurative Stil', *Die Literatur*, 1: 1 (15.3.1952), 3.

[18] Walter Benjamin, 'Einbahnstraße' in: ders. *Gesammelte Schriften*, Bd.4, 1. Hrsg. v. Tillman Rexroth (Frankfurt a. M.: Suhrkamp, 1980), S.83-148, hier S.108.

[19] Walter Benjamin, 'Literaturgeschichte und Literaturwissenschaft', in: ders. *Gesammelte Schriften*, Bd.3, hrsg. v. Hella Tiedmann-Barthels, S.283-90, hier S.287.

[20] Klaus Harpprecht, 'Hilfe — Literatur! Der Dichtung Jammer ficht uns an!', *Christ und Welt*, 24.4.1952.

[21] Hans Beckmann, 'Literarisches Scheibenschießen. Vom Händewaschen und der Wahrheitsfrage bei der Gruppe 47', *Rheinischer Merkur*, 13.6.1952.

[22] Günter Blöcker, 'Die Reaktion als Fortschritt. Zu einem neuen Roman von H.W. Richter', *Der Tagesspiegel*, 16.3.1952.

[23] Heinz Beckmann (s. Anm. 21).

[24] Klaus Harpprecht (s. Anm. 20).

[25] Helmut Heißenbüttel, 'Literarische Archäologie der 50er Jahre', in: Dieter Bänsch (Hrsg.), *Die fünfziger Jahre* (Tübingen: Niemeyer, 1985), S.305-25.

RHYS W. WILLIAMS

Inventing West German Literature: Alfred Andersch and the Gruppe 47

As the former co-editor of *Der Ruf*, who had, like Hans Werner Richter, worked on the earlier PoW periodical of the same name during his captivity in the USA, Alfred Andersch played a major part in the development of the Gruppe 47. His own work was influential, whilst he acted as a 'talent spotter' for the Group and also publicised it as a frequent contributor to the media. A process of estrangement set in in the mid-1950s when Andersch's growing enthusiasm for avant-garde literature made him wish to impose a literary programme on the Group. His emigration to Switzerland and his espousal of leftist positions also led to difficulties with Richter. Nevertheless he was still prepared to defend the Group. Moreover, through his influence he helped to create a western identity for the literature of the Federal Republic, something in which the Gruppe 47 played a major role.

In his somewhat ungenerous section on Andersch in *Im Etablissement der Schmetterlinge*, Hans Werner Richter recalls a judgement made by Andersch on the Gruppe 47 in the mid-1950s: 'In fünfzig Jahren ist das berühmt.'[1] The whole tenor of Richter's comments indicates that Andersch was obsessively concerned with fame, especially his own, yet the continued interest shown by academic research in the Gruppe 47 confirms at least the accuracy of Andersch's prediction: 'In fünfzig Jahren *ist* das berühmt'. Here I propose to explore the relationship between Andersch (one of its founding fathers) and the Group. After setting out the political and literary preconceptions which informed the establishment of the Group, I intend to examine Andersch's contribution both to shaping the Group's identity and publicising its activities. I shall then explore his own literary and essayistic contributions delivered at Group meetings and finally consider his decision to distance himself from the Group in the late 1950s. Since any account of Andersch's involvement with the Group is simultaneously a history of his relationship with Hans Werner Richter, I make no apology for devoting some attention to Richter's assumptions about politics and literature.

It is my contention that the values and attitudes which shaped the early direction of the Gruppe 47 and with it the literature of the Federal Republic in the 1950s were less the product of re-education in the American PoW camps (as Volker Wehdeking[2] has argued) than of the experience of defeat, defeat, not of the German army in 1945, but of the socialist ideals of the young generation in 1933. The failure of socialism to resist Hitler, enforced accommodation with Nazi values in the Third Reich and the sense that the complexities of their situation were not fully appreciated in the Brave New World of the Federal Republic characterised the political and literary values of the founder members of the Gruppe 47. Both Alfred Andersch and Hans Werner Richter were to devote most of their own literary production to a reappraisal of their personal experiences in the Third Reich, playing out retrospectively a range of possible reactions to National Socialism, justifying and explaining their own failure to resist and presenting themselves as psychological victims of a totalitarian regime. Refusing to accept the notion of collective guilt and retaining a belief in a demilitarised, united Germany, they were branded as nationalists (a charge which they emphatically denied); holding fast to socialist values after the onset of the Cold War, they were dismissed as communist fellow-travellers (an accusation which they rejected with equal vehemence). All too aware of the failure of communism to offer effective resistance to the Nazis, they harboured deep suspicions both about communist policies in Eastern Europe and about ideology in general. What they envisaged as the new literature of West Germany was to be a literature which confronted the failures of the past in the interests of a new political and, by implication, literary future. When socialist ideas were attacked, they responded with exaggerated vehemence, recalling the earlier failure of socialists to stand up for their views; but when confronted with Soviet policies they reacted with equal suspicion, remembering the failure of Moscow to unite left-wing opposition to Hitler. That Andersch and Richter had been socialists before 1933, that they had remained in Germany in the Third Reich and that, despite their literary ambitions, had succeeded in publishing little before 1945, was to give both of them excellent credentials as spokesmen of the younger generation.

Andersch's literary and journalistic background before 1945 throws some light on his post-war attitudes. Before 1933 he had been Communist Youth Organiser for Southern Bavaria and dabbled in political journalism. After Hitler's seizure of power and the burning of the Reichstag, Andersch, like most communist functionaries, was arrested; he emerged from Dachau after six weeks, thanks to his mother's effective intervention in drawing attention to the not insignificant contribution which his late father, Alfred Andersch senior, had made to the rise of National Socialism. Andersch himself was briefly rearrested in the autumn of 1933, and reacted, perhaps not unnaturally, in view of the threat of a return to Dachau, by breaking off his communist party affiliations and giving up politics for literature. His experience that literature under National Socialism implied the abandonment of politics was to ensure that Andersch's post-war commitment would be to a literature in which political concerns were central. Andersch's literary beginnings were unpromising: poetry in the style of Rilke and short prose sketches evoking landscapes from which human concerns were largely excised. In February 1942 he submitted a longer prose piece, 'Skizze zu einem jungen Mann', to the literary section of the *Frankfurter Zeitung*, which was just about the time when he was released from military service after taking part in the invasion of France and serving as part of the occupying force. Early in 1943, Andersch applied for membership of the *Reichsschrifttumskammer*. While his application was successful, he was 'von der Mitgliedschaft befreit', the usual procedure for writers who had published little.[3] Andersch's decision to apply was the first step in his effort to gain transfer to a 'Propaganda-Kompanie', one of his frequent and understandable attempts to avoid a posting to front-line military service. Called up again in October 1943, Andersch was posted to Denmark, where in April 1944 he received a letter from the Suhrkamp Verlag, declining his projected volume 'Erinnerte Gestalten'.[4] One of the three stories in that volume was, however, published in April 1944 in the *Kölnische Zeitung*. Although after the war, for obvious reasons, Andersch was to be silent[5] about his literary activities before 1945, he was, if only just, a writer of 'innere Emigration' and his sympathy for the writing which was published in Germany between 1933 and 1945 is, as we shall see, a feature of his appraisal of the post-war literary situation.

After his desertion in Italy, Andersch was transferred as a PoW to Fort Ruston in Louisiana and then in April 1945 to Fort Kearney, Rhode Island, where he joined the editorial team of *Der Ruf*, in its original form as a fortnightly periodical which, from 1 March 1945, was distributed to all other PoW camps in the United States. Andersch contributed regularly to the periodical from April until August, when he left the editorial team to attend re-education courses in nearby Fort Getty. His contributions were threefold: attempts at creative writing, which reflected the powerfully autobiographical impetus which marked his later works; reviews and reports dealing with American literature and music, in keeping with one of the primary functions of the periodical, namely to inform its readers about American values; and reflections on the question of future political and cultural life in Germany. Speaking for a 'young generation', which he firmly identified with those who had experienced the war and faced death, Andersch rejected ideology and was suspicious of party politics. From the re-education courses held at Fort Getty Andersch acquired a new set of American values; these principles of liberalism, national self-determination and freedom of expression, were part of the baggage which he brought back to Germany in the autumn of 1945.

With the foundation of the German version of *Der Ruf*, which first appeared on 15 August 1946, Andersch was able to develop his ideas on the future of Germany. His inaugural editorial, characteristically entitled 'Das junge Europa formt sein Gesicht', propounds a synthesis of socialism and humanism, with the warning that the younger generation in Europe would be swift to abandon the socialist camp if it saw socialism as jeopardising human freedom in favour of orthodox Marxist determinism. Produced under American licence, *Der Ruf* was sympathetic to the ideals of American liberalism, but insisted on the German right to self-determination, a demand which was, sooner rather than later, to bring the editors into conflict with an increasingly anti-communist American line. In various contributions Andersch criticised the Americans for failing to remain true in practice to their democratic ideals, for refusing to institute the 'Freiheit und Gleichberechtigung Deutschlands'.[6] He poured scorn on 'die Tragikomödie der "re-education"'[7] and highlighted 'die Sehnsucht der Deutschen nach der Vereinigung'.[8] Through re-unification, he argued, Germany would become a neutral zone, outside the East-West conflict, a country in which a new synthesis might be attempted between the values of East and West. Andersch's unambiguous commitment to socialism in Western Europe was bound, in a climate of international tension, to arouse American suspicions. It is not difficult to see why the removal of Andersch and Hans Werner Richter as editors of *Der Ruf* in April 1947 should have been the price demanded by the Americans for the continuance of the publication's licence.[9]

Richter, it should be noted, had a strikingly similar 'Lebenslauf' to Andersch: he had been associated, on his own admission, with socialist groups, had opted to remain in Germany, had accommodated himself with the regime, had begun a minor literary career, publishing a few newspaper articles and short stories, had applied for membership of the *Reichsschrifttumskammer* on 26 July 1938 and had finally been awarded his 'Befreiungsschein' on 17 May 1939; like Andersch he had fought in Italy, been taken prisoner by the Americans and had worked on the American *Ruf* before returning to Germany. As Richter himself noted of Andersch: 'Wir hatten beide das Dritte Reich überstanden, ohne Konzessionen zu machen, wir hatten uns beide demütigen lassen, ohne nachzugeben' (*Etablissement*, p.44).

The ill-fated attempt of the *Ruf* contributors to found a literary magazine, *Der Skorpion*, and the decision to call the editorial meeting in Bannwaldsee which inaugurated the Gruppe 47 are now well-known. Andersch, who was prevented by the wedding of his younger brother Martin from attending that meeting, nevertheless played a major role in the early years of the Group. His essay *Deutsche Literatur in der Entscheidung*, which was read to the second meeting of the Gruppe 47 in Herrlingen, remains one of the few theoretical texts which the Group, with its suspicion of theory and dislike of ideology, ever countenanced. Indeed, Andersch's later disillusionment with the Group may be explained, to some extent, by its reluctance to adopt a clear programmatic line. Andersch's essay is remarkable for three reasons: first, it is a brave statement from someone whose literary and intellectual status was by no means firmly established; second, it is a document which translates into literary judgements the political dilemma which Andersch was voicing elsewhere; and third, it provides a framework for the rehabilitation of much of the writing of the Third Reich, for the acceptance of some of the writing of exile, and for the assimilation of both these traditions into a new style of post-war writing. In short, Andersch provides here the justification for a specifically West German literary tradition, one which he was to foster with extraordinary success in his editorial and broadcasting activities over the next decade. Both the Gruppe 47 and Andersch's various editorial and broadcasting ventures helped to invent West German literature; their activities were not congruent, but they clearly overlapped, especially during the formative years of the Group.

Andersch purports to offer in his essay an analysis of the literary situation in 1947. If something rather different emerges, it is as much because of what Andersch leaves out as because of what he includes. He opens his essay by emphasising 'die tiefe Verwandlungsfähigkeit des Menschen im Allgemeinen, des künstlerischen Menschen im Besonderen'.[10] The possibilities of casting off a past life of *mauvaise foi*, of undergoing a Sartrean conversion, or exercising a new Sartrean choice, form a framework for the whole essay, as its title illustrates. It is not difficult to appreciate the attractions of such a view for German writers of Andersch's generation in 1947. If the compromises of literary life under National Socialism may be defined as *mauvaise foi*, then they may be cast off by making a new existential choice. Considering what we now know of the extent of Andersch's literary activities in the Third Reich, activities of which few would have been aware in 1947, this essay acquires new autobiographical urgency. Given his own position, it is particularly poignant that he should assert: 'Jede Untersuchung des Zustandes der deutschen Literatur, [...] muß daher von einer sorgfältigen Betrachtung des wahren Verhaltens des deutschen Geistes in den Jahren der Diktatur ausgehen' (*AAL*, p.113).

Although he is aware that the phrase 'innere Emigration' covers a multitude of different reactions to the regime, Andersch elects to adopt the term, extending it to typify all the literature which was produced within Germany after 1933. His argument is ingenious: since all explicitly Nazi writing is not worthy of the name literature, it may be conveniently set aside. It follows that all genuine literature produced in Nazi Germany was written in opposition to the regime. 'Eine Zeugung des Dichterischen aus dem Geist des Nationalsozialismus gab es nicht' (*AAL*, p.114). This sleight-of-hand enables Andersch to claim that any analysis of literature produced in Germany between 1933 and 1945 is an analysis of the literature of 'innere Emigration'. Some rather dubious figures may thus be saved: Hans Grimm, Erwin Guido Kolbenheyer, Wilhelm Schäfer, Emil Strauß. These figures, for Andersch, displayed 'eine Art subjektiver Ehrlichkeit' (*AAL*, p.116) and could thus be regarded as opponents of the regime. In order to illustrate the tragedy of this group, Andersch helps his argument along by devoting some attention to the least problematic figure, Ernst Wiechert, whose four-month imprisonment in Buchenwald in 1938 turned him into a victim of the regime. A second, older, generation is described as belonging to a tradition of 'bürgerliche Klassik': Gerhart Hauptmann, R. A. Schröder, Hans Carossa, Ricarda Huch, Gertrud von Le Fort. Apart from Carossa, who attempted 'aus sehr noblen Gründen' (*AAL*, p.117) to compromise, all the others are described as opponents of the regime, driven by their humanistic values into isolation. A third and final group of writers who remained within Germany are subsumed under the category 'Widerstand und Kalligraphie', a group containing figures like Stefan Anders, Horst Lange, Hans Leip, Martin Raschke and Eugen Gottlob Winkler. This group maintained their independence from the *Reichsschrifttumskammer* through the form of their work. Andersch concludes his section on those who remained with a study of Ernst Jünger, whose 'conversion' is adduced as proof that genuine artistic achievement was identical with opposition to National Socialism. Andersch's admiration for Jünger (a response which was to cause Andersch difficulties with some of his left-wing colleagues) is based on a reading of Jünger's symbolic style as the only effective weapon against totalitarian control.

Turning to the literature of opposition, Andersch begins by insisting that resistance was infinitely more difficult in Germany than France, not least because nationalism preserved French writers from collaboration with the Nazis but encouraged German opponents of Hitler to mute their criticism. One cannot help feeling that Andersch is indulging in an act of self-exoneration, both of himself and his generation. His attitude to the literature of exile is ambivalent: he admires those who went into exile, but insists that they can influence the future literature of Germany only if they return. Here Andersch enters a topical debate in which the central issue was that of Thomas Mann's return to Germany, an issue which, incidentally, dominated the discussion of exile writing at the Berlin Writers' Conference in October 1947. For Andersch, whose admiration for Mann is attested not only by his imitation of Mann's work during the 1930s but also by his sympathetic essays in the post-war period, Mann's work represents 'die Zugehörigkeit Deutschlands zur atlantischen Kultur' (*AAL*, p.124) which he defines, significantly, as openness, willingness to change,

commitment to humanitarian values. When he turns to 'realistische
Tendenzkunst', the writing of those who bitterly opposed National
Socialism, including Heinrich Mann, Werfel, Arnold Zweig and Döblin,
Andersch is critical. These writers forfeit his approbation in that their
realism is tainted by didacticism, by 'propagandistische Vorzeichen'
(*AAL*, p.125). Similarly, a group entitled 'Satiriker' (Tucholsky,
Polgar, Ossietzky, Walter Mehring, Kästner) are too much satirists, for
him, and not sufficiently true artists. Nor is he convinced by 'die
proletarischen Schriftsteller' (Oskar Maria Graf, Willi Bredel, Anna
Seghers, Theodor Plievier). What inhibits their work, for him, is 'ihre
allzustarke Bindung an eine erklärende Dogmatik der gesellschaftlichen
Vorgänge, ihr Glaube an eine wissenschaftliche Methodik' (*AAL*,
p.127). Here we have an early indication of Andersch's antipathy
towards the cultural policy in the Soviet Zone. If Ernst Jünger
epitomised the writers of 'innere Emigration', it is Brecht who
embodied the strengths (and weaknesses) of the writers of opposition.
For Andersch, Brecht's anti-German sentiments, however
understandable, diminish his achievement, and Brecht's return to
Germany will alone convince Andersch of his value to the new
generation of German writers.

Turning, in a final section, to the future of German literature,
Andersch singles out some new developments: Langgässer's *Das
unauslöschliche Siegel*, the work of Schnurre, Kolbenhoff, Borchert,
Weyrauch and Eich. Foreign influences are commended: Henry Miller,
Camus, Silone and Koestler, the last two for their much publicised
repudiation of communism, which made them significant figures in the
history of the Cold War in Europe. The essay closes with some bitter
comments on the 'colonial' status of German literature under
occupation: the role of the left-wing intellectual in Germany is,
Andersch contends, doubly difficult: he must defend democracy both
against those who give democracy a bad name by their current
imposition of undemocratic practices in Germany, and against those
who become so disillusioned by the contrast between democratic theory
and practice that they revert to their old fascist ways. Andersch's ideal
is a 'Synthese von Freiheit und sozialer Gerechtigkeit' (*AAL*, p.131), a
programme which was, in the context of the incipient Cold War, bound
to bring him into conflict with both America and the Soviet Union.

Certainly, *Deutsche Literatur in der Entscheidung* was well received by the writers present, who regarded it as a statement representative of their position. Why that should have been so is interesting: Andersch has managed in his essay to rehabilitate nearly all the writing which went on in Germany in the Third Reich, to blur the distinction between those writers of an older generation who continued to write in Germany and a younger generation whose voice was first heard after 1945, to define this new possibility as anti-communist, or at least anti-Stalinist, yet as a possibility equally opposed to American control, and to argue for a realism which is ill-defined enough to permit a plurality of styles. Here in essence is the rationale for the eclecticism of the Gruppe 47, its own blurring of distinctions between those writers who were published in Nazi Germany and those who were genuine newcomers in the post-war era. With his subsequent radio and editorial activities Andersch was to continue to pursue similar ends.

What, then, was Andersch's practical involvement in the Gruppe 47? While his theoretical essay was well received in Ulm, in the presence of the Bürgermeister, the father of Sophie and Hans Scholl, its reading did not take place in the privacy of the Group proper, but at a public event. To the Group, a few days earlier, Andersch had read his story 'Heimatfront', in which the central character, Werner Rott (frequently a cipher for Andersch himself) is presented as a figure involved in the German resistance. The reading was not a success, a response which Andersch, himself a severe critic of the writings of other participants, was to encounter not infrequently. Yet he continued to attend meetings; in Jugenheim in April 1948 he first met Günter Eich (whose work he championed); at the fifth meeting in Marktbreit, he read, to general approval, his short story 'Weltreise auf deutsche Art'. At the same time he was embarking on a highly successful career as a radio editor, promoting in his essays and on radio the work of writers who participated in the meetings of the Group, and situating their work within a distinctively Western European context. In 1949 he edited a series entitled *Europäische Avantgarde*, with texts by Camus, Sartre, de Beauvoir and Malraux. Later, when he moved to Radio Frankfurt (which became the Hessischer Rundfunk) he edited a series which included texts by Böll, Arno Schmidt, Weyrauch, Hildesheimer and Bachmann. In July 1949, in a feature entitled 'Fazit eines Experiments neuer Schriftsteller' for the Abendstudio of Radio Frankfurt, he introduced the Gruppe 47 to a wider audience. Here, after offering longer excerpts[11] from the work of Richter, Schnurre and Eich (the older generation, as it were), he recommended younger talents: Hans Jürgen Soering, Wolfgang Bächler, Georg Hensel (representing the post-war new generation of writers). Once more important distinctions were being blurred.

Andersch's role in publicising the activities of the Group and talent-spotting was, at least in the early years, as significant as Richter's. Writing to Franz Josef Schneider on 22 March 1949, Richter issued an invitation to the Marktbreit meeting, but concluded his letter with the words: 'Andersch wird sicher inzwischen schon mit Ihnen gesprochen haben. Vielleicht hat er Sie auch schon eingeladen.'[12] It is clear that Andersch, whose radio work brought him into close contact with influential figures, was empowered to issue invitations to appropriate persons. Andersch could even exercise influence over Richter's invitation policy: Paul Celan's first reading at Niendorf in 1952 had met with a negative reaction, not least on the part of Richter himself; on 9 March 1954, Andersch intervened to ensure that Celan was offered another opportunity to attend: 'Celan erzählte mir die Geschichte Deiner Mißverständnisse mit ihm. Ich halte sie wirklich für Mißverständnisse und Celan für einen sehr guten Mann, auch wenn Du mir im Augenblick widersprichst. Wenn Du Dich überwinden könntest, ihn einzuladen, würde ich mich freuen' (*HWRB*, p.178). Richter immediately issued an invitation and repeated the offer over the following years, despite Celan's steadfast refusal to accept.

At the sixth meeting, Andersch again made a foray into the essayistic with a paper on the German film. At the eighth meeting in Bad Dürkheim in 1951 Andersch met Böll, Aichinger, Milo Dor and Hildesheimer, and continued, outside the Gruppe, to review and propagate their work. The series *Studio Frankfurt* which Andersch edited from 1952 to 1953 brought together some notable early figures of the Group, including Ilse Schneider-Lengyel (at whose house the first meeting of the Group took place) and writers outside the Group, like Arno Schmidt, whom Andersch championed despite Richter's wholly negative reaction. When Friedrich Sieburg attacked the Group in a series of articles in August 1952, it was to Andersch that Richter turned for a rebuttal, and Andersch's public defence was keenly appreciated by those attending the October 1952 meeting, where he read with great success from *Die Kirschen der Freiheit*. Andersch's high-profile career in radio had seen him move in April 1952 to head the feature department of the NWDR in Hamburg. At the thirteenth meeting in Bebenhausen in 1953 he read 'Die bitteren Wasser von Lappland', material inspired by a visit to Lapland and which he exploited in feature form for the radio. At the fourteenth meeting in Cap Circeo in Italy, Andersch's reading of the story 'Diana mit Flötenspieler' was warmly received. From 1 January 1955, Andersch moved to the Süddeutscher Rundfunk and simultaneously edited the journal *Texte und Zeichen*. With his 'Radio-Essay' programme Andersch was in a position to exert an enormous influence on young radio listeners and, once again, the writers whom he met in the Gruppe 47 were the main beneficiaries: what he drew attention to on the radio, he also published in his periodical.

At the seventeenth meeting in Bebenhausen in 1955 Andersch again read a theoretical essay: 'Die Blindheit des Kunstwerks', which manages to offer a blueprint for literature as disparate as that which is found in the Group. Andersch had championed the avantgarde since the late 1940s, and was anxious to dispel the misconception, as he saw it, that the literature of formal experiment was escapist 'l'art pour l'art'. Once more his argument is ingenious: 'Die Abstraktion ist die instinktive oder bewußte Reaktion der Kunst auf die Entartung der Idee zur Ideologie.'[13] In a totalitarian system (of the right or the left) abstract art has the vital function of challenging, or at least resisting, attempts to make art subservient to ideology. Here we have a justification for what might be termed an 'abgemilderte Moderne', a literature of formal experiment which, provided it does not degenerate into pure formalism, can find a necessary place within the canon. Andersch concludes his essay with the often quoted sentence: 'Die Literatur ist Arbeit an den Fragen der Epoche, auch wenn sie dabei die Epoche transzendiert' (pp.50-51). His essay manages to clear the middle ground, justifying simultaneously a literature of political commitment (provided that it is not subservient to ideology) and a literature of formal experiment (provided it does not lapse into pure formalism). The Gruppe 47 was a broad church and Andersch supplies here a justification for its pluralism.

By late 1954 Andersch had, as 'Die Blindheit des Kunstwerks' suggests, begun to part company with Richter. Andersch developed,

during the early 1950s an enthusiasm for the avantgarde and sought to
impose on the Group an aesthetic programme. Richter gives a detailed
and somewhat jaundiced account of their disagreement:

> An diesem Tag war es anders, zum ersten Mal sprach er über die 'Gruppe 47',
> nicht nur ihr späterer Ruhm beschäftigte ihn, sondern auch die Fehler, die ich
> machte, er ließ durchblicken, daß ich das alles ohne klare Zielsetzung [...]
> mache, es sei, so erklärte er mir, dringend erforderlich, ein Programm zu
> machen, ein literarisches natürlich, ein zeitgemäßes, mit Blick nach vorn
> natürlich, ein avantgardistisches Programm. (*Etablissement*, p.36)

Andersch must have swiftly realised that his comments had upset
Richter, for a conciliatory letter of 21 December 1954 seeks to paper
over the differences. Andersch writes: 'Wenn man in einer Sache mal
etwas anderer Meinung ist, wie ich in puncto Gruppe 47, dann darf das
nicht zu einer persönlichen Verstimmung führen', and he adds for good
measure that this is, in fact, not so much a difference of opinion as 'das
Erwägen von Möglichkeiten, die mit meiner grundsätzlichen
Zustimmung zur Gruppe gar nichts zu tun haben' (*HWRB*, p.193).
Nevertheless, Andersch was at this time embarking on the editorship of
just such an avantgarde periodical, *Texte und Zeichen*, and was clearly
seeking to identify that periodical with the Group. In any event, the
tension was short-lived. On 11 February 1955 Richter replied to
Andersch's letter and announced the Berlin meeting in May 1955;
moreover, he conceded that as Andersch is in close contact with many
writers through his work on the periodical 'bitte ich Dich, es schon jetzt
mitherumzusprechen' (*HWRB*, p.196). Richter's reaction to the first
number of *Texte und Zeichen* in the same letter alludes to the recent
differences of opinion: 'Alles in allem ist sie konservativer, als ich
erwartet hatte. Ein Charakterzug, der mich in diesem Zusammenhang
freut' (*HWRB*, p.197). Far from presenting a thoroughgoing
programme for the literary avantgarde, the periodical retains more than
a residual commitment to the pluralism of the Gruppe 47. Richter has
some criticisms: he is still unhappy about Arno Schmidt, but concedes
that the Celan poems which Andersch included have finally won him
over. Andersch's decision to include in the periodical a bibliography of
the Gruppe 47 elicited a mixed reaction from Richter: his initial
pleasure gave way to some mild concern that the bibliography might
suggest to the unwary reader that the Group contained a fixed
membership. But he expressed considerable interest in the detailed

analysis of the Group which was promised for a later number, an analysis which, in the event, never appeared.   Nevertheless, the connection between *Texte und Zeichen* and the Gruppe 47 was close enough to confuse some of Andersch's readership. After the appearance of the bibliography Andersch found himself forced to remind readers 'daß unsere Zeitschrift von allen literarischen Verbänden und Gruppen unabhängig ist und im Geiste solcher Unabhängigkeit redigiert wird'; he regrets that his decision to publish the bibliography led critics erroneously to assume 'es handele sich bei *Texte und Zeichen* um ein Organ der Gruppe 47'.[14] That such a disclaimer had to be issued is token enough of the very close connection of Andersch's editorial work with the Group.

Although Andersch and Richter were to remain on good terms, contacts between them diminished after 1955. Andersch was fully occupied with his editorship of *Texte und Zeichen*, with his work for the Süddeutscher Rundfunk, and with his own literary career. The success of *Sansibar oder der letzte Grund* (1957) made it possible for him to contemplate existence as an independent writer. Andersch's decision to move to Switzerland and pursue a full-time literary career coincided with Richter's increasing involvement with the 'Grünwalder Kreis', a group dedicated to what Richter termed 'democratic firefighting', namely opposing the remilitarisation and restoration policies of the Adenauer government wherever and whenever they made themselves manifest. The first plenary meeting of the Kreis took place in Hamburg in February 1956 and in the subsequent years Richter's active political involvement was to contrast with Andersch's more radical conviction that the Federal Republic was a lost cause. Early in 1962 Andersch responded enthusiastically to Richter's introduction to the newly published anthology of *Der Ruf* edited by Hans Schwab-Felisch.[15] Contact thus having been re-established, Andersch decided to attend the Berlin meeting of the Group in October 1962, the first meeting he had attended for a number of years. The decision to meet in Berlin was a fateful one; the event was overshadowed by the *Spiegel*-Affair. It was Andersch who drafted the protest, together with Enzensberger and Klaus Roehler in Uwe Johnson's flat, a protest which forty-nine authors of the Gruppe 47 were emboldened to sign; Grass and Schnurre refused to endorse the protest letter, which led, indirectly, to Andersch's break with Grass. Looking back on the furore

which the declaration provoked, Richter tended to blame the affair on
Andersch: 'Die Bundesrepublik war für ihn nicht mehr ein Land
bürgerlicher Restauration, sondern schon so etwas wie der Vorhof einer
neuen faschistischen Zeit' (*Etablissement*, p.42). Andersch's view also
provoked a rupture in his relationship with Böll. A chance meeting in
Rome in December 1962 led to a political argument which Böll was to
make public in his essay 'Was heute links sein könnte' (1963). With
Andersch (who chose to live either in Switzerland or Italy) no doubt in
mind, Böll argued:

> Eine Linke, die sich jetzt noch als heimatlos bezeichnet, ist nur noch weinerlich.
> Das Recht, sich heimatlos zu nennen, hatten die Emigranten, ein teuer
> erkauftes, bitter erworbenes Recht. Hier, heute, in diesem Land, aus dem
> niemand zu emigrieren braucht, zum Alibi erhoben, klingt es wie ein
> aufgewärmter Traum.[16]

Böll was clearly reacting in a not dissimilar way to Richter. In a curious
way, the respective reactions of Richter and Andersch to the political
atmosphere in the Federal Republic in the early 1960s echoed their
attitudes to their own past. Richter had always justified his decision not
to emigrate during the Third Reich, not to run away from what he saw
as his political responsibility. Andersch, who had likewise remained in
Germany, had retrospectively seen his failure to emigrate as an
opportunity missed; his own belated 'emigration' to Switzerland in the
late 1950s he perceived, perhaps unconsciously, as rectifying the
omission of the past.

     While Andersch sought to give the Group a sharper political
focus, to transform it into a political pressure group against what he saw
as the increasing right-wing tendency of the Federal Republic, he
simultaneously rejected explicit electoral support for the SPD, which
Richter and Grass advocated. Andersch's own gloomy prognostications
for the Federal Republic led to his estrangement from the West German
political scene and his growing distance from the Gruppe 47, which
became increasingly identified, through Richter and Grass, with the
SPD. After initially signalling his willingness to attend, Andersch pulled
out of the meeting in Sweden in September 1964, not, he emphasised,
for political reasons, but because he was hard at work on his next
project: *Efraim*. Perhaps Andersch was being disingenuous, for a
number of prominent names stayed ostentatiously away from the
Sigtuna meeting, much to Richter's irritation. Johnson, Lenz, Eich,

Aichinger, Böll, Bachmann, Walser and Hildesheimer, for example, declined the invitation. A number of writers were unhappy about the representative nature of the events, about their being seen as contributing in some obscure way to the cultural policy of the Federal Republic. Andersch, while he clearly shared these doubts, insisted that his reasons were personal; Richter responded with ill-disguised annoyance, though he claimed to accept Andersch's excuse. After the event, however, Wolfgang Hildesheimer (whose withdrawal had infuriated Richter's wife) sent Richter a detailed explanation of his motives: 'in meinen Augen begehst Du einen Fehler, wenn Du Deinen Ehrgeiz darin siehst, Deine Gruppe über das internationale Parkett zu steuern [...]. Ich sehe in der neuen Gruppe 47 bedenkliche Zeichen einer Eingliederung' (*HWRB*, p.535). Hildesheimer copied his letter to Andersch, who endorsed its sentiments fully in his own letter to Richter on 8 November 1964: 'ich teile wolfgangs ansicht, dass wir von dem system, das heute in deutschland herrscht, durch politische taktik nichts zu gewinnen haben' (*HWRB*, p.537). What must have particularly upset Richter was that the views held by Hildesheimer and Andersch were representative of a sizeable minority of the established membership of the Group. Given this sharp divergence in their positions, it is unsurprising that Andersch indicated that he was prevented by illness from attending both the Princeton meeting and the final meeting of the Group.

Despite his reservations about its promotional activities, Andersch retained a profound and genuine affection for the Gruppe 47. Whenever it came under attack, he leapt to its defence, much to Richter's delight. In a poem of 1966 entitled 'Zeilen schinden für die Gruppe', Andersch asks himself (and his readers) some awkward questions about the Group. After listing the titles of some of the major works produced by its members, Andersch poses the uncomfortable question:

> warum die betrachter so heterogener gegenstände
>
> die sie in den verschiedensten stilarten behandelten wobei sie zu ganz
>
> entgegengesetzten schlüssen kamen
>
> nach dem zweiten weltkrieg
>
> in deutschland
>
> jedes jahr
>
> drei tage
>
> zusammenkamen

> und sich ihre erzeugnisse vorlasen[17]

No obvious answer suggests itself,

> nichteinmal die freundlichkeit des ausgezeichneten schriftstellers
>
> hans werner richter
>
> scheint uns das phänomen zu erklären

Andersch lists the cynical explanations advanced by critics of the Group:

> das geldbedürfnis
>
> das bedürfnis nach publicity
>
> die markt-manipulation
>
> der kulturbetrieb
>
> eines selbsthilfevereins
>
> literarischer nulle

but leaves the broader evaluation of its achievement to posterity. Future literary sociologists will have to return to 'dem absurden geheimnis' of the Group's existence. Richter, beleaguered and depressed by defections and assaults, was delighted (and not a little flattered) by Andersch's contribution, ambiguous and open-ended as it was.

What, then was the lasting legacy of Andersch's involvement with the Group? Perhaps Andersch's editorial activity for *Texte und Zeichen* from 1955 to 1958 best illustrates his efforts to support writers associated with the Group and at the same time place their work in a wider European context. That periodical came to epitomise the avantgarde, oppositional literature of the Adenauer era. But the opposition to restoration conservatism was only one facet of what Andersch helped to create. Based on his assumption that avantgarde art embodied a rejection of both the National Socialist legacy and the doctrinaire cultural policies of the GDR, Andersch, perhaps unwittingly, created a cultural climate which was specifically West German. Critical, but not dangerously so, of Cold-War attitudes in the West, but dismissive of much that was produced in the GDR, Andersch, in his non-aligned, yet Western-oriented canon, helped to create the liberal, modernist, eclectic taste of the Federal Republic. Alongside his championing of the Group, Andersch in his radio programmes introduced West Germans to Ionesco and Beckett, Faulkner and Wilder, while in *Texte und Zeichen* he published, in some cases for the first time in Germany, works by Beckett, Borges, Char, Dylan Thomas, Neruda, Vittorini, Pavese, and Barthes. Yet Andersch, at that time, virtually ignored what was going on in the GDR; *Texte und Zeichen* did include a brief survey of work published in the GDR and reprinted a short story by Karl Mundstock, but these were its only genuflexions towards East Germany. While East Germany was fostering a tradition of Socialist Realism, Andersch was shaping a Western alternative, one that was modernist, yet pluralistic and undogmatic. It was broad enough to contain the conservative writers of both exile and 'innere Emigration' (Thomas Mann, but also Ernst Jünger and Gottfried Benn) and the more obviously experimental writers (Heißenbüttel, Bense, Arno Schmidt). It effectively blurred the distinction between those who had remained in Germany, those who had emigrated and returned to the West, and those who were beginning a literary career within the 'Gruppe 47'. It created a kind of Western 'Erbe', excluding only those who were receiving official sanction in the GDR. It might be construed as mischievous to call it a NATO theory of literature, but, for all its outspoken opposition to Adenauer's 'Weststaatlösung', it supplied a kind of literary counterpart to just such a policy, looking for its models to France, the United States and Italy, and largely ignoring events behind the Iron Curtain.

To his credit, Andersch was ever prepared to re-evaluate critically his own position. In his Open Letter to Konstantin Simonov of 1975, he was later to admit that he was more of a 'Westler' than he had realised. Recalling the post-war period, he offers a critical gloss both on his own editorial activity and his contributions to the Gruppe 47:

> Was haben wir nachgeholt? Merkwürdigerweise nicht zuallererst die Bücher der deutschen Emigranten, die in New York, Mexiko und Moskau entstanden waren, die kamen erst später, und manche von ihnen, besonders diejenigen des linken Flügels der deutschen Emigration, sind bis heute noch von uns kaum wahrgenommen worden. Worauf wir uns stürzten, waren Amerikaner, Engländer, Franzosen, Italiener. Hemingway, Faulkner und Vittorini. Eliot, Gide und Sartre. Unsere spezielle Aufmerksamkeit widmeten wir der Literatur der Avantgarde: Kafka, Proust, Joyce und der neuen Lyrik jeglicher Observanz [...].[18]

With characteristic frankness Andersch confesses his shortcomings, admitting that he was more determined by the atmosphere of the Cold War than he knew. In his defence one could note that his catalogue of the literature which he did indeed promote reads deceptively like a literary history of the Federal Republic, a literary history in which,

largely thanks to Andersch's efforts, the writers of the 'Gruppe 47'
played a central role.

Footnotes

1 Hans Werner Richter, *Im Etablissement der Schmetterlinge. Einundzwanzig Portraits aus der Gruppe 47* (Munich: Hanser, 1986), p.35. Further references to this work appear in the text under *Etablissement* followed by a page reference.

2 Volker Christian Wehdeking, *Der Nullpunkt. Über die Konstituierung der deutschen Nachkriegsliteratur (1945-1948) in den amerikanischen Kriegsgefangenenlagern* (Stuttgart: Metzler, 1971).

3 Andersch's application form was made available to me by the American Document Center.

4 See '*...einmal wirklich leben'. Ein Tagebuch in Briefen an Hedwig Andersch 1943 bis 1975*, ed. by Winfried Stephan (Zurich: Diogenes, 1986). For the references to the 'Propaganda-Kompanie', see p.21; for the letter of rejection, see pp.37-38.

5 Andersch broke his silence in 1977 in 'Der Seesack', in: *Literaturmagazin 7*, ed. by Nicolas Born and Jürgen Manthey, pp.128-29.

6 'Der grüne Tisch', *Der Ruf,* 1: 3 (15 September 1946); also in: Hans Schwab-Felisch (ed.), *Der Ruf. Eine deutsche Nachkriegszeitschrift* (Munich: dtv, 1962), pp.42-46.

7 'Chaplin und die Geistesfreiheit', *Der Ruf,* 1: 3 (15 September 1946).

8 'Die Zonen und der Weltfriede', in *Der Ruf,* 1: 6 (12 November 1946); also in: Schwab-Felisch, *Der Ruf,* pp.79-83..

9 For a detailed account of these events, see Jérôme Vaillant, *Der Ruf. Unabhängige Blätter der jungen Generation (1945-1949). Eine Zeitschrift zwischen Illusion und Anpassung* (Munich, New York, Paris: Saur, 1978), pp.44-47.

10 *Das Alfred Andersch Lesebuch*, ed. by Gerd Haffmans (Zurich: Diogenes, 1979), p.111. Subsequent quotations from *Deutsche Literatur in der Entscheidung* are taken from this edition (= *AAL*); page numbers are given in brackets in the text.

11 Interestingly, for the radio broadcast Andersch selects from Richter's novel *Die Geschlagenen* a highly problematic and programmatic section from Chapter Fourteen, namely the debriefing by an American Intelligence Officer of the captured Gühler. The section contains the following exchange: to the officer's question, 'Warum sind Sie dann nicht emigriert?', Gühler replies, 'Das wäre feige gewesen' (*Die Geschlagenen*, Munich: Kurt Desch, 1949, p.221). See also the essay by Wilfried van der Will in this volume.

12 *Hans Werner Richter: Briefe*, ed. by Sabine Cofalla (Munich: Hanser, 1997), p.87. Subsequent references to this edition appear in the text as *HWRB* followed by a page reference.

13 *Die Blindheit des Kunstwerks* (Zurich: Diogenes, 1979), p.44.

[14] The bibliography appeared in the first number of the periodical *Texte und Zeichen*; Andersch's disclaimer in the fourth number of 1955. See *Texte und Zeichen. Eine literarische Zeitschrift*, ed. by Alfred Andersch, reprint in three volumes (Frankfurt a. M.: Zweitausendeins, 1971), vol. 1, pp.140-43 and p.558.

[15] See note 6.

[16] Heinrich Böll, *Werke*, vol.7: *Essayistische Schriften und Reden I, 1952-1963*, ed. by Bernd Balzer (Cologne: Kiepenheuer und Witsch, 1978), p.532.

[17] *Sprache im technischen Zeitalter*, 20 (1966), 294-97.

[18] Alfred Andersch, *Öffentlicher Brief an einen sowjetischen Schriftsteller, das Überholte betreffend. Reportagem und Aufsätze* (Zurich: Diogenes, 1977), pp.199f.

CHRISTINA UJMA

Alfred Anderschs Italienbild im Kontext der Nachkriegsliteratur

Italien spielt eine ausschlaggebende Rolle im Leben und Werk Alfred Anderschs. Seine Desertion von der Wehrmacht, die 1944 in Mittelitalien erfolgte, findet ihren literarischen Niederschlag in dem Bericht *Die Kirschen der Freiheit*. In diesem Werk wird die Schönheit der italienischen Landschaft heraufbeschworen, die Brutalität des Krieges und der deutschen Besatzung aber ausgeblendet. Nach dem Krieg erlebte Italien eine kulturelle Blüte, die Andersch faszinierte. In dem in Venedig spielenden Roman *Die Rote* ringt er um ein eigenes Italienbild. Seine Aufsatzsammlung *Aus einem römischen Winter* lobt die italienische Literatur, die er für vorbildlich hält.

'Rom erdrückt einen. Das war schon vor dreißig Jahren so, als ich es zum erstenmal sah. Damals floh ich'.[1] So heißt es einleitend in Alfred Anderschs Reisebild *Aus einem römischen Winter* aus dem Jahr 1963. Das Fluchtmotiv, das so zentral für Anderschs Werk ist, findet sich auch hier, allerdings in verwandelter Form. Zwar ist Italien spätestens seit Goethe traditionelle Zuflucht deutscher Dichter und Denker, die Flucht innerhalb der Flucht — und das war Anderschs erste Italienreise im Juni 1934 sicherlich — stellt aber eine Abwandlung des traditionellen Motivs dar. Die Flucht *in* Italien, d.h. die Desertion in Mittelitalien im Juni 1944, ist das beherrschende Thema von Anderschs frühem schriftstellerischen Werk.

Es existieren gleich zwei literarische Versionen des Fluchtberichts, der literarische Erstling *Die Kirschen der Freiheit* von 1952 und die 1950 in der *Frankfurter Allgemeinen Zeitung* veröffentlichte Vorarbeit *Flucht in Etrurien*, in der der autobiographische Gehalt freilich durch ein alter ego kaschiert ist. Beide Werke beschreiben Anderschs Reflexionen über die Fahnenflucht und die italienische Landschaft, in der diese stattfindet. Beide Prosastücke folgen der Route des Soldaten Andersch, die von Pisa, die Via Aurelia entlang, die Küste hinunter bis Tarquinia führt und von dort aus landeinwärts in

Richtung Viterbo verläuft. In diesem letzten Abschnitt verläßt er die Truppe, um sich zu dem amerikanischen Brückenkopf in Nettuno durchzuschlagen.

Die literarische Verarbeitung des Themas 'Desertion' war in den frühen fünfziger Jahren angesichts drohender Remilitarisierung und Restauration der alten Eliten eine Provokation und wurde von der Kritik denn auch als eine solche empfunden.[2] Beide Erzählungen zeigen eine Hauptfigur, die diesen damals als ultimative Feigheit empfundenen Schritt, als existentielle Herausforderung ansieht. Dabei war die italienische Front kein übler Ort, Andersch ist in den Briefen an seine Mutter geradezu begeistert, wieder im geliebten Land zu sein.[3] In beiden Erzählungen gibt es kein Fronterlebnis, die Hauptfigur schlendert durch Pisa, trinkt italienischen Wein, starrt den Frauen nach, badet in Waldseen und genießt die Schönheit der italienischen Landschaft. Der touristische Aspekt dieses Italienaufenthaltes wird durchaus thematisiert, so heißt es in *Die Kirschen der Freiheit*:

> Und der vollmondige, akazienduftende Feldzug raste die Straße entlang, mit Mond und Staub die Aurelia entlang, im donnernden Gedröhn der Kolonnen, im wilden, aufreizenden Knirschen der Raupenketten, im fliegenden Haar der Männer, die in den Luken der Panzer standen, in ihrem fliegenden, monddurchwehten Haar und ihren Gesichtern, die dunkel nach Norden blickten, im staubig erstickten Schrei der Kommando Rufe, erstickt im verwehten Triumph der Staubfahnen, im mondbleich dahinwehenden Staubfahnen-Triumph der Südarmee, der geschlagenen [...] Und ich dachte: Schade! Es war ein herrlicher Krieg. Ich hätte was darum gegeben, einmal in meinem Leben an einem so herrlichen und großartigen Krieg teilnehmen zu können. Aber unter diesen Umständen fiel das eben flach.[4]

Die italienische Landschaft wird in beiden Werken als von geradezu überirdischer Schönheit gefeiert. Die frühsommerliche toskanische Natur erinnert an Cézanne und Kunst, an Urlaub und Freiheit;[5] damit nicht genug, die archaische Kulturlandschaft birgt Erinnerung an andere Gesetze, an das dionysische Ausbrechen in die Wildnis. Hymnisch heißt es dazu in *Flucht in Etrurien*: 'Zypresse und Schlange und Marmorgott. Götter, die nackt sind, nackt und wirklich, höhnisch und schön [...] Italien! Italien und ein Augenblick der Freiheit zwischen Gesetz und Gesetz' (S.104). Die Fahnenflucht des Protagonisten ist ein existentielles Erlebnis in der Wildnis der Maremmna, einer damals noch einsamen und unzugänglichen Landschaft, die besonders in *Die Kirschen der Freiheit* mit quasireligiösen Zügen aufgeladen wird.

Was jedoch verwundert, ist die gänzliche Ignoranz, die beide Erzählungen den Menschen des Landes gegenüber zur Schau stellen. Als Helfer kommen die "Eingeborenen" vor; obwohl Andersch dies nicht erwähnt, riskieren sie den Tod, als sie dem Deserteur in *Flucht in Etrurien* Unterschlupf und Hilfe gewähren. Diese Unterstützung wird in *Die Kirschen der Freiheit* nicht mehr erwähnt, wie auch die Gestalt des jungen Soldaten Erich, der zusammen mit Anderschs alter ego Werner Rott desertiert, wegfällt. Die Fahnenflucht wird hier theatralisiert, sie ist die einsame Entscheidung eines heroischen Individuums vor der Kulisse der archaischen Landschaft, umgeben von 'abgeschieden brütenden, von Weltangst erfaßten Pinien' und der 'dämonischen Verschlossenheit der Ölbaumhügel' (*Kirschen*, S.79). Die Italiener und Italienerinnen, denen Andersch auf der Flucht begegnet, haben höchstens den Rang von Statisten, sind etwa deshalb erwähnenswert, weil sie ihn an eine Gestalt aus einem italienischen Film erinnern' (S.127f.).

Jene Gegend, die Andersch Etrurien nennt und neuzeitlich eher als Toskana, Umbrien und Latium bekannt ist, war just zu dem Zeitpunkt, an dem die Erzählungen angesiedelt sind und auch die reale Flucht des Soldaten Andersch stattfand, zum Schauplatz eines ganz anderen Krieges geworden, eines Krieges gegen Partisanen wie gegen die Zivilbevölkerung. Auch wenn Andersch nichts davon erwähnt, waren die Italiener, nachdem sie 1943 die Achse Berlin-Rom gebrochen hatten, Opfer einer brutalen deutschen Besatzungspolitik geworden.[6] Die am 1. April 1944 beschlossene verstärkte Bandenbekämpfung konzentrierte sich vor allem auf Mittelitalien, d.h. die Toskana, Emilia und Umbrien. Anlaß für den wahllosen Terror war entweder der Verdacht, mit den Partisanen zusammenzuarbeiten oder Deserteure zu beherbergen. Ein solcher Verdacht genügte, um ganze Dörfer zu verwüsten. Von Andersch werden diese Massaker, an denen häufig die Wehrmacht beteiligt war, nicht erwähnt. Es ist kaum möglich, daß er davon nicht wußte; dazu waren die Aktionen zu massiv.[7] Die Landschaft, die Andersch als Etrurien bezeichnet, erscheint als wunderschön, aber auch als seltsam irreal, entwirklicht gar, selbst der Name Etrurien bezieht sich nicht auf ein reales, sondern auf ein mythisches, ein untergegangenes Land. Die von Deutschen verursachte

Verwandlung dieses Traumlandes in ein Schlachtfeld, der idyllischen Dörfer in Orte des Terrors und der lieblichen Hügel in Hinrichtungsstätten, wird in den autobiographischen Erzählungen nicht erwähnt.[8]

Ein spätes Echo dieser Leerstelle in Anderschs Beschreibung seiner italienischen Flucht findet sich in seinem Nachwort zu einer Aufsatzsammlung mit dem Titel: *Die andere Achse. Italienische Resistenza und geistiges Deutschland* aus dem Jahr 1964, in dem er Bezug auf den Film *Die vier Tage von Neapel* nimmt, der die diplomatischen Beziehungen zwischen Westdeutschland und Italien ernsthaft belastete. Grund für diese ungewöhnliche Wirkung war der Umstand, daß der Film die Brutalität der deutschen Besatzer gegen die italienische Zivilbevölkerung zeigte und auch auf die Mittäterschaft der Wehrmacht verwies. Andersch erklärt die deutsche Empörung als Mißverständnis und Ressentiment, scheut aber vor deutlichen Worten zurück.[9]

Die Herausgeberin des Bandes, Lavinia Jollos-Mazzucchetti, die Grande Dame der italienischen Germanistik, führt dagegen eine Sprache so klar, wie man sie selten in Nachkriegsdeutschland hörte. Jollos-Mazzucchetti nennt Namen, erwähnt, daß sie ihre Freundschaft sowohl mit Gerhart Hauptmann, als auch mit Hans Carossa beenden mußte, da sich diese 1933 auf die Seite der Nazis gestellt hätten.[10] Vordergründig geht es ihr um die positive Wirkung deutscher Literatur auf die Resistenza, den italienischen Widerstand, dabei hebt sie, neben Autoren wie Thomas Mann, vor allem die linken exilierten Schriftsteller der Weimarer Republik, den Expressionismus und die jüdischen Schriftsteller hervor. Die Auswahl der genannten Autoren: Heinrich Mann, Brecht, Toller, Kaiser, Hasenclever und Döblin ist aber auch ein indirekter Seitenhieb auf die westdeutschen Germanistenkollegen, denn in der Literaturwissenschaft der fünfziger und sechziger Jahre hatten diese einst von den Nazis ausgebürgerten Schrifsteller noch immer kein Heimatrecht. Mit dem Nachwort zu diesem Band wird Andersch zum Vermittler von brisanten Positionen, die er selber aber nicht einnimmt.

Seine Wahrnehmung Italiens — soviel wird im Nachwort zu *Die andere Achse* aber auch deutlich — bezieht sich sehr positiv auf den italienischen Widerstand. Die Kunst, die aus dem Geist der Resistenza geboren wurde, der Neorealismus, hat Andersch fasziniert. Diese Affinität beschrieb Wolfgang Koeppen folgendermaßen:

Sein Meister in der Literatur war nicht Hemingway. Andersch fühlte sich als Geselle unter Gesellen den italienischen Dichtern seiner Generation verbunden, denen, wie ihm, in jungen, entscheidenden Jahren die Flügel des Pegasus beschnitten wurden, die unter dem Druck, dem Unverständnis und der Bosheit des Faschismus ihre Kraft brauchten zu überleben: Elio Vittorini, Cesare Pavese, Carlo Emilio Gadda. Sie waren Tagebuchschreiber, belletristisch, philosophisch getarnte politische Essayisten, Gefesselte der Selbst- und Weltbetrachtung, geschult im strengen Stil des Widerspruchs, der Gefährlichkeit, der Diktatur, der Illegalität.[11]

Andersch nutzte seine Stellung in den Kulturabteilungen verschiedener Rundfunkhäuser, um die Rezeption neuer italienischer Kunst und Literatur voranzubringen. Eine wichtige Rolle in dem Unterfangen, die deutsche Nachkriegsliteratur welthaltiger zu machen, spielte auch seine Kulturzeitschrift *Texte und Zeichen*, die 1956 dem Neorealismus eine ganze Ausgabe widmete. Die vom Geist des Antifaschismus getragene Kunstrichtung war damals zwar fast am Ende, dies tat Andersch Interesse zunächst keinen Abbruch.[12] Das *Texte und Zeichen*-Heft konzentriert sich im wesentlichen auf Vita und Werk des führenden Neorealisten Elio Vittorini.[13] Obwohl Andersch auch italienische Autoren, die nicht zur neorealistischen Strömung gehörten, positiv rezensierte, wie Bassani oder Lampedusa, ist für ihn Vittorini *der* italienische Schriftsteller, wie er in der von ihm herausgegebenen deutschen Ausgabe des Vittorinischen *Diario Pubblico* schreibt. Andersch würdigt den italienischen Schriftsteller hier als Vertreter einer realistisch-heroischen Art der Moderne, die analytisch und dialektisch, abstrakt, lyrisch und realistisch, heimatverbunden und internationalistisch zugleich ist. Es ist auch die Persönlichkeit des Autors, die Andersch fasziniert: Vittorini war wie Andersch ein Vermittler zur anglo-amerikanischen Literatur und auch ein abgefallener Kommunist, im Unterschied zu Andersch allerdings einer, der von einer Führungsposition aus abtrünnig wurde.[14] Vittorini erscheint in Anderschs Vorwort als die Verkörperung des idealen Schriftstellers überhaupt, 'er beweist, daß man zugleich ein ausgekochter Ästhet und ein Schriftsteller des Engagements sein kann'.[15] Andersch bewundert hier die Souveränität, mit der sich italienische Schriftsteller bewegen und Grenzen überschreiten, ihre politische Radikalität, und der gesellschaftliche Spielraum, den sie hatten, ist etwas, das in Adenauer-Deutschland undenkbar schien.

Im Vergleich mit den Italienern nehmen sich die Schriftsteller der Gruppe 47 eher zahm und harmlos aus, dies fiel auch anderen auf. Ingeborg Bachmann äußerte sich meist sehr zurückhaltend zu diesem Thema, und obwohl sie zur deutschen und zur italienischen Literaturszene gehörte, hat sie selten direkte Vergleiche angestellt. Die folgende Äußerung ist in ihrer Deutlichkeit singulär:

> Ich gehöre zur Gruppe 47, die mir aus unerfindlichen Gründen von allerlei törichten Legenden umwoben ist. Ich höre neuerdings [...], daß die politische Aktivität, daß die literaturpolitische Macht dieser Gruppe beachtenswert sein soll. Es ist mir nicht aufgefallen. Mir ist höchstens aufgefallen, daß die deutschen Schriftsteller, die sich dem Verdacht aussetzen, radikale, gefährliche Ansichten zu vertreten, fast ausnahmslos derart gemäßigt denken, daß sie sich in einem anderen Land, etwa in Italien oder Frankreich, dem Verdacht aussetzen würden, zuwenig zu denken. Ich habe es darum schwer [...], mich hier an einem politischen Gespräch zu beteiligen.[16]

Während Ingeborg Bachmann es vorzog in Italien zu leben und zu arbeiten, ist Anderschs starkes Interesse an ausländischer — besonders italienischer — Literatur aber wohl oft genug auch ein Versuch, mit dem Umweg übers Ausland die enggesteckten Grenzen des Inlands zu umgehen, die u.a. lauteten: keinen Kontakt mit der DDR-Literaturszene, keine positive Rezeption der DDR-Literatur, keine politischen Stellungnahmen, die dem regierungsamtlichen Antikommunismus widersprochen hätten. Mit der strikten Ausgrenzung der aus dem Exil zurückgekehrten Schriftsteller, genau wie der weitgehenden Abwehr der Rezeption von Autoren und Autorinnen der Weimarer Republik, fügten die Schriftsteller der Gruppe 47 noch ein paar zusätzliche Grenzen hinzu. Es war also eng für die Schriftsteller der Gruppe 47; da erscheint intellektuelle Flucht in großzügigere Gegenden nur zu verständlich.

Die italienische Kulturlandschaft der Nachkriegsjahre hatte in Europa eine Ausnahmestellung, erlebte einen kulturellen Aufbruch ohnegleichen, der ein wenig an die Weimarer Republik erinnert. Valeska von Roques spricht von einer 'kulturellen Blüte in Italien, von der Europa heute noch zehrt', und fährt fort:

> Künstler wie Alberto Burri, Ettore Colla, Tano Festa, Renato Guttuso [...] waren europäische Avantgarde. Der moderne Film ist undenkbar ohne den Beitrag der Italiener — der Visconti, Rossellini, Pasolini, De Sica, Fellini, Bertolucci und vieler anderer. Schriftsteller und Dramatiker wie Pirandello,

> Gadda, Svevo, Moravia, Ginzburg, Sciascia, Calvino wurden überall in
> Europa begeistert gelesen und aufgeführt. Auch den Alltag des modernen
> Europa belebte die überbordende italienische Kreativität [...].[17]

Diese kulturelle Vitalität zog nicht nur Andersch, sondern auch andere
Schrifsteller an. Italien, seit 200 Jahren für deutsche Dichter und
Denker ein Land, das vorwiegend aus kunstgeschichtlicher Perspektive
wahrgenommen wurde, hatte plötzlich eine veränderte Funktion. Denn
gerade in den fünfziger Jahren bot Rom für deutsche Schriftsteller/innen
und Intellektuelle, die noch nicht einmal über eine eigene
Kulturmetropole verfügten, eine alternative Existenz, Auswege aus dem
provinziellen Mief. Es gab diverse Zirkel und Cafes, in denen
italienische Künstler und Intellektuelle untereinander oder mit Kollegen
und Kolleginnen aus anderen europäischen Ländern diskutierten.

Über Italien, besonders über Rom schreiben, heißt immer auch,
sich in eine Tradition zu begeben, zu der man schon Stellung nehmen
muß. Dabei war der entmystifizierende Blick auf Italien, besonders auf
Rom, die scharfe Abgrenzung vom Goetheschen Italienerlebnis, in den
fünfziger Jahren nicht außergewöhnlich. Sie findet sich in Marie Luise
Kaschnitz' *Engelsbrücke* (1955), Ingeborg Bachmanns 1955 erstmals
veröffentlichtem Essay 'Was ich in Rom sah und hörte', genau wie in
Koeppens *Der Tod in Rom* (1954) und in seinem *Neuen römischen
Cicerone* (1958).

Anderschs Roman *Die Rote* ist in diesem Kontext zu sehen, er ist
Produkt gleichermaßen der Italienfaszination wie der Suche nach einem
anderen Italienbild. Sein Schauplatz ist nicht Rom, sondern das
winterliche Venedig, in dem sich die Deutsche Franziska und der
Italiener Fabio aufeinander zubewegen. Die Rote — die rothaarige
Franziska, die Mann und Liebhaber aus Überdruß an den lieblos-
patriarchalen Verhältnissen ebenso wie aus Widerwillen gegen den
platten Materialismus der eigenen Mittelschichtexistenz verlassen hat —
flieht ins winterliche Venedig, mit dem Wunsch, einfach aus ihrem
früheren Leben zu verschwinden. Ein planloser Rückzug, eine
vollkommen unvorbereitete Flucht lassen sie in Mailand zum Bahnhof
stürzen und mehr zufällig den Zug nach Venedig besteigen, wo sie mit
wenig Geld und ziemlich desorientiert ankommt, denn ohne Geld und
ohne ihre Männer sind auch die Gewohnheiten ihres früheren Lebens
hinfällig. Franziska, die Dolmetscherin und Fremdsprachensekretärin,
ist eine Frau, die sich durch Selbstbewußtsein und Eleganz auszeichnet,

die ein unsentimentales Verhältnis zur eigenen Sexualität hat, die die
Männer durchschaut und die auch in der Krise zumindest weiß, was sie
nicht will.

Fabio, ihr männlicher Gegenpart, ist Venezianer. Im
familienorientierten Italien der Fünfziger führt er eine untypische
Junggesellenexistenz, hat aber eine Geliebte, die Sängerin Giulietta.
Seine wahre, aber verlorene Liebe ist die Revolution. Die Arbeit für die
während des Faschismus verbotene kommunistische Partei, die ihn
während des Bürgerkrieges bis nach Spanien führte und in den vierziger
Jahren Battaillonskommandeur einer norditalienischen Partisaneneinheit
werden ließ, hat sein Leben geprägt. Nachdem im Nachkriegsitalien die
Revolution von der Tagesordnung verschwunden war, zog er sich
resigniert ins Zivilleben zurück. Fabio, der eine Karriere als
Solomusiker für die Politik aufgegeben hatte, ist im Orchester des
venezianischen Theaters la Fenice untergetaucht, wo er sich mit
Monteverdis Musik, als einer der 'magischen Trauer' identifiziert:

> Dies also war das sogenannte Ewige in der Kunst: weil ein Mann sich im
> Jahre 1606 zu dem Gedanken der Katastrophe richtig verhalten hatte, stimmte
> seine Musik auch heute noch. Monteverdi hatte die Pest in Venedig erlebt. Er
> schrieb Musik für Zeiten, in denen die Pest herrschte, Eurydike gestorben
> war, Revolutionen verlorengingen und die Wasserstoffbombe geworfen
> werden würde.[18]

Während im Erzählstrang, der sich mit Franziska befaßt, einiges
passiert und vor allem über die entstehende westdeutsche
Wirtschaftswundergesellschaft mit ihren liebensunfähigen Männern
reflektiert wird, sind die Fabio Passagen essayistischer und
theoretischer, thematisieren Kunst, Musik und Politik.

Daneben porträtiert Andersch mit Fabios Welt nicht Tod, sondern
Leben in Venedig, konterkariert den Mythos von der untergehenden
Stadt, bietet einen Blick auf das Venedig der arbeitenden Menschen,
ihrer Bars und Cafes. Sogar die Venezianische Politik spielt eine Rolle;
Professor Bertaldi, parteiloser Bürgermeister von Venedig, der einer
scheiternden Volksfrontkoalition vorsteht, will sich aus der Politik
zurückziehen, weil auch er mittlerweile denkt wie Fabio, daß angesichts
einer Situation, in der sich die politischen Blöcke ideologisch
hochgerüstet und sprachlos gegenüberstehen, es wenig Möglichkeiten
zum vernünftigen Handeln gibt. Über Bertaldis akademische Tätigkeit
wird sogar ein kurzer Ausblick auf die intellektuelle Landschaft Italiens

geliefert, Gramsci, Croce und Vittorini werden erwähnt (S.137-47). Unter dem Wust an Informationen über Italien geht die Figur des Fabio fast unter. Da hilft es auch wenig, daß es Fabio selber auffällt, daß es ihm an Lebendigkeit fehlt, denn dies geschieht ausgerechnet unter dem Eindruck von Antonionis Film *Il Grido* (Der Schrei), dessen Beschreibung Andersch mehr interessiert, als seine Romanfigur (S.238ff.). Aber dann ist es schließlich auch ein Wagnis, einen Fremden, gar einen Italiener zur Hauptfigur seines Romans zu wählen; selbst Ingeborg Bachmann, die Land und Leute wesentlich besser als Andersch kannte, hat immer nur aus der Perspektive der Fremden geschrieben. Zwar sagt der italienische Literaturwissenschaftler Battafarano, daß Fabio einer der wenigen plausiblen Italiener in der deutschen Literatur ist,[19] seine Qualität gewinnt er vor allem durch Anderschs penible Recherche. Die Tatsache, daß er es nicht lassen konnte, die Ergebnisse derselben alle in einem Roman unterzubringen, macht Fabio vielleicht plausibel, aber auch blaß.

Als Kontrast zu Fabios elaborierten Reflexionen über Kunst, Musik und Politik dienen die kurzen, fast gestammelten Monologe des alten Piero, der nicht nur Fabios Vater, sondern auch der letzte Lagunenfischer im industriellen Teil Venedigs, in Mestre ist. Die Piero-Passagen, in der es immer wieder um dessen harten Arbeitsalltag geht, sind klar vom Neorealismus beeinflußt.[20] Die von Fabriken umgebene Lagune von Venedig liefert dem Fischer längst nicht mehr den Lebensunterhalt. Am Ende des Romans erfriert er bei der Arbeit. Sein Tod symbolisiert den Untergang traditioneller Lebens- und Arbeitsformen, ohne sich jedoch kulturkritischer Verfallstopoi zu bedienen.

Venedig als Thema der Reflektion ist eine Gemeinsamkeit von Fabio und Franziska, die Stadt ist für beide Zufluchtsort, schneidet sie aber gleichzeitig auch vom Leben ab:

> und wieder einmal machte er sich klar, daß er immer mehr einrostete, stationär wurde, ein Inseldasein führte, ein venezianisches Insel-Leben in einem festen Netz von Gewohnheiten, die Ghetto-Wohnung, das Teatro Fenice, Ugos Bar, hin und wieder der kleine unverbindliche Guilietta-Zauber, hin und wieder wieder die verborgenen magischen Augenblicke, vor einer alten Landkarte, in einem Gespräch, in einem Traum, manchmal sogar Anläufe zu Taten, ein Legato, in dem die Violine für ein paar Sekunden etwas mehr herzugeben schien als gutes Handwerk. (*Die Rote*, S.175)

Auch in Franzikas Reflexionen erscheint die Stadt ambivalent: einerseits 'verkitschtes Sightseeing-Zentrum' (S.37), in dem im Januar das Leben, d.h. die Touristen fehlen, eine 'eisige, winterstarre Stadt', andererseits ein Ort, dessen Schönheit immer wieder überwältigt:

> *Vielleicht habe ich nie etwas Schöneres in einer Stadt gesehen, gerade jetzt, wo es mich nichts angeht, muß es mir passieren, daß ich in einer Januar-Nacht auf die Piazza San Marco gerate.* Sie mußte sich einen Augenblick lang zwingen, nicht in Tränen auszubrechen. (S.42. Kursiv im Original)

Trotz aller momentan wahrgenommenen Schönheit der Stadt: in den Franziska-Passagen wird einmal mehr die Auseinandersetzung mit den Traditionen der deutschen Italienliteratur geführt. Bereits in *Die Kirschen der Freiheit* hat Andersch gegen die ästhetizistische Italienwahrnehmung polemisiert und proklamiert:

> Die Kunst ist nicht eine Angelegenheit der Musen, die dichten, malen oder Gitarre spielen können [...]. Die Musen aber sind Symbole, also Ersatz für die Realität. Die Musen sind die Pin-up-girls der symbolistischen Schön-schreiber und Schönpinsler und Schön-Notenstecher. (*Kirschen*, S.85f.).

Diese Polemik ist nicht ganz angemessen, weil schließlich Andersch selbst in *Die Kirschen der Freiheit* die Landschaft der Toskana ästhetisiert und mythisiert.

Venedig ist als magische Idealstadt des Symbolismus und Ästhetizismus für solche Art von Polemik der ideale Ort.[21] Franziska sucht im Gegensatz zu den Männern, vor denen sie weggelaufen ist, nicht Italien als Ort der Kunst, sondern als Ort des Lebens. Wie Andersch liebt sie die Darstellung des einfachen italienischen Alltagslebens in den Filmen Antonionis oder des Neorealismus. Für deutsche Kunstphilister, wie sie durch ihren Mann repräsentiert werden, hat sie wenig übrig:

> Er liest gerne 'schöne' Bücher, die feinen, die gebildeten Leute, über deren Lippen niemals und unter keinen Umständen ein rauhes Wort kommt, ich glaube, heimlich liest er immer noch Rilke, hat aber Angst sich zu blamieren, wenn er es offen zugibt. Am meisten Furcht hat er vor Dostojewskij, Beckett und den neorealistischen Filmen, 'Il Grido' fand er natürlich peinlich, dieser Ästhet, ich hab ihn auf der Straße stehengelassen, als er das sagte, wie wir in Mailand aus dem Kino kamen [...]. (*Die Rote*, S.15)

Franziska ist neugierig auf das Leben, wie es in den neorealistischen Filmen dargestellt ist, das einfache Leben in den einfachen Häusern. Es ist weniger ein romantischer Traum, den sie hegt, als der Wunsch, eine geheimnisvolle verborgene Welt zu finden, die ihr als Fremde — auch wenn sie sich in Italien fast wie eine Einheimische bewegt — verschlossen bleibt (S.111).

Insgesamt hatte sich Andersch mit diesem Roman viel vorgenommen: eine Frau, die von den deutschen Männern die Nase voll hat, und ein venezianischer Geiger, der vom Kommunismus nichts mehr wissen will, zwei schwierige Hauptfiguren und die tausendfach literarisch gepriesene Stadt Venedig als weitere Hauptdarstellerin, das ist eine Konstellation, die einen männlichen deutschen Autor vor eine Herausforderung stellt, die er anfangs recht gut meistert.

Dann scheint ihn mitten drin — bei Seite 110 ungefähr — die Courage zu verlassen. Er führt eine Nebenhandlung ein, die sich wie ein schlechter Spionageroman liest und Franzika involviert, aber weder sie noch ihre Lage letztlich verändert; wenn Andersch den Schluß 100 Seiten früher angesetzt hätte, wäre er kein anderer. Denn die Geschichte des monströsen Altnazi Kramer, der als Zuhälter in Venedig lebt und sich dort mit dem ehemaligen britischen Geheimagenten O'Malley das letzte Gefecht liefert, bleibt den Grundproblemen des Romans äußerlich. Einmal abgesehen davon, daß sich der Altnazi Kramer in dem auch von Juden bewohnten Arbeiterbezirk Guidecca, in den ihn Andersch steckt, wohl kaum hätte etablieren können — dafür waren die Deutschen und vor allem die Nazis in jenen Jahren noch zu verhaßt — wirft Andersch das Bild einer realen und lebendigen Stadt Venedig mit diesem Handlungsstrang um und degradiert sie zum reinen Schauplatz.

Das Ende des Romans ist auch problematisch; im ursprünglichen Schlußkapitel 'Das Geheimnis solcher Häuser' drückte sich Andersch Bewunderung für das italienische Proletariat aus (S.283-95). Franziska, die nun weiß, daß sie schwanger ist, kommt mit Fabio zusammen; dieser bringt sie bei seiner Mutter in Mestre unter und vermittelt ihr Arbeit in einer Fabrik. Franziska fühlt sich recht wohl, die Affäre mit Fabio gibt ihr, ebenso wie dessen Familie, ein Gefühl der Geborgenheit und eine Möglichkeit, eine Art von Existenz in Italien anzufangen. Sie kennt nun das Geheimnis jener *neorealistischen* Häuser; dabei erscheint ihr das Leben in diesen kaum als Dauerlösung, denn nach der Geburt des Kindes plant sie, sich eine Arbeit, die ihrer Qualifikation entspricht, zu suchen (S.293). Kein happy end, aber ein plausibler und positiver Schluß. Zu positiv, wie Andersch später befand, so daß er das letzte

Kapitel kurzerhand strich und den Roman damit noch stärker aus der Balance brachte.[22]

Ob mit oder ohne Schlußkapitel ist Anderschs Botschaft in diesem Roman eine andere, als in *Die Kirschen der Freiheit*; nicht Flucht und Einsamkeit stehen am Ende, sondern eine wie auch immer geartete Ankunft:

> Was für einen Kreis von Bekannten ich schon in Venedig habe! [sagt Franziska nach 3 Tagen in Venedig, C.U.] [...] Man kann nicht untertauchen, man kann fortgehen, aber nur um zu entdecken, daß man wieder irgendwo angekommen ist. Man verläßt Menschen, um unter Menschen aufzutauchen. (*Die Rote* (1960), S.246)

Das italienische Leben sollte, wenn nicht die Erlösung, so dann doch die Lösung bringen, wobei ein altes Motiv deutscher Italiendichtung abgewandelt wird. Nicht, wie einst Goethe, Glück und Befreiung unter Fremden in der deutschen Kolonie zu finden, sondern unter Italienern, das war Anderschs Absicht für seine Heldin Franziska. Ein anderes klassisches Motiv, die Flucht nach Italien, wird auch abgewandelt und als höchst problematisch dargestellt. Sie kann nur durch Solidarität der Italiener gelingen, aber, wie die meisten deutschen Schriftsteller vor ihm, läßt Andersch keinen Zweifel daran, daß Italien ein Ort ist, an den es sich zu fliehen lohnt.

Nachdem er in *Die Rote* das lebendige Venedig porträtiert hat, beschwört er in der nächsten Italien betreffenden Arbeit das untergehende Rom. *Aus einem römischen Winter* heißt eine Folge von Städtebildern, die Andersch anläßlich eines Romaufenthaltes 1963 verfaßte. Anders als Bachmann, Koeppen und sogar Kaschnitz versucht Andersch sich nicht darin, das Spannungsverhältnis zwischen Tradition und Moderne, Geschichte und Gegenwart Roms literarisch zu erfassen, sondern kapituliert vor der Gegenwart der ewigen Stadt.[23]

> Ich bin der heutigen Wirklichkeit Roms ausgewichen. Nichts von der Betonwoge der zukünftigen Slums, in der Rom erstickt, nichts vom Inferno der Autos, nichts von der Vernichtung der Albanerberge [...] nichts von Politik [...] der Tod Roms wurde in den metaphysischen Bildern Chiricos beschlossen und ist unwiderruflich. Meine Skizzen sind also schon Erinnerungen. Die Utopie, die sie umschreiben, liegt in der Vergangenheit, auch wenn ich probiere, so genau wie möglich wiederzugeben, was noch existierte, als ich es sah. (*Winter*, S.185)

Die Städtebilder sind in der Tat der Vergangenheit verpflichtet, suchen bewußt Archaisches auf, den Herkulestempel in Cori, den Markgrafen Moretta, den berühmten Gelehrten, dem der Volksmund nachsagt, er habe den bösen Blick, und immer wieder die Campagna oder die Albanerberge, die Anlaß zu Naturreflektionen geben. Die Beschreibung von Landschaften, Tempeln und Kirchen ist bewußt zeitlos gehalten. Nur zwei der Bilder wenden sich der Gegenwart zu, eines ist ein Porträt des bewunderten Regisseurs Antonioni, das freilich auch Bildern der Vergangenheit verpflichtet ist:

> Man sieht solche Gesichter in den Diokletians-Thermen oder im kapitolinischen Museum, unter den Porträts aus der Kaiserzeit. Der Regisseur Michelangelo Antonioni stammt aus Ferrara, aber er hat den Kopf eines römischen Kaisers und zwar der besten Zeit. (S.199)

Außer einer liebevollen Beschreibung des Äußeren des Regisseurs enthält das Porträt kaum Neues; ob die Begegnung unergiebig war oder ob Andersch sich nach dem Ende des Neorealismus einfach nicht mehr besonders für italienische Gegenwartskunst interessiert, ist nicht festzustellen. Zu den Künstlern der Neoavantgarde, der Gruppe 62, hatte er, im Unterschied zu Ingeborg Bachmann etwa, wenig Kontakt. Mit den römischen Bildern ist Andersch fast zur enthistorisierenden Italienmetaphysik des Frühwerks zurückgekommen. Es gibt jedoch eine Ausnahme, die auch mit Anderschs Beziehung zu den dominanten Persönlichkeiten des italienischen Literaturbetriebes zusammenhängt.

'Gli scrittori' — zu deutsch 'Die Schriftsteller' — heißt ein Essay aus dem *Römischen Winter*. Hier porträtiert Andersch ein Zusammentreffen italienischer Schriftsteller und entwirft dabei ein Bild, in dem er den Kontrast zum deutschen Literaturbetrieb und wohl auch zur Gruppe 47 in den Vordergrund stellt.

Die italienischen Scrittori tragen deutlich Eleganz und Stil zur Schau. Ihr Habitus und ihr Äußeres sind keineswegs mit ihren Schriften identisch, dies illustriert Andersch am Beispiel Alberto Moravias:

> Der demokratischste Schriftsteller Italiens sieht aus wie ein preußischer Offizier. Ich wage diesen Vergleich, weil mich die modische Abneigung gegen preußische Offiziere seit langem schon zum Widerspruch reizt. Moravia jedenfalls könnte ein Monokel tragen; sein seltenes Lächeln wirkt immer so, als ließe er ein unsichtbares Einglas fallen. Natürlich hatte man sich den berühmten Kenner des Volkes ganz anders vorgestellt: breit, deftig, fast gemütlich [...]. (S.206f.)

Vielleicht so wie Günter Grass, möchte man hinzufügen. Wenn man Moravia, dieses Oberhaupt der italienischen Schriftstellergemeinde mit Hans Werner Richter und seiner Hemdsärmligkeit vergleicht, dann werden die Unterschiede offensichtlich.

Worauf Andersch hier verwundert hinweist, ist die Intellektualität, Strenge und Eleganz italienischer Schriftsteller, eine Tradition, die ganz am deutschen Bild des sonnig-heiteren, volkstümlich-chaotischen Italien vorbeigeht und dementsprechend von deutschen Beobachtern weitgehend ignoriert wurde. Die italienischen Künstler mußten sich nicht durch Kleidung absetzen, Hemdsärmligkeit war nach dem Ende des Neorealismus ein Habitus, den sie nicht nötig hatten, sie waren schließlich eine international bewunderte Avantgarde, Repräsentanten der modernen Kunst. Auch wenn Andersch recht hat und Moravia in seiner Jugend wirklich ein Monokel trug, bedeutete dies nicht, daß er sich so verhielt, wie man sich das in Deutschland von einem Monokelträger vorstellte.[24] Denn nicht nur Moravia, sondern auch die meisten anderen italienischen Schriftsteller tendierten nach links, sie waren Opposition und Repräsentanten ihres Landes zugleich. Andersch verweist ein wenig verwundert auf die Gleichzeitigkeit von rebellischem Geist und kühler Eleganz, die ihm gleichzeitig wohl sehr fremd war. Er schließt das Essay mit einer Schilderung des Autors Emilio Gadda, der wie ein Mailänder Ingenieur aussieht, aber einen literarischen Stil pflegt, der ästhetisch und barock zugleich ist. Bewunderung schwingt mit in diesem Bild für die Kollegialität der italienischen Schriftsteller und für die Fähigkeit, scheinbar Widersprüchliches und Unvereinbares zu leben. Andersch schließt das Bild mit einer Hommage an Rom als *eines der letzten literarischen Paradiese*, aber dieser Blick auf das Paradies der eleganten Dichterwelt ist gleichzeitig auch sein letzter Blick auf die italienische Gegenwartsliteratur.

Fußnoten

[1] Alfred Andersch, 'Aus einem römischen Winter', in: , *Aus einem römischen Winter und andere Reisebilder* (Berlin und Weimar: Aufbau, 1979), S.185. Weitere Hinweise auf dieses Werk befinden sich im Text unter *Winter*.

[2] Vgl. Wilfried Barner, Alfred Andersch, '"Kirschen der Freiheit", Zeitsignatur, Form, Resonanz', in: H. Krummacher, F. Martini, W. Müller-Seidel (Hrsg.), *Zeit der Moderne. Zur deutschen Literatur von der Jahrhundertwende bis zur Gegenwart* (Stuttgart: Kröner, 1984), S.1-23.

3. Vgl. Stephan Reinhardt, *Alfred Andersch. Eine Biographie* (Zürich: Diogenes, 1996).

4 Vgl. Alfred Andersch, *Die Kirschen der Freiheit* (Zürich: Diogenes, 1968), S.75f. Weitere Hinweise auf dieses Werk befinden sich im Text unter *Kirschen*.

5 Alfred Andersch, *Flucht in Etrurien. Zwei Erzählungen und ein Bericht* (Zürich: Diogenes, 1983), S.103

6. Vgl. Rudolf Lill, 'NS-Deutschland als Besatzungsmacht in Italien', in: ders. (Hrsg.), *Deutschland-Italien 1943-45, Aspekte einer Entzweiung* (Reihe der Villa Vigoni, Bd.3, Tübingen: Niemeyer,1992), S.1-10.

7 Gerhard Schreiber, *Deutsche Kriegsverbrechen in Italien. Täter, Opfer, Strafverfolgung* (München: C.H. Beck, 1996), S.216f.

8 Schreiber spricht in seiner Untersuchung der deutschen Kriegsverbrechen in Italien von 16 600 ermordeten Zivilpersonen, darunter 580 Kinder unter 14 Jahren. In diese Zahl sind die getöteten Partisanen, die nach Deutschland verschleppten Zwangsarbeiter, die Folteropfer und die Opfer von sexueller Gewalt noch nicht einbezogen. Vgl. Schreiber, *Deutsche Kriegsverbrechen*, S.7.

9 Vgl. Alfred Andersch, 'Nachwort', in: Lavinia Jollos-Mazzucchetti (Hrsg.), *Die andere Achse. Italienische Resistenza und geistiges Deutschland* (Hamburg: Claassen, 1964), S.118-21.

10 Vgl. dazu Lavinia Jollos-Mazzucchetti, 'Geschmuggelte Freundschaften', in: dies., *Die andere Achse*, S.9-24.

11 Wolfgang Koeppen, 'Mein Freund Alfred Andersch', in: Volker Wehdeking (Hrsg.), *Zu Alfred Andersch* (Stuttgart: Klett, 1983), S.9-12, hier S.11.

12 Vgl. Wolfgang Eitel, 'Alfred Andersch und Italien. Neorealismus und lebenslange Impulse', in: Wehdeking, *Zu Alfred Andersch*, S.28-36.

13 Vgl. Albert Meier 'Dichter und doch keine. Zu den literaturpolitischen Hintergründen von Alfred Anderschs Interesse an Elio Vittorini', *Zeitschrift für Germanistik*, Neue Folge 3: 1 (1993), 110-19.

14 Der ehemals bei den Partisanen aktive Vittorini stieg nach dem Ende des Krieges schnell zum führenden Parteiintellektuellen und zum Chefredakteur der *Unità* auf. Wegen eines Streits um die Freiheit der Kultur überwarf er sich 1947 mit dem Parteivorsitzenden Togliatti und trat bald danach aus der PCI aus.

15 Alfred Andersch, 'Nachricht über Vittorini', in: ders. *Norden, Süden, Rechts und Links. Von Reisen und Büchern 1951-1971* (Zürich: Diogenes, 1972), S.141.

16 Ingeborg Bachmann, *Wir müssen wahre Sätze finden. Gespräche und Interviews*, hrsg. v. Christine Koschel, Inge von Weidenbaum (München, Zürich: Piper, 1983), S.50.

17 Valesqua von Roques, *Die Stunde des Leoparden. Italien im Umbruch* (Frankfurt a. M.: Suhrkamp, 1996), S.18f.

[18] Alfred Andersch, *Die Rote* (Originalausgabe, Olten: Walter, 1960), S.23. Weitere Hinweise auf dieses Werk befinden sich im Text unter *Die Rote*.

[19] Vgl. Italo Michele Battafarano, 'Alfred Anderschs Italien Roman 'Die Rote", in: Irène Heidelberger-Leonard, Volker Wehdeking (Hrsg.), *Alfred Andersch. Perspektiven zu Leben und Werk* (Opladen: Westdeutscher Verlag, 1994), S.116.

[20] Ebd., S.118.

[21] Vgl. Gunter E. Grimm u.a., *'Ein Gefühl von freiem Leben'. Deutsche Dichter in Italien* (Stuttgart: Metzler, 1990), S.189-219.

[22] Vgl. Alfred Andersch, *Die Rote, Neue Fassung* (Zürich: Diogenes, 1972).

[23] In dem Roman *Efraim* wird das Romthema noch einmal aufgenommen. Anders als in dem Roman *Die Rote* versucht Andersch hier keinen Einblick in das Alltagsleben zu geben, sondern die Perspektive des nordeuropäischen Fremden prägt die Darstellungsweise, bei der diverse Ideen aus dem Essayband *Aus einem römischen Winter* wiederverwendet werden. Vgl. Alfred Andersch, *Efraim* (Zürich: Diogenes, 1967), S.84f.

[24] Vgl. Dacia Maraini, *Der junge Alberto. Gespräche mit Alberto Moravia* (Reinbek bei Hamburg: Rowohlt, 1990), S.146.

FRANK FINLAY

'Ein Schriftsteller, der funktioniert, ist keiner mehr': Heinrich Böll and the Gruppe 47

Böll's relationship with the Gruppe 47 went through a variety of stages. For an author struggling to establish himself and beset by financial difficulties the award of the Group's prize in 1951 was a significant event which initially helped to advance his career. The Group may also have helped Böll to make useful literary contacts. In the longer term, however, his relationship with the Group was seldom easy. He disliked the increasing presence of publishers pursuing their commercial interests and also the moderate political positions with which it became associated. Nevertheless, despite his disappointment at the lack of radicalism, he was never willing to dissociate himself entirely from the Group.

The following essay documents and analyses Heinrich Böll's relationship with the Gruppe 47. In Section One, I shall examine the early part of Böll's career as an unknown writer struggling for recognition in the period before his first triumphant participation at the Bad Dürkheim meeting of the Group in June, 1951. I shall discuss the professional impact of his winning the Prize of the Gruppe 47, and highlight the importance of the support and advice of Alfred Andersch. Section Two focuses on the contacts and friendships with other writers and intellectuals which 'membership' of the Group generated, and which Böll himself considered to be the most important benefit of his association. In Section Three, I shall discuss the salient features of Böll's often trenchant critique of the Group's literary and political activities. A concluding section reassesses the nature and degree of his frequently ambivalent involvement.[1]

1. '"gedruckt" ... dennoch keineswegs "entdeckt"'

A number of recent publications from Böll's literary estate[2] and the latest bibliography of his work[3] have brought us new insights into his career. It has been established that Böll began to write stories and poems in the 1930s but was restricted by his military service to composing letters to his family and later wife, Annemarie.[4] Böll began to write fiction again on his return from the war, completing the unpublished novel *Kreuz ohne Liebe* (1946/47). It was, however, to take until May of the year that saw the founding of the Gruppe 47 before he was able to secure his first publication, when the story 'Vor der Eskalierwand' appeared in a mangled and much abridged form under the title 'Aus der "Vorzeit"', in the *Rheinischer Merkur*.[5] In the next year or so there followed further publications in *Das Karussell, Hessische Nachrichten, Die Literarische Revue* and, in July 1948, the short story 'Wir Besenbinder' was the first of a total of four stories to appear in *Der Ruf*, which was by then under the editorship of Erich Kuby.

The letters in Böll's literary estate to potential publishers, as well as the volume of his correspondence with his close friend Ernst-Adolf ('Ada') Kunz,[6] chart the early progress of Böll's career. These letters are eloquent documents of the material and ideological climate which prevailed at the time, with some of the most revealing devoted to the reverberations in the literary world of the Currency Reform of June 1948. As Böll never tired of pointing out in essays and interviews, this event was an important watershed in what has become known as the postwar 'Restauration'; more significant than the actual founding of the Federal Republic a year later (*E1*, p.367).[7] In the context of literary production, the new economic realism led to the financial ruin of many potential publishers, and the increasing affluence, together with the impact of the Cold War, meant that there was a marked change in public taste and attitudes. As the many rejection letters Böll received at the time indicate, his main literary concerns, the war and the problems faced by returning soldiers, were anathema to commissioning editors who clamoured for optimistic stories of the kind he refused so adamantly to deliver. In a letter of 10 July 1948, for example, he informed Kunz that his war story 'Das Vermächtnis' had been turned down:

> Die Brüder wollen nichts so scharf Antimilitarisches. Ist das nicht toll? Drei Jahre nach dem Krieg muß man sich schon wieder vor dem Publikum fürchten [...] jedenfalls versucht man jetzt sehr schnell, auf populär umzuschalten, mit nackten Weibern, Farbfotos (à la Life) und optimistischen Kurzgeschichten und meine Arbeit ist für Monate unwahrscheinlich.[8]

Nevertheless, in February 1949, Böll secured his first publishing contract with the Friedrich Middelhauve Verlag and an all important monthly cash advance of DM200. His long story, *Der Zug war pünktlich*, duly appeared at the end of the year. It had virtually no impact at all, selling only 356 copies by the time he made his Group début eighteen months later.

A particular obstacle to Böll's career at this time was that his home city of Cologne was very much a literary backwater. As a result, Böll endeavoured to make contacts with groups of young writers, whom he clearly considered important not only for the further development of his career, but also for some kind of intellectual and literary exchange of ideas. His attempts, however, often proved to be a drain on his time and energy. Böll's involvement, with the 'Gruppe junger Autoren', which Johannes M. Hönscheid had set up to rival the Gruppe 47 and its already much coveted contacts to publishers[9] offers an interesting example. Hönscheid also had plans for a press agency which would syndicate the reports, theatre and film reviews of its regional correspondents, and Böll hoped to become one of them. His efforts were to bring him no material benefits whatsoever, although he did at least make the acquaintance at a meeting in Kassel in August 1950 of Gruppe 47 member Janheinz Jahn, and fellow writers Paul Schallück, who was to become a close friend, and Gerd Kalow. The latter's report of the meeting is a particularly succinct and accurate appraisal of Böll's predicament. Having condemned much of what he had heard as inferior, Kalow went on to draw particular attention to the one writer he considered to be a real talent still awaiting discovery: 'Heinrich Böll ist ein Name, den kein Teilnehmer der Tagung vergessen wird [...]. Böll gehört verdientermaßen zu den wenigen der Gruppe, die bereits "gedruckt" wurden. Dennoch ist er keineswegs "entdeckt".'[10]

Faced with the prevarication of publishers who wanted stories which offered 'Licht und Trost' instead of works about the horrors of 'Krieg, Trümmer und Hunger',[11] an increasingly frustrated Böll turned to the broadcasting media in his efforts to be 'discovered' by a wider audience. As several letters to Kunz demonstrate, however, his earliest attempts to gain access were in vain: without an academic title, bogus or otherwise,[12] to secure him an entrée, he was often turned away by the same self-important and arrogant apparatchiks and aesthetes he was later to satirise to such great effect in stories such as 'Dr Murkes gesammeltes Schweigen'. He remained, however, extremely tenacious and persistent in his pursuit of literary acknowledgement, and it was entirely on his own initiative that Böll made what was to prove the crucial acquaintance, in May 1949, of Gruppe 47 stalwart, Alfred Andersch, the editor of Radio Frankfurt's 'Abendstudio', to whom he sent six stories for approval.[13] Andersch's first judgement bears further witness to the public taste of the times, as he conceded in a letter of 22 June 1949:

> Eine Verwendung im Radio [...] ist bei keiner der Arbeiten möglich, da die technisch geeigneten, also die richtige Länge aufweisenden Erzählungen sich mit Themen befassen, die, augenblicklich gebracht zu einer Hörer-Revolte führen würden, so schlecht sie auch ist.[14]

Undaunted, Böll sent off another manuscript, 'das auch dem Publikum nicht gefallen wird',[15] and 'Über die Brücke' was the first ever Böll story to be broadcast: on 2 January 1950.[16] It was to be an isolated success. Nevertheless, as a letter to Andersch of 8 July 1949 indicates, Böll was above all delighted that he had at last found someone willing to offer help, constructive criticism and advice at a time when his finances were becoming increasingly parlous and when he was very close to abandoning his plans to become a writer.

The commercial benefits of his new association with a professional radio editor like Andersch are manifest in Böll's correspondence at this time, not least in a heightened awareness of how to maximise the likelihood of his work getting on air. Böll announced to his publishers, for example, in a letter of 26 May 1950, the completion of a tailor-made 'Geschichte für den Funk', which experience had taught him needed to fulfil three conditions: it required a simple linear narrative of a certain length; it had to be light-hearted and entertaining and, most significantly, it had to avoid any mention of the war. A fifteen-minute broadcast, accordingly, required a story of no longer than eight typed pages, ideally divided up into three sections of approximately two and a half pages each.

If the support and advice of Andersch was vital in selling his stories and refining his skills as a radio author, it also proved itself to be crucial to Böll in gaining an invitation to the Gruppe 47. In his letter of 8 July 1949, Böll had asked Andersch to help him make contacts with wider professional networks when he observed in a letter: 'Es ist wirklich deprimierend, so als absolutes literarisches Individuum da zu hocken.' It was to be Andersch who drew Hans Werner Richter's attention to Böll, which resulted in an invitation to the Bad Dürkheim meeting from 4 - 7 June 1951.[17] Böll accepted eagerly, and attended with a very clear idea of what he might expect, for Janheinz Jahn had already given him a thorough briefing in a letter of 31 January 1951, that is revealing of the Group and the mechanism by which Richter identified and invited his 'guests':

> An den 47ern ist nichts Geheimnisvolles. Die Gruppe ist kein Verein und keine Gesellschaft und hat keine 'Mitglieder', keine Beiträge und kein Vereinsblatt. Im Mai [sic], Anfang Mai ist eine Tagung. Dazu wird man eingeladen oder nicht eingeladen. Wenn man eingeladen wird, gehört man dazu, paßt seine Manuskripte unter den Arm, liest sie vor, läßt sie zerreißen und überläßt den Rest den Verlegern. Der Einlader ist Hans Werner Richter [...]. Er will von Ihnen was lesen. Er ist ein sympathischer Mann, Gegenteil von H[önscheid]. Ohne großen Wind, ohne Geheimnis, ohne Konferenzen, ohne Klimbim. Er liest also was von Ihnen und wenn es ihm und den anderen, dem Andersch, dem Minssen, dem Kolbenhoff auch gefällt, dann kriegen Sie im April nehm ich an einen Brief. C'est tout.[18]

Böll's début has long since been part of the mythology of the Gruppe 47. According to Hans Werner Richter, Böll cut a rather gauche figure whom he initially mistook for a tradesman. Having remained virtually silent throughout, Böll was the surprise recipient of the prize of DM1000 with a winning margin of only one vote over Milo Dor, whom he promptly loaned DM100, before cabling the remainder to his wife and hungry children. For some of the more conservative members of the Group, Böll's success signalled the first of what were to be many premature ends of its activities.[19] What is less well-known is that 'Die schwarzen Schafe', the satirical short story which made him the second winner of the Group's prize, was the very same 'Geschichte für den Funk', which had been conceived to cater primarily to the perceived tastes of a mass radio audience rather than the literary sophisticates and self-appointed representatives of the 'junge Generation' of German authors.

The initial impact of the prize is quite revealing. As his business correspondence with Middelhauve Verlag shows, Böll attracted immediate, albeit fleeting, attention, with *Die schwarzen Schafe* being purchased at Bad Dürkheim for broadcast by the Südwestfunk on 12 June 1951. *Die Welt* was one of the first major daily newspapers to react with a request for permission to print extracts, whilst others, like the *Süddeutsche Zeitung*, took the opportunity to publish various Böll stories in order to capitalise on the heightened public interest. There

were even tentative approaches made to film one of Böll's works. The
meeting also brought Böll the potential assistance of all those present in
Bad Dürkheim, a fact which was underlined by his supplying
Middelhauve with the names of authors to be sent review copies of his
novels and stories,20 amongst them the special glossy edition of *Die
schwarzen Schafe*, which his publisher produced to coincide with the
Frankfurt Book Fair. Moreover, direct mention of Böll's status as a
prize-winner was made when other works were advertised, and his
higher public profile was certainly of assistance in Middelhauve's
successful attempts to get his new novel *Wo warst du, Adam?* onto the
short list of the prestigious René Schickele Prize, judged, amongst
others by the internationally most famous contemporary author,
Thomas Mann.21

Perhaps most importantly from the point of view of his still
precarious finances, Böll was to come into contact with powerful
patrons in the media, such as Group 'member' Ernst Schnabel, the
Director General of the NWDR, and a number of invitations to submit
and broadcast work ensued, establishing a pattern which was to continue
for many years. Böll's third meeting, for example, in 1952, saw him
read the satire on the emerging consumer society and the
commercialisation of religion, 'Nicht nur zur Weihnachtszeit', which
was promptly purchased by a new Schnabel recruit, the seemingly
ubiquitous Alfred Andersch, for broadcast by the NWDR. It was the
first work by Böll to provoke public controversy and bring him
notoriety, thereby helping to further establish his name. There was an
angry exchange of open letters in the press between the writer, and the
Director of the Protestant Church's Office for Broadcasting Affairs,
Hans-Werner von Meyenn.22 Subsequently Böll was quickly to become
synonymous with the Gruppe 47 and, as the 'Tagungsberichte' in
Lettau's book show, he was held in very high regard by the Group, with
all of his readings being very enthusiastically greeted. His non-
attendance, for example, as early as 1954 was interpreted in a
newspaper article by Heinz Friedrich as sufficient evidence of yet
another imminent 'end' of the Group's activities.23

In the event, however, the increased public recognition which the
Prize of the Gruppe 47 brought Böll was to be short-lived, as the
perceptive Janheinz Jahn had already warned it would be in the letter
previously quoted: 'Als Preisträger 47 wirst du mit einer oder zwei

Geschichten bevorzugt drankommen, dann eben wird es dir wie den anderen ergehen.' This raises what I consider to be a very important point. In no way did the impact of the Prize compare with that, say, of Günter Grass's success only seven years later: the meetings of the Gruppe 47, important though they had become, were, in 1951, not yet embedded in the public's consciousness nor did they enjoy the power and influence within the German *Literaturbetrieb* to catapult someone to immediate success. Six months after Bad Dürkheim, Böll's contract with Middelhauve was terminated by mutual consent with the author's debts of more than DM4000 — a small fortune at the time — being generously written off.[24] Although there was interest from a number of publishers, including Rowohlt, Böll still required the intercession of Andersch to secure a new publishing contract with Kiepenheuer & Witsch.[25]

2.   'Verzweigungen und Verwicklungen und auch Kommunikation'

In the medium and longer term, the Gruppe 47 undoubtedly provided Böll with a network of often enduring contacts, and Alfred Andersch, in particular, continued to play an important role for the rest of the decade.[26] Some of the collateral benefits were strictly commercial, such as the invitation to attend a workshop 'Über den Rundfunk und seine Möglichkeiten für junge Autoren', which Böll received from a young editor at the Süddeutscher Rundfunk, a certain Martin Walser,[27] whose acquaintance he had made at the Group's autumn meeting in 1951. Böll was able to put what he learned at this and similar events[28] to good effect throughout the 1950s, at a time when he was heavily reliant on the radio stations as a source of income: his first breakthrough as a relative commercial success did not come until the publication of *Und sagte kein einziges Wort*, in 1953, whilst it was to take until 1959 and *Billard um halbzehn* before he could live entirely on the proceeds of his novels and stories.

When assessing the importance to Böll of the Gruppe 47 as far as professional 'networking' is concerned, which he once termed in a speech 'Verzweigungen und Verwicklungen und auch Kommunikation',[29] the situation is not always quite so clear cut, and some caution does need to be exercised. Böll's presence at two important meetings of French and German writers organised by the French periodical *Documents*, is a good example in this regard. As Böll himself points out in his account of the first meeting in 1953, entitled 'Rendezvous in Paris', a number of writers on the German side were non-Group members and several had never encountered one another before (*E1*, p.90). The link to the Gruppe 47 in this instance, therefore, is probably only indirect, arising from the award of the prize which helped to make Böll's name known in France. It is more likely that Böll's pre-Group contact, Alfred Andersch, who knew the organisers and who also attended, may once again have been influential, although I think that one should not exclude the possibility that Böll was there purely on the strength of his own publications, which by now had brought him a further five major prizes and membership of the Deutsche Akademie für Sprache und Dichtung.[30]

Böll goes on to mention how discussions were hosted by various publishers and he stresses the importance of having the opportunity 'das französische Literaturgetriebe gleichsam von innen kennenzulernen' and of negotiating lucrative deals for French translations of his works (*E1*, p.91; p.93). Böll's business correspondence at this time reveals that rights were sold to the prestigious Éditions du Seuil for *Wo warst du, Adam?*, *Der Zug war pünktlich* and the new novel, *Und sagte kein einziges Wort*. Therefore, it comes as no surprise that France was the first foreign country to recognise Böll's talents, as evidenced by a number of literary prizes he was awarded from the mid-1950s onwards.[31] Böll was to stay in contact with René Wintzen throughout his life, and many years later the latter acted as the interlocutor for the long and important, autobiographical interview 'Eine deutsche Erinnerung', which first appeared in French and to which I shall refer again in section three.

Although these were arguably the most tangible, the benefits to be derived from such events were of course not only commercial. When Böll attended the second meeting, at Bad Griesbach, in January 1955, for example, together with Alfred Andersch, Hans Bender, Wolfgang Hildesheimer, Walter Höllerer, Walter Jens and Wolfgang Koeppen, he had the opportunity to rub shoulders and debate with, amongst others, Roland Barthes, Alain Robbe-Grillet, and Jean Cayrol, whose work Böll had already reviewed in the wake of the 1953 meeting. As a contemporary report reveals, Böll read the essay 'Der Zeitgenosse und die Wirklichkeit' during a discussion on realism and the novel, and it was positively received by, among others, Roland Barthes.[32] It is my contention that opportunities to express and defend his ideas in such august company were very important to Böll's own intellectual development. They also provide a marked contrast to his earlier provincial isolation in Cologne, and I would argue that such contacts can be used to refute the widely held view that Böll was a naive writer unaware of, and consequently uninterested in, wider aesthetic issues.[33] Thus, for example, when Böll was to write an essay on the modern novel, it was with the benefit of having engaged in an exchange of views with Robbe-Grillet, one of the principal exponents of the *nouveau roman*.[34]

Beyond the professional level, there is no doubt that through his presence at the Gruppe 47 meetings, Böll had the opportunity to meet a number of writers who became close personal friends, a fact which he emphasises as the most important benefit of his association in all his statements about the Group. The database of private letters in the Heinrich Böll archives, which catalogues and summarises the content of his correspondence between 1947 and 1963, is a particularly rich source of information. It is clear from this correspondence, for example, that apart from Andersch, Böll was close to Günter Eich and Ilse Aichinger, with whom he maintained regular contact. All three writers enjoyed the benefit of having access to the house which Böll acquired in Ireland in the mid-1950s. An even closer contact was Wolfgang Hildesheimer, who, like the others, offered help and provided the opportunity for mutual criticism of new work. With the latter, for example, Böll was able to have a productive exchange of ideas about the radio play as a literary genre; he was kept informed of the progress of Hildesheimer's work on Mozart, and was to receive warm praise for his own *Irisches Tagebuch*. It was probably Hildesheimer who introduced Böll to composer Hans Werner Henze, who was many years later to write the score for the film version of *Die verlorene Ehre der Katharina Blum*.

Measured in terms of the frequency of correspondence, it would appear that Böll was also a valued friend and confidant of Ingeborg Bachmann. Between 1952 and 1956, Bachmann wrote from Klagenfurt, Vienna, Rome, Paris and Harvard. From the letters it emerges that the two writers discussed their own works and that Böll generally provided helpful advice and contacts. Bachmann clearly trusted Böll's familiarity with the commercial aspects of being a writer, soliciting advice on matters ranging from the level of fees she might command to suggestions as to possible future outlets for her work. Böll, for example, acted as an intermediary with Ernst Schnabel. The exchange also included the works of other writers: Böll sent a copy of James Joyce's *Ulysses* to Rome, while Bachmann drew attention to the latest poetry of Paul Celan, with whom Böll also corresponded. It is little wonder that it was Böll to whom *Der Spiegel* turned for an obituary after Bachmann's untimely death.[35]

It was, therefore, the positive social function as a forum for making and meeting personal friends, rather than the direct literary influence of Hans Werner Richter's Group, which Böll valued most highly and considered to be the most significant benefit he derived from his involvement in it. To this extent, a remark made in a television interview is very revealing of his attitude: the only reason for his attendance after a gap of several years at the Berlin meeting in 1965 was 'weil es die einzige Möglichkeit ist, in dieser weitverstreuten Schriftstellerexistenz Freunde zu treffen'.[36] Similarly, when Böll became the first citizen of the Federal Republic to be awarded the Nobel Prize for Literature he thanked his 'deutsche Freunde' for their encouragement (*E2*, p.622) but failed to make any mention of the Group and Hans Werner Richter, much to the latter's annoyance.[37]

3. 'Angst vor der Gruppe 47?'

Böll's criticism of the Gruppe 47 is articulated in several interviews and essays and is consistent in its simultaneous focus on the literary and political impact of the Group's activities. As far as literary issues were concerned, Böll bemoaned the fact that meetings soon lost their early intimate character as 'reine Arbeitstreffen [...], man las sich vor, man kritisierte sich gegenseitig und konnte einander ein bißchen helfen [...]. Das war eine sehr wichtige Funktion' (*Int*, p.600). This change in mood, tone and character occurred when the Group increased in size, welcomed representatives of the media into its ranks, and quickly degenerated into little more than a literary market place. Böll identifies the approximate time when this shift took place, namely 'in dem Augenblick, als sich die deutsche Öffentlichkeit für deutsche Nachkriegsliteratur zu interessieren begann' (*E2*, p.167); a process which commenced with the deaths of Thomas Mann, Bertolt Brecht and Gottfried Benn, and reached ist climax in 1959, with the virtually simultaneous publication of Grass's *Die Blechtrommel*, Uwe Johnson's *Mutmaßungen über Jakob* and Böll's own *Billard um halbzehn*.

Not only did the new 'Marktcharakter' destroy the atmosphere of 'genialische Improvisation', which Böll had found to be such a positive aspect of his early experiences, it effectively undermined the Group's original function and, in the process, rendered some of its own idiosyncratic customs and rituals problematic. This was particularly true of the established practice by which the authors who read from the famous 'electric chair' had no right of reply to instantaneous and often damning criticism. With the media in attendance, entire careers could be torpedoed:

> Es kamen Verleger, Funk, Fernsehen usw., und sobald die Gruppe 47 zum Markt wurde, wo über das Schicksal eines Autors entschieden wurde, und zwar ad hoc durch Vorlesen, was ja kein legitimer Vorgang ist, Lesen und Vorlesen ist etwas ganz anderes, entstanden Schwierigkeiten. Ich bin dann auch nicht mehr sehr oft hingefahren, weil mir die Prozedur zu grausam war. Wenn man schon über Literatur diskutiert, muß derjenige, der sie macht, mitdiskutieren können, und das war untersagt. (*Int*, pp.600f.)

The ferocity of some of the criticism, even in the early days, and its 'bread and circuses' character (*E2*, p.167) was a phenomenon which caused Böll much displeasure. As he commented to Wintzen, 'da sind eben schlimme Dinge passiert, sind Autoren regelrecht hingerichtet worden' (*Int*, p.601). For Böll the final straw came when the critics virtually took over proceedings: 'und es bildete sich eine sehr arrogante Kritiker-Crew, die praktisch die ganzen Tagungen beherrschte, das war das Ende' — the so-called *Kritikerbank* of Reich-Ranicki, Höllerer, Jens, Mayer, and Kaiser (ibid.). In an essay commissioned for a feature entitled 'Literarische Cliquen — gibt es sie oder nicht?', which appeared alongside contributions by such staunch conservative critics of the Group as Hans Habe and Rudolf Krämer-Badoni, Böll adduces the brutal treatment which he had witnessed as evidence to counter the charge that Group members were uncritical of one another's work. In so doing he highlights the currency of the word 'Zerreißen' in the context of book reviewing, which has a contemporary resonance, when one considers the mauling received by Günter Grass's *Ein weites Feld* at the hands of erstwhile fellow Group member Marcel Reich-Ranicki:

> Zerreißen, gräßliches Wort, hin und wieder nennt man's auch schlachten oder abschießen, aus der Wolfssprache: zerreißen aus der Metzgersprache:

schlachten aus der Jägersprache: abschießen — man sieht in welch blutige
Bezirke sich einer begibt, der Bücher schreibt.[38]

An analysis of the chronological pattern of Böll's attendance at
meetings supports his own avowal of increasing disenchantment, which
resulted in his reduced participation from the late 1950s onwards.
Moreover, it can be used to throw differentiated light on the degree of
his involvement, which has on occasion been exaggerated.[39] From 1951,
Böll attended meetings a total of eleven times, reading from his work on
seven occasions. All but two of the meetings, however, took place in the
first decade of the Group's existence, and well over half during the
period up until 1956 when it met twice-yearly. Böll's last reading to the
group was in 1957, a mere six years after his first participation.[40]

If Böll felt a certain attachment to the Group because it had once
offered the opportunity for 'Werkstattgespräche'; resembling a
'Redaktionssitzung' or 'Vorlektorat' (*E2*, pp.166f.), he was more
unequivocal in his critique of its political activities, to which I shall now
turn. In particular, Böll recognised the paradox that up to 1955, the
group was practically invisible and had no political influence; after
1955, when it became more prominent and started to become
institutionalised, it forfeited the possibility to influence political
developments (*E2*, pp.163ff.).[41]

One of the most important sources of irritation and frustration
was the increasingly close relationship Richter and certain prominent
Group members, such as Grass, began to develop with the SPD. Böll
had become ever more disenchanted with the party after its
'modernisation' at Bad Godesberg in 1959. In an attempt to appeal to a
broader base of the electorate a major revision of policies had taken
place and socialism was renounced in favour of pro-market social
democracy. As several of Böll's essays of the early 1960s reveal, he had
consistent doubts and reservations about the direction of the German
Left in general, and the main parliamentary opposition in particular. He
even went as far as to suggest, for example, that the Federal Republic
might as well be a one-party state (*E1*, p.534). The article 'Was heute
links sein könnte' of 1963 is typical of his attitude and a vintage piece of
polemic:

> Ich weiß nicht, was heute links sein könnte. Die offizielle Linke hat ihren
> rechten Flügel, die Rechte ihren linken Flügel, ich höre die Flügel rauschen
> und weiß doch: kein Vogel erhebt sich in die Lüfte. Es gibt so viele Mitten,

> die Mitte der Rechten, die Mitte der Linken, die Mitte des rechten Flügels der
> Linken und die Mitte des linken Flügels der Rechten. Es gibt auch eine
> heimatlose Linke, ohne Flügel. (*El*, 531)

This 'heimatlose Linke', which included a significant number
from the Gruppe 47 had, however, already begun to embrace the SPD
with ever increasing enthusiasm, evidenced, not least, by the
publication, shortly before the federal elections in 1961, of *Die
Alternative oder Brauchen wir eine neue Regierung?* Böll was a
noticeable absentee from this anthology of statements from writers and
intellectuals pleading for a change of government, which was edited by
Martin Walser.[42] In a letter of 23 February 1963 to Erich Kuby, Böll
revealed that he had been approached but declined because he was
unwilling to accept the condition not to write anything critical. The
importance of the loss of Böll to the project, who by now enjoyed a
high public profile, emerges in a letter from Richter to Walter Jens,
dated 13 June 1961:

> Wir wollen bei Rowohlt jenen Taschenband machen, dessen Arbeitstitel heißt:
> 'Brauchen wir eine neue Regierung?' Viele haben dafür geschrieben, aber
> drei, bzw. vier Namen fehlen. Gerade diese vier Namen, so meint nun
> Raddatz, seien aber *die verkaufsträchtigsten*. Die vier Namen sind Böll, Jens,
> Koeppen, Andersch.[43]

In advance of the next elections, Hans Werner Richter had
approached Böll in the autumn of 1964 with a request to contribute a
portrait of the SPD politician and deputy party chairman, Fritz Erler, to
the follow-up project *Die Alternative in Personen*, which was designed
to elicit support for a change of government by drawing attention to
leading lights in the party executive. Böll, who by now had been further
annoyed by the SPD's willingness to join a Grand Coalition responded
in an exasperated letter dated 10 December 1964. Not only was he
unwilling to make a contribution, Böll criticised the SPD's recent
'Parteitag der Zuversicht' in Karlsruhe, where nationalistic banners
demanding a return to the borders of 1937 had been prominently
displayed as: 'der Schwanengesang der deutschen "Linken", die ja
eigentlich schon 1914 gestorben ist, als die SPD ihr patriotisches Herz
entdeckte'. In so doing he appealed to Richter to understand his
predicament:

> Mein Gott, ist es so schwer, einzusehen, dass einer, der sozusagen von Kopf
> bis Fuss gegen die CDU ist, nicht für die SPD sein muss? Die einzige

> Möglichkeit wäre eben Parteispaltung: den linken Flügel der CDU mit dem
> linken Flügel der SPD (der kleiner ist als der der CDU) — alles andere ist
> Persilreklame! Ich verstehe sehr gut, dass einer gern eine Partei als seine
> politische Heimat erkennen möchte, aber ich glaube mit dieser 'Zuversicht' ist
> nicht viel anzufangen.[44]

Böll was to distance himself still further from supporting the SPD
when it subsequently entered the Grand Coalition with the CDU-CSU
headed by an ex-Nazi, Kurt Georg Kiesinger; a government in which
Franz Josef Strauß, another of Böll's *bêtes noires*, was a prominent
member. Böll had anticipated this development and later gave it as his
reason for turning down a request from SPD-enthusiast and campaigner
Günter Grass for assistance to campaign on the SPD's behalf. One
cogent and concise way of exemplifying the difference between Böll's
stance during this period is to refer to the very public spat that occurred
between the two writers in 1968, when Böll sent flowers to Beate
Klarsfeld as an act of support after she had assaulted Chancellor
Kiesinger, and was chastised by Grass for encouraging violence.[45]
Another reason why Böll could not bring himself to support the SPD at
this time was because he was simply unwilling to accept Grass's premise
that 'schriftstellerischer Kredit, nennen wir es so, unmittelbar in
Wählerstimmen zu verwandeln ist'.[46] It was his view that one had to
take direct action if one wanted to achieve a desired end. In an interview
entitled 'Kein Schreihals vom Dienst sein', with Reich-Ranicki, in 1967,
he formulated this conviction as follows:

> es [ist] sinnlos, Zeitverschwendung, sich parteipolitisch zu engagieren. Als
> Schriftsteller kann einer nur mittelbar politisch wirken, und er muß auf diese
> mittelbare Wirkung vertrauen. Sonst muß er Politiker werden, Aktionen leiten
> oder einleiten. (*Int*, p.60)

As far as the success of the Group's own 'Aktionen' was
concerned, Böll was circumspect about its committed forays into
politics, although this did not prevent him from adding his signature to
a number of resolutions relating to domestic and international issues.[47]
Moreover he had been involved in several initiatives and organisations
which developed from the mid-1950s onwards as off-shoots of the
Group's activities. As far as the former were concerned, he once
referred to them retrospectively and in derisory tones as 'eine Art
Resolutions-Gewissens-Gymnastik' which he considered to be 'völlig
bedeutungslos'[48] because society was able to dismiss them as the efforts

of dilettantes (*E1*, p.471). With regard to the various Group-based projects, Böll maintained that their failure was also because they, like the Gruppe 47, were too heterogeneous for an agreed line to be maintained. The 'Grünwalder Kreis', which he helped to co-found and which campaigned against neofascism and remilitarisation, and the 'Club republikanischer Publizisten', of which he was a member, are two notable examples.

I shall now take a more detailed look at the Group's very public argument with Josef-Hermann Dufhues because it offers the most revealing case study. Dufhues, like Böll a Rhinelander, was the Chairman of the CDU in North-Rhine Westphalia when he referred notoriously to the Group during a press conference in early 1963 as a 'geheime Reichsschrifttumskammer', the organ, which in Nazi Germany was responsible for administering state censorship of literature.[49] Thirteen members of the Group, including Böll, initiated court proceedings and threatened to sue Dufhues for defamation, and Böll was particularly vociferous in the press. In the aforementioned essay in the *Ruhr Zeitung*, for example, Böll described Dufhues's statement as a 'Denunzierung übelster Herkunft [...]. Eine perfide Dummheit, von jemand ausgesprochen, der so dumm gar nicht ist.' The newspaper had printed a potted biography of Böll next to his essay in which he was referred to as being 'close to, but not a member of, the Gruppe 47.' In a subsequent letter to the editor, Böll demanded a correction stating that he was, unambiguously, a member of the Group, and to suggest otherwise would make his article seem ridiculous.[50] It is perhaps then no surprise that, after such a public expression of solidarity, he should become dismayed when the legal action was dropped after an out-of-court settlement. It is a matter for conjecture whether Hans Werner Richter's membership of the *Reichsschrifttumskammer* during the Third Reich, which he managed to conceal for many years, influenced his ultimate reluctance to pursue Dufhues through the courts. As the recent volume of Richter's correspondence shows, Richter was certainly not a prime mover in the litigation against Dufhues.[51]

For Böll, the Dufhues affair was the acme of the Group's ineffectuality, and he singled it out in a highly critical essay, entitled 'Angst vor der Gruppe 47?' which he published in *Merkur*, two years later. The extent to which the matter still rankled with him also emerges in several letters in which he continued to badger Richter on the issue.[52]

As far as Böll was concerned, the Group had passed up a golden opportunity to make real political capital out of the affair and should, in his opinion, have orchestrated a campaign in the foreign press to damage the reputation of the CDU abroad and to lose it electoral support at home. Faced with such a symptomatic lack of solidarity and political pragmatism, which was evident shortly afterwards when the Group failed to mobilise support for Wolfdietrich Schnurre in his dispute with the WDR, on whose supervisory board Dufhues also sat,[53] Böll argued that German society had no cause to fear the Group because it had become harmless (*E2*, p.173). I think it is in this context that Böll's involvement in the establishing of the West German Writers Union in 1969 is to be understood, namely he saw it as a way of providing a framework for supporting his colleagues in their struggle, not only materially against unscrupulous publishers, but with the state and quasi-state institutions. In his address to the inaugural congress on 8 June 1969 with the rallying title 'Ende der Bescheidenheit. Zur Situation der Schriftsteller in der Bundesrepublik', he preached the strength of a solidarity that he had clearly found wanting in the Gruppe 47 (*E2*, pp.374-86). A plea he repeated in a speech at the following year's conference in terms of the formula 'Einigkeit der Einzelgänger' (*E2*, pp.482-85).

There is a final aspect to Böll's criticism of the political impact of the Gruppe 47, which relates to its degenerating into a huge media and publishing circus and to its commanding considerable international interest. In the early days of the 1950s, Böll had been quite happy to attend the first meeting of the Group abroad at Cap Circeo, near Rome in 1954. However, he was absent at the high profile congregation in Sigtuna, Sweden, ten years later, and Richter's decision to accept the sponsorship of the Ford Foundation and to take the 1966 meeting to Princeton he found to be beyond the pale of acceptability. Böll clearly felt sufficiently aggrieved that, having already communicated his declining of Richter's invitation to Princeton by telephone, he sent a strongly worded letter in which he set out the precise nature of his objections. First of all, he found what he termed the 'Auslandsbetriebsausflüge der Gruppe 47' distasteful because it was taking on the reified status of 'Export-Artikel'. Similarly, and more importantly, this development constituted an institutionalisation of the Group which left it open to exploitation by the German government in

order to increase its political credit abroad: 'die Vorstellung, dass die
Bundesrepublik — was unvermeidlich ist — aus unserem Besuch dort
politisch Kapital schlagen wird, verschafft mir eine Gänsehaut.' Böll
goes on to argue that by presenting their '"ach so bewährten kritischen"
Texte', they were inadvertently enhancing the image in the USA of
Germany as a liberal and tolerant state which was a travesty of the
actual political and social reality. Böll concludes that if the Gruppe 47
should ever meet again its meetings ought to take place 'im nächstbesten
elenden Bundeskaff'; an appeal for it to return to its roots.54 That
critical art can have have such an affirmative function is a recurring
preoccupation of Böll's literary and political journalism at this time, as
well as the 'artist novel' *Ansichten eines Clowns*, and is articulated not
least in the *Frankfurter Vorlesungen*. With a passing swipe at his own
popularity as a public speaker, Böll describes those groups and societies
which eagerly welcome an appearance at one of their functions by a
controversial writer:

> Das Überraschende ist nur, daß solche Gesellschaften [...] ihre Erwartung
> nicht auf Schmeichelei, auf Trost, Zuspruch, Bestätigung richten: sie erwarten
> etwas Freches, etwas Kesses, Gesellschaftskritisches, sie erwarten Zeitkritik
> [...] sie erwarten Prügel, und seitdem mir das bewußt geworden ist, bin ich
> nicht mehr bereit, Prügel, wenn auch nur scheinbare, auszuteilen. (*E2*, p.36)

Here we have the succinctly formulated aporia of artists who recognise
'eine Verbindlichkeit außerhalb ihrer Kunst' (*E1*, p.322), and who see
their attempts effectively neutralised, once society has reduced them to
the level of a commodity. It is significant in this context, and following
the very mixed reception of *Ansichten eines Clowns* in 1963, that Böll's
only fictional works of any note to appear in the remainder of the
decade were *Entfernung von der Truppe* (1964) and *Ende einer
Dienstfahrt* (1966). These works' programmatic titles signalled his
intention to resist society's attempts to exploit him as one of the state's
licensed moral watch-dogs; '[als] ein etablierter Aufpasser, als Teil des
'guten Gewissens', als einer der 'funktionalisierten Schreihälse' vom
Dienst, als willkommener Bösewicht, der immer wieder durch seine
Existenz bestätigt wie wunderbar frei wir sind (*Int*, p.62). Little wonder
that in the same year Böll only agreed to put up the prize money with
Grass on condition that Richter disband the group.55

4.   Conclusion

I hope to have shown that the impact of Heinrich Böll's involvement in
the Gruppe 47 was relatively slight in the process of his establishing
himself on the literary scene. Far more important in the early stages of
his career was the support and advice of Alfred Andersch, which pre-
dated his involvement with the Group and remained important
throughout the 1950s. Nevertheless, the Group did provide a network of
contacts, which offered professional support, frequently with tangible
commercial benefits. Moreover, the Gruppe 47 was often, although by
no means exclusively, the point of departure for invitations which
enabled Böll to engage in a productive exchange of ideas with leading
writers and intellectuals beyond its own confines. The Group also acted
as a catalyst for the development of a number of close personal
friendships with Helmut Heißenbüttel and Ingeborg Bachmann, for
example, and it was to be this aspect which Böll valued the most highly.
These contacts and friendships outlived Böll's regular attendance at
Group meetings, which lasted for the relatively short period of six or
seven years.

From the end of the 1950s onwards, Böll maintained a guarded
distance from the Group because he deplored the media circus and the
literary 'Gruselkabinett' into which it degenerated, once a wider public
and the media began to take note of the literary talents of the younger
generation of writers. In the early 1960s there followed his
estrangement from the Group's political activities for a number of
reasons. Böll was not persuaded that society took the criticism of
writers seriously; his own practical experience of various initiatives and
political 'Aktionen', which had their origin in the Group convinced him
that they were anodyne. The Dufhues affair in particular demonstrated
the fundamental weakness of the Group: it was incapable of agreeing a
sustainable line on a given issue, owing to its complex and
heterogeneous composition. This led Böll to argue that the Group was
little more than a paper tiger and that society had no reason whatsoever
to fear it. Böll became particularly disaffected when in the early 1960s
prominent members of the Group began to campaign for the SPD,
which he did not consider to be a viable alternative government at this
time. Perhaps most importantly, Böll recognised that the Gruppe 47 had
become a victim of its own domestic and international success.
Inadvertently it had allowed itself to be institutionalised and

functionalised and had started to play an ideological function as an 'Alibi im Überbau' of West German society, to borrow Hans Magnus Enzensberger's phrase.[56] In Böll's eyes this entailed the inevitable self-negation of the critical writer: 'Ein Schriftsteller, der funktionert, ist keiner mehr' (*E2*, p.173).

Footnotes

[1] There are a number of institutions and individuals to whom I would like to express my thanks for their help with this project: Sally Johnson, Karl Heiner Busse; the Heinrich Böll Archives of the City of Cologne, particularly Viktor Böll, Markus Schäfer and Jochen Schubert; Hamish Reid who read a draft of this paper and made a number of very useful comments. I am particularly grateful to him for the exchange of information regarding the pattern of Böll's group attendance, which he analyses in detail in his forthcoming chapter in Stephan Braese (ed.), *Die Gruppe 47 Reconsidered* (Berlin: Erich Schmidt Verlag). Finally to the German Academic Exchange Service (DAAD), whose generous grant enabled me to spend several weeks researching in Cologne. Any errors and omissions are, of course, entirely my own.

[2] See, for example, the collection *Der blasse Hund. Erzählungen*. Mit einem Nachwort von Heinrich Vormweg (Cologne: Kiepenheuer & Witsch, 1995).

[3] Viktor Böll and Markus Schäfer, *Fortschreibung. Bibliographie zum Werk Heinrich Bölls* (Cologne: Kiepenheuer & Witsch, 1997). See also Werner Bellmann, *Das Werk Heinrich Bölls. Bibliographie mit Studien zum Frühwerk* (Opladen: Westdeutscher Verlag, 1995), pp.11-30.

[4] Three volumes of these *Kriegsbriefe* are scheduled for publication in 1999, edited by Karl Heiner Busse.

[5] See Böll/Schäfer, *Fortschreibung*, p.24.

[6] *Die Hoffnung ist wie ein wildes Tier. Der Briefwechsel zwischen Heinrich Böll und Ernst-Adolf Kunz 1945-1953*, ed. by Herbert Hoven (Cologne: Kiepenheuer & Witsch, 1994).

[7] Unless otherwise indicated, all page references to Böll's essays, speeches and interviews are to Bernd Balzer's standard edition (Cologne: Kiepenheuer & Witsch, n.d. [1978]) and employ the following ciphers: *E1-3* =*Werke*, vol.7: *Essaysistische Schriften und Reden*; *Int* = *Werke. Interviews I*.

[8] *Die Hoffnung ist wie ein wildes Tier*, p.96. It was 1981 before the story was finally published.

[9] Ibid., p.508.

[10] Gerd Kalow, 'Tagung junger Autoren', *Stuttgarter Zeitung*, 1 September 1950.

[11] See the analysis by Herbert Hoven in *Die Hoffnung ist wie ein wildes Tier*, particularly pp.407-12.

[12] Böll's efforts to have work broadcast by the WDR were thwarted by a certain Dr Ringling, the head of the culture department, who had to leave the broadcasting station to write and submit the doctoral thesis which he fraudulently claimed existed. See the excellent study of Böll's radio work by Dietrich Kluge, *Heinrich Böll und das Hörspiel. Der Läufer auf der Aschenbahn* (Diss. Justus-Liebig-Universität Gießen: Frankfurt a. M., 1993), p.79.

[13] The stories included 'Der Mann mit den Messern', 'Wir Besenbinder' and 'Aufenthalt in X'.

[14] *Die Hoffnung ist wie ein wildes Tier*, pp.408f.

[15] Letter to Andersch, 24 October 1949.

[16] *Die Hoffnung ist wie ein wildes Tier*, p.417.

[17] 'Alfred Andersch hatte ihn mir vorgeschlagen, und zwar mit den Worten "Da gibt es einen jungen Mann in Köln. Der kann ganz gut schreiben"'. See Hans Werner Richter, 'Die Kriegsgeneration und die Anfänge der Gruppe 47', in: *Heinrich Böll. Vortragsabende zu seinem 70. Geburtstag an der Universität zu Köln* (Kölner Universitätsreden 70, 1987), pp.6-15.

[18] Quoted by Kluge, *Heinrich Böll und das Hörspiel*, p.86.

[19] *Hans Werner Richter und die Gruppe 47*. Mit Beiträgen von Walter Jens, Marcel Reich-Ranicki, Peter Wapnewski u.a. (Munich: nymphenburger, 1979), pp.96-101.

[20] Among those present were: Günter Eich, Wolfgang Hildesheimer, Ilse Aichinger, Walter Kolbenhoff, Wolfgang Weyrauch, Milo Dor, and Walter Jens. See Reinhard Lettau (ed.), *Die Gruppe 47. Bericht, Kritik, Polemik. Ein Handbuch* (Neuwied and Berlin: Luchterhand, 1967).

[21] The prize was won by Hans Werner Richter for *Sie fielen aus Gottes Hand*, and Böll received a commendation. See Böll/Schäfer, *Fortschreibung*, p.40.

[22] See J.H. Reid, *Heinrich Böll. A German for his Time* (Oxford/New York/Hamburg: Berg/Oswald Wolff, 1988), p.80.

[23] Quoted in Lettau, *Handbuch*, p.104.

[24] Viktor Böll and Karl Heiner Busse, 'Nachwort', in: Heinrich Böll, *Erzählungen* (Cologne: Kiepenheuer & Witsch, 1995), p.987.

[25] Letter of Andersch to Böll, 25 November 1951, in: *Heinrich Böll und sein Verlag Kiepenheuer & Witsch. Der Deutsche Herbst. Heinrich Böll und die Terrorismus-Diskussion der 70er Jahre. Zwei Austellungen* (Austellungskatalog, Cologne,1992), p.8.

[26] It was Andersch who introduced Böll to non-group member, Arno Schmidt. Both Schmidt and Böll had published in Andersch's journal *Texte und Zeichen* and it would seem that there was no lack of mutual respect and support. See Volker Ladenthin, 'Misanthrop und Philanthrop? Über die Beziehung zwischen Arno Schmidt und Heinrich Böll', *Wirkendes Wort* , 38: 3 (1988), 359 ff.

27 Letter to Böll, 17 March 1952.

28 Böll attended a conference at the Süddeutscher Rundfunk in October 1955 which explored the possibilities of the newer medium of television. Böll/Schäfer, *Fortschreibung*, p.64.

29 'Dank des Autors', in: Heinrich Böll, *Vermintes Gelände. Essayistische Schriften 1977-1981* (Cologne: Kiepenheuer & Witsch, 1982), p.230.

30 In this context it is significant to note that when Böll produced in the same year a brief autobiographical text 'Selbstvorstellung eines jungen Autors' for a French publication, he made no mention of the Group or of his prize-winning story 'Die schwarzen Schafe'. For a complete list of the honours bestowed on Böll see Böll/Schäfer, *Fortschreibung*, p.376.

31 *Haus ohne Hüter*, for example, received the French Publishers' Prize for best foreign novel, in 1955. See Viktor Böll (ed.), *Heinrich Böll und Köln* (Cologne: Emons, 1990), p.201.

32 Karl August Götz, 'Wo steht heute der Roman? Ergebnisse eines deutsch-französischen Schriftstellertreffens' *Antares*, 3: 2 (1955), 33.

33 See the discussion in Frank Finlay, 'On the Rationality of Poetry', in: *Heinrich Böll's Aesthetic Thinking* (= Amsterdamer Publikationen zur Sprache und Literatur 122), (Amsterdam and Atlanta: Rodopi, 1996), pp.20-24.

34 'Über den Roman' (*E1*, pp.355-57). See also in this context J.H Reid, 'Heinrich Böll: From Modernism to Post-Modernism and Beyond', in: Keith Bullivant (ed.), *The Modern German Novel* (Leamington Spa,Hamburg,New York: Oswald Wolff/Berg, 1987) pp.109-25.

35 See 'Zum Tode Ingeborg Bachmanns', *Der Spiegel*, No.43, 22 October 1973, 206. Original title: '"Ich denk an sie wie an ein Mädchen". Heinrich Böll zum Tode Ingeborg Bachmanns'. Böll also favourably reviewed Uwe Johnson's 'Eine Reise nach Klagenfurt' and contributed a preface to a bibliography of the scholarship on Bachmann's work. See Böll/Schäfer, *Fortschreibung*, p.201; p.214.

36 'Heinrich Böll im Dialog'. Interview with Klaus Harpprecht, ZDF 7 July 1967 in the series *Portraits von Personen unserer Zeit*. Ms. Heinrich Böll Archiv, Cologne.

37 See Hans Werner Richter, *Im Etablissement der Schmetterlinge. Einundzwanzig Portraits aus der Gruppe 47* (Munich: Hanser, 1986), pp.73f.

38 'Ich fürchte es werden noch andere Waffen angewandt', *Neue Ruhr Zeitung*, 2 March 1963.

39 Heinz Ludwig Arnold, for example, has erroneously maintained that Böll was present at meetings 'von den Anfängen an bis weit in die sechziger Jahre hinein mit einer gewissen Regelmäßigkeit'. Heinz Ludwig Arnold (ed.), *Die Gruppe 47. Ein kritischer Grundriß* (Munich: text + kritik, 1980), p.165.

40 Böll's actual participation is as follows: Bad Dürkheim (May 1951; reading: 'Die schwarzen Schafe'), Laufenmühle bei Schorndorff (October 1951; reading: extracts from a war novel, most likely *Wo warst Du, Adam?*), Niendorf, Ostsee (May 1952), Burg Berlepsch bei Göttingen (October 1952; reading: 'Nicht nur zur Weihnachtszeit'),

Mainz (May 1953), Cap Circeo, Italy (April 1954; reading: a chapter from *Haus ohne Hüter*), West Berlin (May 1955; reading: two episodes from *Irisches Tagebuch*), Bebenhausen bei Tübingen (October 1955), Niederpöcking, Starnberger See (September 1957; reading: 'Hauptstädtisches Journal'), Großholzleute, Allgäu (October-November 1958), Wannsee, West Berlin (November 1965).

[41] See also Reid, *Heinrich Böll. A German for his Time*, p.110.

[42] Ibid., p.114.

[43] Hans Werner Richter, *Briefe* (=HWRB). Ed. by Sabine Cofalla (Munich: Hanser, 1997), p 346 (my italics). In fact none of the four contributed.

[44] See Jürgen Schutte (ed.), *Dichter und Richter. Die Gruppe 47 und die deutsche Nachkriegsliteratur. Ausstellungskatalog* (Berlin: Akademie der Künste, 1988), p.327.

[45] See Reid, *Heinrich Böll. A German for his Time*, p.142.

[46] Interview with WDR, in *Der Spiegel*, No 33, 11 August 1969, 90.

[47] Examples are the protest against the suppression of the Hungarian Uprising of 1956, and against French government action during the Algerian War.

[48] Interview with Frau Papic of Deutsche Welle, 1 August 1969. Ms. Böll Archiv.

[49] See the article 'Dufhues über den Einfluß der Gruppe 47 besorgt', *Frankfurter Allgemeine Zeitung*, 19 January 1963.

[50] Heinrich Böll, letter to the editor, which appeared under the heading 'Böll gehört doch der Gruppe 47 an', and was printed in a number of newspapers on 10 March 1963.

[51] The relevant letters and annotations are in *HWRB*, pp.444-49. For a highly critical account of similar embarrassing aspects of Hans Werner Richter's early career see Karl Heiner Busse, 'Alte Kameraden', *Konkret*, H.12 (1997), 52f.

[52] See for example one dated 11 June 1964 in which Böll offered the following comment: 'Ich fürchte, Du bist auf diesen süffisanten Miefer, den man nur verstehen kann, wenn man rheinische Erfahrung hat, hereingefallen. Der Bursche erscheint mir wie ein rechtes Ungeheuer', in: *HWRB*, p.543, footnote 2.

[53] Schnurre had written the TV script for a *Panorama* documentary criticising the system of political lobbying, and WDR severed contacts with him under political pressure from the CDU. Böll considered this to be tantamount to a boycott of his work.

[54] Letter of 19 February 1966, quoted in: *HWRB*, p.595.

[55] Richter, *Im Etablissement der Schmetterlinge*, p.145.

[56] Hans Magnus Enzensberger, 'Gemeinplätze, die neueste Literatur betreffend', in: Enzensberger, *Palaver. Politische Überlegungen (1967-1973)* (Frankfurt a. M.: Suhrkamp, 1974), p.44.

ANTHONY WAINE

'Templone's Ende' and Walser's Arrival

In 1951, the young Martin Walser, working as a journalist covering the Laufenmühle meeting of the Gruppe 47, famously told Hans Werner Richter that he could do as well as those reading inside. Four years later he was awared the Group's prize; in the meantime he had written an enthusiastic group portrait for Radio Bern and reviewed on radio many works written by those associated with the Group. The prize was undoubtedly a major attraction for a young writer and the story which brought the award, 'Templones Ende', contains many features that reflect the literary ethos of the Group at that time. At the same time the Group was probably keen to encourage a nascent talent, encouraging him to move from a kafkaesque style to a more realistic form of writing. What is beyond doubt is that Walser's career was helped by the award of the increasingly prestigious prize.

When the Gruppe 47 met at the Laufenmühle in October 1951 a young freelance journalist working for the Süddeutscher Rundfunk sat outside the building in a broadcasting van checking that the transmission of the readings and discussions was running according to plan. Four years later at the May meeting of the Group in Berlin that same young man was inside the building and had been awarded the Group's prize 'mit absoluter Mehrheit'.[1] In the space of less than half a decade Martin Walser, between the ages of twenty-four and twenty-eight, had moved from being outsider to celebrated insider with a contract from the Suhrkamp Verlag as his reward. Walser's literary beginnings in relation to the Group were explosive, spectacular, but not solely the product of chance. And therefore what I wish to do in the first part of this essay is reconstruct the network through which Walser found his way to the Laufenmühle in 1951 and received his first invitation from Richter to attend the Mainz meeting in May 1953, and briefly sketch with the help of an unpublished document how Walser's 'Weltanschauung' was very much at one with that emerging in the early fifties amongst the non-conformist younger generation.

    I shall follow this by taking a closer look at the prize-winning text of 1955, 'Templones Ende', and try with over forty years hindsight to

say what is 'Walseresque' about the story. I wish to adopt this
perspective on the early work of a writer who quickly became known in
the Group circles as 'der schwäbische Kafka'[2] and less flatteringly as a
'Kafka-Epigone.'[3] In searching for Walser's emergent identity in this
short story I shall be following in the footsteps of several earlier
interpreters of his work[4], who, having analysed the stories of Walser's
first published collection, *Ein Flugzeug über dem Haus* (1955), which
includes 'Templones Ende', reached conclusions similar to those
expressed by Gabriele Schweikert:

> Die Parallelität der frühen Geschichten Martin Walsers zu Kafka, die in vielen
> einzelnen Punkten — Handlungsablauf, Konstellationen, Erzähltechnik —
> festzutsellen war, legitimiert weder die Folgerung einer generellen
> Übereinstimmung noch kann sie, recht verstanden, Anlaß sein, in Walser den
> noch unsicheren, noch nicht zu sich selbst und seinem eigenen Stil
> gefundenen Epigonen zu sehen.[5]

In the final part I shall refer briefly to 'Templones Ende' in the context
of the publication of *Ein Flugzeug über dem Haus*, and also tentatively
suggest why the Group chose to award Walser the prize.

Let me return to my sketch of the contacts, connections and
common interests which would lead the anonymous would-be writer to
the Group and partly determine whether he or she found acceptance and
approval. The very fact that Walser was at the Bebenhausen meeting on
behalf of the media, and especially at the behest of the Süddeutscher
Rundfunk was symptomatic, for the Group was well disposed to the
media from its inception, and the SDR together with the
Nordwestdeutscher Rundfunk had two of the most enlightened and
prolific arts departments in the whole of West Germany, certainly for
the first ten years of the Republic. Indeed the groupings which
established themselves within these two radio stations were at least as
productive and powerful as the Gruppe 47 in fostering new talents,
promoting new literary forms and techniques, investing in them and
ensuring that their ideas reached a wide audience. But that is another
story.[6] From 1949 onwards, Walser was at the very heart of these
daring, progressive institutions, as a journalist, as a programme
producer, as a radio playwright and as a radio play producer. And one
of the radio play talents with whom he cooperated particularly closely
was Wolfgang Weyrauch, a veteran of the Group's early years to
whom the concept of 'Kahlschlag' is attributed (Arnold, p.75). Walser's

media involvement also brought him into contact with Alfred Andersch, another veteran, and he and other writers, including Heinrich Böll, and on one occasion Gottfried Benn, would be invited to workshops by the SDR.

There can be little wonder, then, that in November 1952, before he had ever been invited to the Group to read, Walser was able to pen for Radio Bern a group portrait which was both authentic, and authoritative: 'Die Richtung? Die Art? Der Ismus? Das ist nicht so wichtig bei der Gruppe 47; wichtig ist, daß einer für uns und in seiner Art gut schreibt. Snobs, arrogante Literaten und intellektuelle Zungenkünstler und Wortakrobaten werden nicht mehr eingeladen', and uncannily accurate in its assessment of the literary and philosophical positions of every major figure (Lettau, pp.278f.). Of particular interest in that section in which he ironically speculates on the most appropriate position for each author is the following passage:

> Und noch zu Ilse Aichinger, die auch auf dem Gruppenbild untergebracht werden sollte. Aber wo? Da, wo Jens an Hildesheimer stößt [...]. Und warum eigentlich vor die Lücke zwischen Jens und Hildesheimer? Erstens, daß die Lücke verdeckt ist, und zweitens, weil sie soviel von Kafka gelernt hat wie Jens und so präzise phantastisch ist wie Hildesheimer. (Ibid., p.281)

This was a prophetic line-up, because Aichinger like Walser had openly acknowledged the influence of Kafka, and yet had won that year's prize; because it was Walter Jens who first recommended to Richter that Walser be invited; and, finally, because it would be Hildesheimer, who, together with the young composer Hans Werner Henze, would defend Walser a year later after his first reading provoked a torrent of accusations over his alleged dependence on Kafka.[7] Jens's promotion of Walser reminds us of a further force field in the magical and magnetic circuit that led to the Group and held its members together. Walser had studied at Tübingen, where Jens was already a charismatic young lecturer, with various literary publications to his name, and where in 1951 Walser had gained his doctorate with a ground-breaking investigation of Kafka's fiction.[8] It was also in this same university town that Walser got to know a student who would be one of the publishing houses' early visitors to the Group meetings and eventually sign up Walser for his company: Siegfried Unseld.[9]

Works by Aichinger, Hildesheimer and Jens, together with those of a range of writers from the Group, were regularly reviewed and promoted, almost in the manner of commercials, by Walser and his fellow sketch writers at the SDR in a fascinating piece of high-brow radio cabaret called *Zeichen der Zeit*, which ran from mid-1952 until July 1953.[10] Here too the ubiquitous spirit of the Gruppe 47 could be seen, for one of the fellow writers was Heinz Huber, one of Germany's most successful *Hörspiel* authors, who regularly read from his plays at Group meetings. There were fourteen monthly editions of this programme and in the penultimate one, broadcast in June 1953, Walser gave a portrait of the Group, whose most recent meeting he had officially attended for the first time as a writer.[11] This portrait, never published, differs markedly from the ironically tinged, report-like one written for Radio Bern and published in Lettau's famous *Handbuch*.

Here we perceive the other Walser: passionate, dramatic, quasi-expressionistic. He shows himself to be at one with the Group's idealism and humanism. Five times the word 'Verantwortung' is used to evoke the writers' essential ethical attitude, whilst the words 'Mensch' and 'Menschenbild' recur no less than eleven times, culminating in the promulgation of Böll's dictum of 1952 as the quintessence of the Group's sense of commitment: 'Unsere Aufgabe ist es, daran zu erinnern, daß der Mensch nicht nur existiert, um verwaltet zu werden und daß die Zerstörungen in unserer Welt nicht nur äußerer Art sind'. If it is clear who or what the Group is for, it is equally clear for Walser what the Group collectively is resisting. Three 'enemies' are identified: culturally, the Group is a counter-movement to the inhabitants of the 'Salon': Gruppe 47's 'literary footsoldiers' ('Landesknechte') are the 'Kräfte [...] die das lackierte Mobiliar des Salons zu erschüttern beginnen'. The second enemy is the economically driven 'Zeitgeist' (note, not a class nor an ideology, but a phenomenologically perceived trend); 'die Gesellschaft [ist] so sehr mit ihren Investitionen, mit ihrer Besitzvermehrung beschäftigt [...], daß sie keine Zeit und keine Lust hat, zu hören, daß Verantwortung mehr ist als Spekulation.' And, thirdly, thoroughly in tune with the existentialist undercurrents of the time, time itself is indicted: 'die reissende Zeit [ist] der übermächtige Gegenspieler des Menschen.'

The final dimension in this eclectic ideology attributed to the Gruppe 47 by Walser (but certainly in accordance with his own emotions and experiences) is anthropological, for he maintains that 'Der Sinn dieser Zusammenkunft liegt im Zusammenkommen selbst. Die jungen Schriftsteller vergewissern sich ihrer Lebensart.' Here I would suggest one can perceive the kernel of Walser's search for 'Heimat' which over his near fifty years of writing has seen him attempting to find sense, peace of mind and belonging in a variety of movements and causes, ranging from the DKP in the 1970s to the espousal of German unity in the 1980s. The Gruppe 47 undoubtedly fulfilled this need, certainly up to about 1957.

Perhaps sophistically I have left one of the main reasons for Walser's gravitation towards the Group to the end of this section. It is a rationale or motive which is highlighted at the very beginning of the *Zeichen der Zeit* sketch when he mentions the Prize: 'Dieser Preis ist die angenehmste Zutat des alljährigen Frühlingstreffens, er ist aber nicht mehr als eine Zutat.' Thirty-one years on in an interview in *The German Quarterly* Walser owned up to exactly how much of a 'Zutat' it had been for him. It is a revealing résumé of his early sentiments:

> Das war ein wunderbarer Verein für Kamaraderie, Freundschaft, Diskussion und Gerede. Ich meine die Abende und Nächte bei den Tagungen. Die Tage waren eher unangenehm. Fand ich. Sportplatzatmosphäre, Arena, Boxring. Natürlich wollte ich auch den Preis. Deshalb bin ich hin, von 53 bis 55. Als ich den Preis hatte, bin ich immer noch hin, aber ich habe kaum mehr gelesen, ich glaube, nur noch einmal.[12]

Despite the protestations I suspect that Walser has always had and still has a liking for the 'Arena' and 'Boxring'. A recent monograph on the author also draws attention to this bellicose trait, appropriately in the context of relations with Richter: 'Er [Richter] erlebte Walser als "streitbaren, wenn nicht streitsüchtigen Alemannen" und er meinte, Streit sei Walsers "Lebenselement"'.[13] Further anecdotal evidence of this relish for doing battle comes from Leonhardt's retrospective on the Group in *Die Zeit* in 1977 and allows me to conclude this part by going full circle to the opening image of the SDR 'technician' overseeing the smooth transmission of the Laufenmühle meeting, for what I did not add then was that whilst Walser was whiling away his time Hans Werner Richter came out during a break 'und fragte einen jungen Mann, der dort saß und den er für einen Techniker hielt: "Na, wie läuft das?", "Technisch einwandfrei", antwortete der junge Mann, "aber was da gelesen wird, das kann ich besser"'.[14] The rest, as they say, is history.

Walser's prize-winning story — he received DM1000 for it — is indeed ambitious and moved one reviewer at the time to opine:

'Templones Ende' [...] ist ein beachtenswertes Exemplar innerhalb des Ringens um eine moderne deutsche Short Story' (Lettau, p.109). The work shows the young author willing to speculate on the realities, internal and external, of a decidedly post-post-war Germany. No looking back for Walser to the certainties of the past. It is the uncertainty of the present which preoccupies him and indeed is the obsessive preoccupation of his central figure, the ageing financier and property speculator, Herr Templone, who before the war had bought a huge villa for little money and had lived quite happily at the centre of the villa owning community of Bernau. After the war this community disintegrates or at least changes profoundly; Templone is confused, becomes paranoid and mounts a tragi-comic campaign aimed at maintaining the value of his property and convincing the new neighbours that the old residents are happy and united.

Anyone reading that briefest of plot summaries will immediately recognise that this is not the territory of 'Trümmerliteratur', nor of the disenfranchised 'little man' and his trials, nor is it a universal parable, with setting, time and meaning unspecified. There is no defining Group insignia attached to it. That is my argument and I shall now try to show how Walser won the Prize on his own merits and how the Group was unwittingly acknowledging an embryonic configuration of motifs and techniques which were to become his trademark. By awarding him the prize, it was furthermore encouraging him to develop that configuration and his individuality; therein lay one of the real psychological functions of the Group. What is then 'Walseresque' about this story?: first, the psychological response of an individual to change, be it external or internal, and specifically to 'Übergänge' or 'Übergangszeiten'; second, the paradoxical state of being at once insider and outsider and the accompanying existential sense of disorientation and isolation; third, the mis-reading or mis-interpreting of the 'Zeichen der Zeit' and the ensuing confusion, panic and loss of identity, with all their tragi-comic potential; fourthly, the pathology of the nexus of money, property and possessions; and, finally, one can already perceive the emergence of an ironic perspective on these states of being which leaves the reader as productively uncertain as the protagonist and as the narrator himself.

Perhaps this last point, the ironic attitude, is a good place to start. Even though Walser was soon viewed within the group as a satirist (Arnold, p.110), I do not see in this story a great deal of evidence for this opinion. Without wishing to enter a theoretical debate on the distinction between satire and irony, I believe that the former presupposes that the writer has a pretty good idea of what is wrong and of what the solution or at least palliative should be, whereas the Walserian irony is a more restrained weapon which both protects the author's own inadequacies and expresses philosophical and ideological doubts about the reading of the situation. Walser's veritable love affair with the subjunctive, which we find particularly in the post-1976 works is central to the ironic style of 'Templones Ende', as his central figure manically tries to make sense of the changing world:

> Templone aber war der Meinung, man müsse das Viertel halten, weil es doch offensichtlich geworden sei, daß die neuen Käufer unter einer Decke stünden, daß wahrscheinlich eine Organisation am Werke sei, das Villenviertel Bernau planmäßig zu erobern, eine ausländische oder staatsfeindliche Organisation gar! Und da dürfe man nicht weichen, nicht nachgeben, der Grundbesitz verpflichte zum Aushalten.(p.72)[15]

The ironic effect is heightened by maintaining the narrative perspective doggedly fixed to the central figure's claustrophobic odyssey, and this technique changes only once at the very end, when the gas man arrives, finds Templone's body and alerts the neighbours: 'Die besahen sich alles und sorgten für die Beerdigung des alten Herrn, der zwischen ihnen gelebt hatte, unverständlich wie ein Stein. Aber sie trugen es ihm nicht nach, daß er nie gegrüßt hatte, wenn man ihm begegnet war' (p.86). This final brief change of narrative perspective is replete with irony for the reader: the narrator has been leading us a merry dance right through to the bitter 'Ende'; Templone's 'Ende' is grotesquely ludicrous, because unwarranted and premature; and his 'Ende' is the beginning of normality, of the 'Alltag'.

This premature concentration on the story's conclusion has allowed me to highlight the ironic tone and to indicate how it relativises the four motifs already enumerated and helps them to become distanced, critically yet comically. They are thus free of melodrama ('the sad lonely victim of circumstances'), dogmatic social criticism ('the obsessive capitalist who gets his comeuppance'), naturalistic milieu portrayal ('the mundane materialism of the economic boom'). Instead an almost timeless, even surreal quality is engendered, as if these events and states of being have been going on since recorded history and I believe that Walser, once again ironically, alerts us to this through the names he has chosen for the characters and setting. The name of the main character is not a realistic name, but rather a symbolic amalgam of associations: Templone. 'Temp' can be read as the stem of the Latin noun 'Tempus', 'time'. He is indeed a man who has lived through changing times, and has certainly understood and exploited the spirit of the times, to his great economic advantage. To speculate is precisely to divine the forces of the moment and to attempt to turn them to one's advantage and profit.

Let us not forget either that the main acquisition of his speculating skills, the 'Villa', is designated by a word which is derived directly from the Latin. I would argue in fact that this story is as much about the 'Villa' as it is about the people who inhabit it. And it is not difficult to find within Templone's polyvalent name the word 'Tempel' whose origin is also Roman, 'Templum'. It is also worth remembering that a temple in Roman times designated a non-Christian building, wherein a cult would meet, worship, and celebrate. Templone and his pre-war villa-inhabiting neighbours would indeed regularly meet and hold 'Feste', and the post-war Templone resurrects precisely this social ritual, the 'Fest' in order to communicate to his new neighbours the vitality and the values of the old inhabitants of their quarter. The villa, as in pre- and post-Christian cultic rites and practices, becomes an object of fetishistic worshipping. For Templone the possibility that he may have to sell his prized possession is not just an economic threat but a psychological and timelessly cultural one. His crusade — and here we are reminded of yet another association of his name with the Templars, members of a military religious order founded in the early middle ages to protect the holy sepulchre against non-believers — reminds us of the struggle of secular and religious institutions throughout the ages to preserve buildings which they have imbued with a sacred or mystical significance.

The name Templone encapsulates his outsider status, through the English suffix 'lone'. As such he becomes the forerunner of so many Walserian figures from Hans Beumann in *Ehen in Philippsburg* via Anselm Kristlein to Alfred Dorn in *Die Verteidigung der Kindheit*. All these figures live within the community, some like Kristlein wanting to be part of it, others like Dorn at odds with it, but all feeling they are not part of that community and speculating a great deal on their seemingly existential condition of being doomed, fallen, forsaken. And in this respect the story contains a further layer of irony, for Templone, as part of his crusade to reanimate his threatened existence takes in a tenant, a professor and his library of eleven thousand volumes. The stratagem goes wrong, for Templone's daughter, thirty-eight and unmarried, falls in love with the scholar and they spend most of their days and nights fornicating — ostentatiously. The professor's name is once more highly literary and allusive: Professor Priamus. Priamos is a creation of Greek mythology, the King of Troy who fathered fifty sons and several daughters and who as an old man had lived to see the Trojan War, but the name Priamus also recalls another Greek mythological figure, Priapus, the god of fecundity whose own cult spread three centuries before Christ across the Greek and then Roman world. He is invariably portrayed as possessing a phallus of grotesque proportions. Nor is the setting of the events in a fictitious Bernau without some esoteric interest. On the shore of Walser's native Lake Constance lies the historic pilgrimage church of Birnau, which changed hands in 1803 and again in 1919. There is actually a town called Bernau in the state of Brandenburg which successfully repelled an attack by the Hussites in 1432. But most intriguingly this story set in *Ber*-nau was chosen by Walser to be read at the Group's meeting in *Ber*-lin, a city of course in which two estranged post-war communities lived side by side, locked in a psychologial battle of nerves as each speculated on the other's motives and objectives. A purely accidental congruence of the Group's meeting place and the ambience of the prize-winning story?!

The winning of the Prize signalled Walser's arrival within the peripatetic coterie of the Gruppe 47 and within the literary anti-establishment which, by 1955, it was coming to represent. However, it was Peter Suhrkamp who believed that the young author's arrival needed to be publicised and consolidated. Only a month after the successful Berlin reading, Peter Suhrkamp wrote to Walser about the need for publication:

> Nach dem Bild, das ich jetzt gewann, halte ich es aber in Ihrem Interesse, daß jetzt ein Buch von Ihnen erscheint. Dabei spielt für mich der Preis der Gruppe 47, wenn überhaupt nur eine periphere Rolle. Wichtig ist, daß jetzt Arbeiten von Ihnen, aus der Schublade, aus Ihrer Werkstatt und aus Zeitschriften, für in sich geschlossene Kreise hinaus in die Luft unserer Tage, in die Winde der literarischen Kritik, und vor allem an eine breite Leserschaft kommen. (Pezold, p.25)

Three months later *Ein Flugzeug über dem Haus* appeared. The eight stories of the collection had, however, not been written in one concentrated period prior to publication, but had been produced intermittently over a period of some four or five years, during which time their author was engaged in many other activities. Not surprisingly, the stories are thematically diverse, adopt different narrative perspectives and vary considerably in tone between the satirical, the ironical and the grotesque. In some the shadow of Kafka is visible; in others, such as 'Templones Ende', it has almost disappeared. In short, the volume is evidence of that eclecticism, which I suggested earlier could be detected in his *Zeichen der Zeit* portrait of the Group.

Returning to the Group's unanimous enjoyment of 'Templones Ende', one can justifiably claim that Walser was not being awarded the Franz Kafka Memorial Prize for this story. On the contrary, he may well have been rewarded for finding his own idiom and applying this to a snapshot of mid-fifties Germany with its amorphousness, confusions and divisions, all of which he was to continue to probe in his first full-length epic work *Ehen in Philippsburg* of 1957. In respect of Walser's emergent idiom, I believe the Group was also applauding his eschewing of full-blown satire, of parody and caricature, in favour of the more distancing effects of irony, although, as stated, this is not the irony of social or moral certainty, but one that expresses the petit-bourgeois search for an appropriate sense of one's position not only in society, but also in the world. For the story exudes that sense of existential 'Sorge', for which irony is one potent antidote. And finally, I contend that the Group did, subliminally, recognise the genuine narrative skills of this story, which enjoys playing with its reader, which entertains the reader, which surprises the reader with its 'Seitensprünge' of plot, characterisation and style. It is no wonder that three years later, when the next prize was awarded, it went to a novel which was to show that West German literature had found its voice and an audience ready to be subversively entertained: *Die Blechtrommel*. Walser 1955: Grass 1958: the Group's collective sensorium was becoming very attuned and astute.

Footnotes

[1] Reinhard Lettau (ed.), *Die Gruppe 47: Berichte, Kritik, Polemik. Ein Handbuch* (Neuwied and Berlin: Luchterhand, 1967), p.106. Further references to this volume are to be found in the text under Lettau.

2 Heinz Ludwig Arnold (ed.), *Die Gruppe 47. Ein kritischer Grundriß* (Munich: text + kritik, 1980), p.89. Further references to this volume are to be found in the text under Arnold.

3 'Ein Kafka-Epigone', title of a review of *Ein Flugzeug über dem Haus* by Paul Noack in the *Frankfurter Allgemeine Zeitung*, 23 March 1956.

4 Klaus Pezold, *Martin Walser. Seine schriftstellerische Entwicklung* (Berlin: Rütten & Loening, 1971), pp.24-49. Thomas Beckermann, *Martin Walser. Oder die Zerstörung eines Musters* (Bonn: Bouvier, 1972), pp.113-18. Further references to the volume by Pezold are to be found in the text under Pezold.

5. Gabriele Schweikart, '"...weil das Selbstverständliche nie geschieht": Martin Walsers frühe Prosa und ihre Beziehung zu Kafka', in: Heinz Ludwig Arnold (ed.), *Martin Walser, Text + Kritik*, 41/42 (1974), 37.

6 See Anthony Waine, 'Literature and the Radio in Post-War Germany: A Portrait of the Süddeutscher Rundfunk', *Journal of European Studies*, 16 (June 1986), 77-108.

7 See Anthony Waine, *Martin Walser* (Munich: Beck, 1980), p.19.

8 Published as Martin Walser, *Beschreibung einer Form. Versuch über Kafka* (Frankfurt a. M.: Suhrkamp, 1992).

9 Siegfried Unseld, 'My Walser, or the Author as Friend', in: Jürgen E. Schlunk and Armand E. Singer (eds), *Martin Walser. International Perspectives* (New York etc.: Lang 1987), pp.127-36.

10 See Anthony Waine, *Martin Walser. The Development as Dramatist* 1950-1970 (Bonn: Bouvier 1978), pp.13-24.

11 Manuscript from the archive of the Süddeutscher Rundfunk, transcribing tape KW 4094/1-11 of episode 13 of *Zeichen der Zeit*, broadcast on Monday 1 June 1953, 21.15 - 22.00, pp.27-31.

12 'Porträt Martin Walser. Ein Gespräch mit Anton Kaes', *The German Quarterly*, 57 (Summer, 1984), 439.

13 Gerald A. Fetz, *Martin Walser* (Stuttgart, Weimar: Metzler, 1997), p.6.

14 Rudolf Walter Leonhardt, 'Gruppenbild nach 30 Jahren', *Die Zeit*, 8 July 1977.

15 This and all further references to the text are based on the edition of Martin Walser: *Gesammelte Geschichten* (Frankfurt a. M: Suhrkamp, 1983).

16 Quoted in Pezold, *Martin Walser*, p.25.

STUART TABERNER

Fictional Reflections on the Gruppe 47 in Martin Walser's Kristlein Trilogy

In the early stages of his career, Martin Walser, whose work was frequently unfavourably received by critics, undoubtedly felt the need of support from the Gruppe 47. Later on his attitude became more distant, as can be seen from his essays which both satirise and directly criticise the Group. Within his fictional work there are also many passages which can be interpreted as reflecting increasing disenchantment. All the novels of the Kristlein trilogy contain a critique of the world of the intellectual. In *Halbzeit* Kristlein is seeking entry into the world of the literary salon, in *Das Einhorn*, he is indulging in the public-sphere rituals of the sociocritical writer, whilst in *Der Sturz* he is at the periphery of literary life, as Walser himself was in the mid-1960s, given his rejection of the increased moderation shown by the Group in its political pronouncements.

The importance of Martin Walser to any consideration of the Gruppe 47 is beyond dispute. Tony Waine has described in the previous essay Walser's gravitation towards the Group, the manner in which his prose piece 'Templones Ende' (1955) mirrored its aims and ideals, at least in the mid-1950s, and the author's influence upon the Group's literary programme. It is also not difficult to find other contemporary allusions, from the late 1950s and early 1960s, to the central place occupied by Walser in public perceptions of the Group. In 1957 Joachim Kaiser, reviewing the first ten years of the Gruppe 47 for the *Frankfurter Allgemeine Zeitung*, declared with some wit: 'In den letzten zehn Jahren schrieben sich noch H.M. Enzensberger und Martin Walser nach vorn'.[1] Many other instances could be cited, placing Walser alongside the older Böll and Aichinger, or, of his own generation, alongside Grass and Bachmann as key figures associated with West Germany's most celebrated literary club.

In this essay, I want to argue that Walser's relationship to the Gruppe 47 was more complex, and more fraught, than has previously been assumed. The author's early prose was rarely well-received by critics. It was often considered to be convoluted, diffuse and

overworked. Writing in 1965, Günter Blöcker noted that Walser's talent
was not easy to define: 'Anders als sein Altersgenosse Günter Graß [sic],
anders auch als der um einige Jahre jüngere Uwe Johnson, die [...] als
klar umrissene Begabungen vor das Publikum traten, hat sich Walser
bisher jeder Festlegung entzogen'.[2] The reason given was that Walser
was 'wortmächtig und formschwach' (p.390). Put another way, Walser's
fiction was demanding. This hostility may, in the early days at least,
have increased Walser's feelings of dependence upon the Group's
sponsorship, since, as is well known, reading performances at Hans
Werner Richter's literary gatherings greatly improved an author's
chances of being published. Dependence, of course, is a major theme
throughout Walser's work, a lack of self-sufficiency typically indicated
by the casting of his characters as 'Angestellte'. Perhaps mindful, even
resentful, of the writer's dependence upon the Gruppe 47, Walser began
to read less frequently at meetings from about 1955. Indeed, a number
of the author's essays and short stories from this time onwards (1954-
1964) reveal an emerging suspicion of the Group's institutionalisation,
of the growing dominance of critics, and of the shift away from
spontaneity to media orientation. Yet Walser's opprobrium was aimed
primarily at the discrepancy between the Group's image of itself as an
uncompromising censor of the CDU state and its more substantive
function as a source of cultural legitimacy for the fledgling Federal
Republic. The relative transparency of these essays and prose pieces
means that they help to throw light upon the extended fiction where
references to the Gruppe 47 are often less than obvious, and where, in
fact, such allusions might otherwise be simply a matter of speculation.

Walser's prose piece 'Die letzte Matinee' was read aloud at the
April meeting of 1954, which took place in Cap Circeo in Italy. A
young couple returns from the cinema to find their house occupied by
strangers. Following involved discussions of their predicament, they
decide to call the police. The police arrives only to be presented with
the couple's request that they be interned by the security forces. The
bizarreness of the situation, the couple's dogged yet pointless
engagement with their circumstances, and their self-inculpation at the
story's close clearly signal an early indebtedness to Kafka. Yet Walser's
immediate audience also recognised more contemporary allusions within
the piece. Hans Werner Richter concluded 'daß sich womöglich die
"Gruppe 47" in dieser Geschichte selber karikiert sehen muß'.[3]

Certainly, the story can be read as an extended metaphor. Obsessed by purely aesthetic matters, West Germany's literati could be said to have failed to recognise that they had already been evicted from their anti-establishment domicile, perhaps by more politically-aware activists (although given the prevailing atmosphere of social conformity and the lack of explicitly political intellectual intervention in the 1950s, we can only speculate that Walser's 'Störenfriede' are ironically invoked by the author as a piece of wishful thinking). The debates carried on by West Germany's intellectual elites appear long-winded and fruitless, and their reliance upon the state in the form of the police abject. In addition, this gently ironic lampoon also helps illuminate a rather paradoxical paragraph in Walser's earlier and otherwise generally more positive 'Gruppenbild' of 1952. Composed as a radio broadcast for Radio Bern, the essay describes the Group's discursive style:

> Die Schriftsteller der Gruppe 47 vermeiden es, sich in die uferlosen Meere allzu abstrakter Diskussionen zu stürzen, um nach den sogenannten letzten Dingen zu fischen: daß ein Satz ein guter Satz sei, daß einer die Sprache, die Ausdrucksmittel der Sprache beherrsche und die seinem persönlichen Ausdruckswillen gefügig mache, das ist diesen Schriftstellern das erste und wichtigste Problem.
>
> Darüber diskutieren sie seit 1947.[4]

With great irony the author creates a contradictory and overwrought image to describe the rejection of the same complex structures he himself employs.[5] The conventional linking of 'Diskussionen' and 'uferlos' to produce 'uferlose Diskussionen' is extended to breaking point. The device is over-exploited to associate 'uferlos' with 'Meere', 'Meere' with 'fischen', and 'fischen' with the original abstract discussion. Subjunctives and pompously inflated constructions imply the vacuousness of aspirations towards verbal and conceptual concreteness. Finally, the supposed abhorrence of discussion is juxtaposed with the phlegmatic: 'Darüber diskutieren sie seit 1947.' In the five years between 1947 and 1952 the Gruppe 47 had reached no conclusions. Instead, as Walser's contrastingly lucid summary laconically implies, it had devoted itself to the selfsame hypothesising that it had claimed to abjure.

Two essays written at the beginning of the 1960s reveal a hardening of emphasis in Walser's assessment of the Group. 'Brief an einen ganz jungen Autor', published in 1962, lists the humiliations to be overcome by an author present for the first time at a meeting of the Gruppe 47. Walser describes the difficulty of integrating into an already established social clique, and sardonically advises the aspiring writer to respect the need for adept role-playing: 'Bitte, weigere Dich, schon am ersten Vormittag vorzulesen. Gib Dich so scheu, wie Du bist.'[6] The focus here upon the Group as a social entity, with its own conventions to be aped by the newcomer, recalls the element of mimicry in *Halbzeit*, which had been published two years earlier in 1960. Of equal significance, however, is the new more caustic note in the author's portrayal of the critics who had become such a dominant force: Dein Vorgelesenes landet, mit Höllerers Fähnchen gespickt, von Jens groß etikettiert und erwogen, von Kaiser ein- und ausgeatmet und intim entlarvt bei Reich-Ranicki, der sofort aufsteht, wenn er sich mit Dir abzugeben beginnt. (p.159) The obvious comic intent here cannot disguise the author's conviction that intimidation, vanity and self-importance had become the hallmarks of the *Großkritiker*.[7] Furthermore, the barely disguised elitism displayed by what Walser and many others regarded as an evolving hierarchy of critics appeared to mirror the Group's broader abandonment of its democratic ethos. Two years later in 1964, Walser published an article in *Die Zeit* provocatively entitled 'Sozialisieren wir die Gruppe 47!'. The tone of this essay exhibits both the author's growing impatience and his increasingly strident political stance. Its terminology recalls the Frankfurt School's influential analysis of the culture industry. Far from furthering progressive ideals, Walser claims, the Gruppe 47 had become 'eine literarische Monopolgesellschaft, etwas Herrschsüchtiges, eine Dauerverschwörung'.[8] Its authors had become 'Markenartikel' (p.370).[9] During the next few years similar accusations could be heard from the anti-authoritarian movement. These included Robert Neumann's vilification of the Group in his 1966 *Konkret* article 'Spezis' — 'Die ihres Inhalts entleerte Gruppe 47 als Grass-Richtersche Privatliteraturplantage'[10] — the outrage caused by the decision to accept sponsorship from Ford to gather in Princeton at the height of the Vietnam War, and student demonstrations at the 1967 Pulvermühle meeting. At the same time as the Group was being attacked for its moderate political stance, however, it was also being berated on mainly aesthetic grounds by Peter Handke for its supposed 'Beschreibungs-impotenz'.[11] At the Princeton meeting of 1966, Handke had accused writers of sacrificing the principles of aesthetic innovation in favour of social engagement.

By the end of the 1960s Walser had dissociated himself from the dissolving Gruppe 47. Speeches now became the preferred form of expression for the author, reflecting a more energetic and immediate form of political intervention. Walser stayed away from Princeton, campaigned vigorously against the Vietnam War (the author's activism offered a sharp contrast to the Group's ineffectual joint declaration), and spoke out in favour of a writers' trades union as means of democratising the profession.[12] In retrospect, then, a line of development can be traced in Walser's attitude towards the Gruppe 47 from the mid-1950s onwards. Youthful awe, tempered by mildly facetious scepticism, evolved into dissatisfaction with the Group's media status, finally to develop into outright cynicism regarding its democratic credentials.

If Walser's shorter prose, essays and speeches engage directly with the Gruppe 47, his extended fiction operates at a more allusive level. The purpose of the rest of this essay is to trace the development of the author's literary engagement with the Group through his Kristlein trilogy: *Halbzeit* (1960), *Das Einhorn* (1966), and *Der Sturz* (1973). I aim to show that the novels follow the same evolving pattern of equivocal respect, consternation and antagonism that marks the shorter pieces. The vehicle for Walser's engagement with the Gruppe 47 is an ever evolving engagement with literary self-consciousness. Initially, the author looks to this technique as a means of identifying with the Group's aims, whilst distancing himself from its incorporation into the mainstream. Subsequently, he turns self-consciousness against itself to reveal the literary establishment's appropriation of this technique as a corrupt, but commercially viable literary strategy. In the final instalment of the Kristlein story, however, Walser demonstrates the way in which even this 'higher' level of self-consciousness is incorporated within the current predilection for confession. The consequence of the frustrations Walser encountered in his efforts to criticise from the inside a *Literaturbetrieb*, within which dissent was neutralised or even commercially exploited, was his temporary withdrawal from the literary sphere towards the end of the 1960s. This reluctance to engage also affects Anselm Kristlein as he appears to 'write himself' out of the narrative in third part of the trilogy.

The most transparent reference to the Group appears in *Der Sturz*. A petition is signed by a group of SPD-supporting trade unionists led by the allegorically and aptly named Herr Lämmle. This document of protest contains '47 Unterschriften', and its ineffectual and pathetically conformist signatories are ironically invoked as the 'Gruppe 47'.[13] Yet the beginnings of Walser's tale of political timidity lie in the earlier *Halbzeit*. In this novel, Anselm Kristlein is established as a 'Vertreter', a profession whose superfluity Walser has compared with the redundancy of the writer:

> Es gibt keinen Beruf, der einem Menschen das Gefühl seiner eigenen
> Überflüssigkeit so aufdringlich klar machen könnte, wie der des Vertreters.
> Das hat mir diesen Beruf sympathisch gemacht, er erinnerte mich fast an den
> des Schriftstellers.[14]

Anselm is also justifiably famous as the representative of his materialistic age, as 'the archetypal "economic miracle man"', to employ a phrase coined by Stuart Parkes,[15] and his widespread role-playing and desire for conformity reflects what Donald Nelson terms the 'breakdown of social communication and the depersonalization of human behavior'.[16] Anselm, however, is also an author of sorts, as evidenced by his fictionalisation of both personal biography and shared experience.[17] As such, his principal ambition is to gain access to the literary gatherings held at the residences of prominent capitalist patrons.

The fascination of Anselm's attempts to establish himself as a writer resides mainly in the novel's anthropological concern with questions of generation, integration, and face-to-face interaction. The literary congregations that take place at the house of the industrialist Frantzke recall the Group's meetings and its gradual incorporation as a commercial enterprise. Artists compete for an invitation, a 'Sprechrolle',[18] and finally for the 'prize' of public affirmation. Anselm's account of his performance at these gatherings may yield an insight into the initiation rites endured by unknown writers struggling to gain access to West Germany's most prestigious literary clique. Anselm follows his own author's advice to the younger generation of writers, as set out in 'Brief an einen ganz jungen Autor'. He feigns shyness, defers to more prominent colleagues, and, towards the end of the novel, achieves modest success:

> Mir war diesmal kein lauter Triumph beschieden. Das hatte ich gar nicht
> erwartet. Lamberts Art war weder zu imitieren, noch zu übertreffen. Ich

wollte mit meinem unaufdringlichen Genrebildchen bloß darauf hinweisen,

daß ein Neuling aufgetaucht sei. (p.634)

A number of important expressions feature in this passage as it develops from elegant simplicity into a more elaborate arrangement confirming Anselm's skill as a story-teller. The need to respect entrenched hierarchies militates against an unqualified triumph for the newcomer. A representative of the upcoming generation, Anselm confesses a debt to those who have influenced him, whilst also defining his own style. His reworking of a 'Genrebildchen' presents him as an apprentice demonstrating his newly acquired skills by means of a generic piece of prose. Finally, Anselm is accepted into the group as a talented 'Neuling'. His is a literary talent in the making.

Form as well as content testify to Walser's engagement with the Gruppe 47 in *Halbzeit*. Critics have often noted the novel's 'performative' quality. *Halbzeit* relies heavily upon dialogue, dramatic stylisation, and ostentatious formal innovation. Yet such typically short and highly climatic 'scenes' are arranged within a novel which is provocatively long and complex. This contradiction may imply both acquiescence and resistance to the requirement to distort a work's 'natural' rhythm for the sake of immediacy of impact at the Group's meetings. In his 'Brief an einen ganz jungen Autor', Walser reminds young hopefuls that material read aloud should be 'Literatur fürs Zuhören'. The accent should be on the piece's musical quality, on its ability to flatter the listener: 'er habe Rhythmus und Melodie beim Zuhören sozusagen dazugemacht' ('Brief', p.162). Friedhelm Kröll summarises that the format of recitations favoured 'das kurze Prosastück, dem eine pointierende Wirkungspotenz innewohnte'.[19] Anselm's recitals certainly possess this quality of prose as drama, indicating his desire for conformity. Yet Walser's organisation of individual 'performances' into a more elaborate concert of juxtaposition and allusion exposes the poverty of the solitary piece when delivered out of context and foreshortened for dramatic effect. It also signals a calculated assertion of the author's control of the narrative, of his refusal to be intimidated into restraining or distorting a talent for invention.

Walser's self-conscious foregrounding of his manipulation of material is a distinctly modernist gesture. It is also a technique that the author devolves to Anselm in his capacity as narrator.[20] This allows for the creation of Anselm the unthinking protagonist and Anselm the more reflective, and thus more distanced, story-teller. It also reflects Walser's relatively early (1963), generally optimistic, assessment of the critical insight that can be generated when writers engage with their own social function in their fiction:

> Das erste Positive: der Schreiber kümmert sich endlich ganz um sich selbst und wenn er sich aus dem Sattel gehoben hat, stellt sich heraus, daß er alle mitriß, die im Sattel saßen. Das ist sicher eine Utopie. Aber vielleicht nützt es, an ihrer Realität zu scheitern.[21]

The self-conscious Anselm thus satirises writers' trivial discussions of what is 'typisch deutsch' (p.605), their callous efforts to win acclaim with competing versions of a horrific industrial accident (pp.612-20), and his own collusion in all of this and more. Such criticisms invariably reflect badly on the social and political order in which the artists in the novel operate. In 'unseating' himself as a writer, therefore, Anselm to some degree also, to continue the metaphor, causes all his colleagues to fall ('alle mitriß, die im Sattel saßen'). Moreover, Anselm's potentially destructive schizophrenic vacillation between dependence upon the 'Literaturbetrieb' and criticism of its incorporation can be resolved within a literary device. This compromise generates some bizarre formulations of personal identity: 'In meinem taubenblauen Anzug stieg er aus meinem Auto' (p.345). Equally, its power to reconcile is always fragile and provisional: Anselm suffers as a result of his role-play as his 'true' identity becomes ever more tenuous. Anselm comments of himself: 'Versteh ich Anselm noch? Und er selbst, versteht er sich noch?' (p. 718). This self-alienation may explain his equivocal response to the sun's rays, a motif that runs through the entire novel:

> Die Sonne schien bloß auf mich, mich hatte sie ausgesucht, auf meinen Schädel bündelte sie die Junivormittagshitze, eigentlich bestimmt für die ganze Stadt, aber jetzt von Schritt zu Schritt nur noch auf meinen Schädel sammelnd, um mir eine glühende Mitra aufzusetzen. Warum mir? Ich hatte keine Schlange getötet, keinem Sonnenpriester ein Auge ausgestoßen, ich kannte gar keinen. (p.25)

The sun may connote enlightenment, the source of the writer's obligation to chastise power. Yet Anselm's reaction to this duty is paranoia. The literary establishment had fashioned itself as the 'conscience of the nation', and Anselm now suffers from public expectations that he will fulfil this function. His censure of the capitalist state, of course, simultaneously reveals his own complicity. At the same time, Anselm's protest may be duplicitous. The author's rejection of hero status simply intensifies his public appeal.

If *Halbzeit* depicted Anselm's acceptance into the literary establishment, *Das Einhorn* shows him at the height of his success.[22] It is surely no coincidence that the period of the novel's composition coincided with the most influential phase of the Gruppe 47. Appearing on *Podiumsdiskussionen*, television debates and in town halls, Anselm confirms Heinrich Böll's contention of 1965 that the Group had developed into an 'öffentliche[n] Institution'.[23] Yet the self-conscious narrator once again employs modernist techniques in his exposé of the 'representativeness' that adheres to writers as media stars. This label had already been invoked by Helmut Heißenbüttel in 1960, who determined with a degree of approval that the Group possessed a 'gewisse Repräsentanz'[24] within West German culture, and by Peter Härtling, whose use of the term was rather more negative: 'Sie sind "Repräsentanten" einer angesehenen Firma, einer Holdingsgesellschaft (Poesie und Kritik)'[25] Härtling's more caustic criticism conjures up an impression of the Group's commercialisation, and certainly fits well with Walser's analysis. Thus the commercial aspect of representativeness is explored by Anselm by means of parody and burlesque. Separating his self-conscious persona from his unreflective alter ego, Walser's character recounts his own duplicitous media performance. Following comments on the democratic sham of political opposition, the 'Schauspiel der Auseinandersetzung' (p.133), Anselm invokes his own complicity:

> Und hätte Anselm verraten, daß die Grenze in Wirklichkeit streng zwischen Saal und Podium verläuft, hätte er wahrscheinlich auch alle Ansicht zerstört, je ganz aufgenommen zu werden unter die Geheimnisträger, die Erstklassigen, die Hochbezahlten [...] und er mußte doch dringend hoffen, seiner eigenartigen Berufsverhältnisse wegen, irgend wann einmal aufgenommen zu werden in die höheren Priesterklassen der Bunzreplik. (p.134)

The two conditionals that introduce this passage may represent the narrator's retrospective attempts to justify the omissions committed by his narrated self. More generally, Anselm appears to concede with his unholy trinity, 'die Geheimnisträger, die Erstklassigen, die Hochbezahlten', the anti-democratic consequences of the emergence of

supposedly representative media elites. Typically, of course, Anselm
views access to this charmed circle as a means of escaping from the
dependence which plagues him as a freelance writer.

Walser's perception of the inhibiting effect of media elites upon
the development of a popular democratic consciousness was to become
increasingly stark in the course of the late 1960s and early 1970s.
Speaking to Aurel Schmidt in 1974, Walser commented: 'Alles
Repräsentieren ist ja von Übel nicht erst dort, wo es in einem grotesken,
in einem prunkhaften Sinn ins Repräsentieren übergeht, denn das Für-
andere-da-sein schließt die Teilnahme anderer aus.'[26] Here Walser
distinguishes two senses of 'representativeness'. On the one hand,
writers collectively appear to make manifest what is 'splendid' within
the national culture. This is a form of display which Walser seems to
consider to be as grotesque as it is magnificently ostentatious.
Alternatively, an individual author might claim that he is acting as the
mouthpiece of the views of his constituency. This could be a further
implication of the prevalence of the 'Vertreter' in Walser's fiction; this
character represents the outlook of his lower-middle class
contemporaries. Yet the politically engaged writer appears to exercise
both functions at the same time, and, Walser implies, is suspect on both
counts. The author as public figure may appear to be making a false
claim to embody the nation, or, at least, his readership. Equally, his
greater prestige, access to the media and superior linguistic competence
may deter 'ordinary' citizens from participating fully in the democratic
process.

Anselm's irony is also directly against the relationship between
the state and its intellectuals, the so-called priestly classes. This is
presumably a reference that includes the Gruppe 47.[27] The context in
which the term 'Priesterklassen' is used here implies Walser's own
satire on the self-importance of the intellectual elite, a clique which has
been described by Wilfried van der Will and Rob Burns as the 'secular
clergy that has inherited something of the elevated aura which once
attached to prophets, philosophers and poets'.[28] In an essay published in
1974, Walser delivers his own, rather more scathing, analysis of
writers' adoption of this priestly role: 'Auch der Schriftsteller ist in
Versuchung, als Religionserbe aufzutreten und durch bloße Literatur
eine Religion für Ungläubige zu gründen. Und schon wird sein
Negatives ganz positiv.'[29] In *Das Einhorn* Anselm addresses the

consequences of this rejection of negativity in favour of affirmation. He draws attention to writers' cosy collusion with the state, and mocks their institutionalisation through his use of the comically deviant form 'Bunzreplik'. This spelling most probably echoes the compressed speech of West Germany's cultural and political elites who have developed their own language fads. The passage in its entirety, of course, reiterates Walser's central theme of dependence. Anselm's success rests solely upon his successful initiation into representative cultural institutions. This representativeness is a symptom both of a literary elite's conviction that it speaks for the nation and of the public's credulity. Following his appearance in a *Podiumsdiskussion*, for example, Anselm is eagerly seized upon by Barbara, who desires nothing less than the 'Ersatzpfarrer vom Podium' (p.162). Indeed, Anselm had previously noted with some irony: 'Der fehlende Pfarrer war nicht da' (p.137).

Walser's travesty of the workings of the literary establishment shows Anselm as a 'homo ludens' (p.126). This figure is invoked in Anselm's parody of intellectual discourse (pp.122-30), and may embody yet another reference to the self-conscious analytical mode of both author and narrator. This method becomes increasingly apparent in Anselm's lampoon of literary critics, which is both topical and playfully irreverent. Friedhelm Kröll claims that criticism within the Gruppe 47 had become a 'selbstständige Darstellungsform' by the early 1960s. (Kröll, p.41).Anselm illustrates this phenomenon by means of his caricature of the critics surrounding the artist NDB.[30] Anselm cites Dr Keckeisen's assessment of NDB's costume at a fancy dress party:

> Dr Keckeisen sagte uns etwas über die magische Funktion des NDB-Kostüms, NDB in der Haut des Gegners, dessen Existenz als Kostümexistenz demonstrierend, gleichzeitig sublimierende Verarbeitung des eigenen Affektüberschusses und bewandtnisreiche Anspielung auf einen historischen Vorläufer mit Beschwörungstendenz. (p.52)

The parody should be obvious. Academic pomposity, elitist jargon and overbearing egotism would appear to be the emblems of the *Großkritiker*. Yet even this passage indirectly reveals Walser's adoption of self-consciousness, itself being a 'sublimierende Verarbeitung des eigenen Affektüberschusses'. The satirical commitment to excessive embellishment persists in Anselm's subsequent allusions to a famous member of the Gruppe 47. Uwe Johnson appears as his own character Karsch,[31] and critics struggle to decipher his typically enigmatic utterance 'STAUB'. Wollensak identifies 'eine Erinnerung an die DDR', whereas Beumann, a character from Walser's first novel *Ehen in Philippsburg* (1957), determines that Karsch's comment is surely 'religiös' (p.297). In both cases, a tendency to assume omniscience is ridiculed.

Yet Anselm too is part of the *Literaturbetrieb*. He has a publisher, the suggestively named Melanie Sugg, whose principle interest lies in procuring pornography disguised as fiction. He also composes with an audience in mind, ostensibly his 'lieben Verwandten und Bekannten' (p.364). This readership originally formed Habermas's eighteenth-century domestic sphere for the reception of literature, the 'Sphäre klein familialer Intimität' which prepared individuals for participation in a wider public: 'die zum Publikum zusammentretenden Privatleute räsonieren auch öffentlich über das Gelesene und bringen es in den gemeinsamen vorangetriebenen Prozeß der Aufklärung ein.'[32] More recently, however, the relationship between the literary and political spheres has changed as readers have evolved from a 'kulturräsonierenden zu [einem] kulturkonsumierenden Publikum' (p.176). They have become consumers of the culture industry, which, as is well-known, displays a strong predilection for fake intimacy. The effect on the novel form of this transformation of the literary sphere had already been adumbrated by Adorno in an essay of 1958: 'die allverbreitete biographische Schundliteratur ist ein Zersetzungsprodukt der Romanform selber.'[33] Anselm contributes to this trivialisation of the novelistic genre by marketing his self-consciousness, itself a form of confession which appears to offer access to the narrator's intimate sphere. The split into reflective and unreflective selves is the novel's true theme. Anselm's crisis of identity is stylised into the recognisably modernist motifs of illness and self-disclosure:

> Ich liege. Ja. Ich liege. Ich hätte diesen Zustand lieber verschwiegen [...].
> Aber die dumme Bekenntnissucht war nicht zu bändigen. Protegiert von
> meinen niedrigsten Fähigkeiten, wurde das Sätzchen immer frecher, radierte
> rabiat in mir herum, kratzte als Hustenbox, boxte als überreife
> Schwangerschaft, machte mir Enge und Ohrensausen und klopfte mich ab
> nach der durchlässigen Stelle. (p.7)

Alliteration, anaphora and metaphor supply an entertaining pastiche designed to assure Anselm's success within the literary sphere he feigns to censure. Yet this is not the involuntary sickness of the artist, as portrayed by Thomas Mann, for example: it is a deliberate manipulation, and a corruption, of the modernist obsession with illness and sensitivity for commercial ends. It represents the 'Verrat an der Negativität' which Walser considers to the trademark of writers in the period: 'Der Schriftsteller ist nur insofern schlimmer als andere, als er diesen Verrat schriftlich ummünzt in eine Art Reifevorgang. Er macht Stil daraus' ('Schriftsteller', p.45). If Anselm wishes to remain popular as an artist, he must fictionalise and stylise the schizophrenic split between conformity and criticism that he suffered in *Halbzeit* in order to render it appetising. Thus Anselm comments: 'Ich mußte von einer Minute zur anderen eine Krankheit parat haben' (p.9). All that remains of Anselm's enlightenment heritage is occasional 'Sonnenstrich' (p.13). As for identity, Anselm realises that he is now simply a 'Figur. Sichtbar am besten schwarz auf weiß' (p.483). The ironic allusion to the printed page is obvious.

Walser's portrayal of the manner in which Anselm corrupts the critical impulse associated with the self-consciousness novel is, of course, itself an attack upon the degeneration of the literary sphere into confession. As such, a positive vision of the potential of literature to reflect upon itself, and upon society more broadly, may still emerge from *Das Einhorn*, despite the fact that the narrator appears to have rejected any oppositional stance for himself. Yet the critical perspective adopted by the novel as a whole — its depiction of the betrayal of the principle of intellectual dissent enacted by its own narrator — already appears as a form of retreat. It is also probable that the novel's broader commitment to a critical self-consciousness will itself eventually be incorporated as entertainment, much as was the case with Anselm's brief moments of insight in *Halbzeit* and *Das Einhorn*.

If *Das Einhorn* depicts Anselm's adept commercialisation of self-consciousness, then *Der Sturz* describes the devastating consequences of this betrayal of an earlier critical impulse. In part one of the novel, Anselm seeks refuge with some of the many marginal factions that had emerged following the fragmentation of an elitist public sphere. His pilgrimage leads from hippies to political extremists, to Eastern mystics, and to prison. This somewhat incredible, even fantastical journey may be an attempt to find a political home following the breakdown of left-liberal cliques such as the Gruppe 47 at the end of the 1960s. Yet Anselm's attempt to mimic the emphasis on diversity, plurality and peripheral life-styles typical of that period attracts universal disgust. Anselm is arraigned on charges of abusing a minor, but his real crime is to have disappointed his public with false claims of omniscience. The prestige of the *Podiumsdiskussion* intellectual has been shattered by anti-authoritarian protests. Anselm is condemned for his 'Lügen und Renommieren' (p.124), and denounced as 'Zwielichtig. Verschuldet. Spielbesessen. Überheblich. Ehrsüchtig' (p.128). He retires from public life following an exemplary beating by 'concerned' citizens. He then becomes, as reported earlier in the novel, the 'Heimleiter eines ziemlich großen Erholungsheims, zumindest der Mann einer Heimleiterin' (p.79).

Anselm narrates his criminal past from the sanctuary of the convalescent home. His choice of retreat appears to signal his desire to exit the public stage. It also indicates a determination to overcome the schizophrenic split that he had marketed so successfully in *Das Einhorn*. Within his pastoral refuge Anselm shuns social, political and cultural engagement. He sidesteps the heated debates between Fritz Hitz and Edmund, two would-be political activists squatting at his house, on the subject of poetry as an adequate response to the Vietnam War (pp.202-07), or on the merits of direct action (p.209).[34] He even fails to respond to the 'Gruppe 47' (p.239) of signatories to a petition protesting against the left-wing irreverence of youthful critics. Instead, Anselm favours introspection and withdrawal. His main occupations are the excavation of an escape shaft and the composition of a book on the sexual habits of spiders. Anselm associates these creatures with privacy (p.171), masturbation (p.285), auto-eroticism, and the devouring of the male by the female. The allusions to the 'Neue Innerlichkeit' of the late 1960s and early 1970s should be evident. A sublimated fear of women may be a response to the emergence of the feminist movement, to Anselm's previous sexual rapacity, and to his dependence upon his wife, the 'Heimleiterin'.

The final instalment of Walser's Kristlein trilogy signals Anselm's passage from modernist self-consciousness to pure introspection. This marks the implosion of Anselm's critical perspective on the conditions of his literary production. The inward-looking narrator is incapable of analytical distance. The self-consciousness associated with Anselm's particular corrupt form of modernism is thus divorced from its political intent, leading to cultural pessimism. Even if Anselm still wished to intervene politically, the dissolution of the established literary sphere would make this impossible. The left-liberal intellectual of Anselm's generation is left without a secure basis for political engagement. Hence Anselm is merely a lodger in a property located at the periphery of his boss's estate, without influence on the social, political and cultural events which take place in the main house. Anselm, the consummate role-player, has even lost the desire to ingratiate himself and to present himself to his public:

> Und ich bin ein schlechter Selbstdarsteller [...]. In meinem Fall ist der Mangel an Darstellungsfähigkeit ein Ausdruck für einen Mangel im Darzustellenden: das ist meine Person. Ich will tatsächlich diese Arbeit, die ich kriege, nicht tun. (p.336)

The unadorned directness of this passage distinguishes it from the highly stylised confessions that feature in *Das Einhorn*. Anselm's rejection of celebrity status appears authentic here, as shown by his uncompromising admission of his inadequacy: 'in meinem Fall', 'das ist meine Person', and by his pre-emptive rebuttal: 'tatsächlich'. A genuine need for seclusion differentiates Anselm from those writers at the end of the 1960s who, in the eyes of their detractors, saw introspection as the route to commercial success: criticism of this new trend in literature is evident in Walser's 1970 essay 'Über die Neueste Stimmung im Westen'.35 Anselm's friend Edmund exemplifies this new introspective sensibility, emphasising 'style', self-disclosure and exhibitionism over political or social impact. In any case, Anselm ensures that his departure from centre stage is irreversible by choosing suicide in an Alpine crash at the end of the novel. Suicide may represent an extreme form of intellectual honesty on the part of the public figure. Anselm is no longer able to justify political intervention within a public discourse that has changed beyond recognition. His gesture of withdrawal may, in fact, be contrasted with those other characters within the novel who opt for continued engagement, either as political extremists, or as liberal democrats in the traditional mould. Hence, the dementia of the aged fanatic is manifest in plans to plague Heinrich Böll by unloading 'Scheiße vor's Haus [...] bis er aufhört, seine öffentliche Güte zu produzieren' (p.192). More subtly, Anselm invokes his 'Gegentyp'. The prototype for this character is most likely Günter Grass, a staunch supporter of the Gruppe 47 in the face of the attacks on its legitimacy launched by the students. Anselm's 'Gegentyp' positions himself at the

centre of the political spectrum: 'Er wendet sich oft genug gegen links
und gegen rechts', and appears to exude a powerful self-righteousness:
'Und seine Heftigkeit ist einfach bedingt durch seine eigene
Tadellosigkeit' (p.251). The 'Gegentyp' continues with his public
functions, giving interviews and 'politische Belehrung' (p.252), and
holding speeches (p.323). Anselm's 'Gegentyp', it seems, is both envied
for his success and yet also criticised for his unshakeable conviction of
the legitimacy of his public pronouncements.

The life of Anselm Kristlein reflects the highs and lows of his
creator's relationship with the Gruppe 47. Anselm breaks his way into
the Group as a young writer, employing techniques of literary
modernism as a means of making his mark. Like the Group, he is split
between critical commentary on his environment and social integration.
His formal innovation brings him public prestige, and his political
commitment makes him representative of the nation. At the same time,
however, success neutralises Anselm's critical perspective. He becomes
as much an institution as the Group itself, travelling from radio
interview, to *Podiumsdiskussion*, to public meeting. Social comment
becomes harmless entertainment, and confession of this incorporated
status becomes the latest modernist device: modernism itself becomes
corrupt. At this point, the modernist technique of self-consciousness is
stripped of its critical impulse and is transformed into titillating
confession. Writers become as ineffective as the lovers in 'Die letzte
Matinee' who return home to find that their place has been usurped by
more radical groups taking direct action. Endless discussion, navel
gazing, and appeals to state bodies are certain to emasculate dissent.
Authors begin to 'function', recalling Heinrich Böll's rhetorical
question: 'Ob eine Gruppe von Schriftstellern, wenn sie anfängt zu
funktionieren, sich nicht auf eine absurde Weise mit der Gesellschaft
konform erklärt?'[36] At this point, the only honest choice may be the
retreat from literature itself. This, of course, is exactly Walser did from
the late 1960s to the early 1970s.

Footnotes

Thanks are due, as always, to Dr Beth Linklater.

[1] Joachim Kaiser, 'Zehn Jahre Gruppe 47', *Frankfurter Allgemeine Zeitung*, 2 October
57. Quoted in Reinhard Lettau (ed.), *Die Gruppe 47. Bericht, Kritik, Polemik. Ein
Handbuch* (Neuwied and Berlin: Luchterhand, 1967), p.123.

[2] Günter Blöcker, 'Der Realismus X', *Merkur*, 19 (1965), 389-92, here 389.

[3] Heinz Ludwig Arnold (ed.), *Die Gruppe 47. Ein kritischer Grundriß* (Munich: text + kritik, 1980), p.111.

[4] 'Gruppenbild 1952', Radio Bern, 1952. Quoted in Lettau, *Handbuch*, pp.278-82.

[5] In the same essay, Walser notes that 'Sprachakrobaten' (p.279) are rarely invited again. This may provide an early hint of Walser's future difficulties with a critical establishment whose tastes had been shaped by an early rejection of literary exuberance. Walser's prose, as previously noted, was often condemned for its 'irrelevant' playfulness and excessiveness.

[6] Martin Walser, 'Brief an einen ganz jungen Autor', in: Walser, *Erfahrungen und Leseerfahrungen* (Frankfurt a. M. : Suhrkamp, 1965), pp.155-62, here p.155. Further references to this essay are to be found in the text under 'Brief'.

[7] Walser was still more ferocious in his condemnation of critics in a later essay 'Über Päpste' (1977). Martin Walser, *Wer ist ein Schriftsteller?* (Frankfurt a. M. : Suhrkamp, 1979), pp.47-54.

[8] Martin Walser, 'Sozialisieren wir die Gruppe 47!', *Die Zeit*, 3 July 1964. Also in: Lettau, *Handbuch*, pp.368-70, here p.368.

[9] Walser had already used this word in discussion with the *Frankfurter Rundschau*: '"Die Gruppe 47" ist ein politisch hoch geputschter Markenartikel' (13 September 1963, p.15). Although the article is entitled '"Gruppe 47" eine Clique?', only a single paragraph comments directly on the Group (the rest deals with relations between East and West German authors). Newspapers clearly responded to an insistent public interest (itself created by the media) in the Group.

[10] Robert Neumann, 'Spezis: Gruppe 47 in Berlin', *Konkret* , H.5, 1966.

[11] Peter Handke, 'Zur Tagung der Gruppe 47 in USA', in: Handke, *Ich bin ein Bewohner des Elfenbeinturms* (Frankfurt a. M. : Suhrkamp, 1972), p.29.

[12] Walser's attack on members' lack of engagement is contained in 'Engagement als Pflichtfach für Schriftsteller' (1967). His speeches against the Vietnam War include 'Praktiker, Weltfremde und Vietnam' (1966), 'Auskunft über den Protest' (1966), and 'Amerikanischer als die Amerikaner' (1967). All four appear in: *Heimatkunde. Aufsätze und Reden* (Frankfurt a. M.: Suhrkamp, 1968). The author's plea for a writers' trades union was made in his speech 'Für eine IG-Kultur' (1970), in: Martin Walser, *Wie und Wovon handelt Literatur. Aufsätze und Reden* (Frankfurt a. M.: Suhrkamp, 1973), pp.67-75.

[13] Martin Walser, *Der Sturz* (Frankfurt a. M.: Suhrkamp, 1973), p.237 and p.239. All future references in brackets in the text are to this edition.

[14.] 'Dem Sog ergeben. Ein Werkstattgespräch zwischen Martin Walser und Horst Bienek' (1962), in: Martin Walser, *Auskunft* (Frankfurt a. M.: Suhrkamp, 1991), pp.8-21, here p.9.

[15] Stuart Parkes, 'An all-German Dilemma: Some Notes on the Presentation of the Theme of the Individual and Society in Martin Walser's *Halbzeit* and Christa Wolf's *Nachdenken über Christa T*', GLL, 28: 1 (1974-75), 58-64, here 59.

[16] Donald Nelson, 'The Depersonalized World of Martin Walser', *The German Quarterly*, 42 (1969), 204-16, here 204.

[17] Writing in 1973, Kurt Batt countered the conventional reading of the novels 'als satirische Inventuren des gehobenen mittelständischen Lebens der BRD'. This theme, the East German critic insisted, is a 'bloßer Hintergrund für die Selbstabrechnung mit dem eigenen Beruf' (Kurt Batt, 'Die Exekution des Erzählers (II). Westdeutsche Romane um 1970', *Sinn und Form*, 25 (1973), 397-431, here 425. The present article expands upon this argument.

[18] Martin Walser, *Halbzeit* (Frankfurt a. M.: Suhrkamp, 1960), p.584. All future references in brackets in the text.

[19] Friedhelm Kröll, *Gruppe 47* (Stuttgart: Metzler, 1979), p.43. Further references to this volume are to be found in the text under Kröll.

[20] Anselm also employs other modernist conventions as a means of highlighting the fictional status of his narrative. Extreme stylisation, pastiche, and the introduction of non-novelistic genres draw attention to Anselm's attempts to elaborate his story for commercial success. With reference to this, see my article: 'Martin Walser's *Halbzeit*: Stylizing Private History for Public Consumption', *MLR*, 92: 4 (October 1997), 912-23.

[21] Martin Walser, 'Freiübungen', in: Walser, *Erfahrungen und Leseerfahrungen*, pp.94-112, here p.98.

[22] Martin Walser, *Das Einhorn* (Frankfurt a.M.: Suhrkamp, 1966). All future references in brackets in the text.

[23] Heinrich Böll, 'Angst vor der Gruppe 47?', in: Lettau, *Handbuch*, pp.389-400, here p.394.

[24] Helmut Heißenbüttel, 'Und es kam Uwe Johnson', *Deutsche Zeitung*, 10 November 1960, pp.156-58, here p.156.

[25] Peter Härtling, 'Repräsentanten', *Der Monat*, 16 (1964), in: Lettau, *Handbuch*, pp.203-05, here p.204.

[26] 'Weit weg von der Berufskultur. Ein Interview mit Martin Walser über Amerika, den Kulturbetrieb und die Ironie', in: Walser, *Auskunft*, pp.37-44, here p.38.

[27] The term also anticipates Helmut Schelsky's 1975 assault on the complacency of West Germany's leftist intelligentsia, *Die Arbeit tun die anderen: Klassenkampf und Priesterherrschaft der Intellektuellen* (Opladen: Westdeutscher Verlag), although there is no indication that Walser agreed with the detail of Schelsky's analysis.

[28] Rob Burns and Wilfried van der Will, *Protest and Democracy in West Germany. Extra Parliamentary Opposition and the Democratic Agenda* (London: Macmillan, 1988), p.17.

[29] Martin Walser, 'Wer ist ein Schriftsteller?', in: Walser, *Wer ist ein Schriftsteller?*, pp.36-46, here p.45. Further references to this essay are to be found in the text under 'Schriftsteller'.

30 Anselm's self-conscious and modernist credentials are evident in his use of allegorical names. NDB's 'zündende Initialen' (p.47) may refer to the publication *Neue Deutsche Biographie* which detailed the lives of 'representative' public individuals.

31 Karsch appears in 'Eine Reise wegwohin' (1960) in: Uwe Johnson, *Karsch, und andere Prosa* (Frankfurt a. M.: Suhrkamp, 1964), pp.29-81 and in: *Das dritte Buch über Achim* (Frankfurt a. M.: Suhrkamp, 1962).

32 Jürgen Habermas, *Strukturwandel der Öffentlichkeit* 2nd edn (Neuwied: Luchterhand, 1965), p.63.

33 Theodor W. Adorno, 'Der Standort des Erzählers im zeitgenössichen Roman', in: Heinz Ludwig Arnold, Theo Buck (eds), *Positionen des Erzählens* (Munich: C.H. Beck, 1976), pp.9-14, here p.10.

34 Fritz Hitz may be based on Friedrich Hitzer, at the time the editor of the radical magazine *Kürbiskern*.

35 Martin Walser, 'Über die Neueste Stimmung im Westen', *Kursbuch*, 20 (1970), 19-41.

36 Böll, 'Angst vor der Gruppe 47', in: Lettau, *Handbuch*, p.400.

KATRIN KOHL

'Diesmal wollte man [ihn] gern anders' —
Peter Rühmkorf und die Gruppe 47

Obwohl Peter Rühmkorf ziemlich spät zur Gruppe 47 kam, bietet die unterschiedliche Rezeption, die ihm 1960 und 1961 zuteil wurde, einen interessanten Einblick in die Praxis der Gruppe. 1960 verfehlte er knapp den Preis; 1961 wurden seine Gedichte verrissen, obwohl er in beiden Jahren Gedichte vorlas, die in der gleichen Sammlung erscheinen sollten. Ihm wurde aber 1961 vorgeworfen, ähnliche Texte wie im vorigen Jahr vorgelesen zu haben. Die Vermutung liegt nahe, daß die Urteile der Kritik auf den Tagungen der Gruppe 47 durch kurzfristige Moden und die Vorlesesituation beeinflußt wurden. Nach seinen Erfahrungen im Jahre 1961 las Rühmkorf nie wieder auf einer Tagung der Gruppe. Es spricht einiges dafür, daß seine literarische Karriere lange Zeit unter diesem Mißerfolg litt. Er selbst übte scharfe Kritik an der Gruppe, obwohl er weiter an den Tagungen teilnahm.

In der Geschichte der Gruppe 47 bildet Peter Rühmkorf eher eine Randerscheinung. Obwohl er derselben Generation angehört wie Bachmann, Grass, Walser oder Enzensberger, die schon in der ersten Hälfte der fünfziger Jahre teilnahmen, wurde er erst ab 1960 eingeladen. In diesem und im Folgejahr setzte er sich auf den 'elektrischen Stuhl' und unterzog sich damit einem Vorgang, der in den Worten Hans Werner Richters 'über Erfolg und Mißerfolg, über Aufstieg und Niederlage' entschied.[1] Nach 1961 nahm Rühmkorf zwar regelmäßig bis 1967 an den Treffen teil, begab sich jedoch nicht mehr auf diesen 'Prüfstand der deutschen Gegenwartsliteratur' (Kröll, S.56). Interessant ist Rühmkorf mit Bezug auf die Gruppe 47 vor allem aufgrund der Rezeption seiner Lesungen, da er 1960 offensichtlich starken Beifall fand, 1961 jedoch auf vernichtende Kritik stieß, wie aus einem Bericht des Gruppe-47-Veteranen Wolfdietrich Schnurre zur 1961er Tagung in Göhrde hervorgeht:

> Helmut Heißenbüttel las knappatmige lyrische Prosa [...], artifizielle Fingerübungen, kaum mehr, wenn die Kritik sich hier auch als überraschend wohlgesonnen erwies.

> Schon bei Peter Rühmkorf begannen die Rauchschwaden im sonnedurchfluteten Vorleseraum sich jedoch erheblich zusammenzuziehen, und gleich auch zeigte die sonst leidlich intakte Kritik sich von ihrer ungünstigeren Seite. Warf sie Rühmkorf doch vor, Rühmkorf geblieben zu sein. Er hatte Gedichte gelesen, traurige, schnodderige, ein Stiefsohn Villons, nur sehr viel verletzbarer noch. Vorm Jahr hätte er um ein Haar für solche Verse den Preis der Gruppe 47 bekommen; diesmal wollte man Rühmkorf gern anders.[2]

Der radikale Umschwung in der Rezeption von Rühmkorfs Gedichten legt nahe, daß nicht nur die von der Metapher des 'Prüfstands' implizierte literarische Qualität der Texte — wie auch immer definiert — ausschlaggebend war. Aus den Teilnehmerberichten über die Tagungen geht eine Fülle von weiteren Faktoren hervor, die bei der Bewertung ins Spiel kamen: sie reichen vom Tagungskontext bis hin zu den spezifischen Merkmalen des Gelesenen. Die Rezeption von Rühmkorfs Lesungen wirft so ein Schlaglicht auf die Problematik der Beurteilung unbekannter Texte auf der Basis eines einmaligen Vorlesens, wobei die Unzulänglichkeit der 'Stegreifkritik' schon früh zu den 'Lieblingsthemen der Kritik an der Gruppe 47' gehörte.[3] Gerade die Lesungen mit der anschließenden spontanen Kritik verkörperten jedoch als zentrales Ereignis der Tagungen die Rolle einer Gruppe, die schon in den frühen fünfziger Jahren mit Metaphern von der 'Werkstatt' über den 'Prüfstand' bis hin zur 'Literaturmesse' oder 'Börse' bezeichnet wurde — Metaphern, die nicht zufällig den gesamten Produktions- und Vermarktungsprozeß abdecken.[4]

Rühmkorf las beide Male unveröffentlichte Gedichte, die dann 1962 als Teil der Gedichtsammlung *Kunststücke* erschienen.[5] Schnurres Bericht läßt sich entnehmen, daß auf der 1961er Tagung Rühmkorfs Gedichte dem Erwartungshorizont der sich äußernden Tagungsteilnehmer nicht entsprachen: im Gegensatz zur ersten Lesung verstieß er bei der zweiten offenbar gegen die unausgesprochene Forderung nach 'Innovation', die sich bei weiteren Lesungen als 'Entwicklung' darzustellen hatte.[6] Diese Erwartungshaltung wird vor allem den professionellen Kritikern zugeschrieben, die im Laufe der fünfziger Jahre zunehmend mit ihren eloquenten, literaturkritisch versierten Beiträgen die Diskussion dominierten, während die Kollegen des lesenden Autors nur als Zuhörer teilnahmen.[7] Wenn auch Richter bei der 1961er Tagung in Göhrde 'das Massenmeeting und die Fachkritik' abbauen und 'zur Autorenkritik' zurückkehren wollte,[8] waren die Stammkritiker trotz einer Kontroverse um die Einladung von Marcel Reich-Ranicki wie immer präsent.[9] Dem Bericht von Schnurre darf man wahrscheinlich entnehmen, daß er selbst seine vom vorherrschenden Urteil abweichende Meinung zu den Lesungen Heißenbüttels und Rühmkorfs nicht in die Diskussion einbrachte.

Bei der Beurteilung der gelesenen Texte spielte nicht nur eine autorbezogene Erwartungshaltung mit, sondern auch ein die jeweilige Tagung prägender inhaltlicher Trend. So konstatiert Fritz Raddatz beispielsweise für die 1966 abgehaltene Tagung eine plötzlich zunehmende Politisierung nicht nur der Texte, sondern auch ihrer Beurteilung:

> Das war die Überraschung der Tagung: Eine Repolitisierung der Texte, eine Ermüdung, gar Irritiertheit auch der Kritik gegenüber dem bloßen Sprachexperiment. [...] Wenn vor zwei Jahren die sogenannte Avantgarde triumphiert hatte und vor einem Jahr fast eine Sex-Welle anzurollen schien, war auf der diesjährigen Tagung deutlich ein Trend zum Konkreten, nicht unbedingt Realistischen, aber doch die Realitäten interpretierenden Text zu spüren.[10]

Dies deutet darauf hin, daß die Bewertungskriterien wenig mit etwaigen zeitlos objektiven Qualitätsnormen zu tun hatten, sondern eher allgemeine Tendenzen der Zeit widerspiegelten. Wenn Schnurre zufolge Heißenbüttels Sprachexperimente bei der 1961er Tagung auf Wohlwollen stießen,[11] so geht dies mit einer allgemeinen Dominanz politisch neutraler Texte während der fünfziger Jahre konform: Raddatz konstatiert in seiner Einleitung zu der von Hans Werner Richter vorgenommenen und als 'Querschnitt' intendierten Textauswahl für den *Almanach der Gruppe 47*, daß einzig Enzensberger mit seinem 1959 gelesenen Gedicht 'schaum' sowie Heinz von Cramer mit einem 1961 gelesenen Romankapitel 'politisch engagiert genannt werden dürfen'.[12] Obwohl Richter 1961 'angesichts der "Mauer"' 'wieder eine auch politisch engagierte Gruppe haben' will, erwartet er dieses Engagement offenbar weniger in den Lesungen aus literarischen Texten als in einer 'Reihe von Besprechungen' während der Tagung.[13] Möglicherweise waren auch gerade auf dieser in einer gespannten Situation statt-findenden Tagung politisch neutrale Texte willkommen, um den Freiraum für die Auseinandersetzung um die politische Identität der Gruppe zu schaffen.

Wie sehr auch die Vorlesesituation an sich die Beurteilung der Texte bestimmte, geht aus einer Reihe von Teilnehmerberichten hervor (s. Kröll, S.40-83, Arnold, S.180-84). In einer Zeit, wo die Rezeption literarischer Texte fast ausschließlich über das Auge stattfindet, war die Praxis des Vorlesens und der sofortigen Diskussion über das Gehörte außergewöhnlich; es erinnert dies eher an das 18. Jahrhundert mit seinen Gruppierungen gleichgesinnter Dichter (z.B. 'Bremer Beiträger' und 'Göttinger Hain'), literarischen Gesellschaften und Lesezirkeln. Es bietet sich jedoch auch der Vergleich mit den 'ästhetischen Tees' in den frühen Jahrzehnten des 20. Jahrhunderts an: ein Teilnehmer an der Herbsttagung von 1947 in Herrlingen benutzt diesen Vergleich, um die Bedeutung der Kritik hervorzuheben, welche die Tagungen der Gruppe 47 grundlegend von jenen Zusammenkünften mit ihrer Aura 'fromm-ästhetischer Schwelgerei' unterschied.[14]

Die zentrale Rolle der Lesungen mit anschließender Kritik verhalf zweifelsohne der Gruppe 47 zu ihrer hervorragenden Bedeutung in der Geschichte der deutschen Nachkriegsliteratur. Immer wieder wird der 'Werkstatt'-Charakter der Tagungen betont, wodurch den teilnehmenden Autoren die seltene Möglichkeit zu kollegialem Austausch über ihr Werk gegeben war. Wenn auch auf den ersten Tagungen mit ihrem kleinen Teilnehmerkreis 'das Gefühl einer ihnen allen gemeinsam auferlegten Verpflichtung' gegenüber der 'Wahrheit' und der 'Sprache' die Arbeit am Text in den Vordergrund rückte (Minssen, S.29), ist schon dort diese Metapher nur bedingt anwendbar. Treffender erscheint das Bild des 'Prüfstands', denn gefertigt wurde auf den Tagungen allenfalls die Kritik, nicht das Gelesene, und von Anfang an stand die Beurteilung im Vordergrund, wie es der Ausschluß des Vorlesenden von der Diskussion, das Bild vom 'elektrischen Stuhl' bzw. 'Hinrichtungsstuhl' und die Fülle von Jagd- und Prüfungsmetaphern für die Kritik sowie ab 1950 die Verleihung eines Preises verdeutlichen.[15] Es war daher nur folgerichtig, wenn sich zunehmend eine Spaltung in vorlesende Autoren und urteilende Kritiker herausbildete,[16] wobei letztere es ihrem professionellen Ruf schuldig waren, sich durch Soforturteile zu profilieren — auch wenn sie sich wie Joachim Kaiser der 'Inkompetenz der spontanen Kritik' bewußt waren.[17] So sah sich die Gruppe als zuständige Instanz für die Ausmusterung ungeeigneter Anwärter auf die Schrift-stellerlaufbahn, wie der Stammkritiker Hans Schwab-Felisch an einem Beispiel erläutert: 'Der Bärtige fiel durch, die

Kritik war kurz und vernichtend. Stracks machte der junge Mann kehrt und fuhr zurück gen Norden. [...] Welch ein Verdienst der Gruppe!'[18] Vor allem aber erfüllten die Tagungen die Funktion, den Autoren durch medien-wirksame Darstellung ihrer Texte Veröffentlichungs-möglichkeiten aufzutun. Literatur wurde hier im Zeitalter der Reproduzierbarkeit zum einmaligen Ereignis, und sie konnte eine sofortige Resonanz erzielen, die durch die teilnehmenden Kritiker, Verleger und Vertreter des Rundfunks über den Kreis der 'live' Teilnehmenden hinausgetragen wurde: 'Es kam vor, daß eine gute Erzählung bereits wenige Stunden, nachdem sie gelesen worden war, an drei Sendestationen verkauft war.'[19] Wenn die Rolle der 'Manager' und der Medien häufig als Verfallserscheinung gewertet wird, die bedauerlicherweise den ursprünglichen spontanen Werkstatt-Charakter zerstörte, so verdrängt dies eine der Hauptfunktionen schon der ersten Tagung: es ging 1947 am Bannwaldsee vorrangig um die Sammlung von Manuskripten für eine von Richter geplante neue Publikation und die Förderung der jungen Literatur (s. Kröll, S.41). Daß bereits Anfang der fünfziger Jahre die Bilder von einer 'Börse' bzw. 'Messe' auftauchen, läßt nicht auf einen Prozeß des 'Abgleitens' in die Ökonomisierung schließen,[20] sondern darauf, daß der materielle Aspekt der Förderung von Anfang an zu den Grundfunktionen der Gruppe 47 gehörte und die Gruppe am Aufschwung des bundesdeutschen Verlags- und Medienwesens teilhatte.

Die Auswirkung der Vorlesesituation auf die Beurteilung spezifischer Texte wird aus einer Reihe von Beispielen deutlich. So gilt als 'wohl berühmtestes Fehlurteil' (Kröll, S.166) die ablehnende Reaktion auf die Lesung von Paul Celan 1952 in Niendorf, die allgemein darauf zurückgeführt wird, daß das Kollektiv 'von der hochpathetischen Art des Celanschen Gedichtvortrags irritiert wurde; äußere Gründe also nahmen der Gruppe den Blick für die außerordentliche Qualität der Gedichte Celans'.[21] Aber auch Johnsons *Das dritte Buch über Achim* fiel als 'vollkommen unverständlich' durch.[22] Der Erfolg anderer Texte beruhte demgegenüber nicht zuletzt darauf, 'daß man überzeugend lesen konnte'.[23] Hörfehler waren vermutlich nicht selten; dokumentiert ist die Verkehrung des Bachmann-Titels 'Liebe: dunkler Erdteil' in 'Lieber dunkler Erdteil', was eine verfehlte Diskussion über die Exotik des Gedichts anregte.[24] Daß der Zwang zum 'spontanen Kritisieren' auch die Urteilskriterien beeinflußte, konstatiert Martin Walser: 'eingebunden war diese sprachliche, diese stilistische Diskussion in einen sehr beschränkten, primitiven, realistischen Vorschriftenhorizont';[25] Fritz Raddatz bemängelt, 'die "Kritiker" beschränkten sich mehr oder minder auf eine Wiedergabe ihrer Eindrücke, unterzogen sich nicht der Mühe einer gründlichen Analyse'.[26] Auch die Gattung hatte eine nicht zu unterschätzende Auswirkung auf den auditiven Erfolg:

> Lyrik hat zwar den Vorteil, in der Regel nicht aus einem Werk extrahieren zu müssen, doch inhärieren ihr spezielle Probleme, die mit dem mündlichen Vortrag und mit der der Lyrik eigenen Dichte verknüpft sind. Generell paßt sich das kurze, abgeschlossene Prosa-Stück der Lesung-Kritik-Situation *funktional* am ehesten ein. (Kröll, S.68)

Das Drama führte aus diesem Grund ein Aschenbrödeldasein, während das Hörspiel florierte.[27] Über die Gattung hinaus werden jedoch auch die spezifischen Eigenschaften der gelesenen Texte die Beurteilung beeinflußt haben: je komplexer der semantische Gehalt sowie Faktoren wie Syntax, rhythmische Struktur und intertextuelle Beziehungen, desto unzuverlässiger dürfte eine sofortige Beurteilung nach rein auditiver Rezeption gewesen sein. Erfahrene Teilnehmer richteten sich offenbar auf die besonderen Bedingungen der Vorlesesituation ein: es wird berichtet, daß sich zunehmend die Tendenz durchsetzte, schon Publiziertes vorzutragen;[28] man wählte 'Paradestücke' aus, die sich auch für die Vorlesesituation eigneten, und bot dem Zuhörer 'statt Schwarzbrot eine Rosine' an (S. Kröll, S.70, S.220f.). Unerfahrene Teilnehmer waren dabei natürlich strategisch im Nachteil.

Ich möchte diese Gesichtspunkte nun mit Bezug auf Texte beleuchten, die Rühmkorf auf den Tagungen las. Es soll dabei nicht darum gehen, definitive Rückschlüsse auf die tatsächlich zum Tragen gekommenen Bewertungskriterien zu ziehen, zumal die Dokumentation zu den gelesenen Texten unvollständig ist und insgesamt wenig detaillierte Dokumentation zu den auf Tagungen geäußerten Meinungen vorliegt; auch bedürfte es einer viel systematischeren Untersuchung der Auswirkung auditiver Rezeption auf den Beurteilungsprozeß bei den Tagungen, um verläßliche Ergebnisse zu erzielen. Ziel ist hier vielmehr ein eher spekulativer Vergleich von Gedichten eines einzigen Autors, die aufgrund des mündlichen Vortrags völlig unterschiedlich beurteilt wurden. Im Zentrum stehen dabei zwei 1960 gelesene Gedichte und ein Gedicht, das Rühmkorf 1961 vortrug.

Die 1960 vorgetragenen Gedichte sind in dem 1962 von Hans Werner Richter herausgegebenen *Almanach der Gruppe 47* abgedruckt (S.359-64). Ob Rühmkorf außer den acht dort wiedergegebenen Gedichten noch weitere vorlas, ist nicht klar; auf jeden Fall jedoch sind sie Teil eines von Richter ausgewählten 'Querschnitts' des Gelesenen.[29] Auffällig ist, daß all diese Gedichte als 'Lied' betitelt sind, mit Ausnahme des Gedichts 'Auf eine Weise des Joseph Freiherrn von Eichendorff', welches allerdings als 'Variation' auf Eichendorffs Lied 'In einem kühlen Grunde' ebenfalls diesem Genre angehört.[30] Entsprechend ist für diese Gedichte die Liedform charakteristisch: jeweils fünf oder sechs regelmäßige kurze Strophen, mit einer Ausnahme Vierzeiler; regelmäßige Jamben oder Trochäen, nur ab und zu durch eine Unregelmäßigkeit variiert; regelmäßiger Reim. Die vertraute, eingängige Form vermittelt gleich beim ersten Hören einen Eindruck leichter Verständlichkeit, welcher auch durch das zumeist einfache Vokabular und die unkomplizierten Satzstrukturen gestützt wird. Dies sei zunächst anhand des 'Zeitvertu-Lieds' erörtert:

Das Zeitvertu-Lied

Sommer, und die Schwalbe piepste
Monde zwischen Dach und Tür —
Dumm wie Dotter meine Liebste,
weich wie Melde unter mir.

Der an unsern Ohren zerrte,
Südwind, legt die Freuden bloß;
auf der schwankenden, der Erde,
halt ich an um deinen Schoß.

Komm als Luft- und Feuerbarde,
sing und zehr vom Wankelmut.
Zwielicht steckt mir die Kokarde
Hermes' an den Gockelhut.

Ehe, ehe die somali-
braune Nacht die Sterne bleckt,
schmelze, was mir als moralisches Gesetz im Halse steckt.

> Zwischen zween Rosenzitzen
>
> stoß ich auf nach Seligkeit.
>
> Und vertu, um zu besitzen,
>
> meine mir gesetzte Zeit. (Rühmkorf, S.70)

Das Gedicht rekurriert unterhaltsam auf die Dichtung vor allem der Anakreontik und spielt schon im Titel 'Zeitvertu-Lied' mit der Tradition des *carpe diem*. Prägend ist die Naturmetaphorik mit Sommer, Vogel, Pflanze, Erde, Wind, Mond und Sternen; der Hinweis auf den Gott Hermes gibt dem Ganzen eine klassische Note. Die Liebesmetaphorik ist betont sinnlich: die Liebste, 'Dumm wie Dotter', ist 'unter' dem Ich, und es interessieren ihn einzig ihr Schoß und ihre Brüste. Aber wenn auch das Wort 'Zitze' an sich mit Bezug auf eine Frau als derb gilt, wird dieser Effekt vermieden durch die Verbindung mit dem archaischen 'zween' und den an das Hohelied erinnernden Rosen. Auch sonst spielt Rühmkorf ironisch mit Logik, Stil und Form: 'die Schwalbe piepste / Monde zwischen Dach und Tür' und der Vergleich 'Dumm wie Dotter' widersprechen logischen Erwartungen sowie tradierter Metaphorik; 'die Nacht bleckt die Sterne' verstößt zudem gegen Idiomatik; 'stoß ich auf nach Seligkeit' ist krasser Stilbruch; und die Worttrennung 'morali- / sches' am Versende bringt eine auffällige humorvolle Unregelmäßigkeit in die sonst streng eingehaltene Form. Das Gedicht wirkt unmittelbar. Es erfüllt durchgehend die mit dem Titel geweckte Erwartung der Unterhaltsamkeit, enthält jedoch in der Ausführung genügend anspruchsvolle Überraschungen, um nicht zu langweilen.

Vielschichtiger ist das Gedicht 'Auf eine Weise des Joseph Freiherrn von Eichendorff', in dem Rühmkorf mit den für seine Lyrik typischen Mitteln der Parodie arbeitet, so daß das Verständnis erst durch den intertextuellen Vergleich zustandekommt.[31] Allerdings ist Eichendorffs 'In einem kühlen Grunde' so bekannt und durch die eingängige Form so gemütlich vertraut, daß schon beim erstmaligen Hören die Folie präsent ist, auch wenn nicht unbedingt sämtliche Allusionen in der Vorlesesituation sofort verständlich sind. Zudem ist durch die schon fast klischeehafte Popularität des Eichendorffschen Liedes ein sofortiger allgemeiner romantischer Assoziationskontext gegeben, den Rühmkorfs Parodie im Gedicht wiederholt explizit miteinbezieht.

Auf eine Weise des Joseph Freiherrn von Eichendorff

In meinem Knochenkopfe
da geht ein Kollergang,
der mahlet meine Gedanken
ganz außer Zusammenhang.

Mein Kopf ist voller Romantik,
meine Liebste nicht treu —
Ich treib in den Himmelsatlantik
und lasse Stirnenspreu.

Ach, wär ich der stolze Effendi,
der Gei- und Tiger hetzt,
wenn der Mond, in statu nascendi,
seine Klinge am Himmel wetzt! —

Ein Jahoo, möcht ich lallen
lieber als intro-vertiert
mit meinen Sütterlin-Krallen
im Kopf herumgerührt.

Ich möcht am liebsten sterben
im Schimmelmonat August —
Was klirren so muntere Scherben
in meiner Bessemer-Brust?! (Rühmkorf, S.85)

Rühmkorfs Gedicht bietet — sehr verkürzt gesagt — eine Auseinandersetzung mit der romantischen Stimmungslyrik. Statt der Begründung der Melancholie des Ich durch Liebeskummer und statt der Sehnsucht des eichendorffschen Ich nach einem mittelalterlichen Sängerleben und abenteuerlichen Heldendasein stehen bei Rühmkorf 'Scherben' der romantischen Tradition, bezeichnet durch das umgangssprachlich abwertende 'Mein Kopf ist voller Romantik'. Das Gedicht des Ich wird reflektiert als von der Realität abgehobene 'Stirnenspreu'. Die eichendorffsche Sehnsucht ist ironisiert durch Anspielungen auf Karl Mays Effendi in *Unter Geiern* und die tierischen Menschen (Jahoos genannt) in Swifts *Gullivers Reisen* sowie in der durch Stilmischung parodierenden Mondmetapher. Der Todeswunsch bei Eichendorff wird parodiert durch die Verkehrung des Klischees

'Wonnemonat Mai' in den 'Schimmelmonat August' und durch die einen technischen Läuterungsprozeß bezeichnende Vokabel 'Bessemer', die wie die 'Kollergang'-Maschine in der ersten Strophe aus dem unpoetischen Bereich der Fachsprache entlehnt ist.

Es soll hier keine erschöpfende Interpretation versucht werden. Vielmehr geht es darum zu zeigen, daß die Bekanntheit des parodierten Textes sowie die eingängige, bekannte Form beider Gedichte den Eindruck des Verständnisses vermitteln, auch wenn sich viele Nuancen beim ersten Hören noch nicht erschließen. Gerade die Möglichkeit einer 'leichten, bloß kulinarischen Rezeption', die Arnold bei Rühmkorf im Vergleich zu Bobrowski bemängelt (S.147), scheint auf jener Tagung eine positive Aufnahme gefördert zu haben.

Für Rühmkorf selbst trug seine erfolgreiche Lesung zu einer insgesamt sehr positiven Beurteilung der Tagung in Aschaffenburg und darüber hinaus des Bewertungsvorgangs allgemein bei, die er in seinem Beitrag 'Zum ersten Mal bei der Gruppe 47' im *Almanach der Gruppe 47* veröffentlichte (S.424-27). Das 'Risiko' des elektrischen Stuhls findet er gerade für nicht-etablierte Autoren wenig abschreckend, da diese nichts zu verlieren hätten. Gar für 'mustergültig' erklärt er, daß im Anschluß an die Lesungen über 'das Können, die handwerkliche Akkuratesse [...,das] Nachprüfbare, technisch Verbindliche debattiert' wurde (S.425). Obwohl gerade diese Tagung vielen älteren Mitgliedern als 'Massenmeeting' erschien,[32] begrüßt Rühmkorf den Werkstatt-Charakter der Diskussion.

Als Rühmkorf im folgenden Jahr wieder Gedichte vorlas, verlief die Reaktion entgegengesetzt. Nur zwei der Gedichte sind dokumentiert[33] — beide schätzte Rühmkorf selbst offenbar besonders, da er sie in dem autobiographischen Band *Die Jahre die Ihr kennt* wiedergibt.[34] Das 'Lied' 'Aussicht auf Wandlung' (Rühmkorf, S.53f.) unterscheidet sich inhaltlich und stilistisch nicht wesentlich von den 1960 gelesenen Gedichten und mag so zu dem Urteil beigetragen haben, daß Rühmkorf der alte geblieben sei. Der andere dokumentierte Text ist die 'Variation auf "Gesang des Deutschen" von Friedrich Hölderlin'. Mit siebzehn Strophen ist es ein viel längeres Gedicht als die 'Lieder', und die Unterschiede auch zur Eichendorff-Variation könnten kaum größer sein. Hölderlins Ode dürfte zwar belesenen Dichtern und Kritikern nicht unbekannt sein, aber es ist kaum anzunehmen, daß das komplexe fünfzehnstrophige Gedicht auf eine Weise präsent ist, wie dies beim Eichendorff-Lied der Fall ist. Vor allem aber liegt Hölderlins Ode aufgrund der klassischen Form — es sind alkäische Strophen — klanglich-rhythmisch nicht so im Ohr wie das gereimte, jambische Eichendorff-Lied. Der gehobene Stil mit ungewöhnlichem Vokabular, komplizierter Syntax sowie klassischen Allusionen erschweren das sofortige Verständnis. Insgesamt steht das Gedicht in einer Tradition erhabener Lyrik für gebildete Kenner, die schon bei ihrer Einführung in die deutsche Dichtung durch Klopstock der 'Dunkelheit' bezichtigt wurde. Zitiert sei hier nur der Anfang:

Gesang des Deutschen

O heilig Herz der Völker, o Vaterland!
Allduldend, gleich der schweigenden Mutter Erd,
Und allverkannt, wenn schon aus deiner
Tiefe die Fremden ihr Bestes haben!

Sie erndten den Gedanken, den Geist von dir,
Sie pflüken gern die Traube, doch höhnen sie
Dich, ungestalte Rebe! daß du
Schwankend den Boden und wild umirrest.

Du Land des hohen ernsteren Genius!
Du Land der Liebe! bin ich der deine schon,
Oft zürnt' ich weinend, daß du immer
Blöde die eigene Seele läugnest. [...][35]

Hölderlins 'Gesang des Deutschen' ist eine Ode an das Vaterland, in der er dessen politische Machtlosigkeit beklagt, aber die geistige Rolle Deutschlands preist und dadurch die deutschen Dichter zu befeuern sucht: es ist das 'Land des hohen ernsteren Genius' und der 'Liebe' (9f.); es ist das Land der Wissenschaftler und Künstler (21-24), das zudem durch eine schöne Natur gesegnet ist (13-20). Beschwörend blickt er voraus auf die Zeit, wo der 'Genius' (37) Griechenlands in Deutschland wirksam werden wird. Rühmkorfs Kontrafaktur der Hölderlin-Ode setzt sich äußerst kritisch mit diesem Deutschlandbild auseinander, um mit dem krassen Materialismus und der Kriegshetzerei der Bundes- republik zur Zeit des Wirtschaftswunders und des Kalten Krieges besonders scharf ins Gericht zu gehen:

Variation
auf 'Gesang des Deutschen'
von Friedrich Hölderlin

Wie der Phönix aus den Scherben, oh Vaterland,
Edelstahl platzt in den Nähten, Fette erholt,
Farben bei lebhaftem Angebot Aufgalopp, Kursgewinn,
Hanomag, hundertprozentige Rheinstahltochter...

also erhobest du dich, verlorengegebener
gräulich geviertelter Aar, doch bald auf der Höhe schon
deines alten Gewichts, und, ei, den Tauben gleich
an Kropf und Krallen!

Du Land, chromblinzelnd, wo man die Meinung verzieht
bei stillem Anteil, bin ich der deine schon?
Sieh, auch ich bin fix in der Lüge,
freundlich blinket mein Damaszenergebiß. [...]
(Rühmkorf, S.79)

Das von Rühmkorf dargestellte Deutschland bildet einen diametralen
Gegensatz zu Hölderlins: das geistige Deutschland ist gekennzeichnet
durch Lüge und Käuflichkeit; die Dichter liefern kein göttlich
inspiriertes Werk, sondern ein opportunistisches 'Gemythe' (45); und
statt der Beschwörung einer Wiederkunft der vergangenen goldenen
Zivilisation Griechenlands findet sich hier eine Invektive gegen die allzu
schnelle Wiederkehr der deutschen Wirtschaftsmacht mit ihren in den
Faschismus verwickelten Unternehmen (Phönix-Rheinrohr AG,
Rheinstahl-Hanomag, IG Farben). Getragen wird dieses
entgegengesetzte Argument durch eine 'Variation' der Form, des Stils
und der Metaphorik der Hölderlin-Ode, was hier nur anhand der ersten
drei Strophen erläutert werden soll. Rühmkorf benutzt zwar keine
alkäischen Strophen, aber mit ihrer erheblichen Länge und dem
unregelmäßigen Wechsel zwischen alternierenden und daktylischen
Sequenzen umspielen seine freien Verse klassische Versformen. Häufig
finden sich Anklänge an das alkäische Versmaß (z.B. 'hundertprozentige
Rheinstahltochter' als Schlußvers der alkäischen Strophe) oder an
charakteristische Hexameter- oder Pentameterkadenzen (z.B. 'fix in der
Lüge', 'Damaszenergebiß'), aber es stellt sich keinerlei rhythmisch
regelmäßige Bewegung ein. Der Stil ist vorwiegend gehoben, mit

ungewöhnlichen Wortstellungen (das Subjekt des ersten Satzes, 'du', erscheint erst in der zweiten Strophe), poetischen Verbformen mit eingefügtem 'e' ('erhobest', 'blinket') und poetischen Vokabeln ('Aar'), aber es finden sich häufige Stilbrüche: so wird gleich zu Anfang das erhabene Pathos des Hölderlin-Zitats 'oh Vaterland' gebrochen durch Vokabeln aus dem Wirtschaftsjargon ('Kursgewinn', 'hundertprozentige Rheinstahltochter' usw.) und eine abgewandelte umgangssprachliche Redewendung ('platzt in den Nähten'). Ein dichtes Netz von Metaphern besonders aus den Bereichen Geld und Essen trägt die Auseinandersetzung mit Hölderlins Ode bis ins einzelne Wort. Wo Hölderlin Deutschlands geistige Früchte als 'Traube' einer 'ungestalten Rebe' darstellt und später die Nachtigall (18) besingt, steht bei Rühmkorf ein 'gräulich geviertelter Aar', den er mit dem Friedenssymbol 'Taube' vergleicht, um dann jedoch den Vergleich auf 'Kropf und Krallen' zu beschränken — Gefräßigkeit und Gewalt. Statt der von Hölderlin besungenen 'Ströme' (17) finden wir das Unternehmen 'Rheinstahl' mit den militaristischen Konnotationen der Stahlindustrie; statt der 'Mutter Erd' das Unternehmen 'Rheinstahltochter'; statt des 'hohen ernsten Genius' den mit der Autoindustrie assoziierten oberflächlichen Glanz von 'Chrom'; und statt 'Liebe' den finanziellen 'Anteil'. Wie in der Hölderlin-Ode profiliert sich das dichtende Ich bei Rühmkorf durch pathetische Apostrophen an das personifizierte Vaterland, aber während das Ich bei Hölderlin sich so als rechtschaffen empfindsames, von Tränen und Zorn gerührtes Subjekt zu erkennen gibt, ist das Ich bei Rühmkorf 'fix in der Lüge'; die zitierten Worte 'bin ich der deine schon' verkehrt er in eine Frage, die eine opportunistische Annahme der materialistischen Identität des Vaterlandes impliziert. Das gesamte Gedicht ist eine Auseinandersetzung mit dem 'Gesang des Deutschen' und darüber hinaus mit der Tradition des Deutschlandbildes und der Beziehung zwischen Deutschland und seinen Dichtern.

Es wird in Rühmkorfs Gedicht wie in Enzensbergers 'schaum' sowie in 'landessprache' (beide 1960 veröffentlicht[36]) eine Abrechnung mit der Bundesrepublik geliefert. Wie Enzensberger in 'landessprache' verquickt Rühmkorf Essens- und Geldmetaphern, um die Wohlstandsgesellschaft anzuprangern; beide verweisen auf romantische Märchen, zitieren aus Bibel und Literatur und benutzen umgangssprachliche Redewendungen bzw. Klischees. Während jedoch auch Enzensberger mit der Apostrophe 'deutschland, mein land, unheilig herz der völker' (S.12) auf Hölderlins 'Gesang des Deutschen' verweist, ist es dort ein Zitat unter vielen. Bei Rühmkorf will dagegen das ältere Gedicht durchgehend als Folie mitgedacht sein, wodurch die Geschichtlichkeit des Deutschlandbegriffs und der deutschen Identität in den Vordergrund rückt und das Ich stärker ironisiert wird. Wenn Rühmkorfs Gedicht auch zunächst als Wiederholung des schon von Enzensberger Geleisteten erscheint und möglicherweise nicht zuletzt dadurch die Zuhörer irritierte,[37] erschließt sich bei gründlicherer Rezeption die Bedeutung der Folie des Hölderlin-Gedichts für die Aussage der 'Variation'.

In Rühmkorfs Band *Kunststücke* von 1962 findet sich ein Aufsatz zu deutschen Mondgedichten mit dem Untertitel 'Anleitung zum Widerspruch'.[38] Eine 'Anleitung zum Widerspruch' ist auch diese Replik auf Hölderlins Deutschlandgedicht, aber so wirken kann sie nur in einem allmählichen Prozeß der Auseinandersetzung mit dem Dialog zwischen These und Antithese. Keinesfalls kann eine einmalige Rezeption über das Gehör dem Rezipienten die 'Fülle von Folien und bereits bebilderten Papieren' (S.91) vor Augen führen, mit denen Rühmkorfs modernes Deutschland-Gedicht korrespondiert. Die Annahme, man könne über Dichtung dieser Art im Schnellverfahren ein Urteil fällen, zeugt zum einen von Selbstüberschätzung auf Seiten der Kritiker, zum anderen vielleicht auch von einem schematischen Literaturbegriff, der von realistischen Schreibweisen ausgeht. Rühmkorfs Gedicht ist für einen solchen Urteilsprozeß besonders ungeeignet: der Dialog mit der intertextuellen Folie erhöht im Vergleich beispielsweise zu Enzensbergers 'schaum' die Komplexität des Textes und erschwert das Verständnis; im Gegensatz zu Heißenbüttels 'Sprachspielen'[39] jedoch verlangt sein Gedicht bei aller 'Dunkelheit' eine rationale Auseinandersetzung mit dem semantischen Gehalt; und im Gegensatz zu Bobrowski ist die erhabene Diktion und Form nicht Mittel zur Beschwörung der Vergangenheit, um so die gegenwärtige Schuld zur Sprache zu bringen, sondern ein Mittel, durch komplexe ironische Brechungen eine Distanz zu schaffen, welche die komplexe kritische Auseinandersetzung mit Vergangenheit und Gegenwart ermöglicht. Gerade für einen solchen Text trifft am ehesten zu, was Rühmkorf schon hinsichtlich der 1960er Tagung als Vorbehalt äußert: 'Wohl zu gering geachtet das Komplizierte, Subtile, nicht auf den ersten Blick

Überschaubare; zu früh gezückt die Schablonen, zu ungern kritische Klischees im Stich gelassen'.[40]

Daß die Aburteilung seiner Gedichte 1961 Rühmkorf davon abhielt, in den folgenden Jahren mit Lesungen zu den Tagungen beizutragen, zeigt die folgende Stelle aus dem autobiographischen Kompendium *Die Jahre die Ihr kennt*:

> Ich selbst debütierte vor diesem Forum im November 1960 mit Oden und Liedern erster Wahl (schwer von sich selbst zu sprechen, ohne privat zu werden). Die durchweg freundliche Resonanz beflügelte mich dann im folgenden Jahr, noch einmal mit lyrischen Arbeiten vorstellig zu werden, traf aber auf eine Großekoalition von Nörgelingen, die keinen Neuling über die eigene Hutschnur erhöhen wollten, dafür aber Grassens Schöneberger Lutschbonbons[41] mit den schillerndsten Gütebanderolen versahen. Hatte tagwendend klassische Alpträume. Ließ Grass und der Komplettierung halber die ganze Ignorantenfronde in die Grube fahren, stand tränennaß vor frisch gefüllten Reihengräbern und verschaffte mir so das Glücksgefühl einer Massenbeerdigung nebst dem Luxus der Trauerkundgebung. Nahm fernerhin zwar noch an vielen Tagungen teil — indes das Mißtrauen in die Bewertungskriterien blieb. [...] Las seit 1961 nie wieder vor diesem Gremium. (*Die Jahre*, S.134f.)

Angesichts der ablehnenden Reaktion auf seine Dichtung ist nun von einem Werkstatt-Charakter der Diskussion nicht mehr die Rede. 1948 hatte Heinz Friedrich die ausschließlich konstruktive Wirkung der Kritik betont: 'Die Kritik ist fördernd, nicht zersetzend. Selbst an mißglückten Arbeiten wird sie so geübt, daß der Autor wieder auf den Weg findet, daß er den Anschluß behält und nicht in Ressentiments verfällt'.[42] Daß dies schon auf den frühen Tagungen nicht immer die Erfahrung des kritisierten Dichters war, dürfte aus der Reaktion Paul Celans hervorgehen, der nach seiner gescheiterten Lesung 1952 trotz Einladungen 1957 und 1962 nie wieder teilnahm. Anfang der sechziger Jahre beklagt dann Richter, die Kritik werde 'allzu akademisch, offiziell, [...] und dient nicht dem Autor, sondern schadet ihm.'[43]

Inwieweit der mangelnde Erfolg bei der 'dominierenden Literaturinstitution der Bundesrepublik'[44] Rühmkorfs schriftstellerischen Erfolg beeinflußte, ist schwer auszumachen. Es ist allerdings vielleicht nicht uninteressant, daß große Preise lange auf sich warten ließen. So erhielten die anfangs genannten Schriftsteller Bachmann, Grass, Walser und Enzensberger den begehrten Büchner-

Preis in den frühen 60er Jahren bzw. im Falle von Walser 1981. Rühmkorf wurde er erst im Jahre 1993 verliehen.

In Zusammenhang mit dem Bericht von 1972 über seine eigenen Lesungen unterzieht Rühmkorf die Gruppe 47 unter Einräumung seiner 'privaten Animosität' einer grundlegenden Kritik, die für die Diskussion um die Rolle der Gruppe 47 in der deutschen Kulturlandschaft der sechziger Jahre bezeichnend ist (*Die Jahre*, S.134f.). Im Zentrum der Kritik stehen nicht nur die Literaturkritiker und die Bewertungskriterien, die Rühmkorf als 'hochformalistisch' bezeichnet, sondern die Rolle einer Gruppe, 'die Hans Werner Richter 1947 privatunternehmerisch gegründet hatte, und die 20 Jahre lang so etwas vorstellen wollte wie eine Degussa der schönen Literatur'.[45] Für Rühmkorf sind nun die Tagungen der Gruppe 47 vor allem ein Forum, wo sich Verlagslektoren 'im Geschwindkurs Überblick über sämtliche Literatenschreibtische verschaffen' können, und 'ein unnachahmlicher Alpdruck. Eine Wertpapierbörse, wo die Tageskurse gemacht wurden, die oft nur Schwindelkurse waren, obwohl sie über Jahre einen Rang stabilisieren konnten — unten oder oben' (S.135).

Aus Rühmkorfs Kritik spricht die Position eines Autors, der am eigenen Leib erfahren mußte, daß außer konstruktiver Diskussion auch voreilige Aburteilung durchaus an der Tagesordnung war. Vergleicht man seine Erfahrung der 1960er Tagung als fruchtbaren 'Prüf-, Eich-, Revisionsanlaß der Kritik',[46] mit der späteren Definition der Tagungen als 'Wertpapierbörsen', so eröffnet sich hier das Spektrum der Funktionen, welche die Gruppe 47 durchgehend als zugleich ideelle und materielle Selbsthilfeorganisation für teilnehmende Autoren erfüllte' (s. Arnold, S.165). Auch wenn es schon allein durch die steigende Teilnehmerzahl tendenziell eine Entwicklung weg vom Arbeitsgruppen-Charakter und hin zur Literaturmesse gab, so darf man annehmen, daß die Autoren auch später noch den Kontakt zu Kollegen und die werkbezogene Diskussion schätzten; umgekehrt war aber auch schon bei den frühen Tagungen die Möglichkeit der Kontaktknüpfung mit Verlegern und Sendern eine zentrale Funktion der Tagungen. Die regelmäßige Teilnahme Rühmkorfs bis 1967 dürfte sowohl ideell als auch materiell begründet sein: selbst bei der umstrittenen 1966er Tagung in Princeton war er dabei, obwohl er diese als 'tiefsten Fall' der Gruppe bewertete, 'da ihre Rolle im Restaurationsgefüge damit völlig klar wurde' (*Die Jahre*, S.135), und 1969 treibt ihn die 'nackte wirtschaftliche Existenznot' zur Annahme einer Gastdozentur in der Hochburg des Kapitalismus, Amerika (S.232).

In einem Aufsatz zu dem Thema 'Lyrik auf dem Markt' reflektiert Rühmkorf 'die realen Marktchancen' seiner 'gereimten und gebundenen Kurzwaren' und kommt zu dem Schluß, 'die Sache mit dem Markt und der Poesie' sei 'wie ein schwarzer Schimmel' (S.192). Gerade aufgrund ihres Charakters als regelmäßiger, aber 'flüchtiger, zeitlich begrenzter Ausnahmezustand im bundesdeutschen Literaturleben'[47] vermochte es die Gruppe 47, zwischen den Bedürfnissen der Autoren und jenen des literarischen Marktes zu vermitteln und das Spektrum zwischen Werkstatt und Börse abzudecken. Während der Nachkriegszeit konnte sie auf diese Weise die junge Literatur der Bundesrepublik fördern und repräsentieren, ohne sich als marktorientierte Institution festzuschreiben. Mit dem Generationswechsel in den sechziger Jahren jedoch kam eine radikale Veränderung der bundesdeutschen Gesellschaftsstruktur und damit der Zeitpunkt, wo Rühmkorfs Alp- bzw. Wunschtraum in Erfüllung ging und die Gruppe 47 'in die Grube fuhr'.

Fußnoten

[1] Hans Werner Richter, 'Kurs auf neue Erde', *Westfälische Rundschau*, 2./3.3.1963; zitiert nach: Friedhelm Kröll, *Die 'Gruppe 47'. Soziale Lage und gesellschaftliches Bewußtsein literarischer Intelligenz in der Bundesrepublik* (Stuttgart: Metzler, 1977), S.56. Weitere Hinweise auf diesen Band befinden sich im Text unter Kröll.

[2] Wolfdietrich Schnurre, 'Seismographen waren sie nicht' (1961), in: Reinhard Lettau (Hrsg.), *Die Gruppe 47. Bericht, Kritik, Polemik. Ein Handbuch* (Neuwied und Berlin: Luchterhand, 1967), S.159-63, hier S.159f.

[3] Lettau, *Handbuch*, S.11. Zu diesem Thema allgemein: Kröll, *Die 'Gruppe 47'*, bes. S.38-83; Heinz Ludwig Arnold (Hrsg.), *Die Gruppe 47. Ein kritischer Grundriß*, (weitere Hinweise unter Arnold) 2. Aufl. (München: text + kritik, 1987), bes. S.175-89; ders., '"dann kann hier jemand nicht mehr kritisieren!". Kritik in der Gruppe 47 — Unsystematischer Versuch einer Annäherung', in: Jürgen Schutte (Hrsg.), *Dichter und Richter. Die Gruppe 47 und die deutsche Nachkriegsliteratur*, *Ausstellungskatalog* (Berlin: Akademie der Künste, 1988), S.80-90.

[4] Zum Bild der 'Werkstatt' s. Herbert Hupka, 'Die Gruppe 47' (1949), in: Lettau, *Handbuch*, S.46-48, hier S.47; dieser Gedanke wurde auch in der Ausstellung *Dichter und Richter* hervorgehoben: 'auf den Podien betritt man die literarische Werkstatt' (Jürgen Schutte, 'Ein kurzer Rundblick', in: ders., *Dichter und Richter*, S.6f., hier S.7. Zum Bild des 'Prüfstands' s.o. S.163, sowie Rolf Schroers, 'Dichter unter sich' (1953), in: Lettau, *Handbuch*, S.90-93, hier S.90. Zum Bild der 'Literaturmesse' s. Th. G., 'Deutsche Literaturmesse 1952. Gruppe 47 tagte im Ostseebad Niendorf' (1952), zitiert in: Arnold, *Die Gruppe 47*, S.177. Zum Bild der 'Börse' s. Ernst Theo

Rohnert, 'Symposion junger Schriftsteller' (1951), in: Lettau, *Handbuch*, S.58-63, hier S.59.

5 Peter Rühmkorf, *Kunststücke. Fünfzig Gedichte nebst einer Anleitung zum Widerspruch* (Reinbek bei Hamburg: Rowohlt, 1962). Weitere Hinweise auf diesen Band befinden sich im Text unter Rühmkorf.

6 S. Kröll, *Die 'Gruppe 47'*, S.68, S.166f. Kröll zitiert auch weitere Beispiele für diesen Innovationsdruck.

7 S. Kröll, *Die 'Gruppe 47'*, S.40-83; Arnold, '"...dann kann..."', bes. S.87-90; Roland H. Wiegenstein, 'Die Gruppe 47 und ihre Kritiker', in: Schutte, *Dichter und Richter*, S.103-09, hier S.104.

8 Hans Werner Richter and Marcel Reich-Ranicki, 5.10.1961, zitiert in: Arnold, '"...dann kann..."', S.90.

9 S. Arnold, '"...dann kann..."', S.88-90. Von den 'fünf Großen — Walter Jens, Hans Mayer, Marcel Reich-Ranicki, Walter Höllerer, Joachim Kaiser' (Thomas von Vegesack, 'Synthese in Sicht' (1964), in: Lettau, *Handbuch* S.189-93, hier S.193) fehlte nur aufgrund des Mauerbaus Hans Mayer; auch Hans Schwab-Felisch war dabei (s. Artur Nickel, *Hans Werner Richter — Ziehvater der Gruppe 47. Eine Analyse im Spiegel ausgewählter Zeitungs- und Zeitschriftenartikel* (Stuttgart: Hans-Dieter Heinz, 1994), S.373f.

10 Fritz J. Raddatz, 'Die Bilanz von Princeton' (1966), in: Lettau, *Handbuch*, S.241-47, hier S.244.

11 Möglicherweise zeigt diese Reaktion auf Heißenbüttels Lesung eine im Vergleich zu früheren Tagungen zunehmende Toleranz gegenüber dem sprachlichen Experiment; Arnold zufolge stand Heißenbüttel 'für viele in der Gruppe jenseits der Grenzen dessen, was sie für Literatur gerade noch halten konnten. Für Experimente war die Gruppe 47 nicht zu haben' (Arnold, '"...dann kann..."', S.85).

12 Fritz J. Raddatz, 'Die ausgehaltene Realität', in: Hans Werner Richter, *Almanach der Gruppe 47* (Reinbek bei Hamburg: Rowohlt, 1962), S.52-59, hier S.59.

13 Hans Werner Richter an Roland H. Wiegenstein, 26.9.1961, in: Schutte, *Dichter und Richter*, S.257.

14 Friedrich Minssen, 'Notizen von einem Treffen junger Schriftsteller' (1948), in: Lettau, *Handbuch*, S.27-30, hier S.28f.

15 Ein Bericht über die Tagung von 1950 bezieht sich auf den 'Elektrischen Stuhl' und benutzt das Bild 'Hyänen der Kritik' (Albrecht Knaus, 'Die Meistersinger von Inzighofen' (1950), in: Lettau, *Handbuch*, S.52-57, hier S.52). Ein Teilnehmer an der Herbsttagung 1949 berichtet vom 'Hinrichtungsstuhl' und betont die Häufigkeit des Urteils 'Durchgefallen' (MM, 'Herbsttagung der Gruppe 47 am Ammersee' (1949), in: Lettau, *Handbuch*, S.48-51, hier S.49).

16 'Die Sofort-Kritik auf den Sitzungen [wurde...] von der Mitte der fünfziger Jahre an immer ausschließlicher zum Privileg und Ritual einer Sondergruppe akademisch ausgewiesener, brillierender Kritiker', Ludwig Fischer, '"Es ist zu Ende". Über den langsamen Hingang der Gruppe 47', in: Schutte, *Dichter und Richter*, S.68. S.a. Kröll, *Die 'Gruppe 47'*, S.40-83.

[17] Joachim Kaiser, 'Physiognomie einer Gruppe', in: Richter, *Almanach*, S.44-49, hier S.46.

[18] Hans Schwab-Felisch, 'Dichter auf dem "elektrischen Stuhl"' (1956), in: Lettau, *Handbuch*, S.116-20, hier S.118.

[19] Ernst Theo Rohnert, 'Symposion junger Schriftsteller' (1951), in: Lettau, *Handbuch*, S.58-63, hier S.59.

[20] So Arnold, *Die Gruppe 47*, S.177. Dies suggeriert eine vertikale Wertungsskala, derzufolge Schriftsteller und literarische Texte außer Reichweite von niederen ökonomischen Erwägungen angesiedelt sein sollten.

[21] Arnold, '"...dann kann..."', S.84; s.a. ders., *Die Gruppe 47*, S.98, sowie Kröll, *Die 'Gruppe 47'*, S.166.

[22] Helmut Heißenbüttel im Gespräch mit Heinz Ludwig Arnold, zitiert in: Arnold, '"..dann kann..."', S.88.

[23] Helmut Heißenbüttel im Gespräch mit Heinz Ludwig Arnold, ebd., S.85.

[24] S. Kaiser, 'Physiognomie einer Gruppe', S.44f., sowie Arnold, '"...dann kann..."', S.88.

[25] Martin Walser im Gespräch mit Heinz Ludwig Arnold, zitiert in: *Dichter und Richter*, S.83.

[26] Fritz J. Raddatz, 'Wiedersehen mit der Gruppe 47' (1955), in: Lettau, *Handbuch*, S.110-13, hier S.111.

[27] Lettau übersieht die Rezeptionsbedingungen, wenn er bemerkt, daß 'dem heutigen Leser die damalige Einschätzung des Hörspiels als einer literarischen Gattung etwas unbegreiflich ist' und dies als Beweis wertet, 'daß die Gruppe nicht von irgendwelchen festen Vorstellungen von Literatur ausgegangen ist' (Richter, *Almanach*, S.12f.).

[28] S. Arnold, '..."dann kann..."', S.87

[29] S. Raddatz, 'Die ausgehaltene Realität', S.59.

[30] Die Gedichte in *Kunststücke* sind unterteilt in 'Oden', 'Sonette', 'Hymnen und Gesänge', 'Lieder' und 'Variationen'.

[31] Zur Parodie bei Rühmkorf s. Herbert Uerlings, *Die Gedichte Peter Rühmkorfs. Subjektivität und Wirklichkeitserfahrung in der Lyrik* (Bonn: Bouvier, 1984), S.159-223; zu diesem Gedicht bes. S.193-212.

[32] Arnold, '"...dann kann..."', S.90.

[33] Schutte, *Dichter und Richter*, S.260; Nickel, *Hans Werner Richter*, S.375.

[34] Peter Rühmkorf, *Die Jahre die Ihr kennt. Anfälle und Erinnerungen* (Reinbek bei Hamburg: Rowohlt, 1972), S.136-38. Weitere Hinweise auf dieses Werk befinden sich im Text unter *Die Jahre*.

35 Friedrich Hölderlin, *Sämtliche Werke,* Stuttgarter Hölderlin-Ausgabe, hrsg. v. Friedrich Beißner (Stuttgart: Kohlhammer, 1943-), Bd. II/i, S.3. Ziffern nach den Zitaten beziehen sich auf den jeweiligen Vers.

36 In: Hans Magnus Enzensberger, *landessprache* (Frankfurt a. M.: Suhrkamp, 1960), S.35-47 bzw. S.5-13.

37 Den Hinweis auf die Übereinstimmungen zwischen 'landessprache' und Rühmkorfs Gedicht verdanke ich Hans Hahn. Wenn Rühmkorfs Gedicht zunächst fast als Plagiat erscheint, so liegt dies an einer ähnlichen politischen Perspektive und an der Verarbeitung gängiger Motive der zeitgenössischen Auseinandersetzung mit der Wohlstandsgesellschaft. Bezeichnenderweise zitiert Enzensberger in einer anerkennenden Rezension der *Kunststücke* aus diesem Gedicht (Hans Magnus Enzensberger, 'Peter Rühmkorf "Kunststücke"', *Der Spiegel,* 9.1.1963, zitiert nach D. Lamping u. S. Speicher (Hrsg.), *Peter Rühmkorf. Seine Lyrik im Urteil der Kritik* (Bonn: Bouvier, 1987), S.59-62, hier S.60.

38 'Abendliche Gedanken über das Schreiben von Mondgedichten. Eine Anleitung zum Widerspruch', in: Rühmkorf, *Kunststücke,* S.89-134.

39 Nickel, *Hans Werner Richter,* S.374, gibt in seiner Liste der 1961 gelesenen Texte für Heißenbüttel 'vier Sprachspiele' an.

40 Rühmkorf, 'Zum ersten Mal bei der Gruppe 47', S.427.

41 Grass las Gedichte, u.a. 'Whisky'; s. Nickel, *Hans Werner Richter,* S.374.

42 Heinz Friedrich, 'Vereinigung junger Autoren', in: Lettau, *Handbuch,* S.261-64, hier S.264.

43 Arnold, '"...dann kann..."', S.88.

44 Schutte, 'Ein kurzer Rundblick', S.6.

45 Der Name Degussa AG steht für Deutsche Gold- und Silber-Scheideanstalt.

46 Rühmkorf, 'Zum ersten Mal bei der Gruppe 47', S.427.

47 Rühmkorf, Ebd., S.425.

ROBERT GILLETT

'Nein. Es war sehr kompliziert.' The problem of Hubert Fichte.

Hubert Fichte is seen as at most a peripheral figure in the history of the Gruppe 47. Whilst it is true that he only attended on three occasions, it is nevertheless the case that his work was well received. He also contributed to one of the volumes associated with the Group in which writers expressed their support for the SPD. Moreover the themes of Fichte's work show marked parallels with the concerns of writers usually more closely associated with the Group. The relationship between the writer and language, a major concern of the *Kahlschlag* period, is just one example of this. It is therefore possible to claim that Fichte was truly part of the Group, although of a different generation from its founders.

In his reply to one of the '55 Fragebögen' sent out to authors by Joachim Leser and Georg Guntermann and collected by them in 1995 under the title *Brauchen wir eine neue Gruppe 47?*, Franz Dobler maintains 'nach bestem Wissen und Gewissen': 'Kaum ein Schriftsteller dabei, der mir heute und über die Jahre wichtig wäre mit seiner Arbeit — aber Hubert Fichte, der aber glaube ich gar nicht richtig dabei war.'[1]
   Now this question of 'richtig dabei sein' touches on issues which are at the heart of almost all discussions of the Gruppe 47. Despite its name, the Gruppe 47 was not so much an organisation as a series of events, so membership was defined literally by 'being there'. Conversely, since in the view of many the Gruppe 47 was a clique and a cabal — was indeed the dominant clique and cabal of the post-war West German *Literaturbetrieb* — a great deal depended upon being 'in with it'. Moreover, whatever its detractors and disingenuous defenders might say, the Gruppe 47 was a place where literary fashions were, if not formed, then at least registered and discussed, accordingly considerable importance attached to keeping 'up with it'. A continuing element in these discussions about the proper function of literature had to do with the question of the political efficacy of the written word, with the issue of 'commitment'. In the Germany of 1947, however, this notion of 'commitment' was far from being unequivocally positive. The whole process of denazification, after all, relied upon the possibility of

establishing different degrees of allegiance. And if it did nothing else, the controversial concept of 'Kollektivschuld' had a defining effect on all those who had, in that sense, been 'dabei'.

In this last as in several other respects, it is perfectly true to say that Fichte was 'gar nicht richtig dabei'. Of the thirty-odd meetings of the Gruppe 47, he attended three. In at least two of the more popular guides to the group, Fichte's name does not appear.[2] He did not win, and as far as I know was never in the running for, the famous prize. With one exception, which neatly coincided with the failure of the group to meet, Fichte's work has never been fashionable. The book in which he gives an account of his first reading bears a subtitle in praise of prostitution — and in it Fichte insists that he would rather sell his body than put his writing at the service of a particular programme (*Kleiner Hauptbahnhof*, p.211).[3] The date of his birth, 1935, conferring on him the 'Gnade der späten Geburt', makes him a generation younger than Richter (in his account he refers to himself as 'Nachwuchs' — *Kleiner Hauptbahnhof*, p.208) — and means that, at the time of that fateful first meeting at Bannwaldsee, he was all of twelve years old. The first of his writings to find their way into print were still some four years off.[4]

Yet just as we know why, for a German, late birth is a blessing, so Fichte in his third novel presents us with the unsettling spectacle of a 'Mischling ersten Grades' participating with enthusiasm in the rituals of the last days of the Hitler Youth ('Schneidig, die HJ!', *Grünspan*, p.78.) His second novel is, among other things, a novel of protest addressed to a protesting generation, and in it he recounts a trip to an anti-nuclear rally (*Palette*, pp.107-10). There is a passage in *Detlevs Imitationen*: "*Grünspan*" (pp.228-29) in which Fichte shows himself to be an acute commentator on the vicissitudes of literary fashion. He did win a number of prizes, sharing at least one of them with a fellow member of the group and using another to further his acquaintance with such a central figure as Ingeborg Bachmann.[5] When, in *Der kleine Hauptbahnhof* he tells of his abortive attempt to get away from Hamburg, one of the reasons he gives for his return is 'Er wollte zur Gruppe 47 gehören' (p.226). His wish seems to have been granted at least to the extent that repeated reference is made to him both in Lettau's *Handbuch*, and Arnold's *Text + Kritik Sonderband*, and Siegfried Mandel's monograph.[6] And the fact of the matter is that he was there, in Saulgau and Sigtuna and Berlin. We can prove this, because he left an account of the Saulgau meeting in *Der kleine Hauptbahnhof* (pp.203-09); because he was largely responsible for putting together the catalogue which accompanied the Sigtuna meeting[7]; and because there is a picture of the meeting in Berlin in which he appears, slightly out of focus, but unmistakable.[8] Indeed, if the 'Biographische Skizze' is to be believed, he would have been at Princeton too, if illness had not prevented him.[9] And the fact that he was not there was specifically remarked upon.[10] In other words, it is possible to claim that even when he was not there, he was nonetheless 'dabei'.

Whether he was 'richtig dabei', of course, is another matter. His account of the meeting at Saulgau is doubly second-hand — taking the form of a transcript of a telephone conversation, repeatedly interrupted by Günter Grass, in which important things are left unsaid. In it, Fichte admits both that he would not want to read the works of the authors he met there, and that he did not say very much. From the context too it is possible to deduce that Fichte had his doubts about whether there would be space in such a meeting for the frank description of gay sex. ('Marcel Reich-Ranicki und Walter Jens würden diesen Text nicht loben', *Kleiner Hauptbahnhof*, p.210.) As we have noted, the book which reprints the photograph of Fichte in Berlin makes no further mention of him. Conversely, the catalogue of the meeting in Sigtuna, which Fichte himself is credited with compiling, contains no photograph of him. Nor for that matter are there any references to him in the distichs which Bobrowski was persuaded to write for that volume.

On the other hand, perhaps because of his modesty and his reticence, each of his three appearances seems to have been a success. At the Berlin meeting he was as it were on the home territory of Walter Höllerer, the convenor of the Literarisches Colloquium and editor of *Akzente*, to both of which Fichte was a committed contributor.[11] Indeed, his contribution to the former was singled out for praise in the columns of *Konkret*.[12] In Sigtuna, moreover, Fichte was as it were on his own home territory. He must have been one of the relatively few participants at that meeting who spoke Swedish fluently. And Fredrik Benzinger, in describing the cultural significance of the event from the point of view of German-Swedish literary relations, praises Fichte especially for his extensive knowledge of Swedish literature.[13] The

reasons for this are very particular and psychologically charged: it was
to Sweden that Fichte's Jewish father fled shortly after begetting him. It
was therefore to Sweden that Fichte repaired in search of his father —
though working in an anthroposophical institution enabled him to keep
faith to a certain extent with the ideals of his mother. Hence it was in
Sweden that Fichte enacted, and later chose to set, his Oedipal
conflict.[14] And it was from Swedish literature that he derived a
significant variant of the quest motif, which, enriched with a
characteristic sexual dimension, was to dominate his writing from the
(Swedish-based) *Aufbruch nach Turku* onwards.[15] Meanwhile, back in
Saulgau (and it is important to remember that Saulgau itself provided
reasons for preventing an 'Aufbruch'), what impressed the young Fichte
was the human warmth of his fellow writers and their clever,
hardworking, sceptical, tolerant, responsible faces. And their company
extorted from Fichte the exclamation: 'Ach Dulu, es ist wirklich die
Aufklärung, der Kahlschlag' (*Kleiner Hauptbahnhof*, p.208).

Now it may seem surprising to find this last word in such a
context. Had it not been overcome over ten years previously, with the
entry upon the scene of Aichinger, Bachmann, Celan and Hildesheimer,
when the spirit of Kafka had been unleashed against Hemingway and
Dos Passos? And did not the predicates of the 'Kahlschlag' apply
uniquely and exclusively to Richter's generation, to the situation of the
German language immediately after twelve years of Nazi rule, and
hence to the predicament of the old-timers and founder members of the
Gruppe 47?

Certainly this is the view put forward by Hans Werner Richter. In
a lecture given in Stockholm in 1963, and to which I shall be returning
both because of its succinctness and because of its proximity in time to
Fichte's own association with the Group, Richter sketches out not only
the historical and literary historical situation in Germany after the war,
but also and especially the situation of the language, insisting for
example: 'Was wir 1945-46 vorfanden war eine verdorbene Sprache'.[16]
He lists three particular sources of corruption: Nazi propaganda, of
course, which meant that words like 'treu' were hard to use; what he
calls the 'pervertierte Sklavensprache' of the 'innere Emigration'; and
the language of the returning exiles, which he characterises as sterile
and out of touch. And he sees the 'Kahlschlag' as a not necessarily
conscious response to this situation, quoting Weyrauch on the subject of

the 'Verfasser der Kahlschlagprosa', who 'von vorne anfangen, ganz von vorn, bei der Addition der Teile und Teilchen der Handlung, beim ABC der Sätze und Wörter, beim Stand der Anabasis' (p.341).

Now the protagonist in Hubert Fichte's first novel *Das Waisenhaus* is likewise beginning from scratch, cutting out the letters of his ABC and arranging them into words and sentences in his 'Setzkasten'. The words he writes at first are suspect and second-hand words. He thinks he means them, and on occasion they genuinely do have a profound significance for him. But nonetheless they retain their allegiance to a system of thought and belief which is utterly alien to him. His world too is fragmented, so that in order to work out his story it is necessary to piece together a series of narrative fragments, of 'Teile und Teilchen der Handlung'. Indeed his 'Setzkasten' has a counterpart in a 'Baukasten' which exists so that he can enact the deconstruction of the world around him first into fragments and then into nothingness. And the 'Baukasten' and the 'Setzkasten' are needed as a vital means of responding to the threat inherent in the multiple corruption of language. On the one hand, there is the language of terror — the language manipulated by Alfred to cow him into submission, the language of interrogation and ideological browbeating, the language of greed and blackmail and naked power. This too of course is a second-hand language, garnered from a variety of sources which have perhaps not been understood, but whose coercive force is plainly and perfectly imitated. And then there is the language of fear, punctuated by glances round the room in case a non-conformist sentence has reached the ears of enemies, a language in which you never say yes and try your hardest not to say anything at all, a language in which tortured Poles have only themselves to blame and a Jew is a sloven and a slouch who does not wash and turns his feet inwards when he sits down. This is a well-meaning language, the language of someone you would like to love, a language adopted for the best of all possible reasons — but it is also a perverted language, in which things are said not because they are held to be true, but because they are expedient. Just occasionally, too, there is another language, a language of letters, quite different from familiar everyday speech, Gothic, angular and impenetrable, which can be rather stiff and formal, but which is also somehow instinct with all the overtones of a grandmother's love and memories of happy childhood games — a language which defines the present as an exile and elicits a longing for return. At the same time of course the whole point about this language is that it cannot be recaptured or revived.

In other words, Fichte's first novel, the opening pages of which he read at Saulgau, can be read with only slight exaggeration as an allegory of the 'Kahlschlag' situation itself. And this means that the problematics of the 'Kahlschlag' were not in any way restricted to those who were learning their trade as writers during or immediately after Nazism. On the contrary, those of the younger generation were, if anything, even more seriously affected — because they, in the same period, were learning language itself. Like the Detlev of his novel, Fichte really did learn to read and write in a minefield of conflicting tainted ideolects, which was all the more explosive for a fatherless half-Jew such as himself. One positive upshot of this is that the younger generation are even more acutely aware than their elders of the ideological permeability of language — as when, in Peter Schneider's controversial story, their representative Rolf Mengele wearily deprecates his father's terminology in the phrase 'Ach Vati, deine Substantive'.[17] Or when Fichte himself gives to the fourth volume of his study of the Afro-American religions the programmatic title *Petersilie*, recalling an incident in 1937 in which 20, 000 blacks in the Dominican Republic were murdered because of the way they pronounced the Spanish word for 'parsley' and thus linking what was perceived as a 'pervertierte Sklavensprache' with what we have nowadays irresponsibly allowed to be called 'ethnic cleansing'.

Thus even the language of the 'Kahlschläger' was more in need of cleansing than they may have liked to admit, as Urs Widmer explains;[18] and Fichte himself deftly demonstrates this by the simple expedient of quoting representative catch-words out of context (*Grünspan*, p.228). In particular, the notion that the 'Kahlschlag' situation might be a passing phase is eerily reminiscent of the whole debate about denazification and thus ideologically suspect. As Fichte himself again illustrates when in his third novel his protagonist, without thinking, mentally addresses the word 'Kazett' (sic) to someone who actually turns out to be a former inmate of a concentration camp (*Grünspan*, pp.216-18). Or when, in the index to the *Geschichte der Empfindlichkeit* he wearily registers his alarm at finding again on the walls of public urinals slogans pertaining to gassings and Jews (*Hamburg Hauptbahnhof*, p.9).

From his very first novel to his posthumously published last work, then, Hubert Fichte was engaged in the business of what Hans Werner Richter (p.343) calls 'Abklopfen', pointing up instances where language proved to be not only rotten or hollow, but also and especially an instrument of, or alibi for, violence and oppression. And if in the incident from *Der kleine Hauptbahnhof* quoted earlier he anticipates the dispraise of Jens and Reich-Ranicki, that is a not wholly ironic act of homage, showing as it does how Fichte applies the practice of the Gruppe 47 to his own work as well as other people's. Thus in an early review of a recording of Goebbels's speeches, Fichte is at pains to scotch the myth of the former propaganda minister's intelligence and rhetorical ability, and expresses the hope that the record might serve to strengthen what he calls 'den Ekel vor einer solchen Stillage'.[19] In *Das Waisenhaus* the language of pedagogy and the church are stridently attacked as being embryonically totalitarian — even while due recognition is given to the saving power of what is not said. In *Detlevs Imitationen: "Grünspan"* the same silence is seen as unremittingly complicit — while an equal and opposite inauthenticity hangs over the jangling self-justification which greets the liberation. This inauthenticity is underlined for us by being imitated, disingenuously, but to devastating effect, by a child actor *in spe* aged between eight and thirteen. And the process is intermittently extended to cover the language of novelists, historians, scientists — and even the politically correct revisionism which forbids the use of a word like 'Terrorangriff'.[20] Later on the net is widened still further to include both Luther himself, whose translation of the appalling story of the Shibboleth from the Book of Judges is presented as a precedent for the genocide in the Dominican Republic, and who is condemned in an ironic sermon as 'jugendgefährdend' (*HuL II*, pp.39-60), and the whole hegemonical incuriosity of Western logic in general, as manifested in particular in the colonialism of conquistadors and anthropologists.[21] And finally, in a last menopausal chiasmus, Fichte almost succeeds in taking back *Das Waisenhaus* itself (*Hamburg Hauptbahnhof*, pp.283-84).

For it is not enough just to put one's finger on the weak spots of other people's language — important though that is. Implicit in the 'Kahlschlag' situation is also the need to construct a new language, which must itself then become the object of unremitting 'Abklopfung'. Almost from the very beginning of the Gruppe 47 there were two opposing views of what such a language should look like. So much so, indeed, that the continuous exchange of views can be said to constitute a 'Realismusdebatte'. On the one hand there was the view that a language which defines itself against the pathos of Nazi rhetoric should be simple, straightforward and understated, eschewing all attempts at aggrandisement and obfuscation and maintaining a kind of minimalist realism. And on the other there was the need to make up for lost modernism, to throw off the shackles which had so effectively restricted the avant-garde and to explore all the formalist possibilities that National Socialist realist art had outlawed. In practice of course, the distinction is rarely as definite as that. Schnurre's 'Das Begräbnis', for instance, which is often taken as a prime example of the former tendency (Trahan, for example says of it (p.xiii) that it 'introduces the Kahlschlag-Prosa of the postwar years') is in fact marvellously mannered, while the poetry of Paul Celan, which has such clear links to the latter tradition and has been seen as the greatest German contribution to it, can also surely be seen as pushing to its extremest conclusion the aesthetics of the former.[22] And it is precisely this dialectic which is at the heart of Fichte's oeuvre.

In a review of *Die Palette* still quoted on the cover of the paperback edition, Walter Jens describes the book as 'ein Roman, der von phantastischen Einfällen, Wortspielen, syntaktischen Zaubereien und den verwegensten Raum- und Zeitsprüngen strotzt'.[23] Faced among other things with the stroboscopic impenetrability of the climax to *Detlevs Imitationen: 'Grünspan'* one commentator has chosen to characterise Fichte's technique with the epithet of 'Unbarmherzigkeit'.[24] Fichte himself writes of a 'Vergiftung durch Wörter' (*Pubertät*, p.57). Among the technical devices he employs in imitation of it are the litanies of invocation (compare *Grünspan*, pp.25-27, *Pubertät*, p.56), the 'versus rapportati' which help to conjure the figure of Pozzi (*Pubertät*, pp.47-49) and the 'contenu mental' by which Alex is defined as an avatar of Stefan George (*Pubertät*, pp.160-61). And at the heart of it lies the need for an antidote — as in the reverse codes which subvert the confirmation ritual (*Pubertät*, pp.81 and 85) or the 'Gesetz der wachsenden Glieder' which makes of *Platz der Gehenkten* a deliberately sexualised rebuff of the Koran.

What characterises all these texts is a lyrical complexity which can be assimilated to what Hans Werner Richter (p.341) calls icebergs.

For not only are many of the meanings concealed well beneath the surface; they also have continually to do with sexuality on the one hand and with politics on the other, with repression and oppression, with 'Verdrängung' and 'Unterdrückung'. In these respects, the text which, in the columns of *Konkret*, represents Fichte as the most impressive of the authors who read at Sigtuna, is already characteristic. It starts with the protagonist in bed, just covered with Gregor Samsa's bedclothes but still conscious of the need to inventorise the room. He doesn't get very far, though, because gradually, as he negotiates the transparent barrier between sleeping and waking, it becomes clear that the socially acceptable thoughts of the young capitalist about how to maximise the production of milk and dung are in fact a transposition of a situation in which his master, who is so rich that if he were a cow he would give 40 litres a day, is perceived by the protagonist as a potential rape threat who needs to be artificially inseminated, or artificially to inseminate himself, with the semen of sexually exploited seed bulls. (It is worth noting, incidentally, that this Mr Elmshäuser is also described as the temporary father of a host of 'Eingeladenen'.[25])

The story is called 'Im Tiefstall', and it clearly has two major mythological referents: Augias and Oedipus. To that extent it is of a piece with the rest of Fichte's work. For so far from eschewing what Richter (p.343) disparages as 'Mythologisierung', Fichte has deliberate recourse to several mythological systems in his bid to explore truthfully what lies beneath the surface of the psyche and the status quo. Thus the poor but important play *Ödipus auf Håknäss* of 1960/1 has an equivalent in the *Geschichte der Nanã* of twenty years later. And Xangô, the two-axed God of sexual indeterminacy, presides over Fichte's accounts of exploitation in Brazil and the Papa Doc régime in Haiti. In the earlier works, the myth of the matricide Orestes, as reworked by Goethe on the one hand and Sartre on the other, is especially important as a means by which Fichte can explore and express both his problematical sexuality and his fraught relations with his mother on the one hand and his surrogate fathers on the other. At the same time, Fichte sees in the 'Brechungen' of mythological discourse a possible magic alternative to the exploitative hegemonical logic of the Western world. Thus the — incidentally often bisexual — African deities who were smuggled into Brazil and elsewhere under the auspices of the Christian saints become important pockets of resistance to imperialism not only as a structure of power but as an attitude of mind.

To equate such an attitude of mind with imprecision and unreality, to assimilate 'Mythologisierung' with mystification, though comprehensible enough in the immediate post-Nazi period, nonetheless betrays a continued embroilment in colonialist logic. In point of fact, Fichte's use of myth is an integral part of the double project of autobiography and ethnography which marks out the whole of his work as a 'Geschichte der Empfindlichkeit'. In other words, it is an extension of realism, not a distraction from it. Thus *Ödipus auf Håknäss* and the *Geschichte der Nanā* are answered, in purely titular terms, by <u>*Versuch über die Pubertät*</u> and *Forschung<u>sbericht</u>* (my emphasis). And the volume *Xango*, with its photographic illustrations by Leonore Mau, is an outstanding example of a form which can be seen as typical of the Gruppe 47, and which Hans Werner Richter himself (p.343) calls 'Reportage'.

Now when the members of the Literarisches Colloquium were casting around for a topic on which to practise their art, one of the suggestions put forward was the subject of dying. Fichte objected to this on the grounds that this was not something of which he had any experience; but when he was nonetheless called upon to contribute, he produced a text about somebody slaughtering a chicken for the first time.[26] The idea was not original, nor is the text especially distinguished. But the important point is that Fichte, as a qualified farmer, knew what he was talking about. And the same would seem to be true of almost everything Fichte ever wrote. There is virtually nothing anywhere in his oeuvre which could be described as pure fiction. Everything is rooted in the events of his own life, or in the first-hand stories of others, often as elicited through interviews, or in the vicarious reality of texts, which, as we have seen, then make up, or are tested against, actual occurrences. And just as his vast reading covered a bewildering array of languages, so a very great deal of his time was given up to travelling. One of his very earliest publications was a two-part account of a journey through France called 'Autostop und romanische Kirchen'.[27] In the years that followed he made numerous, repeated and sometimes lengthy visits to places in Europe, Africa and both Americas, on which he then based articles for various *Merianhefte*, *Der Spiegel*, *Stern* and the *Zeitmagazin*.[28] Following a two-part description of a trip to Greece published in *Konkret*, many of these pieces were complemented by the photographs of Leonore Mau.[29] And a large number of them were also adapted for, or written at the instigation of, those radio stations which, according to Hans Werner Richter, were the first to wake up to the existence of a new German literature.[30] Thus it is not for nothing that Fichte says at one point of his alter ego that 'Jäcki fietschert sich so durch' (*Grünspan*, p.88).

Moreover, as Hartmut Böhme has pointed out, the characteristic features of the feature can be seen as the constitutive elements of Fichte's individual style.[31] The dialogue between text and image which distinguishes the form in the printed medium is as it were enacted in the relationship between Hubert Fichte and Leonore Mau.[32] The skilful deployment of voices, and the space between voices, which is the secret of radiophonic success, lies also at the heart of Fichte's ubiquitous paratacticism. The importance of research and the incorporation of the fruits of that research is reflected in Fichte's famous 'Zettelkasten' and the astonishing variety of intertexts adduced. And the art of the interview, which is so closely allied to the feature and often such an essential component of it, was one which Fichte practised continually and conscientiously all his life.

The interview as a genre operates on the interface between the self and the other. Success in it often depends upon an ability to engage with the concerns of others. And very often these concerns have an implicit or explicit political dimension. In other words, the interview is almost by definition a form of committed literature. Thus where Richter (p.337) frankly admits that the founding of the Gruppe 47 was bound up with an attempt to compensate for political ineffectiveness by literary activity, and where Urs Widmer points out that 'manche heute wohlinstallierten Schriftsteller [...] begannen als engagierte politische Journalisten', Fichte not only gives his name to the protest in *Konkret* against the Vietnam War and in Richter's *Plädoyer für eine neue Regierung* puts in an ambivalent word for the appointment of Carl Friedrich von Weizsäcker as 'Atomminister' — he also conducts interviews with Salvador Allende, Forbes Burnham, Julius Nyerere and Leopold Sedar Senghor, among others.[33]

Indeed, even where the interviewee is not a professional politician, the discussions often touch on political issues. The conversation with Jean Genet, for example, begins with reference to a

Trade Union demonstration and covers among other things the Black
Panthers, the Student Revolt of 1968, the regime of Allende in Chile,
Syrian dictators, and the effect of Genet's own writings on the Hamburg
censors.[34] Even in the early feature on Athens, the discussion with the
waiter includes the question 'Sind Sie Papandreou-Anhänger?'[35] While
the first interview with Wolli raises questions concerning the 'APO',
Marx and Gandhi (*Wolli*, pp.99-101).

It has to be said, though, that Wolli admits to being only
tangentially interested in the first of these, and spends much more time
discussing literature, art and music. The Greek waiter, too, 'will von
der Politik nichts wissen', being interested only in the possibilities of
making money. The various professionals of the 'Palais d'Amour' have
very little to say about the actual political situation. In the early
interview with Alain Robbe-Grillet, almost no reference at all is made
to political reality; instead there is a brief discussion of whether Robbe-
Grillet's is a 'Kunst für den Menschen' or an example of 'l'art pour
l'art' (*Alte Welt*, pp.624-29, here p.628). While in *Hotel Garni* the
questions asked have almost exclusively to do with sexual experiences
(*Garni*, pp.123ff.).

These questions are also oddly insistent and demanding, and seem
to have more to say about Jäcki than about Irma. Ironically, the same is
true of *Versuch über die Pubertät*, where the questions have been left
out altogether and what is left are accounts of 'alternative puberties'
(*Pubertät*, pp.123-39, 247-70). For these alternative puberties help to
illuminate the account of Fichte's own and thus invest the interface
between the self and the other with a particular resonance and urgency.
As *Hotel Garni* makes abundantly clear, this urgency is always at least
potentially sexual. Thus where Robbe-Grillet says of himself 'ich glaube
[...], daß ich das Publikum aktiv zur Teilnahme herausfordere' and that
his books are 'ein Appell an die Phantasie der Leser' (*Alte Welt*, p.628),
thereby significantly recalling Sartre, who in his demand for a
'littérature engagée' defines writing as an active appeal to the freedom
of the reader, so Hubert Fichte throughout his life and work commits to
the cause of the oppressed his whole sexual sensitivity and the savagely
circumscribed freedom it entails.[36] Hence the paradox that the apogee
of committed literature is the 'Geschichte der Empfindlichkeit'.

As we have seen, the whole of Fichte's work is just such a
'Geschichte der Empfindlichkeit'. It arises out of concerns identical to

those which faced the authors of the Gruppe 47, and it pursues them with arguably greater single-mindedness. In the relationship between the writer and language Fichte displays and demonstrates the scepticism of the 'Kahlschlag', and applies the business of 'Abklopfung' not only to the slogans of the 'Kahlschläger' but also to his own work. With regard to the relationship between the writer and external reality, Fichte puts to creative use the tension characteristic of the Gruppe 47 between 'Reportage' and 'Mythologisierung', placing the whole dialectic at the service of a higher realism which always implicates both the self and the other. And above all, with regard to the relationship between the writer and politics in the widest sense, Fichte is concerned to put his own liberated self with all its complexes and contradictions at the service of those on the margins of society, pitting it also at every point against the prevalent structures of power. Which is precisely why, even when he is not strictly in the frame, he is nonetheless 'richtig dabei'.

Footnotes

[1] *Brauchen wir eine neue Gruppe 47? 55 Fragebögen zur deutschen Literatur*, eingesammelt von Joachim Leser und Georg Guntermann. Beiträge zur deutschen Literatur des 20. Jahrhunderts (Bonn: RNV, 1995), vol.2, pp.64-65, here p.64.

[2] The fact that he is not mentioned in Richter's Almanach (Hans Werner Richter (ed.), *Almanach der Gruppe 47* (Reinbek bei Hamburg: Rowohlt, 1964)) is explainable simply by chronology. It is possible too that his absence from Elizabeth Trahan's American *Querschnitt* (Elizabeth Welt Trahan (ed.), *Gruppe 47: Ein Querschnitt. An Anthology of Contemporary German Literature* (Waltham, Ma.: Blaisdell, 1969)) is due to an editorial policy which excluded extracts from novels and texts which were thought too difficult. That he is not mentioned either in Friedhelm Kröll's *Gruppe 47* (Stuttgart: Metzler, 1979) is rather more significant and harder to explain.

[3] To avoid overburdening the footnotes, the works of Fichte will be referred to by the abbreviations which are now more or less standard. For a list of these, please refer to my appendix.

[4] See Fichte's own 'Biographische Skizze', in: Thomas Beckermann (ed.), *Hubert Fichte. Materialien zu Leben und Werk* (Frankfurt a. M: Fischer Taschenbuchverlag, 1985) pp.317-22, p.318, s.v. '1951'.

[5] In 1963 he was awarded the Julius-Campe Stipendium together with Gisela Elsner. For an account of his stay at the Villa Massimo, where he spent time together with Gabriele Wohmann as well as Bachmann, see *Alte Welt*, pp.202-86, with Bachmann from p.267.

[6] Reinhard Lettau (ed.), *Die Gruppe 47. Bericht, Kritik, Polemik. Ein Handbuch* (Neuwied and Berlin: Luchterhand, 1967); Heinz Ludwig Arnold (ed.), *Die Gruppe 47. Ein kritischer Grundriß*, 2nd edn (Munich: text + kritik, 1987); Siegfried Mandel,

Group 47. The Reflected Intellect (Carbondale and Edwardsville: Southern Illinois University Press, 1973).

[7] *Stockholmer Katalog zur Tagung der Gruppe 47 im Herbst 1964*, zusammengestellt von Hubert Fichte (Stockholm: Schwedisch-Deutsche Gesellschaft & Deutsches Kulturinstitut, 1964). I am extremely grateful to Ms Koch of the library of the Universität-Gesamthochschule Paderborn and to Jens Bodenburg of Berlin for making it possible for me to consult this publication.

[8] Trahan, *Gruppe 47: Ein Querschnitt*, p.123.

[9] Beckermann, *Fichte*, p.319, s.v. '1966'.

[10] Fritz Raddatz, 'Die Bilanz von Princeton', in: Lettau, *Handbuch*, pp.241-47, here p.241.

[11] See Arnold, *Gruppe 47*, p.220.

[12] *Konkret* H.4 (1965), p.26.

[13] Fredrik Benzinger, *Die Tagung der Gruppe 47 in Schweden und ihre Folgen. Ein Kapitel deutsch-schwedischer Kultur- und Literaturbeziehungen*, Schriften des deutschen Instituts der Universität Stockholm, Nr 16 (Stockholm 1983).

[14] See Hartmut Böhme, 'Der junge Fichte. Auf den Spuren des Mythos. Nachwort', in: *Ödipus*, pp.117-34.

[15] See Torsten Teichert, *"Herzschlag aussen". Die poetische Konstruktion des Fremden und des Eigenen im Werk von Hubert Fichte* (Frankfurt a. M.: Fischer Taschenbuchverlag, 1987), pp.105-33, esp. pp.105-12.

[16] Hans Werner Richter, 'Die Gruppe 47. Vortrag, gehalten auf Einladung der Schwedisch-Deutschen Gesellschaft, Stockholm im März 1963', *Moderna Språk*, 58 (1964), 331-44, here p.335.

[17] Peter Schneider, *Vati*, ed. by Colin Riordan (Manchester University Press, 1993), p.62.

[18] Urs Widmer, 'So kahl war der Kahlschlag nicht', in: Lettau *Handbuch*, pp.328-35.

[19] Hubert Fichte, 'Hubert Fichtes Plattenragout. Goebbels', *Konkret*, H.1 (1966), p.26.

[20] *Grünspan*, pp.73-74, pp.100-01, pp.35-54.

[21] Cf. Robert Gillett, 'On not Writing Pornography: Literary Self-consciousness in the Work of Hubert Fichte', *GLL*, 48: 2 (1995), 222-40, here 235-36.

[22] Wolfdietrich Schnurre, *Die Erzählungen* (Olten and Freiburg i. Br.: Walter, 1966), pp.11-18. For Trahan see note 2. For one comment of many on Celan see Martine Broda's 'Liminaire', in: M.B., *Contre-Jour. Etudes sur Paul Celan. Colloque de Cérisy* (Paris: CERF, 1986), p.5 who calls Celan 'un poète de la modernité'.

[23] Walter Jens, 'Das ist nicht nur ein Roman', in: Beckermann, *Fichte*, pp.56-60, here p.56.

[24] Jörn Götzke, 'Die Unbarmherzigkeit des Schriftstellers Hubert Fichte gegenüber seinen Lesern' (Unpublished MA Dissertation, University of Hamburg, 1993).

[25] Hubert Fichte, 'Im Tiefstall', *Konkret*, H.4 (1965), pp.26-29.

[26] See Walter Hasenclever (ed.), *Prosaschreiben. Eine Dokumentation des Literarischen Colloquiums Berlin* (Berlin: Literarisches Colloquium, 1964), p.70.

[27] Hubert Fichte, 'Autostop und romanische Kirchen. Skizzen einer Frankreichreise', *Antares* 1: 7 (1953), 93-96 and 1: 8, 79-82.

[28] See Michael Fisch, *Personalbibliographie zu Leben und Werk von Hubert Fichte* (Berlin: Edition dià, 1996), for example, nos 175-77, 182, 188, 189.

[29] Hubert Fichte, 'Athen' (Fotos: Leonore Mau), *Konkret*, H.6 (1966), pp.24-29; 'Griechenland. 2. Folge' (Fotos, Leonore Mau), *Konkret*, H.7 (1966), pp.32-36.

[30] See *Alte Welt*, pp.17-22; Hans Werner Richter, 'Die Gruppe 47', p.342.

[31] Hartmut Böhme, *Hubert Fichte. Riten des Autors und Leben der Literatur* (Stuttgart: Metzler, 1992), pp.42-44.

[32] Cf. Peter Braun, 'Irmas Kunst. Zu den gemeinsamen Arbeiten von Leonore Mau und Hubert Fichte', in: Hartmut Böhme und Nikolaus Tiling (eds), *Medium und Maske. Die Literatur Hubert Fichtes zwischen den Kulturen* (Stuttgart: M & P, 1995), pp.54-87.

[33] See Lettau, *Handbuch*, pp.459-62; Hubert Fichte, 'Gewitztheit oder moralischer Mut?', in: Hans Werner Richter (ed.), *Plädoyer für eine neue Regierung, oder: Keine Alternative* (Reinbek bei Hamburg: Rowohlt, 1965), pp.112-20; 'Biographische Skizze', in : Beckermann, *Fichte*, p.320.

[34] Hubert Fichte, *Jean Genet*. Fotos von Leonore Mau (Aachen: Rimbaud, 1992).

[35] *Konkret*, H.6 (1966), p.29.

[36] Jean-Paul Sartre, *Qu'est-ce que la littérature* 2nd edn (Paris: nrf Gallimard, 1972), p.65: 'Ainsi l'auteur écrit pour s'adresser à la liberté des lecteurs'.

Appendix

The appendix lists in alphabetical order the details of each of the texts by Fichte referred to, by what are now more or less the standard abbreviations, in the text itself. The publisher, unless otherwise stated, is Fischer (Frankfurt am Main).

Alte Welt. Die Geschichte der Empfindlichkeit, Bd.V. (1992), (=*Alte Welt*)

Der Aufbruch nach Turku (1988), (=*Turku*)[1]

Detlevs Imitationen "Grünspan" (1982), (=*Grünspan*)[1]

Forschungsbericht Roman. Die Geschichte der Empfindlichkeit, Bd.XV (1989), (=*Forschungsbericht*)

Die Geschichte der Nanà. Die Geschichte der Empfindlichkeit (1990), (=*Nanà*)

Hamburg Hauptbahnhof. Die Geschichte der Empfindlichkeit (1993), (=*Hamburg Hauptbahnhof*)

Hans Eppendorfer, Der Ledermann spricht mit Hubert Fichte (Munich: Goldmann, 1988), (=*Ledermann*)

Homosexualität und Literatur 1. Die Geschichte der Empfindlichkeit, Paralipomena Bd.1 (1987), (=*HuL I*)

Homosexualität und Literatur 2. Die Geschichte der Empfindlichkeit, Paralipomena Bd.1 (1988), (=*HuL II*)

Hotel Garni. Die Geschichte der Empfindlichkeit, Bd.1 (1987), (=*Garni*)

Der kleine Hauptbahnhof oder Lob des Strichs. Die Geschichte der Empfindlichkeit, Bd.II (1988), (=*Kleiner Hauptbahnhof*)

Lazarus und die Waschmaschine (1985), (=*Lazarus*)

Ödipus auf Håknäss (1992), (=*Ödipus*)[1]

Die Palette (1981), (=*Palette*)[1]

Petersilie (1984), (=*Petersilie*)[1]

Platz der Gehenkten. Die Geschichte der Empfindlichkeit, Bd.VI (1989), (=*Platz*)

Versuch über die Pubertät (1982), (=*Pubertät*)[1]

Das Waisenhaus (1984), (=*Waisenhaus*)[1]

Wolli Indienfahrer (1983), (=*Wolli*)[1]

Xango (1984), (=*Xango*)[1]

[1] Fischer Taschenbuchausgabe

JOHANN SONNLEITNER

Grenzüberschreitungen. Ilse Aichinger und die Gruppe 47

Da in den Nachkriegsjahren die Situation für junge Schriftstellerinnen auf dem literarischen Markt in Österreich gar nicht leicht war, bot die Gruppe 47 eine Art Alternative zu den vielen Schwierigkeiten im eigenen Land. Dabei darf aber nicht übersehen werden, daß Hans Werner Richter gar nicht gern auf die national-sozialistische Vergangenheit einging, die z. B. für Ilse Aichingers Leben und Werk so wichtig war. Er schwieg, als sie ihm die Stelle in Wien zeigte, wo ihre Verwandten abtransportiert wurden. Obgleich sowohl Aichinger als auch Ingeborg Bachmann den Preis der Gruppe 47 gewannen, hatten es Frauen in der Gruppe gar nicht leicht. Sie dienten eher als Aushängeschild und sollten hauptsächlich zum größeren Ruhm der Gruppe beitragen. Die Behauptung, die Gruppe habe selbstlos junge Talente gefördert, muß also in dieser Hinsicht in Frage gestellt werden. Sie scheint gar nicht auf Ilse Aichinger zuzutreffen.

1. Wiener Verhältnisse

Im literaturgeschichtlichen Diskurs ist die Gruppe 47 ausschließlich eine Angelegenheit des literarischen Lebens der Bundesrepublik, wobei aber völlig aus dem Bewußtsein gerät, daß doch eine beträchtliche Anzahl ihrer 'Mitglieder' — von Ilse Aichinger bis Peter Handke — aus Österreich resp. aus den Nachfolgestaaten der Donau-Monarchie stammte. Milo Dor spricht in einem Essay über Paul Celan explizit vom 'österreichischen Teil der Gruppe 47',[1] zu dem er Ingeborg Bachmann und Reinhard Federmann zählt, der im Almanach von 1962 mit der Erzählung 'Die Stimme' vertreten ist. Auf deren Betreiben, so Milo Dor, sei die Einladung Paul Celans zur Niendorfer Tagung im Jahre 1952 erfolgt. Hinzurechnen müßte man den heute wohl zu Unrecht von der Bildfläche verschwundenen Herbert Eisenreich, der wie Hans Weigel 1953 sein wohlwollend aufgenommenes Debüt mit der Erzählung *Böse schöne Welt. Tiere von ganz gewöhnlicher Grausamkeit* feierte,[2] die in Wien geborenen Emigranten Jakov Lind, der in Berlin 1962 aus seinem Roman *Landschaft in Beton* las, und Erich Fried, der im Jahre 1963 in Saulgau Gedichte präsentierte wie auch Konrad Bayer, der Auszüge aus dem *sechsten sinn* las. Bei der letzten Tagung in der Pulvermühle stellte Barbara Frischmuth ihre Erzählung 'Meine Großmutter und ich' vor.

Die Bedeutung der Gruppe 47 für das literarische Leben in den Westzonen und der späteren Bundesrepublik Deutschland einzuschränken, scheint also doch eine etwas zu enge Sicht zu sein, offensichtlich bestand eine gewisse, zum Teil zweifelsohne auf Mißverständnissen basierende Kongruenz in ästhetischer und politischer Hinsicht. Nicht zu unterschätzen ist die zunehmende mediale Resonanz der Gruppe, die diese für junge AutorInnen aus Österreich so begehrenswert machte. Für deren Attraktivität kann man noch ein weiteres handfestes Argument anführen: Die im Dezember 1947 realisierte zweite österreichische Währungsreform hatte die einheimischen Verlage und den Buchhandel in eine massive Krise gestürzt, sodaß der deutsche Markt eine unabdingbare Überlebensvoraussetzung auch für österreichische, vor allem für junge Schriftsteller geworden war,[3] die, so Ingeborg Bachmann, im Nachkriegswien nichts zu lachen hatten: 'Wir waren alle Mitte zwanzig, notorisch geldlos, notorisch hoffnungslos, zukunftslos, kleine Angestellte oder Hilfsarbeiter, einige schon freie Schriftsteller, das hieß soviel wie abenteuerliche Existenzen, von denen niemand recht wußte, wovon sie lebten, von Gängen aufs Versatzamt jedenfalls am öftesten.'[4]

Es gab aber auch noch andere triftige Gründe, Wien möglichst rasch den Rücken zu kehren, — und zwar vor allem für schreibende Frauen, denn die ökonomische Tristesse und der damit verbundene Erfolgsdruck verschärften die Machtverhältnisse. Eine einläßliche Untersuchung der Beziehungsgeflechte und der Geschlechterbeziehungen in der Wiener literarischen Szene nach 1945 steht aus. Was aber aus den Memoiren aus männlicher Feder rekonstruiert werden kann, ist die massive Abhängigkeit der Autorinnen von ihren Förderern, die als Herausgeber wichtiger Zeitschriften und Anthologien deren Publikationsmöglichkeiten steuerten und auch zweifelsohne Druck auf ihre jungen Kolleginnen ausübten, wobei private und zum Teil wohl auch phantasierte erotische und emotionelle Beziehungen die beruflichen überlagerten. Christine Schmidjell schreibt dazu:

> Junge Autorinnen nach 1945 müssen in den ersten Jahren des Wiederaufbaus erfahren, daß eine Anerkennung ihrer geistigen Kraft noch keinesfalls ihren freien Zutritt in die Literaturinstitutionen bedeutete. Zeitschriften, Kulturämter

und kulturelle Institutionen sind bereits (wieder) von Männern besetzt und stellen damit Machtzentren dar, die der Literatur von Frauen oftmals zensierende Maßnahmen entgegensetzen.[5]

Die selbsternannten männlichen Förderer nützten ihre Positionen weidlich und schamlos aus, dafür verloren sie aber jegliche Gesprächsbasis zu ihren ehemaligen Schützlingen. Zu nennen sind hier die jüdischen Emigranten Hermann Hakel und Hans Weigel. Hermann Hakel, der in einem italienischen Lager interniert war, nach 1945 die Zeitschrift *Lynkeus* herausgab, zählte Ilse Aichinger zu jenen undankbaren Geschöpfen, die sich für seine angebliche Unterstützung nicht erkenntlich zeigen wollten; er dürfte aber verdrängt haben, daß im *Lynkeus* eine negative Rezension Erika Dannebergs über *Die größere Hoffnung* publiziert worden war. Als PEN-Vorstand hatte Hakel junge unbekannte Talente zu Lesungen eingeladen, um ihnen zu größerer Bekanntheit zu verhelfen, aber 'Aichinger brauchte mich nicht mehr, weil sie schon ein Jahr vor meiner Aktion in der Fischer-Rundschau erschienen und also eine Arrivierte war'.[6] Auch Hans Weigel, der Goebbels' Sprachkunst höher einschätzte als Werfels Prosa,[7] hielt sich für den eigentlichen Entdecker Aichingers. Mit ihrem Text 'Aufruf zum Mißtrauen' im *Plan* war sie bereits 1946 in aller Munde, sie lieferte damit selbst noch das Stichwort für die zwei Dezennien später erschienene berühmte, von Otto Breicha und Gerhard Fritsch herausgegebene Anthologie *Aufforderung zum Mißtrauen*, in der sich sowohl Weigels Essay 'Es begann mit Ilse Aichinger' als auch Aichingers Text finden. Die Kategorie des Mißtrauens in die Sprache wurde zu einem 1961 erschienenen umfangreichen Essay über die Differenzqualität österreichischer Literatur aus der Feder Herbert Eisenreichs.[8] Die Erstveröffentlichung der 'Spiegelgeschichte' war schon Anfang August 1949 in drei Fortsetzungen in der Wiener *Tageszeitung* zu lesen. Sie debütierte also wie Hertha Kräftner in jener kurzen Phase liberaler Aufbruchsstimmung, die einen gewissen Freiraum für schreibende Frauen bot, der mit der raschen Institutionalisierung des Literaturbetriebs wieder verschwand.[9] Folgt man nun Weigels 'fragmentarischen Erinnerungen an die Wiedergeburt der österreichischen Literatur nach 1945' 'Es begann mit Ilse Aichinger', so wäre er es gewesen, der letztlich die Niederschrift des Romans *Die größere Hoffnung* initiiert hätte: 'Ich bat den damaligen Feuilletonredakteur des "Wiener Kurier", Zeno von Liebl, er möge der

unbekannten jungen Dame einen schönen Gruß von mir bestellen —
ihre Prosa scheine mir sehr eindrucksvoll — sie möge doch, bitte,
möglichst bald einen Roman schreiben.'10 Er habe Aichinger zum
Verleger Bermann-Fischer vermittelt. Die Diskretion, die er gegenüber
Aichinger wahrt, läßt er gegen Ingeborg Bachmann völlig vermissen.
Im eher drittklassigen, 1950 entstandenen Schlüsselroman *Unvollendete
Symphonie*, zu dem er im Nachwort der Neuauflage den Schlüssel
'lachend preisgibt', breitet er seine intimen Beziehungen zu Bachmann
aus, die aus der Perspektive einer jungen Malerin aus der Provinz
geschildert werden.11 Er hatte noch die Kühnheit zu behaupten, das
Machwerk habe Bachmann gefallen. Weigel hätte sich besonders für die
Publikation von Bachmanns erstem Roman *Stadt ohne Namen*, der als
verschollen gilt, eingesetzt, den — vorbehaltlich gewisser Änderungen
— der Wiener Herold Verlag auf seine Intervention hin auch publiziert
hätte. Die Entfremdung von ihrem Gönner und die nachhaltige
Kommunikationsstörung reflektiert der Schlußdialog anläßlich der
Verleihung des Österreichischen Staatspreises an die Autorin, die
Weigel auf die Frage, wann denn ihr nächstes Buch erscheine, erwidert,
das müsse er schon ihren Anwalt fragen.12 Nicht nur Mangel an
Abstand und Diskretion verband Weigel mit Hermann Hakel, sondern
auch die Lust, die Autorinnen gegeneinander auszuspielen: Ilse
Aichinger, so Hans Weigel, wäre für Bachmann eine Leitfigur
geworden, und er fügt kryptisch hinzu, das wäre 'nicht ohne Schaden'
(S.16) abgegangen. Hakel wird in seiner postumen Denunziation der von
ihm und seinesgleichen emanzipierten Bachmann schon deutlicher:

> Auf welche Art sich Inge an sie [Aichinger] herangemacht hat, ist mir nicht
> bekannt. Sie verfolgte sie in Gedanken und lief ihr unterwürfig und hündisch
> nach. Es gab keine Zusammenkunft, bei welcher Inge nicht vom Roman 'Die
> größere Hoffnung' gesprochen hätte. Und wenn ich bei aller Anerkennung
> des suggestiven, traumartigen Stils an der Konstruktion und Sentimentalität
> doch etwas aussetzte, linderte meine Kritik an der bewunderten 'Freundin und
> Dichterin' wie eine kühlende Salbe die brennende Wunde, an welcher Inge
> litt. (Hakel, S.204)

Bachmann kann sich von ihren Wienern Gönnern lösen, die sich
untereinander entsprechend befehden, Hakel nimmt vor allem
Bachmann diese Emanzipation besonders übel, als auch sie ihn nicht
mehr braucht. 'Ohne darüber zu sprechen', so vermerkt er eifersüchtig,
habe sie zu Deutschland Verbindungen aufgenommen, 'wahrscheinlich

durch Ilse Aichinger zur Gruppe 47', gegen die er als Konkurrenz-Institution besonders ausfällig wird:

> Dieses geschäfts- und reklamesüchtige Literaturkonsortium zu erobern war
> Inges nächstes Ziel. [...] Daten und Namen genügen den zeitgenössischen
> Fachkollegen der Literaturbranche in Deutschland und Österreich,
> Verlagslektoren und journalistische Rezensenten inbegriffen, um sich unter der
> 'Gruppe 47' etwas vorzustellen, wovon man in zwanzig Jahren keine Ahnung
> mehr haben wird. Aus sogenannten 'Informationen' bildet sich ein Scheinleben
> der Aktualitäten, ein scheußliches Konglomerat von Fotos, Zeitungsmeldungen,
> Proklamationen, papierenen Protestaktionen, lancierten Lobhudeleien,
> Begeisterungen und Verrissen, all das zusammen heißt 'Kulturpolitik' und
> schaut auch so aus. (Ebd. S.206)

Merkwürdigerweise schien diese junge Autorengeneration keinerlei Hemmnisse zu haben, wie sie etwa Jean Améry[13] formuliert hatte, der erst Mitte der sechziger Jahre zum ersten Mal nach Deutschland reiste, jenes Land zu betreten, das so unermeßliches Unheil über Europa gebracht hatte. Das Verhältnis der österreichischen Intellektuellen zum sogenannten Altreich war unmittelbar nach 1945 nicht gerade friktionsfrei, und die politisch motivierte Distanznahme wurde durch die offizielle österreichische Kulturpolitik noch verschärft, die ja viele Autoren mittrugen.[14] Wie prekär das Verhältnis zu allem Deutschen war, belegen die Reaktionen auf einen eher unscheinbaren Text Weigels mit dem Titel: 'Das verhängte Fenster',[15] in dem er nachhaltig dafür plädierte, die Kontakte zum literarischen Leben in Deutschland zu suchen und sich wieder der deutschen Kultur zu öffnen. Weigel konnte es als rassisch verfolgter Emigrant wagen, ein zentrales Tabu der österreichischen Nachkriegsgeschichte zu verletzen: Man möge das Fenster öffnen, das 'uns den Blick auf Deutschland freigeben soll'. Obwohl er einräumt, daß die Österreicher durch die Schuld von Deutschen unsäglich gelitten hätten, sollte man zu einer Normalisierung der Beziehungen finden, er begründet diesen Wunsch mit dem christlichen Gebot: 'Liebet eure Feinde'. Er nennt den 'Anschluß' eine 'Ehe, unter Zwang geschlossen', die auseinander gebrochen sei; wer aber die Deutschen nun kollektiv verurteile, verhielte sich nicht anders als die Antisemiten. Die etwas krausen Formulierungen Weigels, der in Kooperation mit Friedrich Torberg als rabiater Antikommunist für Bertolt Brecht das Fenster nach Österreich ein Jahrzehnt lang höchst unchristlich verschlossen hielt, blieben nicht unwidersprochen; der

Widerstandskämpfer und Kommunist Otto Horn replizierte einige Nummern später mit größter Vehemenz.[16] Die Berührungsängste gegenüber dem Nachkriegsdeutschland waren also vorhanden, und es war also keineswegs eine Selbstverständlichkeit, daß in den fünfziger Jahren immerhin ein Dutzend österreichischer Autoren bei den Gruppentagungen ihre Texte vorstellten.

Aus dem Wien der galanten Förderer wegzukommen, bedeutete also offensichtlich ein Aufatmen und eine Befreiung, und Aichinger und Bachmann waren keineswegs vom Regen in die Traufe gekommen, wie es Hakel sehen wollte, sie lernen das Lachen wieder, vermerkt Bachmann in ihrem Textentwurf zur Gruppe 47, den sie aber nie an Hans Werner Richter absandte:

> Es scheint, daß wir in Wien alle ziemlich wenig zu lachen gehabt haben, denn sonst wäre meine stärkste Erinnerung nicht die, eine verwandelte Ilse Aichinger zu sehen, bald angesteckt worden zu sein von etwas, das Jungsein, Lachen, Gelöstsein in einem war, Ansteckung durch Hoffnungen, durch mehr Weite, und das Unbekümmertsein, so daß meinetwegen der Bericht weniger wie einer über ein Zusammentreffen mit einer literarischen Gruppe klingt, es auch am wenigsten war, sondern eine kurze Spanne 'Jugend'. (Bachmann, S.323f.)

2. Hans Werner Richters Gedächtnis

Richter bestritt jede Schuld und Mitverantwortung seiner Generation am Nationalsozialismus und markierte für die Lebensgeschichten seiner Freunde ostentatives Desinteresse. In seinem Essay über Günter Eich heißt es:

> Ich wußte fast nichts von ihm, nichts von seinem Leben vor dem Krieg und während des Krieges, nichts von seiner Jugend, seiner Kindheit. Es hat mich auch nicht interessiert, und ich habe nie danach gefragt. In dieser Zeit, wenige Jahre nach dem Krieg, war es unwichtig.[17]

Noch klarer formuliert er diese verständliche Befangenheit und Verdrängung im Porträtessay über Milo Dor; er hätte sich nie über dessen Leidensgeschichte vor 1945 informiert, denn 'vielleicht war uns unsere eigene Vergangenheit in den Jahren der Nachkriegszeit zuweilen lästig und suspekt. Wir sprachen eigentlich nur noch von der Gegenwart und Zukunft und warfen nur selten einen Blick zurück.'[18] Das interessierte Desinteresse schlägt noch deutlicher durch, als ihn Ilse Aichinger im Frühling 1952 durch Wien führt.[19] Klaus Briegleb hat sich mit Richters Wien-Text genau auseinandergesetzt, sodaß ich hier nur die zentrale Passage in Erinnerung rufe:

> Nie erwähnte sie in dieser Unterhaltung ihre eigene Vergangenheit, etwa im Dritten Reich. Es war, als hätte sie selbst den Mantel des Vergessens darübergehängt. Nur einmal sagte sie: 'Hier, an dieser Stelle habe ich gestanden, als meine Verwandten abtransportiert wurden.' Diesen Satz habe ich behalten. Bis heute. Damals fragte ich nicht weiter, vielleicht aus Angst, mehr zu erfahren, als ich hören wollte.[20]

In den Aufzeichnungen aus den fünfziger Jahren reagiert Aichinger auf diese augenfällige Bereitschaft zur Verdrängung: 'Die Erinnerung ist jetzt in Gefahr, verloren zu gehen. Und was nützt jede andere Erinnerung, wenn diese eine fehlt.'[21] Opfer und virtueller Täter — Richter als Wehrmachtssoldat — verständigen sich durch Schweigen und Vergessen. Während die klischierten Bilder der Monarchie, die farbenprächtigen k. u. k. Offiziere, ja selbst die Türkenkriege präsent gehalten werden, verschwindet jene Geschichte, die beide gemeinsam betrifft und verbindet, aus dem Blickwinkel, ebenso die Fragen, die Aichinger an ihn gerichtet hatte, — waren sie belanglos, die Fragen einer Frau — oder ihm unangenehm, Fragen, die seine Soldatenexistenz betrafen? Richter reagiert mit einer Verschiebung: Was er nicht wahrhaben möchte oder worüber er nicht sprechen möchte, darüber breitet sein Gegenüber 'den Mantel des Vergessens'. Das dem nicht so ist, belegt Aichingers erster, im September 1945 publizierter Text 'Das vierte Tor'. In welch eklatanten Gegensatz zu Aichinger sich Richter begibt, wird deutlich, wenn er seine Generation von jeder Mitschuld und Verantwortung für die Verbrechen und den Terror der Nazis freispricht:

> Der Vorwurf des Nationalismus ärgert mich besonders. Ich fühle mich als Deutscher, ich bin Deutscher, ich kann nicht aus meiner Haut heraus. Aber ich bin nicht verantwortlich für Hitlers Verbrechen und für den Chauvinismus vergangener Zeiten. Und die jungen, heimkehrenden Soldaten sind es ebenso wenig, ganz gleich, ob sie an den Nationalsozialismus geglaubt haben oder nicht.[22]

Richter expliziert diese Haltung in seinem 1949 erschienenen Roman *Die Geschlagenen*, in dem er die Legitimität der Desertion aus der Wehrmacht und der Kooperation mit den gegnerischen Truppen verneint, da man dadurch das Leben der Kameraden gefährdet hätte. Den Roman widmet er seinen vier Brüdern, 'die Gegner und Soldaten dieses Krieges waren [...] und die weder sich selbst, ihren Glauben, noch ihr Land verrieten'. Gühler, die Hauptfigur des Buches, wird am Monte Cassino von den Amerikanern gefangengenommen und weigert sich, mit dem alliierten Dolmetscher zu kooperieren, denn:

> "jede Stellung, die ich Ihnen sage, bedeutet dreißig bis vierzig Volltreffer für die Kameraden, die jetzt noch eine Chance haben, mit dem Leben davonzukommen."
>
> "Ich verstehe Sie nicht", begann der Dolmetscher wieder, "wenn Sie gegen Hitler sind, müßten Sie auf unserer Seite gegen Deutschland kämpfen."
>
> Gühler [...] sagte langsam: "Ich bin Sozialist und ein Deutscher. Es gibt für mich nur eine Möglichkeit. In meinem Land meine Idee durchzusetzen. Aber nicht gegen mein Land. Nicht für fremde Interessen."[23]

Ein unangenehm berührendes Detail in Richters auto-biographischen Aufzeichnungen verhehlt nur schlecht die Ranküne gegen die Emigranten, die auf der Seite der Alliierten gegen das Dritte Reich kämpften, die also ihr Land verrieten, so darf man die Widmung auslegen, wie Walter Maria Guggenheimer, der Redakteur der *Frankfurter Hefte* und Bewunderer von Ilse Aichinger: 'Wir, er und ich, haben uns 1943 in St. Peter, nicht weit von Monte Cassino, an der Front gegenübergelegen' (Richter, S.84). Nach dem Treffen in Bann-waldsee hätte Guggenheimer Richter ermuntert, diese Meetings zu wiederholen und wäre deshalb der 'eigentliche Gründer' der Gruppe 47. Das ist denn doch etwas zuviel der Ehre, die er Guggenheimer sofort wieder abspricht. Richter reiste 1952 nach Wien, um ein Feature für den Bayerischen Rundfunk zu schreiben, hat aber noch anderes im Sinn: Milo Dor hätte ihm versprochen, 'mir in Wien tausend schöne Frauen zu Füßen zu legen, dies weil er im Münchner Fasching angeblich keine schöne Frau gesehen hatte'. Es wäre ein 'sinnloses Versprechen', räumt er ein, aber er hat es doch nach 30 Jahren der Aufzeichnung wert befunden, wie auch das nächste Ereignis:

> Walter Maria Guggenheimer hat mir ein Geschenk für Ilse Aichinger mitgegeben. Es ist ein mit Rubinen besetztes Halskreuz, kostbar anzusehen. Ich übergebe es ihr schon am ersten Vormittag in ihrer Wohnung am Schwarzenberg-Palais. Sie lächelt in ihrer etwas versteckten, verhaltenen und vielleicht ironischen Art und sagt, als sie das Kreuz sieht: 'Aber nein, das ist ja herrlich.' (Richter, S.102)

Der Überbringer konstatiert aber erleichtert: 'Mehr aber scheint sie sich für die kommende Tagung der "Gruppe 47" zu interessieren.' Richter begleitet seinen Gastgeber Milo Dor zur Pfandleihe und erblickt auch Aichinger, die von einem Beamten das Geschenk Guggenheimers zurückerhält, denn es sei 'völlig wertlos'. Richter dreht sich schnell um (S.103). Wollte er nicht Zeuge der peinlichen Situation sein? Er läßt uns nicht im unklaren, denn es gibt noch eine spätere, mit größerem erzählerischem Aufwand und Kommentaren versehene Version, die nichts an Deutlichkeit zu wünschen übrig läßt: Ich 'hatte Grüße von ihren Verehrern und Bewunderern zu bestellen, trug aber auch ein Geschenk bei mir, das ich ihr übergeben sollte. Es war ein Geschenk des Chefredakteurs der 'Frankfurter Hefte', der zu Ilses beharrlichsten Verehrern gehörte.' Richter beschreibt, welches Prunkstück — wohl ein Familienerbstück — er da zu überreichen habe und übergibt das Geschenk: 'ich dachte, sie würde jetzt vor Freude außer sich geraten, aber nichts Derartiges geschah. Sie klappte die Schachtel auf und wieder zu und stellte sie dann beiseite. Anscheinend war es ihr peinlich, ein solches Geschenk zu bekommen. Ich legte es so aus und freute mich darüber.'

Nicht ganz nachvollziehbar ist, warum Aichinger, die sich ja in der früheren Version (von 1974, bzw. 1979) noch darüber gefreut hatte, nun Guggenheimers Geschenk als peinlich empfinden sollte und weshalb ihre angebliche Indignation Richter so angenehm überraschte. In der Pfandleihe beobachtet er, wie der Beamte ihr die Schachtel mit dem Schmuckstück zurückreicht, das 'offensichtlich keinen Wert' besaß. Zuerst möchte er sie ansprechen, versteckt sich dann aber, sodaß sie ihn nicht bemerken kann. Als diskreter Seigneur verschweigt er den blamablen Vorfall gegenüber Reinhard Federmann und Milo Dor, um ihn dann zweimal schriftlich der Nachwelt zu überliefern. Es ist also kaum anzunehmen, daß er die Geschichte auch wirklich für sich behalten hat. Ich 'freute mich aber', so heißt es weiter, 'daß sich das Geschenk von Ilses Verehrer als wertlos erwiesen hatte'.[24] Es wäre wohl zu kurz gegriffen, hier Richter schlichte Eifersucht zu unterstellen, weil Guggenheimer sich für den eigentlichen Entdecker der Aichinger hielt und diese Leistung Richter streitig machte. Die unverhohlene Schadenfreude darüber, daß sich der jüdische Emigrant Guggenheimer, der für die Alliierten gekämpft hatte, bei Aichinger, so Richters Vorstellung, diskreditiert hat, ist hingegen zusammenzudenken mit der Widmung des Romans *Die Geschlagenen*. Jene Emigranten, die gegen das Dritte Reich und damit gegen die Deutschen gekämpft haben, wären, denkt man Richters Überzeugung konsequent zu Ende, als Verräter zu bezeichnen. Er läßt damit jede Sensibilität gegenüber den Verfolgten und ins Exil Getriebenen, sondern auch jede Bereitschaft vermissen, sich auch mit den Verbrechen der Wehrmacht, die ihm und seinen literarischen Mitstreitern bekannt waren, offen auseinanderzusetzen. Eben diese kollektive Verweigerung gegenüber der Geschichte registrierte Hannah Arendt, als sie 1950 Deutschland bereiste, um über die Verbrechen der Nazi-Diktatur zu sprechen.[25] Ihre Diagnose trifft ohne Einschränkung auch auf Hans Werner Richter zu.

3. Weiblichkeit, Männlichkeit und Geschichte

Die Schwierigkeiten, als Schriftstellerin nach 45 zu reüssieren, lagen wohl auch darin begründet, daß der männliche Erwartungshorizont sich auf jene markige Kahlschlag-Literatur festgelegt hatte, die die Erfahrung des Kampfes und des Krieges aus der Sicht der Heimkehrer verarbeitete. Um zu reüssieren, mußte 'frau' die karge neusachliche neorealistische Prosa der ehemaligen Soldaten kopieren, sozusagen männliche, auf den soldatischen Erfahrungshorizont berechnete Rollenprosa verfassen, um den Preis, durch Camouflage, Verstellung und ästhetische Zurichtung die weibliche Geschichte auszublenden: Aichingers erste, über die Landesgrenzen hinaus renommierte Publikation 'Die geöffnete Order' in den *Frankfurter Heften* und das Anfangskapitel 'Der Kommandant' aus Bachmanns *Stadt ohne Grenzen* imitieren eben diesen Tonfall, so daß Weigel ihn als 'männlich-kräftigen Duktus des Erzählens' beschreibt und Heimito von Doderer, der das Manuskript gelesen hatte, von 'einem jungen Autor, Ingeborg Bachmann' sprach.[26] Zu diesem die Geschlechterdifferenz nivellierenden Lapsus gesellt sich ein berühmt gewordener Versprecher eines Lektors des S. Fischer-Verlages bei der Tagung der Gruppe 47 im Jahr 1951:

> Als Ilse Aichinger eine symbolische Geschichte von dem 'Gefesselten' las, dem Manne, der sich so an seine Fesseln gewöhnte, daß er darin seine wirkliche Freiheit fand und der in Sklaverei verfiel, als man seine Fesseln löste, da versprach sich der Lektor ihres eigenen Verlages, indem er sie schützen wollte, und begann: "Ich glaube, man tut Fräulein Kaf... äh Aichinger Unrecht."[27]

Die Ausgrenzung weiblichen Schreibens aus dem literarischen Diskurs implizierte auch die Ausblendung all dessen, was die

Bewältigungstexte der Heimkehrer mit ihren schönen Inbildern nicht in den Blick bekamen oder schlichtweg verdrängten. In den Vordergrund rückte der Krieg als Bewährungsprobe, mit fatalistischen Deutungsansätzen, wobei politische und ideologische Erklärungsmuster, wie er denn zustande gekommen sei, bestenfalls in Ansätzen aufschienen. Diese ästhetische Monodimensionalität hängt nicht nur mit der Geschlechterordnung in der deutschen Nachkriegsliteratur zusammen, sondern erklärt sich, so Sigrid Weigel 'auch damit, daß die Kriegs- und Faschismuserinnerungen der Männer als *literaturfähig* bewertet wurden, daß sich der herrschende Literaturbegriff an Ereignissen und erzählbaren Tatsachen orientierte.'28

Fritz J. Raddatz hat im einleitenden Kommentar zu den ausgewählten gelesenen Texten in dem von Hans Werner Richter herausgegebenen *Almanach* von 1962 die Verdrängungsmechanismen und die erschreckenden Defizite des männlichen literarischen Kriegsbewältigungsdiskurses, das Fehlen der 'öffentlichen Dinge' und der 'Erinnerung' deutlich herausgestellt: 'Ein erschreckendes Phänomen, gelinde gesagt. Die wichtigen Autoren Nachkriegsdeutschlands haben sich allenfalls mit dem Alp der Knobelbecher und Spieße beschäftigt; die Säle voll Haar und Zähnen in Auschwitz [...] wurden nicht zu Gedicht oder Prosa.'29

Angesichts der Überzeugungen Richters und der berechtigten Kritik von Fritz Raddatz erstaunt es, daß Aichinger für Hans Werner Richter nicht nur ein Gedicht,30 sondern auch einen bemerkenswert freundlichen Kurztext verfaßte:

> Als mich Hans Werner Richter zum ersten Mal zu einer Tagung der Gruppe 47 einlud, sah ich das Bild einer großen grünen Wiese mit weit darüberhin verstreuten weißen Zelten vor mir. Ob die Tagungen in Gasthöfen, Burgen oder Strandhotels stattfanden, dieses innere Bild blieb bestehen. Vielleicht hängt es mit der Atmosphäre der Heiterkeit, der Geborgenheit im Offenen zusammen, die fast allen Tagungen gemeinsam war. Daß man zuweilen kritisiert, auch scharf kritisiert wurde, daß es, wie nicht anders möglich, innerhalb der Gruppe zu Spannungen kam, schmälerte diese Geborgenheit kaum. Alles war ins Offene gesagt. Die Freundschaften innerhalb der Gruppe und die Freundschaft, die diese Gruppe ausstrahlte, schliefen auch in den halbjährlichen oder jährlichen Pausen zwischen den Tagungen nicht ein. Ambitionen, Rivalitäten gab es und mußte es auch geben, aber das Maß gab die Freundschaft.31

Eine besondere Leistung der Gruppe habe darin bestanden, das Vertrauen in eine Sprache wiederherzustellen, das durch vieles Vorhergegangene so schwer erschüttert worden war. Rätselhaft bleibt diese positive Einstellung zur Gruppe und zu Hans Werner Richter allemal. Die vollkommene Abtrennung von negativer Lebenserfahrung aus dem Krieg findet zweifelsohne ihr Pendant in einer zunehmend derealisierten Prosa, die durch die Unterschlagung deiktischer Raum-Zeitverankerung die Figuren in existentielle ahistorische Grenzerfahrungen hineintreibt. Die Verbannung der 'realisierenden Kraft des Mimetischen',[32] das, so Günther Anders anläßlich eines Theaterskandals in Berlin, durch die Bilder das Wirkliche sichtbar machen könne, das Verdikt, das über die denunzierte Kalligraphie der Emigranten gefällt wurde, ist nicht nur dem Impuls einer fragwürdigen Sprachreinigung geschuldet, sondern hat ihr eigentliches Movens darin, die unmittelbare Vergangenheit aus den erzählenden Texten zu eliminieren. Hannah Arendt hatte zu dieser Denkfigur sarkastisch angemerkt, der Durchschnittsdeutsche suche 'die Ursachen des letzten Krieges nicht in den Taten des Naziregimes, sondern in den Ereignissen, die zur Vertreibung von Adam und Eva aus dem Paradies geführt haben' (Arendt, S.45).

Zur derealisierenden Konstitution vor allem epischer Texte, die sicher eine unverkennbare Epochensignatur hervorbrachte, konnte man schreibend aus zwei Richtungen kommen. Auf der einen Seite das Trauma der Opfer, die es sich verbieten, die Vernichtung, der sie soeben entronnen waren, in einen fiktionalen Zusammenhang zu integrieren, dem ja oft etwas Kulinarisches anhaftet, auf der anderen Seite die Erfahrung der Soldaten, die dem Krieg entweder die ästhetisierenden Lesarten des gefährlichen Lebens abgewinnen, wie Alfred Andersch in *Die Kirschen der Freiheit*,[33] oder den Krieg als narratives Modell einsetzen, in dem es sich bequem im Eigentlichen und Wesentlichen einrichten ließ. Die vordergründige und aufdringliche Bedeutungsschwere ist erkauft durch den Verzicht auf konkrete referierbare historische Realien. Der dominante Diskurs über den Krieg weicht der analytischen Auseinandersetzung mit dem National-sozialismus aus, der sich Aichinger auf unkonventionelle und ästhetisch provokante Weise in *Die größere Hoffnung* gestellt hatte. Richters fiktionaler und weitschweifiger Rechtfertigungsprosa ist von der Angst, 'unter dem Eindruck des Endes den Mund nicht mehr' aufzubringen,[34] wie es Aichinger in der 'Rede unter dem Galgen' formuliert, nicht tangiert. Dem literarischen Erwartungshorizont der Gruppe, der von der Existentialphilosophie und -ontologie mitgeprägt war, kamen Erzählungen wie 'Die geöffnete Order' am weitesten entgegen und verhalfen der Autorin zu jener Popularität, die ihr selbst rasch verdächtig wurde und wohl mit dazu führte, daß sie zu immer 'umwegsameren' Formen des Schreibens überging, wie Hilde Spiel zu Aichingers Gedichtband *Verschenkter Rat* anmerkte.35

4. Wem nützt der Erfolg ?

Einer der unverwüstlichen Gemeinplätze über die Gruppe 47 besagt, daß sie junge Talente entdeckte und einer größeren Öffentlichkeit bekannt machte. In vielen Fällen, wie z. B. bei Günter Grass, mag das zutreffen, für Ilse Aichinger hat das Joachim Kaiser überzeugend in Abrede gestellt. Peter Härtling erklärte bei einem 1980 in Wien abgehaltenen Symposium über Ilse Aichinger den Umstand, daß *Die größere Hoffnung* nur langsam den Weg zum größeren Publikum gefunden habe, damit, daß der Ruhm der 'Spiegelgeschichte' den Roman gleichsam überlagert hätte. Kaiser entgegnete, daß Aichinger bereits vor der Niendorfer Tagung allen Literaturinteressierten ein Begriff war, vor allem nach den Rezensionen Guggenheimers in den *Frankfurter Heften* vom Februar 1951, die 'damals viel gelesen und eminent meinungsbildend waren'36 und in denen auch im selben Jahr 'Die geöffnete Order' publiziert worden war. Auch 'Die Spiegelgeschichte' war vor Niendorf schon mehrfach gedruckt worden, am prominentesten in der *Neuen Rundschau*. Richter habe, so erzählt er, Aichinger geraten, gerade diesen Text zu lesen, obwohl er schon publiziert war; er könne aber nicht mehr erklären, weshalb er in diesem Fall gegen den Usus verstoßen habe. Folgendes wäre denkbar: 1952 setzt die Einbindung der Medien in die Gruppentagungen ein. Man konnte also einen schon erprobten und bewährten Text feiern, der schon mehrere Zeitungs- und Verlagslektorate erfolgreich passiert hatte, und man hatte zum ersten Mal eine Frau als Siegerin, sodaß die Gruppe das Stigma, ein reiner Männerverein zu sein, loswurde. Auch bei Bachmann müßte man die Frage umdrehen: Nicht was sie von der Gruppe hatte, sondern inwiefern die Gruppe von ihr profitierte, scheint entscheidend.

Aichingers erster Auftritt 1951 wurde von der Gruppe 47 wohlwollend aufgenommen. 'Die Spiegelgeschichte' wurde richtig-

gehend beklatscht, was Richter sofort unterbunden hätte. Wie hat es
Aichinger solange mit Richter ausgehalten? Ein wichtiges Bindeglied
war zweifelsohne Günter Eich, den sie bei einer Gruppentagung
kennengelernt hatte. Heinz Ludwig Arnold führt für diese erstaunliche
Kohärenz weitere einleuchtende Gründe an: 'Eich, Bachmann,
Aichinger stehen gleichsam über, wenn nicht außerhalb der Kritik —
sie sind ja die Matadore des Kollektivs [...], die den Ruhm der Gruppe
in der Öffentlichkeit begründen und [...] festigen.' Arnold analysiert
dann die Qualitäten der spontanen Kritik, die lediglich einmal peinlich
versagt hätte, nämlich bei Paul Celans Lesung. Arnold spricht von der
'Beschränktheit einer männlichen Kriegsheimkehrer-Kameraderie mit
rauhem Ton und reiner Seele, die, möglicherweise aus sehr männlicher
Galanterie, den Damen zugestand, was sie den Geschlechtsgenossen
versagte: literarische Grenzüberschreitung.'[37]

Bachmann hob durch ihre mediale Präsenz — man denke an das
Spiegel-Porträt — insgesamt das Gruppen-Renommee, Ilse Aichinger
stieß schon als mehr oder minder etablierte Autorin vermutlich über die
Vermittlung von Werner Maria Guggenheimer zur Gruppe 47. Hält
man sich die zugegeben etwas summarische Kritik eines Raddatz oder
den Umgang der Gruppe mit einem Paul Celan vor Augen, den Briegleb
einläßlich untersucht hat,[38] so überrascht es, daß Aichinger in den
fünfziger Jahren zu den regelmäßigen Teilnehmerinnen zählte und sich
erst in den frühen sechziger Jahren immer mehr zurückzog.[39] Sie diente
offensichtlich dazu, als Halbjüdin und Verfolgte die Ausblendung und
systematische Verdrängung der nazistischen Skandal-Masse im
Gruppendiskurs durch ihre kontinuierliche Präsenz bis in die frühen
sechziger Jahre zu überdecken. Bachmann fand in einem Interview von
1964 ziemliche harsche Worte für die Gruppe: es sei ihr klar, 'daß die
deutschen Schriftsteller, die sich dem Verdacht aussetzen, radikale,
gefährliche Ansichten zu vertreten, fast ausnahmslos derart gemäßigt
denken, daß sie sich in einem anderen Land, etwa in Italien oder
Frankreich, dem Verdacht aussetzen würden, zuwenig zu denken'.[40]

Gelohnt hat sich die 'Grenzüberschreitung' in geographischer und
ästhetischer Hinsicht für beide Seiten, für Aichinger, zu der Bernhard
einmal sagte, sie sei den Wiener Intrigen nicht gewachsen, und
Bachmann, die beide am Wiener Nachkriegsliteraturbetrieb auf
unterschiedliche Weise litten, für die Gruppe, die die Leistungen der
Österreicherinnen bitter nötig hatte.

Fußnoten

1 Milo Dor, 'Paul Celan', in: *Meine Reisen nach Wien und andere Verirrungen. Gesammelte Erzählungen* (München, Wien: Langen-Müller, 1981), S.245-49, hier S.245.

2 Einen gehässigen Kommentar dazu lieferte der rechtsextreme Kurt Ziesel in der Salzburger *Neuen Front*: 'Es scheint mir notwendig, auch die deutsche Öffentlichkeit in das richtige Bild über diese Randfiguren des literarischen Lebens Österreichs zu setzen, und die Motive für die üblen Blasen aufzuzeigen, die die aus diesem moralischen Sumpf einer eitlen Kaffeehaus-Clique aufsteigen, für die die Kunst und der Mensch nur ein Mittel der Befriedigung ihrer Eitelkeit und ihrer Ruhmsucht sind.' Zit. nach Christian Ferber, 'Die Gruppe 47 und die Presse', in: Hans Werner Richter (Hrsg.), *Almanach der Gruppe 47* (Reinbek bei Hamburg: Rowohlt, 1962), S.48-55, hier S.54.

3 Vgl. Heinz Lunzer, 'Der literarische Markt 1945 bis 1955', in: Friedbert Aspetsberger, Norbert Frei u. Hubert Lengauer (Hrsg.), *Literatur der Nachkriegszeit und der fünfziger Jahre in Österreich* (Wien: ÖBV, 1984), (= Schriften des Instituts für Österreichkunde 44/45), S.24-46.

4 Ingeborg Bachmann, 'Gruppe 47. Entwurf', in: dies., *Werke IV*, hrsg. v. Christine Koschel, Inge v. Weidenbaum u. Clemens Münster (München, Zürich: Piper, 1993), S.323-25. Weitere Hinweise auf diesen Aufsatz befinden sich im Text unter Bachmann.

5 Christine Schmidjell, '"Geh nicht ohne Mantel und vergiß, was deine Heimat war". Hertha Kräftner und die Generation "Junger" Autorinnen nach 1945', in: *Das Schreiben der Frauen in Österreich seit 1950* (Wien, Graz, Köln: Böhlau, 1991), (=Walter Buchebner-Literaturprojekt 5), S.9-22, hier S.11.

6 Hermann Hakel, *Dürre Äste — Welkes Gras. Begegnungen mit Literaten. Bemerkungen zur Literatur*, hrsg. v. Hermann Hakel-Gesellschaft (Wien: Lynkeus, 1991), S.204. Weitere Hinweise auf dieses Werk befinden sich im Text unter Hakel.

7 'Die Gerechtigkeit kommt um die Feststellung nicht herum, daß der rede- und wortmächtige Joseph Goebbels seine Muttersprache vermutlich besser beherrscht hat als etwa Franz Werfel', *Sprache im technischen Zeitalter*, Sonderheft 6 (1963), S.456.

8 Herbert Eisenreich, 'Das schöpferische Mißtrauen oder Ist Österreichs Literatur eine österreichische Literatur?', in: ders.: *Reaktionen. Essays zur Literatur* (Gütersloh: S. Mohn, 1964), S.72-104.

9 Schmidjell, '"Geh nicht ohne Mantel"', S.11: 'Ein äußerst inhomogenes kulturelles Klima nach dem Zusammenbruch 1945, dessen vorherrschende Tendenz wohl in der Verarbeitung eigener existentieller Erlebnisse lag, die subjektive Perspektive im Schreiben also einerseits, sowie die kurzfristige kulturelle Öffnung, der gesellschaftliche Freiraum für Frauen in der Aufbruchsstimmung andererseits, gewähren schreibenden Frauen "die kurze Spanne Zeit zwischen zwei Zeiten", in fliegender Eile ihr Lebensgefühl auszubilden und auszudrücken.'

10 Hans Weigel, 'Es begann mit Ilse Aichinger. Fragmentarische Erinnerungen an die Wiedergeburt der österreichischen Literatur nach 1945', in: *Protokolle* (1966), 3-8, hier S.3.

11 Hans Weigel, *Unvollendete Symphonie* (Graz: Styria, 1992). Vgl. dazu: Klaus Amann, *"Denn ich habe zu schreiben. Und über den Rest hat man zu schweigen." Ingeborg Bachmann und die literarische Öffentlichkeit* (Klagenfurt: Drava, 1997).

12 Hans Weigel, 'Ingeborg Bachmann', in: ders., *In memoriam* (Graz: Styria, 1979), S.14-27, hier S.27.

13 Vgl. Jean Améry, 'Meine deutsche Szene', in: ders., *Örtlichkeiten*, mit einem Nachwort v. M. Franke (Stuttgart: Klett-Cotta, 1980), S.112-32.

14 Vgl. Albert Berger, 'Die austriakische Restauration. Gerhard Fritschs Verhältnis zu Österreich', in: Friedbert Aspetsberger (Hrsg.), *Österreichische Literatur seit den 20er Jahren* (Wien: ÖBV, 1979), (= Schriften des Instituts für Österreichkunde 35), S.68-80.

15 In: *Plan* 1: 5 (1945/46), 397-99.

16 Horn malte im autobiographischen Roman über den österreichischen Widerstand *Zeitzünder* (Wien: Globus, 1972) in der Figur des Weinberg ein nicht gerade sympathisches Porträt Weigels und schilderte nochmals die Beweggründe für seine harsche Entgegnung im *Plan*.

17 Hans Werner Richter, 'Tränen in Marktbreit. Günter Eich', in: Hans A. Neunzig (Hrsg.), *Lesebuch der Gruppe 47* (München: dtv, 1983), S.23-34, hier S.23.

18 Hans Werner Richter, 'Milo Dor', in: ders., *Im Etablissement der Schmetterlinge. Einundzwanzig Portraits aus der Gruppe 47* (München: Hanser, 1986), S.80-87, hier S.81.

19 Bachmann, 'Gruppe 47': 'Am Vormittag kam Milo Dor in das kleine Büro in der Seidengasse in Wien und fragte mich, ob ich ihm 50 Schilling borgen könne, er brauche sie, für einen deutschen Gast, um ein Taxi nehmen zu können, es sei eine Ehrensache, oder er wird sich wohl anders ausgedrückt haben, wie standen wir da vor der deutschen Literatur, wenn wir nicht einmal Geld für Taxi etc.' Daß es sich dabei um Hans Werners Richter Wienreise 1952 handelt, steht außer Frage.

20 Hans Werner Richter, 'Ilse Aichinger', in: Richter, *Im Etablissement*, S.13f. S.auch Klaus Briegleb, 'Ingeborg Bachmann, Paul Celan. Ihr (Nicht-)Ort in der Gruppe 47 (1952-1964/65). Eine Skizze', in: Bernhard Böschenstein und Sigrid Weigel (Hrsg.), *Ingeborg Bachmann und Paul Celan. Poetische Korrespondenzen* (Frankfurt a. M.: Suhrkamp, 1997), S.43-51.

21 Ilse Aichinger, *Kleist, Moos, Fasane*, hrsg. v. Richard Reichensperger (Frankfurt a. M.: Fischer, 1991), S.55.

22 *Hans Werner Richter und die Gruppe 47*. Mit Beiträgen von Walter Jens, Marcel Reich-Ranicki, Peter Wapnewski u. a. (München: nymphenburger, 1979), S.59. Weitere Hinweise auf dieses Werk befinden sich im Text unter Richter.

23 Hans Werner Richter, *Die Geschlagenen*. Roman. (München: Bertelsmann, 1978) [München: Desch 1949], S.142. Vgl. die Kritik von Heinz Friedrich, in: Lutz W. Wolff (Hrsg.), *Aufräumarbeiten. Berichte, Kommentare, Reden, Gedichte und Glossen aus vierzig Jahren.*, (München: dtv, 1987), S.59f.

[24] Hans Werner Richter, 'Ilse Aichinger', in: *Im Etablissement*, S.7-19, hier S.11 und S.13.

[25] Hannah Arendt, 'Besuch in Deutschland' (1950), in: *Zur Zeit. Politische Essays*, hrsg. v. Marie Luise Knott (München: dtv, 1989), S.43-70, hier S.44f.: 'Überall fällt einem auf, daß es keine Reaktion auf das Geschehene gibt, aber es ist schwer zu sagen, ob es sich dabei um eine irgendwie absichtliche Weigerung zu trauern oder um den Ausdruck einer echten Gefühlsunfähigkeit handelt. [...] Und die Gleichgültigkeit, mit der sie sich durch die Trümmer bewegen, findet ihre genaue Entsprechung darin, daß niemand um die Toten trauert; sie spiegelt sich in der Apathie wider, mit der sie auf das Schicksal der Flüchtlinge in ihrer Mitte reagieren oder vielmehr nicht reagieren. Dieser allgemeine Gefühlsmangel, auf jeden Fall aber die offensichtliche Herzlosigkeit, die manchmal mit billiger Rührseligkeit kaschiert wird, ist jedoch nur das auffälligste äußerliche Symptom einer tief verwurzelten, hartnäckigen und gelegentlich brutalen Weigerung, sich dem tatsächlich Geschehenen zu stellen und sich damit abzufinden.' Weitere Hinweise auf diesen Aufsatz befinden sich im Text unter Arendt.

[26] Vgl. Heimito von Doderer am 2.1.1952, in: *Commentarii 1951 bis 1956. Tagebücher aus dem Nachlaß*, hrsg. v. W. Schmidt-Dengler (München: Biederstein, 1976), S.99.

[27] Heinz Ulrich, *Die Zeit*, 24.5.1951, in: Reinhard Lettau (Hrsg.), *Die Gruppe 47. Bericht, Kritik, Polemik. Ein Handbuch* (Neuwied und Berlin: Luchterhand, 1967), S.65.

[28] Sigrid Weigel, *Bilder des kulturellen Gedächtnisses. Beiträge zur Gegenwartsliteratur* (Dülmen-Hiddingsel: tende, 1994), S.142.

[29] Einführung v. Fritz J. Raddatz zur Auswahl der Lesungen, in: Richter, *Almanach*, S.66-75, hier S.70.

[30] Ilse Aichinger, 'Für H. W.' // 'Die Gelassenheit / zu datieren, / zu versammeln in den Dörfern der Welt. // Der Rat, / die Stille des Rats zu schweigen, / wenn einer das Schreiben / und das Lesen zu Euch gebracht hat // Und wenn die Tage um sind, / zu sagen: Geht. // Aber täusch Dich nicht, / Du hast diesen Tagen / das Umsein abgewöhnt, / sie werden umgehen von Atemzug zu Atemzug, / Dein Rat bleibt bei den Ratlosen, / Du bleibst.', in: *Hans Werner Richter und die Gruppe 47*, S.179.

[31] Ilse Aichinger, 'Als mich Hans Werner Richter zum ersten Mal zur Gruppe 47 einlud...', *Sprache im technischen Zeitalter*, 26: 106 (Juni 1988). Beiheft *Literatur im technischen Zeitalter*, II/88, S.51.

[32] Günther Anders, *Tagebücher und Gedichte* (München: C. H. Beck, 1985), S.235.

[33] Alfred Andersch, *Die Kirschen der Freiheit. Ein Bericht* (Hamburg: Claassen, 1952), S.78: '"Dieser Krieg hier unten ist eine großartige Sache", sagte ich. Und ich dachte: schade! Es war ein herrlicher Krieg. Ich hätte was darum gegeben, einmal in meinem Leben an einem so herrlichen und großartigen Krieg teilnehmen zu können.'

[34] Ilse Aichinger, *Der Gefesselte. Erzählungen I*, hrsg. v. Richard Reichensperger (Frankfurt a. M. : Fischer, 1991), S.9.

[35] Hilde Spiel, 'Eh die Träume rosten und brechen', in: Samuel Moser (Hrsg.), *Ilse Aichinger. Leben und Werk*. 2. akt. u. erw. Aufl. (Frankfurt a. M.: Fischer, 1995), S.303-07.

[36] Joachim Kaiser, 'Freundschaftlicher Widerspruch', in: Moser, *Ilse Aichinger*, S.179-82.

[37] Heinz Ludwig Arnold, '"...dann kann hier jemand nicht mehr kritisieren!". Kritik in der Gruppe 47 — Unsystematischer Versuch einer Annäherung', in: *Dichter und Richter. Die Gruppe 47 und die deutsche Nachkriegsliteratur. Ausstellungskatalog* (Berlin: Akademie der Künste, 1988), S.80-90, hier S.84.

[38] Klaus Briegleb, 'Ingeborg Bachmann, Paul Celan', S.29-81.

[39] Vgl. Heinz Ludwig Arnold (Hrsg.), *Die Gruppe 47. Ein kritischer Grundriß* (München: text + kritik, 1980), S.166.

[40] Ingeborg Bachmann, *Wir müssen wahre Sätze finden. Gespräche und Interviews*, 4. Aufl., hrsg. v. Christine Koschel u. Inge v. Weidenbaum (München, Zürich: Piper, 1994), S.50.

JOHN WIECZOREK

Johannes Bobrowski und die Gruppe 47

Johannes Bobrowski war der einzige DDR-Schriftsteller, der über längere Zeit unmittelbaren Kontakt zur Gruppe 47 hatte. Trotz mancher bürokratischen Schwierigkeiten konnte er an mehreren Tagungen teilnehmen und gewann 1962 den Preis der Gruppe. Da die DDR jegliche ideologische Koexistenz entschieden ablehnte, waren Spannungen unvermeidlich. Obwohl Bobrowski selber bereit war, Kritik an auf Tagungen der Gruppe vorgelesenen Texten und an dem Medienrummel um die Tagungen zu üben, blieb seine Haltung gegenüber der Gruppe als solcher positiv. Es ist interessant zu überlegen, ob und inwieweit Bobrowski bei der Konzeption der 'Zigeunergruppe' in seinem Roman *Levins Mühle* an die Gruppe 47 und die Art ihres Agierens gedacht hat.

Der offizielle Kontakt zwischen Johannes Bobrowski (1917-1965) und der Gruppe 47 fand während der ersten Hälfte der 60er Jahre statt und stellt ein kleines, bezeichnendes Kapitel in der Geschichte der deutsch-deutschen Beziehungen während des Kalten Krieges dar. Die Gruppe 47 war ja nicht irgendeine Gruppe, sondern die westdeutsche Autoren-versammlung schlechthin, und Johannes Bobrowski war nicht irgendein Schriftsteller, sondern ein renommierter Schriftsteller aus der DDR, einem Staat mit eigenen kulturellen und sozialen Zielsetzungen.[1] Der erste Teil meines Beitrags — eine kurze Geschichte der Einladungen an Bobrowski und deren Ergebnisse — zeigt schon die Schwierigkeiten dieser Epoche; dann möchte ich einige der direkten literarischen Reflexionen auf diese Besuche in Bobrowskis Werken aufzählen, ehe ich einen Aspekt des Romans *Levins Mühle* (1964) aufgreife, der sich mit der Bobrowski eigenen Hermetik der Gruppe 47 zuwendet.[2]

   Die erste mir bekannte offizielle Kontaktaufnahme durch Hans Werner Richter erreichte Bobrowski in Form einer kurzen Einladung vom 22. September 1960 zur November-Tagung in Aschaffenburg: 'Die Tagung der Gruppe 47 findet vom 4. bis 6. November im Rathaussaal von Aschaffenburg statt. Anreisetag ist Donnerstag, der 3. November. Wegen Zimmervorbestellung wird sich der Fremdenverkehr von Aschaffenburg an Sie wenden.'[3] Das lag alles noch vor dem Mauerbau am 13. August 1961, und Bobrowski konnnte also relativ problemlos anreisen. Er las mehrere Gedichte vor, einige aus dem Band *Sarmatische Zeit*, der im folgenden Jahr in beiden deutschen Staaten erscheinen sollte, andere aus dem Manuskript für seinen zweiten Band *Schattenland Ströme*.

Er war ein fast Unbekannter, doch seine Gedichte wurden von Walter Jens, Walter Höllerer und Günter Grass lobend aufgenommen; sie wurden aber von Joachim Kaiser abgelehnt, der, wie es Bobrowski ausdrückte, 'das Neuartige, Ungewöhnliche, Interessante' vermißte.[4] In einem Brief vom 12. November an Peter Jokostra beschreibt Bobrowski seine Rezeption: 'Ich bin mit meinen Sachen über Erwarten gut angekommen, Jens hat mich zur "großen Literatur" gerechnet usw.' (das 'usw.' ist von Bobrowski). Trotz der allgemein wohlwollenden Aufnahme war ihm nicht alles geheuer, und gestört haben ihn vor allem die Marktatmosphäre und die Beteiligung der Verleger. In einem weiteren Brief an Ludvik Kundera schrieb er: 'In Aschaffenburg [...] liefen die Verleger wie Hündchen herum und rochen an jedem Hintern nach Talent. Es war lustig' (Tgahrt, S.122). Nichtsdestotrotz hoffte er, beim nächsten Male dabeizusein: 'Es soll nächstes Mal wieder strenger mit den Einladungen zugehn. Ich bin bereit, und wenn es geht, werd ich fahren' (unveröffentlichter Brief an Jokostra 17. November 1960). Da das nächste Treffen im Oktober 1961 stattfand, ein paar Monate nach dem Mauerbau, ging das natürlich nicht, und für Schloß Göhrde liegt also keine Einladung vor.[5]

Für Oktober 1962 bekam Bobrowski dann doch eine Einladung von Richter, der er folgen konnte, nicht nur zur Tagung im Alten Casino am Wannsee, sondern spezifisch: 'Wollen Sie sich an den Lesungen beteiligen?' Bobrowski antwortete mit Bezug auf die Situation nach dem Mauerbau, daß es 'sicher klappen' würde, weil 'die Gruppe nach wie vor hier hohen Respekt genießt', und fügte mit etwas falscher Bescheidenheit hinzu: 'Zum Vorlesen wird es sicher bessere Leute geben, für alle Fälle aber bring ich etwas mit' (Tgahrt, S.124). An Klaus Wagenbach, den er schon kannte, hatte er am 1. Oktober mit dem Vorschlag geschrieben, auch andere DDR-Schriftsteller einzuladen 'falls solche Einladungen an hierorts Lebende akzeptabel sein sollten': Peter Huchel, Christa Reinig und Manfred Bieler, aber auch Hermann Kant, da diese — so habe er gehört — auch vom DDR-Schriftstellerverband Passierscheine bekommen würden (*HWRB*, S.416). Richter wollte jedoch keine weiteren Einladungen abschicken, und Bobrowski war wieder der einzige Vertreter der DDR-Literatur.

Auf dieser Tagung am Wannsee las Bobrowski sieben Gedichte vor, die später in *Wetterzeichen* erschienen: 'Kalmus', 'Der lettische Herbst', 'Schattenland', 'Im Strom', 'Erfahrung', 'Begegnung', 'Die Wolgastädte'. Gegenüber Peter Weiss bekam er in der zweiten Wahl-Runde den Preis der Gruppe und 7000 Mark, die erste Preisverleihung seit 1958. Für die eigentliche Preisverleihung war er nicht dabei — sein Visum war schon abgelaufen.[6]

Die Gründe, warum er den Preis gewonnen hat, wußte er nicht so genau zu erklären. In einem kurz danach an Jokostra geschriebenen Brief behauptete er: 'Die Literaturmanager aus Hamburg oder Frankfurt stimmten für Peter Weiß. Für den ich auch gestimmt hätte, aus Qualitätsgründen' (Tgahrt, S.129). Jahrelang verunsicherte ihn auch die Frage, ob er den Preis 'fair' gewonnen habe oder ob ihm der Preis aus anderen, taktisch-politischen Gründen zuerkannt worden sei. Es wurde ja behauptet, die Schriftsteller hätten gegen Weiss gestimmt, weil dessen Verleger Siegfried Unseld vom Suhrkamp Verlag sich zu sehr für 'seinen' Autor engagiert habe. Es gab aber auch andere mögliche Gründe: er sollte sicherlich nicht als Vertreter des DDR-Regimes belohnt werden, aber war es vielleicht eine Solidaritätserklärung mit einem Daniel in der Löwengrube?[7] Der Grund war wahrscheinlich der naheliegendste: Bewunderung für seine (so Wolfdietrich Schnurre) 'sehr stillen, sehr menschlichen und naturverbundenen Gedichte' (Tgahrt, S.127). Nebenbei bemerkt: die Auswahl der Gedichte, die er vorlas, war idiosynkratisch: im Jahre 1962 und in Berlin war es nicht ohne Brisanz, ein Gedicht wie 'Die Wolgastädte' (1: S.169) vorzulesen, das mit den Zeilen anfängt 'Der Mauernstrich. / Türme'. War Bobrowski, dessen Arbeitszimmer im Union Verlag direkt an der Grenze über Checkpoint Charlie lag, so wirklichkeitsfremd, daß er sich der Wirkung dieser Worte nicht bewußt war?[8] Wohl nicht, wie das Gedicht 'Stadt' vom 13. November 1963 zeigte.

Die Verleihung des Preises wurde November 1962 in der DDR-Presse kommentarlos bis positiv berichtet. Hinter den Kulissen scheint sie jedoch Betroffenheit ausgelöst zu haben, wie der Bericht von Stephan Hermlin demonstriert (Tgahrt, S.158-60). Der längere Zeitungsbericht in *Neue Zeit* von G. Rostin (4: S.458-61) stellt auch eindeutig den Versuch dar, Bobrowski zu verteidigen, indem die

Gruppe 47 in einem politisch sehr günstigen Licht gezeigt wurde. Die nächsten zwölf Monate wurden aber zu den schwierigsten, die Bobrowski mit 'seinem' Staat erlebte: eine seit einiger Zeit laufende Kampagne der SED gegen 'ideologische Koexistenz' schlug sich in Repressalien nieder, als die Partei versuchte, sich stärker vom mächtigen westlichen Nachbarn abzugrenzen. Betroffen wurden vor allem Ende 1962/Anfang 1963 Peter Huchel und Stephan Hermlin. Die Kritik an Huchel hing mit der Unabhängigkeit seiner editorischen Arbeit für die Zeitschrift *Sinn und Form* zusammen. Hermlin wurde zunächst kritisiert, weil er den später berühmt gewordenen Lyrikabend mit Gedichten von u.a. Volker Braun, Wolf Biermann, ja der ganzen ernstzunehmenden jungen DDR-Lyrik veranstaltete. Auch Bobrowski fand sich hier sehr gegen seinen Willen in Mitleidenschaft gezogen: er saß z.B. im Publikum bei diesem Dichterabend und hatte den Abend und den neuen Impuls für die Lyrik in einer Umfrage für *Neue Zeit* gelobt.[9]

Ausschlaggebend für öffentliche Angriffe auf ihn war jedoch etwas anderes: seine Teilnahme an einer Tagung der Evangelischen Akademie in dem östlichen Stadtteil Berlin-Weißensee im Januar 1963 zum Thema 'Sprache im technischen Zeitalter'. Diese Tagung wurde von Kritikern und Schriftstellern aus der DDR und der Bundesrepublik besucht. Klaus Wagenbach befaßte sich unter anderem mit der Prosa von Günter Grass, Hans Mayer mit Dürrenmatt und Brecht. Die Tagung wurde zu einem Gegenstand der Auseinandersetzung bei der Beratung des Politbüros des ZK der SED mit Kulturschaffenden im März 1963, wo Kurt Hager die zur Schau getragene 'ideologische Koexistenz' kritisierte und erklärte, hier 'wurde westdeutschen Kreisen eine Gelegenheit gegeben, auf diese Weise bei uns Einfluß zu erlangen'.[10] Bobrowski selbst, als Mitglied der Ost-CDU, wurde am 18. April 1963 'vor das Tribunal der christlich-demokratischen Parteiführung gezerrt und im Ungeist stalinistischer Kulturpolitik verleumdet'.[11]

Dokumente aus den internen Diskussionen der CDU zeigen, wie in den folgenden Monaten Bobrowskis Gruppe 47-Preis umgedeutet wurde: Die Tagung der Evangelischen Akademie wurde zu einer Tagung, 'an der auch Schriftsteller der *westdeutschen* Gruppe 47 teilnahmen und auf der die Vertreter der DDR ideologische Koexistenz praktizierten' (Tgahrt, S.248), und — persönlicher — in der internen CDU-Diskussion vom 29. März 1963 wurde auch die Frage von einem Teilnehmer erhoben, 'wie die Lyrik des Unionsfreundes Bobrowski einzuschätzen sei, der von der westdeutschen Gruppe 47 ausgezeichnet wurde' (Tgahrt, S.248).

Die Änderungen in der offiziellen Einstellung zeigen sich auch in verschiedenen Artikeln in dem Organ des Schriftstellerverbandes *Neue Deutsche Literatur.* Vor der Kursänderung liest man die kurze neutrale Mitteilung: 'Den Preis der westdeutschen Schriftstellervereinigung "Gruppe 47" erhielt der Lyriker Johannes Bobrowski.'[12] Ein paar Monate danach erscheint dann ein Artikel von Günther Cwojdrak, 'Gruppe 47 Anno 62',[13] der die Gruppe kritisierte — ohne den neuesten Preisträger zu nennen — wegen ihrer angeblich allgemeinmenschlichen, Klassengegensätze ignorierenden Einstellung. Vor allem Enzensberger wurde hierbei namentlich kritisiert als 'ein Möchtegern-Villon, [...] ein Pubertätsbrecht' (S.107). Ein paar Monate später häufte Hans Koch in einer Rede, auch ohne Bobrowski beim Namen zu nennen, noch mehr glühende Kohlen auf dessen Haupt. In seiner Rede 'Der Wirklichkeit auf den Grund gehen' vor der Delegiertenkonferenz des Schriftstellerverbands vom Mai 1963 kritisierte Koch die Gruppe 47, weil sie die spezifische Kultur der DDR ignorierte (d.h. in diesem Kontext die noch laufende Bitterfelder Bewegung) und erklärte:

> Um so mehr [...] muß es zu einer elementaren Pflicht jedes Verbandsmitglieds gehören, beispielweise im Ausland nicht nur subjektive Ansichten, sondern die tatsächliche Rolle und Bedeutung der sozialistischen Literatur der Deutschen Demokratischen Republik im nationalen Kampf in Deutschland zu repräsentieren. [14]

An derselben Stelle kritisierte er Hans Mayer, weil dieser die 'nationale Bedeutung' der Gruppe 47 betont habe.

Daß Bobrowski ab jetzt Schwierigkeiten mit seinen Beziehungen zur Gruppe 47 haben würde, war vorauszusehen, und sie traten prompt im Herbst 1963 im Vorfeld der Tagung in Saulgau in Erscheinung. Hans Werner Richters erste Einladungen an einige DDR-Schriftsteller 'gingen verloren', und erst nach einer Rückfrage von Richter bekam Bobrowski endlich am 23. September einen Durchschlag der Einladung. Andere eingeladene DDR-Schriftsteller, Manfred Bieler, Peter Huchel, Günter Kunert und Christa Reinig wurden mehr oder minder sofort blockiert,[15] und es sah zeitweise aus, als ob Bobrowski selber keine Ausreiseerlaubnis bekommen würde. Stattdessen schlug Hans Koch, der Erste Sekretär des Deutschen Schriftstellerverbandes vor, 'eine Delegation seiner Mitglieder unter Leitung von Johannes Bobrowski zur

Tagung [zu senden]' (*HWRB*, S.481). Die Annahme einer solchen Delegation wurde von Richter sofort entschieden abgelehnt:

> Es gehört zu den Prinzipien der Gruppe 47, daß keine Delegationen geladen werden. Alle Einladungen sind privater und persönlicher Natur [...]. Ich habe [...] die Schriftsteller Günter Kunert, Johannes Bobrowski, Manfred Bieler, Walter D. Schulz [gemeint ist Max Walter Schulz], Christa Reinig, Peter Huchel eingeladen. Ich hoffe sehr, daß sie kommen können, zumindest möchte ich Johannes Bobrowski gern auf der diesjährigen Tagung haben, da es so üblich ist, daß der letzte Preisträger der Gruppe 47 auch auf der nächstfolgenden Tagung anwesend ist. (*HWRB*, S.481f.)

Von den Eingeladenen konnten nur Bobrowski und Max Walter Schulz kommen, wobei die Ausreiseerlaubnis für Schulz sich wohl aus seiner Arbeit bei dem MfS erklärt,[16] aber sie konnten erst am 25. Oktober verspätet nach dem Tagungsbeginn ankommen. Hier liest Bobrowski zwei Prosatexte ('Ich will fortgehen' und 'Das Käuzchen') vor, lernt Hubert Fichte, Erich Fried und Manfred Peter Hein kennen und kehrt krank zurück 'aus dem Vergnügen, so viele liebe Leute zu sehen, [...] [aus] dem Trinken und Wachen' (Tgahrt, S.134). Die Bedeutung von dieser Tagung (und die immer noch spürbaren negativen Wirkungen von der Akademie-Tagung) gehen klar aus einem kurzen Artikel Günther Wirths hervor, der, in dem Versuch, Bobrowski zu rehabilitieren, in der *Neuen Deutschen Literatur* (12: 1 (1964), 182) Bobrowskis Benehmen an der Gruppe 47-Tagung in Saulgau beschrieb und kommentierte: 'Ja, man kann sagen, in Saulgau wurde Berlin-Weißensee korrigiert'.[17] Um Weihnachten 1963 wurde dann Bobrowski von Hubert Fichte gebeten, satirische Doppeldistichen auf Mitglieder der Gruppe 47 zu schreiben, von denen dann siebzehn im Jahre 1964 im Stockholmer Katalog der Gruppe 47 erschienen.

Die behördlichen Schwierigkeiten im Jahr 1964 waren für Bobrowski noch erheblicher. Obwohl alles gut zu laufen schien, bekamen weder er noch die anderen Eingeladenen (Huchel, Kunert, Bieler) für die eigentliche Tagung in Stockholm (10.-12. September) eine Reiseerlaubnis. Stattdessen durfte Bobrowski, und nur er, zur 'Stockholmer Woche der Gruppe 47' (13.-19. September) fahren, und das erst nachdem sich Günther Wirth über das Staatssekretariat für Kirchenfragen an das Ministerium für Kultur in seiner Sache verwandt hatte (Tgahrt, S.136f.). Es sollte sein letzter offizieller Kontakt zur

Gruppe sein: vor der nächsten Tagung im Oktober 1965 war er schon gestorben.

Bobrowskis schriftliche Reaktionen auf diese Tagungen lassen sich in zwei Gruppen teilen: die *direkten*, also epigrammatische Gedichte und Briefe und ein paar Zeitungsartikel und öffentliche Erwähnungen in Interviews, und die *indirekten*, auf die ich später eingehen werde. Nach dem ersten Besuch lobte er die Gruppe direkt in *Neuer Zeit* (29. November 1960) für ihre 'Literatur ohne Unverbindlichkeit' (4: S.394f.). Hier betonte er die Lockerheit der Gruppenzusammensetzung: 'Es sind Schriftsteller, [...] die zusammenkommen' (4: S.395). Er kritisierte auch die Anwesenheit zahlreicher Verleger, aber hob die Protestaktion zur Unterstützung französischer Intellektueller hinsichtlich ihrer Stellungnahme gegen die Algerienpolitik der französischen Regierung hervor.

Im Januar 1963 kritisierte er in einem weiteren Artikel Günter Grass und seinen auf der 1962 Tagung vorgelesenen Text: die letzten drei 'Es war einmal'-Abschnitte aus dem zweiten Buch von *Hundejahren*.[18] Indem er aber, ohne Grass beim Namen zu nennen, nur erklärte: 'ich war neulich auf einer Tagung, wo ich einen Text hörte' schützte er die Gruppe (oder vielleicht sich selbst) durch Schweigen. Im Juni 1963 erwähnt er in einem Interview 'diesen Run, der so jedes Jahr um die Tagung der Gruppe 47 von westdeutschen Verlegern vollführt wird, diesen Indianertanz' (4: S.487), aber über die eigentliche Gruppe hat er nur Gutes zu berichten. Ja, in dem Vortrag 'Die Koexistenz und das Gespräch' (4: S.449-55) lobt er sogar 'die auch für uns in einer ganzen Anzahl ihrer Angehörigen durchaus reputierliche Gruppe 47' (4: S.451) und beschreibt, wie sie in der westdeutschen Öffentlichkeit als eine 'Terroristenorganisation bezeichnet [wird], die sich nun auch noch damit entlarvt habe, daß sie ihren Preis an einen Kommunisten [er meinte sich selbst] verleiht' (Ebd.).

Die Unterscheidung zwischen Verlegern und Autoren, die er so oft betont, wird noch deutlicher in den an bestimmte Mitglieder der Gruppe gerichteten Epigrammen: an den 'Nußknacker' (d.h. Günter Grass) oder Ilse Aichinger ('Huldigung' und 'Reigen seliger Geister') oder Christa Reinig. Über Hans Magnus Enzensbergers Geschäftigkeit macht er sich zwar lustig, aber die Bewunderung, die in den folgenden Zeilen steckt, ist auch klar:

> h m e
>
> Heute am Nordkap und morgen auf Delos, dem russischen Bären
>
> sink ich ans Herz, und wohin sink ich dem Lama Peru's?
>
> Dichte ich nach (aus siebzehn der unverständlichsten Sprachen)
>
> oder dichte ich vor, — überall bin ich zuerst. (1: S.246)

In einer späteren Version steht hier in unverständlichem Englisch: 'überall bin ich at first'. Die Verleger werden schärfer behandelt: Unseld erscheint als 'Gefechtseinheit Unseld' (3: S.249), während 'Herr Ledig von Rowohlt' (so der volle Titel) seine Siege stolz genießt:

> Warum soll er auch nicht: Er schmeißt sich aufs Kreuz, und er räuspert
>
> sich, wie er will und 's ihm paßt; hat er doch eben entdeckt
>
> wieder mal einen, der dichtet und den alle anderen kaufen
>
> wollten, er hat ihn gekriegt· diesmal aus Lokstedt — 'nen Joyce. (1: S.244)[19]

In ein paar Xenien, in dem Stockholmer Katalog und anderswo gedruckt, behandelt er die lockere Existenz der Gruppe, wie in der berühmten 'Definition':

> Eine Gruppe ist eine Gruppe ist zwar eine Gruppe,
>
> diese ist keine, es sind Leute, die kennen sich, denn
>
> keine Gruppe ist keine Gruppe ist gar keine Gruppe —
>
> Hans Werner Richter erklärts deutlich und klar: wie's hier steht. (1: S.245)

Mit dieser 'Definition' unterstreicht er auch übrigens die für die DDR wichtige, aber häufig mißverstandene Tatsache, daß es sich bei der Gruppe nicht um eine offizielle westdeutsche Organisation handelte, sondern um eine private Initiative, zu der man eben keine 'Delegation unter Leitung von Johannes Bobrowski' senden konnte. Ein anderes im Stockholmer Katalog nicht gedrucktes Gedicht behandelt 'die Zukunft der Gruppe 47', ausgehend von dem damaligen Schlagwort des Bonner CDU-Politikers Dufhues, sie sei eine geheime Reichsschrifttums-kammer: 'Ist sie schon heute Reichsschrifttumskammer, so bildet sie morgen/gar die Regierung in Bonn (1: S.249). Der DDR-eigene Vorwurf, die Gruppe betreibe eine 'literarische Hallstein-Doktrin' (Alexander Abusch), wurde übrigens in keinem Gedicht erwähnt.[20]

Texte wie diese stellen die offensichtlichen Ergebnisse von Bobrowskis Kontakt mit der Gruppe dar. Ich möchte aber auf ein weiteres und unsicheres Gebiet hinweisen — als Spekulation, nicht im Sinne von Einfluß oder Wirkung, sondern im Sinne einer durch solche Kontakte verursachten Akzentverschiebung, Bereicherung, und zwar ganz konkret in Bobrowskis Roman *Levins Mühle* (3: S.7-223). An der

Idee eines Romans arbeitete er seit einiger Zeit: im Mai 1961 erfuhr er von einem Ahnen aus dem 19. Jahrhundert, der Mühlenbesitzer gewesen war und die Mühle eines jüdischen Konkurrenten weggeschwemmt hatte. Er machte mit diesem 'Roman über Wassermühlen' in diesem Jahr aber keinen Anfang, und erst im Oktober 1962, kurz vor der Tagung der Gruppe 47, erwähnt er zum ersten Mal die Arbeit daran. Zur Zeit der Tagung ist das erste Kapitel des Romans mit großer Wahrscheinlichkeit schon fertig[21] und bis Februar 1963 ist das fünfte Kapitel auch da (*Chronik*, S.70). In der Zwischenzeit hatte er, wie gesagt, den Preis der Gruppe 47 gewonnen, aber auch die Maßregelungen von Huchel und Hermlin erlebt, und er sollte in den nächsten paar Monaten selber ähnliches erleben, bis der Roman Mitte Juli 1963 plötzlich fertig war. Er wurde 1964 in beiden deutschen Staaten veröffentlicht.

Levins Mühle behandelt Bobrowskis altes Thema: die Deutschen und die östlichen Nachbarvölker. Das Werk stellt also einerseits eine Weiterführung seiner sarmatischen Lyrik dar. Zu einem Zeitpunkt jedoch, wo die DDR-Regierung auf das Ende der 'ideologischen Koexistenz' mit immer schärferen Mitteln drängte und beharrlich auf einer Interpretation der Geschichte, ja der Wirklichkeit, nach marxistisch-leninistischer Ideologie bestand, ist es ein Werk, das man ohne Übertreibung als ein Plädoyer für die Ideale der Gruppe 47 bezeichnen kann, die man oft genug mit dem Schlagwort eines anti-ideologischen 'Pluralismus' auf einen Nenner gebracht hat.

Der Roman spielt bekanntlich in und um Neumühl, einem Dorf in Westpreußen im Jahre 1874. Der sogenannte Großvater hat die Mühle seines jüdischen Konkurrenten Levin weggeschwemmt. Levin will ihn vor Gericht bringen, aber dem Großvater gelingt es, über seine deutsch-gesinnten Freunde die Verhandlung zu verschieben. Levin will schon aufgeben, als andere Leute, einschließlich viele Zigeuner und Musikanten, eine lockere und sehr heterogene Gruppe bilden, die ihn unterstützt. Ein erfolgreiches Mittel dazu ist ein Lied, in dem der Großvater ständig mit seiner Schuld konfrontiert wird. Am Ende des Romans führt der Großvater einen Krawall in der Ortskneipe herbei, den er verliert. Das Dorf bekommt eine Garnison, aber als auch diese Soldaten einen kritischen Bericht über den Großvater schreiben (er besticht sie nicht genug), verkauft er seine Mühle in Neumühl und zieht in die Landeshauptstadt Briesen.

Vor dem Hintergrund dieser Dorfgeschichte untersucht Bobrowski allgemeine Verhaltensweisen. Neben dem schon erwähnten Thema 'Die Deutschen und ihre östlichen Nachbarn' findet man aber noch Allgemeineres: vom Anfang an wird nämlich die Notwendigkeit betont, genau zu denken und zu unterscheiden: z.B. bei dem Versuch zwischen Deutschen und Polen in Westpreußen zu unterscheiden, kommt der Erzähler zu dem unerwarteten Ergebnis: 'Ich sage [...]: Die Deutschen hießen Kaminski, Tomaschewski und Kossakowski und die Polen Lebrecht und Germann. Und so ist es nämlich auch gewesen' (3: S.10). Gleich danach greift der Erzähler Leute direkt an, die gerne 'feste Urteile' haben:

> Feste Urteile hat man schon gern, und vielleicht ist es manch einem egal, woher er sie bekommt, mir ist es jetzt nicht egal, deshalb werde ich die Geschichte auch erzählen. Man soll sich den klaren Blick durch Sachkenntnis nicht trüben lassen, werden die Leute sagen, denen es gleich ist, woher ihre Urteile kommen [...], aber wir werden doch lieber Sachkenntnis aufwenden und genau sein, d.h. also, uns den klaren Blick trüben. (3: S.10)

Wenn dann die moralisch überlegenen Charaktere (diese Gruppe von Zirkusleuten, Zigeunern, Alkoholikern, wandernden Musikanten — alles asoziale Elemente von sozialistischem Gesichtspunkt aus) die Handlungen des Großvaters zu erklären versuchen, indem sie ihn und seine Freunde auf einen Nenner zu bringen versuchen, haben sie nur sehr begrenzten Erfolg: in einem zentralen Gespräch (3: S.169f.) erwägen sie viele Antworten zu der zentralen Frage: 'Weshalb sind die bloß so?' (3: S.169). Die Antworten: 'wegen Frömmigkeit [...] wegen Deutschigkeit [...] [wegen] Mangel[s] an Musik' (Ebd.) werden alle eine nach der anderen abgelehnt, da es überzeugende Gegenbeispiele gibt, bis dann einer vorschlägt: 'es ist wegen Geld' (Ebd.). Und dabei bleibt es. Der Erzähler kommentiert ohne große Begeisterung 'Meinetwegen', und die Antwort wird von Habedank, aber auch ohne große Begeisterung, bestätigt: 'Wirst schon recht haben' (3: S.170). So kann man den Text als eine sozialistische Kritik an den Übeln des Kapitalismus lesen. Die Behauptung wird nirgendwo dementiert.

Sie stellt aber keineswegs die einzige Erklärung für das Benehmen des Großvaters dar, und sie wird durch eine weitere versteckte Erklärung untergraben. Hier dürfen wir Bobrowskis 'heimliche Neigung zum Hermetismus' (s.o.) nicht vergessen: Bobrowski amüsierte es nämlich anscheinend, seinen Text mit

Anspielungen und Zitaten zu spicken. Es handelt sich um ein bestimmtes Buch des Magus im Norden Johann Georg Hamanns: *Golgatha und Scheblimini*, einen Text, den er gerade wieder gelesen und den er erstaunlich gut kannte, wie eine Rezension aus den 50er Jahren (4: S.367-69) beweist.[22] An einer Stelle versucht nämlich Weiszmantel, einer der Musikanten, den Großvater, den er schon mehrmals als einen Teufel bezeichnet hat, zu verstehen. Der Text lautet:

> Wie der Deiwel heißt, der hier los ist, das weiß der Weiszmantel schon, jetzt bekommt er ihn zu sehen. Er wundert sich nicht, aber er denkt doch: Immer war der nicht so. Aber wie war er denn? [...] Du weißt das alles nicht richtig Weiszmantel: nicht, wie man sich anstellt, wenn man etwas hat und es behalten will, noch weniger, wie es einem zusetzt, wenn man mehr haben will als man hat, schon gar nicht, wie einem zumute ist, der hier sitzt, in diesem Land, und weiß: er ist deutsch wie der Kaiser in Berlin, aber rundherum gibt es nur diese Polen und anderes Volk, Zigeuner und Juden, und nun, Weiszmantel, stell dir mal einen vor, bei dem das alles zusammenkommt: behalten wollen, mehr haben wollen, besser sein wollen als alle andern.
>
> (3: S.72)

Dieser letzte Ausdruck faßt alles zusammen, was den Großvater so ärgerte.

In Hamanns *Golgatha und Scheblimini* findet man die Vorlage:

> [Der Mensch] hat also weder ein physisches noch moralisches Vermögen zu einer anderen Glückseligkeit, als die ihm zugedacht, und wozu er beruffen ist. Alle Mittel, deren er sich zur Erlangung einer ihm nicht gegebenen und beschärten Glückseeligkeit bedient, sind gehäufte Beleidigungen der Natur und entschiedene Ungerechtigkeit. Jede Lüsternheit zum Besserseyn ist der Funke eines höllischen Aufruhrs.[23]

Dieser 'Funke eines höllischen Aufruhrs' ist der Grund, warum der Teufel/Luzifer aus dem Himmel vertrieben wurde, warum Adam und Eva aus dem Paradies vertrieben wurden (sie wollten ja 'sein wie Gott') und stellt auch den Grund dar, warum der Großvater aus seinem 'Paradies', aus Neumühl, vertrieben werden soll.

Die Abstrusheit dieses theologischen Erklärungsmusters spricht natürlich dagegen, daß es als ein ernstzunehmendes, eben dogmatisches Paradigma verstanden werden soll. Im Gegenteil: es stellt bloß ein weiteres Erklärungsmuster dar, ein populär-theologisches, neben dem vulgärmarxistischen ('es ist alles wegen Geld'), aber auch neben dem protestantisch-bigotten ('es sind eben alles Katholiken'), dem

nationalistischen ('deutsch ist schlimmer als fromm'), dem
künstlerischen ('alle keine Musiker'), mit denen immer die jeweilige
Gegenpartei verdammt wird. Alle halbwegs abstrakten ideologischen
Erklärungsmuster für die im Roman geschilderten Ereignisse werden
auf diese Weise in Frage gestellt.

    Am Ende des Romans unterbricht sich der Erzähler mit einer
rhetorischen Frage:

> Wie kommt es, daß [Weiszmantels] Lieder fröhlicher geworden sind?
>
> Es ist doch da etwas gewesen, das hat es bisher nicht gegeben. Nicht dieses
> alte Hier-Polen-hier-Deutsche oder Hier-Christen-hier-Unchristen, etwas ganz
> anderes, wir haben es doch gesehen, was reden wir da noch. Das ist
> dagewesen, also geht es nicht mehr fort. (3: S.221f.)

Vor allem in dem letzten Satz betont Bobrowski undogmatisch das
Faktische des Historischen. Schillernder wird er, wenn man in Hamanns
Golgatha und Scheblimini liest: 'Weil ich [...] von keinen ewigen
Wahrheiten, als unaufhörlich Zeitlichen weiß' (Nadler 3: S.303), und im
selben Kontext den Glaubenssatz findet: 'nicht [...] ewige Wahrheiten
sondern lediglich zeitliche Geschichtswahrheiten, die sich zu einer Zeit
zugetragen haben [...], Thatsachen, die [...] in einem Zeitpunct und
Erdraum wahr geworden' (Nadler 3: S.304). Mit diesen Sätzen
unterstreicht Hamann im Kontext den Unterschied zwischen der
jüdischen Gesetzgebung ('den ewigen Wahrheiten') und dem christlichen
Glauben an die ('unaufhörlich zeitliche') einmalige Geburt Christi aber
auch, natürlich, die Bedeutung des Einmalig-Faktischen gegenüber dem
Theoretischen. Sie sind also ein Plädoyer für das Faktische gegen das
Theoretische, für einen ideologiefreien Blick auf 'das Wirkliche' (1:
S.161). Genau dasselbe betont Bobrowski in *Levins Mühle*: die
Vertreibung des Großvaters war nicht das Ergebnis irgendwelcher
marxistisch-leninistischer Gesetzmäßigkeiten sondern etwas Einmaliges,
nichts Verallgemeinbares, aber auch nichts deswegen Wertloses.[24]

    Eine weitere Dimension bekommen jedoch diese Überlegungen,
wenn man die problematische Bedeutung des Ausdrucks 'Ewigen
Wahrheiten' in der DDR-Mythologie erkennt: am 28. Oktober 1956
hatte nämlich die DDR-Zeitung *Sonntag* einen Aufsatz des
Wissenschaftlers Robert Havemann mit dem Titel: 'Rückantworten an
die Hauptverwaltung "Ewige Wahrheiten"' veröffentlicht, in dem
Havemann argumentierte: Der Dogmatismus 'hat unsere Philosophie zu
einem System allgemeinster Sätze über die allgemeinste Struktur der

Welt zu machen versucht, zu einer Hauptverwaltung "Ewige Wahrheiten" (HEW)'.[25] Mit diesem Bonmot bezeichnete Havemann die Parteizentrale und besonders die für Wissenschaft und Kunst zuständige Abteilung, die Bobrowski zu seiner Zeit so gnadenlos schikanierte. Wenn nicht dem Wortlaut nach, dann jedenfalls dem Sinne nach erklärt Bobrowski in diesem Roman seine Gegnerschaft zu Havemanns 'HEW'.

Unter dem dichten Geflecht von Details aus dem westpreußischen Landleben im späten neunzehnten Jahrhundert kann man also in *Levins Mühle* einen Versuch erkennen, die von der Ideologie überlagerte Realität zu erfassen und sie nicht eindeutig, sondern in ihrer ganzen Vielschichtigkeit paradigmatisch zu erhellen, ein kleines anti-dogmatisches Plädoyer, ein Plädoyer für pluralistische Denkweisen, die Bobrowski in seinen Begegnungen und Freundschaften mit Mitgliedern der Gruppe 47 bestätigt und praktiziert fand. Ja, zugespitzt ausgedrückt: mehr als ein Jahrzehnt vor dem *Treffen in Telgte* — oder anders gesehen ein paar Jahrhunderte danach — haben sich die Künstler der Gruppe 47 vielleicht ein einmaliges Treffen in Form von dieser Musikanten- und Zigeunergruppe in Neumühl, Kreis Strasburg, Westpreußen gegönnt.

Fußnoten

[1] S. Hans Lindemann, Kurt Müller, *Auswärtige Kulturpolitik der DDR: Die kulturelle Abgrenzung der DDR von der Bundesrepublik Deutschland* (Bonn-Bad Godesberg: Verlag Neue Gesellschaft, 1974).

[2] S. den Vortrag 'Benannte Schuld — gebannte Schuld?', in: Johannes Bobrowski, *Gesammelte Werke*, hrsg. v. Eberhard Haufe (Berlin: Union Verlag, 1987), Bd.4, S.447, wo er von seiner heimlichen Neigung zum Hermetismus spricht. Weitere Hinweise auf die *Gesammelten Werke* befinden sich im Text.

[3] Hans Werner Richter, *Briefe*, hrsg. v. Sabine Cofalla, (München/Wien: Hanser, 1997). Weitere Hinweise auf dieses Buch befinden sich im Text unter *HWRB*.

[4] *Johannes Bobrowski oder Landschaft mit Leuten*, hrsg. v. Reinhard Tgahrt, (Marbach: Deutsche Schillergesellschaft, 1993), S.123. Weitere Hinweise auf dieses Buch befinden sich im Text unter Tgahrt.

[5] Hans Werner Richters persönliche Reaktion auf den Bau der Mauer sieht man in dem Brief an John Collins vom 9. September 1961 (*HWRB*, S.355f.).

[6] Ein Interview mit Gerhard Rostin stellt die Situation anders dar: Bobrowski habe den Preis nicht gleich empfangen können, 'da er an diesem Nachmittag Hans Magnus Enzensberger in seinem Hause in Berlin-Friedrichshagen zu Gast hatte' (4: S.460).

[7] Bobrowski selbst sah sich nicht als einen solchen. S. seine Rede 'Die Koexistenz und das Gespräch' (4: S.449-55, hier S.451).

[8] Siegfried Mandel, in: *Group 47: The Reflected Intellect* (Carbondale and Edwardsville: Southern Illinois University Press, 1973) schreibt von der 'unintentional irony' von diesen Worten (S.128).

[9] 'Daß in unserer Lyrik einiges in Bewegung gekommen ist [...] eine einsichtsvolle Unterstützung, mit der Stephan Hermlin begonnen hat' (4: S.462).

[10] Elimar Schubbe (Hrsg.), *Dokumente zur Kunst-, Literatur- und Kulturpolitik der SED*, Bd. 1 (1949-1970) (Stuttgart: Seewald, 1972), S. 875.

[11] G. Wirth, *Standpunkt*, 18: 2 (1990), 53. Zitiert nach: Tgahrt, S.248.

[12] *Neue Deutsche Literatur*, 11: 1 (1963), 219.

[13] *Neue Deutsche Literatur*, 11: 5 (1963), 101-11.

[14] *Neue Deutsche Literatur*, 11: 8 (1963), 12-54, hier 44.

[15] In diesem Kontext schreibt Richter unverständlicherweise auch von Einladungen an Christa Wolf und Karl Heinz Jakobs (*HWRB*, S.481). Von solchen Einladungen scheint nichts bekannt zu sein.

[16] S. Joachim Walther, *Sicherungsbereich Literatur: Schriftsteller und Staatssicherheit in der Deutschen Demokratischen Republik* (Berlin: Ch. Links, 1996): Schulz habe für das MfS gearbeitet und verfaßte einen 'Vertraulichen Bericht über die Tagung der Gruppe 47 in Saulgau/Württemberg' (S.271).

[17] *Neue Deutsche Literatur*, 12: 4 (1964), 182. Es war eine sehr notwendige Korrektur. Gegen Bobrowski lief schon ein Operativer Vorlauf, der sich insbesondere mit seinem 'Neuen Friedrichshagener Dichterkreis' befaßte, aber auch seine 'enge Verbindung zu Vertretern der imperialistischen Ideologie in Westdeutschland' verdächtig fand und ihm 'aktive Beteiligung an der politisch-ideologischen Diversion, die auf die Untergrabung der politisch-ideologischen Grundlagen der Gesellschaftsordnung der DDR gerichtet ist', vorwarf (siehe *Sicherungsbereich Literatur*, S.448f.). Ihm wurde auch vorgeworfen, er würde die 'ideologische Konzeption' der Gruppe 47 propagieren (S.449).

[18] Seine eigentliche literarische Antwort auf das Vorgelesene war der schwache Text 'Ein Herz für den Hund' (4: S.58-60), in dem er realistischer den Einsatz von Hunden im Zweiten Weltkrieg anschnitt.

[19] Im Hamburger Stadtteil Lokstedt befinden sich die Studios des Norddeutschen Rundfunks.

[20] Alexander Abusch, *Humanismus und Realismus in der Literatur: Aufsätze* (Leipzig: Reclam, 1972), S.296.

[21] Siehe Eberhard Haufe, *Bobrowski-Chronik: Daten zu Leben und Werk* (Würzburg: Königshausen & Neumann, 1994), S.69.

[22] Eine Auflistung der vielen Bezugnahmen auf *Golgatha und Scheblimini* im Roman *Levins Mühle* würde den Rahmen dieses Beitrags sprengen. Hamanns Werk stellt eine

Auseinandersetzung mit Moses Mendelssohns übertrieben rationalisierendem und systematisierendem Text *Jerusalem oder über religiöse Macht und Judenthum* (1783) dar.

23 Johann Georg Hamann, *Sämtliche Werke*, hrsg. v. Josef Nadler (Wien: Herder, 1951), Bd.3, S.299. Weitere Hinweise auf diese Ausgabe befinden sich im Text unter Nadler.

24 In Bobrowskis Hamann-Ausgabe *Entkleidung und Verklärung: Eine Auswahl aus Schriften und Briefen des 'Magus im Norden'*, hrsg. v. Martin Seils ([Ost]Berlin: Union Verlag, 1963) beginnen die Auszüge aus *Golgatha und Scheblimini* eben mit diesen Worten: 'Weil ich aus von keinen *ewigen Wahrheiten*, als *unaufhörlich Zeitlichen* weiß' (S.235).

25 Robert Havemann, *Die Stimme des Gewissens: Texte eines deutschen Antistalinisten*, hrsg. v. Rüdiger Rosenthal (Reinbek bei Hamburg: Rowohlt, 1990), S.37.

ESTHER V. SCHNEIDER-HANDSCHIN

'Die Wahrheit ist dem Menschen nämlich zumutbar' —
Ingeborg Bachmann und die Gruppe 47 auf dem Hintergrund
der österreichischen bzw. deutschen Kulturpolitik

Ingeborg Bachmann erhielt 1953, ein Jahr nach ihrem Debüt, den Preis der Gruppe 47. Ihr Verhältnis zur Gruppe blieb aber gespannt, obwohl ihre Auftritte immer große Aufmerksamkeit bei den Medien erweckten und dadurch Hans Werner Richters Wunsch nach Publicity nachkamen. Sie fühlte sich nicht wohl in einer Ambiente, wo meistens Schweigen über die deutsche Vergangenheit herrschte und politische Äußerungen oft nur den Schein der Radikalität trugen. Trotzdem bot Teilnahme am literarischen Leben Deutschlands eine Alternative zu ihrer schwierigen Existenz in Wien. Ihr Erfolg in Deutschland dauerte bis Anfang der sechziger Jahre, als ihr erster Prosaband *Das dreißigste Jahr* bei der Kritik nicht gut ankam. Sie entsprach nicht mehr dem Bild, das von ihr gemacht worden war. Seit 1962 nahm sie nicht mehr an den Treffen der Gruppe 47 teil.

Ingeborg Bachmanns Debüt in der Gruppe 47 und damit im deutschen Literaturbetrieb fiel auf die Niendorfer Tagung im Mai 1952. Ein Jahr später erhielt sie in Mainz den Gruppenpreis für ihre vorgetragenen Gedichte 'Große Landschaft bei Wien', 'Die große Fracht', 'Holz und Späne' sowie für 'Nachtflug', die im Band *Die gestundete Zeit* im gleichen Jahr in der von Alfred Andersch herausgegebenen Reihe *studio frankfurt* publiziert wurden. Zehn Jahre lang besuchte sie laut Tagungsberichten[1] als hochgeschätzter Gast die Tagungen der Gruppe regelmäßig, eingeladen war sie bis zur Auflösung der Gruppe 47 im Jahr 1967.

Wie konfliktreich ihre Position von Anfang an gewesen war, läßt sich aus einer römischen Variante rekonstruieren, die in signifikanten Punkten von dem in der Werkausgabe publizierten Entwurf über die Gruppe 47 abweicht. Daß sie mit dem von Richter 1961 angeforderten Bericht über Niendorf für die Rubrik des *Almanachs* von 1962 'Zum ersten Mal dabei' nicht zurechtkam, kann als Indiz für ihre Außenseiterinnen-Position als Nicht-Ort[2] interpretiert werden:

> Am zweiten Abend wollte ich abreisen, weil ein Gespräch, dessen
> Voraussetzungen ich nicht kannte, mich plötzlich denken ließ, *ich sei unter*
> *deutsche Nazis gefallen* [...].
>
> Am dritten Tag las ich ein paar Gedichte vor, vor Aufregung am Ersticken,
> ein *anfreindlicher* [sic] *Schriftsteller* las sie nochmals laut und deutlich vor
> [...]. (Briegleb, S.56)

Zu diesem Zeitpunkt hatte Ingeborg Bachmann ihre Prosa-Arbeit
wieder aufgenommen und sich innerlich und äußerlich bereits von der
Gruppe distanziert. Die Anspielung auf das Nazikontinuum, das
übrigens in vielen Nachlaßtexten aus den 60er und 70er Jahren
ausgeweitet auf die Gesellschaft der BRD thematisiert wird, steht in
engem Zusammenhang mit ihrer Erfahrung der Tabuisierung des
Jüngstvergangenen durch das Gros der Gruppenmitglieder.

In scharfem Kontrast zu ihren spärlichen Äußerungen über ihre
Gruppenzugehörigkeit stand die Publicity, mit der ihre Auftritte in der
literarischen Öffentlichkeit kommentiert wurden. Bereits nach der
Initiationsszene wurde sie von ihrem Entdecker Hans Werner Richter
auf ein Image von weiblicher Hilflosigkeit, 'Unsicherheit,
Chaotische[m], Leise[m], Verlorene[m], Schüchterne[m]'[3] festgelegt, zu
dem ihre legendäre Ohnmacht, geflüsterten Gedichte und das
Durcheinander ihrer Blätter beitrugen. Im Kontext ihrer Erfahrungen
weiblicher Abhängigkeit in der Wiener Szene um Hans Weigel und
Hermann Hakel dürfte die Inszenierung eines in den 50er Jahren
durchaus noch zeitgemässen tradierten Dichterinnen-Bildes der
Weltentrücktheit, Zerfahrenheit und Hilflosigkeit als schützende
Maskierung in der männlich dominierten Gruppe 47 notwendig gewesen
sein.[4] Wie sehr sich auch Medien, Literaturkritik und
Literaturwissenschaft gängiger Klischees des Geschlechterdiskurses
bedienen, wird nicht nur in dem viel zitierten *Spiegel*-Leitartikel mit
dem anspielungsreichen Untertitel 'Gedichte aus dem deutschen Ghetto'
in der Gegenüberstellung von 'scharf trainiertem Intellekt der Doktorin'
versus 'Unschlüssigkeit eines überwuchernden Gefühls'[5] deutlich,
sondern auch in posthumen Veröffentlichungen. War Ingeborg
Bachmann eine auratische Erscheinung in postauratischer Zeit, wie dies
Jochen Hieber posthum in der *Zeit* suggeriert.[6] Durch das textexterne
Moment ihrer Persönlichkeit bzw. der Aura ihrer öffentlichen Auftritte
werden Bewertung und Rezeption ihres literarischen Werks massiv
gesteuert. Der Grad der Emotionalisierung bei der Diskussion ihrer

literarischen Produktion sticht besonders scharf ins Auge in Horst
Neumanns Rezension der Werkausgabe von 1978, in der er die
'Befangenheit der Kritik' auf 'biographische Gründe', 'personale
Botschaften', auf 'die Weiblichkeit der Dichterin und ihr Sterben'
zurückführt, die die Beziehung zu ihren Texten auf eine schwer zu
kontrollierende Weise beeinflussen würden.[7]

Die Fragwürdigkeit eines biographischen Interpretationsansatzes
wird auch in Peter Beickens Bachmann-Biographie evident, wenn er
unbefragt biographische Fakten aus ihrem literarischen Werk, wie zum
Beispiel aus *Malina* und aus Max Frischs Erzählung *Montauk*, zitiert.[8]
Aussagen der Dichterin wie im Zusammenhang mit dem *Malina*-Roman
'eine geistige imaginäre Autobiographie' oder 'Was nicht in seinen [des
Schriftstellers] Büchern steht, existiert nicht'[9] könnten oberflächlich
gelesen einem solchen Interpretationsansatz Vorschub leisten, der jedoch
meines Erachtens einerseits durch die ungesicherte Faktenlage,
andererseits dadurch, daß der Komplexität ihrer Texte ungenügend
Rechnung getragen wird, methodologisch unhaltbar ist.

Auch Schriftstellerkollegen aus der Gruppe 47 identifizierten die
Autorin mit ihrem Werk, so Johannes Bobrowski, indem er schreibt:
'Die Bachmann kam kinderäugig, des Festes Herrin, Undine'.[10] In
Tagungsberichten der Gruppe findet zwar auch ihr Status als
Primadonna oder sogar First Lady, die im 'Fürstenzimmer' oder
'Kaiserzimmer' (Lettau, S.309 und S.364) logiert, Erwähnung, der
Akzent liegt jedoch auf ihrem beachtlichen Talent. Ihre Arbeiten
werden mit wenigen Ausnahmen als 'beste Arbeit', als 'wirkliches
Kunstwerk', mit einer 'Sprachgewalt', die bewegt, mit 'spätwienerischer
Musikalität' apostrophiert (ebd., S.154, S.86, S.89, S.107). Negative
Reaktionen provozierten hingegen ihr Gedicht 'Liebe dunkler Erdteil'
sowie ihr Genrewechsel von der Lyrik zur Prosa. Laut Richter habe die
Dichterin weder ihre eigenen Texte verteidigt noch an Diskussionen
über vorgetragene Texte teilgenommen.[11] Ihre Herkunft aus dem
österreichischen Kulturraum ist einer der Gründe für die Faszination,
die Ingeborg Bachmanns erste Lesung hinterlassen hat. Diese lyrische
Tonart der fremden Stimme aus Österreich war man nicht mehr
gewohnt.

Aus heutiger Sicht werden die ästhetischen Kriterien der
Kahlschlag-Literatur einer eher pejorativen Wertung unterzogen,
während hingegen der Zusammenschluß der Gruppe 47 heroisiert wird.

Im Mythos der Gruppengeschichte wird der Auftritt Ilse Aichingers, Ingeborg Bachmanns und Paul Celans, der von Bachmann Richter als jemand, der viel bessere Gedichte schreibe als sie, empfohlen wurde, als Wendepunkt in der deutschen Nachkriegsliteratur, als Öffnung zur Moderne und zu Innovationen, als Ende der Kahlschlag-Periode interpretiert.[12] Auf die Problematik einer solchen Interpretation verweist nicht nur der Umstand, daß weder Bachmann noch Celan in ihren frühen Publikationen konkret zu poetologischen Fragen Stellung genommen haben, sondern auch die Ambiguität des Terminus Innovation. Zwar nahmen sie die Brüchigkeit der Verbindlichkeit von Tradition wahr, ohne deshalb wie z. B. in der experimentellen Literatur die ästhetischen Mittel und Strategien einer radikalen Infragestellung zu unterziehen. Ihre poetologische Verfahrensweise scheint sich eher an Heimito von Doderers Kritik am positivistischen Wirklichkeitsbegriff und seinem Postulat einer Annäherung an die Wirklichkeit im 'Indirekten' orientiert zu haben.[13]

Richters Feststellung, daß sich die Wiener Autoren weniger für die Debatte über Kahlschlag-Literatur als hauptsächlich für die Honorare des deutschen Rundfunks interessiert hätten,[14] wird von Ingeborg Bachmann bestätigt, wenn sie schreibt:

> Im Jahr 1952 wußte man in Österreich so gut wie nichts über neue deutsche Schriftsteller. [...] Wir waren alle Mitte zwanzig, notorisch geldlos, notorisch hoffnungslos, zukunftslos, kleine Angestellte oder Hilfsarbeiter, einige schon freie Schriftsteller, das hieß soviel wie abenteuerliche Existenzen, von denen niemand recht wußte, wovon sie lebten, von Gängen aufs Versatzamt jedenfalls am öftesten. (*Werke*, Bd.4, S.324)

Da die jungen Autorinnen und Autoren, die von Hans Weigel gefördert wurden, relativ im Abseits des offiziellen Literaturbetriebs standen, hatten sie nur die Möglichkeit, in Zeitschriften kurze Texte zu publizieren, wie zum Beispiel Ingeborg Bachmann Gedichte in der Dezembernummer 1948 in der von Hermann Hakel herausgegebenen Literatur- und Kulturzeitschrift *Lynkeus*. Ilse Aichingers Publikation ihres Romans *Die größere Hoffnung* beim Fischer Verlag stellte eher eine Ausnahme dar. Weigels Schlüsselroman *Die unvollendete Symphonie* wie auch Hakels Enthüllungen über seine angebliche Liaison mit der jungen Bachmann sind nicht nur gespickt mit peinlichen Indiskretionen und mit Vorwürfen der Undankbarkeit, sondern unterlaufen geradezu die Grundintention der Verfasser, die erfolgreich gewordene Dichterin zu diffamieren, indem ein dubioses Licht auf ihre widersprüchliche Rolle als Förderer und Exploiteure fällt.[15] In diesem Kontext kann Ingeborg Bachmanns fassungsloses Staunen über ihr erstes Honorar nach der Lesung beim deutschen Rundfunk kaum überraschen, das ihr Monatsgehalt im Script-Department des US-Senders Rot-Weiss-Rot in Wien bei weitem überstieg (*Werke*, Bd.4, S.323).

1945 wurde in Österreich nicht als Stunde Null aufgefaßt; die wirkliche Zäsur bildete der langersehnte Staatsvertrag von 1955. Aus den hochkomplexen Prozessen, die von der Nachkriegszeit bis in die 50er Jahre wirksam waren, und die bis heute noch nicht vollständig aufgearbeitet sind, möchte ich im Kontext der österreichischen Kulturpolitik vier herausgreifen: 1. Zunächst stand der Kampf um das materielle Überleben vor allem in Ost-Österreich im Zentrum, auch heute noch in einem West-Ost-Gefälle ablesbar; 2. wegen der enormen Menschenverluste im Krieg dominierte eine ältere Generation; 3. das Spannungsfeld Neutralität im Soge des Kalten Krieges und einer gleichzeitig einsetzenden ideologisch-kulturellen West-Integration, die wieder eine politische und ökonomische Abhängigkeit von Deutschland zur Folge hatte; 4. der Versuch, an eine erst zu konstruierende österreichische Kultur vor den beiden Weltkriegen anzuknüpfen bei gleichzeitiger 'Selbstaufschließung' dem US-Einfluß gegenüber, hauptsächlich auf Gebieten der materiellen Kultur, wie der populären Musik und des Films.[16] Der Österreich-Begriff, an dessen Konstruktion die Historiker wesentlichen Anteil hatten, scheint indessen fingiert, installiert. Statt einer klaren Auseinandersetzung mit der jüngsten Vergangenheit wurde eine durch den Freispruch von der Kollektiv-schuld begünstigte Ideologie des Erbes propagiert, die in der Rekonstruktion einer Kontinuität von den Babenbergern bis zu der Nach-Staats-Vertragszeit gipfelte (Schmid, S.11). Gleichzeitig mit den restaurativen Tendenzen setzte — allerdings nicht ganz kritiklos — auch eine offiziöse Kaschierungsrhetorik im Kulturbetrieb ein. 'Aber können wir eine neue Geschichtsepoche mit einem pharisäerhaften Taschen-spielertrick beginnen?' fragt sich Peter Rubel 1946 in dem im *Plan* veröffentlichten Artikel 'Wir sind alle schuldig'.[17] Und im Roman *Wolfshaut* schreibt Hans Lebert 'Wir leben im Lande der Anstreicher. Hier wird doch dauernd übertüncht und frisch gestrichen.'[18]

Eine systematische Studie über die Kulturpolitik in der Nachkriegszeit bis in die 50er Jahre steht meines Wissens noch aus.

Auskunft über die Richtung der Staats-Förderung geben Aufstellungen der Inhaberinnen und Inhaber von Staatspreisen, so zum Beispiel diejenigen des *Großen Österreichischen Staatspreises*, des *Förderpreises der Stadt Wien* und des *Förderpreises des Landes Ober-Österreich*.[19] Einblicke in die Verlagsprogramme gewähren Inserate des 192-seitigen Anzeigers für das Weihnachtsgeschäft von 1947.[20] Zusammenfassend kann festgehalten werden: Neben arrivierten Autorinnen und Autoren erwiesen sich auch wieder diejenigen als preiswürdig, die während der Faschismus-Periode publiziert hatten. Ein problematisches Kapitel stellt außerdem das Fehlen vieler Exilautoren dar. Der bescheidene Anteil an Erstausgaben österreichischer Autoren muß auf die geringe Risikobereitschaft der Verleger, unbekannte Namen auf dem Markt zu präsentieren, also auf die Situation des Buchmarkts, zurückgeführt werden (Lunzer, S.34). Der personalen Konstanz, die Aspetsberger nachweist,[21] stand eine veränderte Realität gegenüber: Statt des Faschismus dominierte der Konflikt des Kalten Krieges auch das Kulturelle, was sich unter anderem am US-Einfluß auf den Buchmarkt ablesen lässt. Wurden 1951 112 Bücher aus dem Englischen übersetzt und in österreichischen Verlagshäusern publiziert, so waren es ein Jahr später bereits 132.[22]

Obwohl die österreichischen Produktionsstätten wesentlich intakter waren, das heißt, weniger von der Zerstörung durch Bombardierungen und Bodenkämpfe der letzten Kriegsmonate betroffen waren als die deutschen, und daher günstigere Voraussetzungen auf dem Buchmarkt, Vorteile zu erwirtschaften, gehabt hätten, konnten diese durch Probleme bei der Materialbeschaffung, durch die Auswirkungen der Währungsreform sowie durch die mangelnde Risikobereitschaft der Verleger kaum genutzt werden. Infolgedessen geriet Österreich durch die materiellen Grundlagen der Buchproduktion und -distribution begleitet von einer fragwürdigen (Literatur)-Kulturpolitik früh in eine Randposition (Lunzer, S.33f.). Die Regierung erwies sich nämlich als außerstande, die für einen wirkungsvollen Neu-Anfang benötigten Rahmenbedingungen zu schaffen, so daß nicht nur die Chance, die ausländische Literatur einzuholen, verpaßt wurde, sondern auch Talente der neuen Schriftstellergeneration mit der fadenscheinigen Begründung, es gebe nicht genug junge talentierte Autoren und 'epochale Manuskripte' (Lunzer, S.34), in die BRD abgedrängt wurden, wo sie günstigere Rahmenbedingungen vorfanden. 'Es ist nicht die erste

Generation [...], sondern seit vielen Generationen haben alle unsere Schriftsteller, im 20. Jahrhundert jedenfalls, in Deutschland verlegt, weil es keine andere Möglichkeit gegeben hat', resümiert Ingeborg Bachmann die Situation talentierter österreichischer Autorinnen und Autoren (*Gu I*, S.133).

Ihre Einstellung zur Bundesrepublik hat sich im Verlaufe eines Jahrzehnts radikal verändert. In ihrer Erinnerung assoziiert sie 1952 diese und die Gruppe 47 im Gegensatz zu Österreich mit einer oszillierenden Exotik und Fremdheit, wenn sie rückblickend schreibt:

> Deutschland, das ferner schien als jedes andere Land [...] nie war ein Land
> exotischer als dieses Deutschland, und nie waren Leute wunderlicher als diese
> Gruppe 47. [...] Ich war noch nie in Deutschland gewesen und ich weiß
> nicht, was damals die grössere Spannung ausmachte: zum ersten Mal in
> dieses Land zu kommen oder Furcht und Neugier oder die gemischten
> Gefühle vor dem Zusammentreffen mit Menschen, von denen man noch nie
> die Namen gehört hatte. (*Werke*, Bd.4, S.13)

Jugend, Lachen, Unbeschwertheit, Weite und Hoffnung standen in scharfem Kontrast zur notorischen Hoffnungs- und Zukunftslosigkeit ihrer Wiener Existenz. Die Auszeichnung mit dem Gruppenpreis und die Zusammenarbeit mit Henze mochten sie zu ihrem Entschluß zur Freiberuflichkeit als Schriftstellerin und zur Übersiedlung nach Italien bewogen haben. Da die Gruppe 47 durch ihre Zusammensetzung aus ehemaligen Wehrmachtsangehörigen wesentlich geprägt war, liegt die Vermutung nahe, die Preisverleihung an die beiden österreichischen Autorinnen sei weniger auf 'männliche Galanterie'[23] zurückzuführen, sondern stehe vielmehr im Kontext fehlender Teilnahme an Kriegserfahrung. Eine umfassendere literarische Aufarbeitung spezifisch weiblicher Kriegserfahrung setzte erst im Zusammenhang mit der Frauenliteratur in den späten 70er Jahren ein.[24] Die Rolle der Frau in der Gruppe 47 ist bisher nur am Rande behandelt worden. Auffallend ist noch in den 60er Jahren der geringe Autorinnen-Anteil. Der 1962 von Hans Werner Richter herausgegebene *Almanach der Gruppe 47* erwähnt 86 Männer und 10 Frauen im Verzeichnis aller Autorinnen und Autoren, die in den ersten 16 Jahren auf Tagungen lasen. Frauen waren in der Regel als dekorativer Chor von Ehefrauen der Mitglieder willkommen, die zuweilen weinten oder zornig wurden, wenn ihre Ehemänner durchgefallen waren.[25] In den Jahren nach 1962 hat sich nicht viel geändert.

1952 war die Gruppe 47 im Begriff, sich als moralisches Gewissen und als Institution der Bundesrepublik zu legitimieren, in der die 'neuen Schriftsteller' gemacht wurden. Ingeborg Bachmann schloß wichtige Freundschaften mit Hans Werner Henze, Günter Eich, Uwe Johnson, Heinrich Böll und Hans Magnus Enzensberger, wehrte sich mit ihnen gegen die Restaurations- und Remilitarisierungstendenzen der Bundesrepublik. Ihre Unterschrift unter den 'Protest gegen die atomare Bewaffnung der Bundesrepublik' im Jahr 1958 provozierte einen harschen Verweis ihres früheren Förderers Hans Weigel, fortan von Ingeborg Bachmann Freund-Feind genannt, in dem er gleichzeitig ihre allgemeine, insbesondere auch die geographische Distanzierung vom österreichischen Kulturbetrieb monierte.[26]

Von ihrer erfolgreichen Präsenz im deutschen Literaturbetrieb zeugen nicht nur zahlreiche Preisverleihungen und Ehrungen sowie ihre Mitgliedschaft in der Deutschen Akademie für Sprache und Dichtung seit 1957 und seit 1961 in der Akademie der Künste, sondern auch ihre Berufung als erste Gastdozentin an die Universität Frankfurt. Ausgestattet mit guten Ratschlägen von Gruppenmitgliedern (Lettau, S.155), hielt sie am 25. November 1959 ihre Antrittsvorlesung. Ihr profundes Wissen und ihre innere Autorität sollten den Barrieren Herr werden, denen sie sich naturgemäß bei dieser ungewohnten Aufgabe gegenübergestellt sehen werde, schrieb Hans Schwab-Felisch in bezug auf die Auswahlkriterien und die institutionelle Krise, die durch die Einrichtung einer Gastdozentur eine kurzfristige Lösung finden sollte.[27] Die Diskrepanz zwischen der Institution Germanistik und der Dichterin war von Anfang an eklatant, denn diese wurde nicht nur als Fremde behandelt, sondern von Professoren und Studierenden verbalen Attacken ausgesetzt, die Ingeborg Bachmann in ihrer Abschiedsvorlesung 'Literatur als Utopie' zu einer scharfen Kritik an der Institution veranlaßt haben mag. Die Literaturwissenschaft sei ein 'Phantom', das sich an einem 'Wunschbild' orientiere und im übrigen einen 'Terror' ausübe (*Werke*, Bd.4, S.255-71). Das Nachrichtenmagazin *Der Spiegel* kommentierte in der üblichen Bachmann-Stereotypie die Reaktion der Dichterin in einer Seminar-Debatte. Ingeborg Bachmann habe zu ihrer riesigen Lacktasche gegriffen und zu rauchen angefangen. Zu einer anderen Art der Entgegnung habe sie sich angeblich nicht bewegen lassen.[28] Die Frankfurter Vorlesungen haben nicht nur die Ungleichzeitigkeit der Bachmann-Rezeption, sondern zugleich das

Scheitern der Utopie, die Wahrheit offen auszusprechen, an der Realität aufgedeckt.

Daß Ingeborg Bachmann nach 1962 nicht mehr an Tagungen der Gruppe 47 teilgenommen hat, kann mit der allgemeinen Gruppenentwicklung sowie mit ihrem Genrewechsel von der Lyrik zur Prosa erklärt werden. Die ambivalente, ja ablehnende Reaktion vieler Mitglieder auf die Publikation ihres ersten Prosa-Bandes *Das dreißigste Jahr* im Jahr 1961 schlug sich auch in der öffentlichen Literaturkritik in einer Imageverschiebung von der gefeierten Lyrikerin zu der gefallenen Lyrikerin nieder. Bereits am Anfang ihrer *Frankfurter Vorlesungen* markiert Ingeborg Bachmann einen Standortwechsel ihrer literaturtheoretischen Position, die sich von derjenigen der Gruppe 47 zunehmend entfernte. Die für das 20. Jahrhundert charakteristischen 'Stürze ins Schweigen und die Wiederkehr aus dem Schweigen' verknüpft die Autorin mit der 'verschärften Lage' der Gegenwart. 'Der Fragwürdigkeit der dichterischen Existenz steht zum ersten Mal die Unsicherheit der gesamten Verhältnisse gegenüber. [...] Das Vertrauensverhältnis zwischen Ich und Sprache und Ding ist schwer erschüttert' (*Werke*, Bd.4, S.88). Einerseits bezieht sich die von ihr konstatierte Unsicherheit auf die Sprachskepsis vieler Autoren seit der Moderne, anderseits auf ihre eigene Unsicherheit bei der 'Übersiedelung' von der Lyrik zur Prosa, von ihr bildlich als 'Umzug im Kopf' beschrieben (*Gu I*, S.31). Erst durch das 'hilflose Wort' Erfahrung, als Fundus von Gesehenem und Erlebtem, sei sie eines Tages fähig geworden, Prosa zu schreiben (S.78). Ab 1961 setzte mit der Arbeit am *Todesarten*-Projekt eine lange experimentelle Phase ein, während der sie eine neue Schreibweise entwickelte, die die ästhetische Vermittlung der Gegenwärtigkeit in der Vergangenheit im Bewußtsein der Shoah leisten sollte, eine Schreibweise, die in ihrer neuen Radikalität in der Büchner-Preis-Rede 'Ein Ort für Zufälle'[29] 1964 zum erstenmal publik wurde (*Werke*, Bd.4, S.278-93). Der besonders vernichtenden Berlin- und Deutschlandkritik dieser Rede korrespondiert eine Anzahl von Texten aus dem Nachlaß, die die mangelnde Auseinandersetzung mit der nationalsozialistischen Vergangenheit in der Bundesrepublik scharf beleuchten: 'ich hasse die [Deutschen], nicht weil sie schlecht sind, denn was sollten sie [schlechter] sein als andere, aber weil sie uns wieder das Fürchten lehren, und ich hasse sie, weil sie nicht begreifen, daß sie es tun.'[30]

Die Beschäftigung der Literaturwissenschaft mit Ingeborg Bachmanns Sprache und Sprachskepsis ist umfangreich. Ich möchte im folgenden versuchen, eine Verbindungslinie zwischen den Kategorien Sprache, Wahrheit, Erinnerung nach Auschwitz zu skizzieren.[31] Eine Konstante scheint mir ihr stetes Bemühen um eine Sprachethik im Sinne Karl Kraus' zu sein, ein Bemühen, das sie im übrigen als das einzig Sinnvolle beim Schreiben wertet (*Gu I*, S.25). Die Schriftsteller hätten es mit der und zugleich gegen die abgenutzte schlechte Sprache voller Floskeln, Phrasen und verbrauchten Metaphern aufzunehmen, indem sie sich schreibend um die neue Sprache, die das neue Denken artikulieren solle, bemühen, um sie nicht nur bruchstückweise, sondern ganz in den Besitz zu bekommen: 'Hätten wir das Wort, hätten wir die Sprache, wir bräuchten die Waffen nicht'.[32] Solche programmatischen Forderungen an die neue Sprache, wie sie die Autorin in den theoretischen und essayistischen Schriften stellt, werden im erzählerischen Werk konsequent dekonstruiert, denn Ingeborg Bachmann gibt lediglich die Richtung, die Gangart an. Erst im Widerspiel des Unmöglichen mit dem Möglichen, des Wünschbaren mit dem Vorgefundenen, finde der Mensch Orientierung, wobei sich das Ziel bei jeder Annäherung aufs neue entferne.[33] Demzufolge liegt ihrem Schreiben eine Anstrengung zugrunde, eine Sprache, 'die standhält', 'wahre Sätze, die unserer eigenen Bewußtseinslage und dieser veränderten Welt entsprechen',[34] zu finden. Die Worte sollten in die Schranken gewiesen werden, um zu ihrer Wahrheit zu kommen. Der große geheime Schmerz, mit dem der Mensch vor allen anderen Geschöpfen ausgezeichnet sei, befähige ihn, die Wahrheit zu erkennen und somit sehend zu werden. Die Wahrheit nämlich sei den Menschen zumutbar.[35] Schmerzerfahrung als Voraussetzung jeder wahrhaften Erkenntnis konstituiert nach Bachmann auch die Grundlage jeder wahrhaften Kunst.

Im Zusammenhang mit Prousts großem Erinnerungsepos schreibt sie dem Ich die Begabung zur Erinnerung zu.[36] Wenn Christa Wolf in ihrem Essay 'Die zumutbare Wahrheit' in bezug auf Ingeborg Bachmanns Wahrheitsbegriff das Widerständige, Subversiv-Oppositionelle des Erinnerungs- und Schreibprozesses betont,[37] wird deutlich, daß es sich bei Bachmanns Erinnerungsarbeit nicht mehr um eine nostalgische Rekonstruktion einer vergangenen Zeit à la Proust handeln kann, sondern im Bewußtsein der Shoah um das Aufdecken verdrängter Dauerspuren im kollektiven Unbewußten, die in den 80er

Jahren bei den Nachgeborenen als transgenerationelle Traumatisierung durch den Nationalsozialismus diagnostiziert worden war.[38] Diese Arbeit am NS-Gedächtnis erforderte ein Experimentieren mit neuen Schreibmethoden, durch die das Problem der Ästhetisierung und Metaphorisierung des Schreckens und Grauens von Auschwitz gelöst werden sollte.[39] Erst nach einem Jahrzehnt intensiver Beschäftigung mit einer 'einzigen grossen Studie aller möglichen Todesarten', einem 'Kompendium, Manuale', das zugleich das Bild der letzten zwanzig Jahre vermitteln solle, immer mit dem Schauplatz Wien und Österreich[40] — Ingeborg Bachmanns Erfahrungs- und Schreibraum — war es ihr möglich, 1971 *Malina* als Ouvertüre vorzulegen, in der die oppositionelle subversive Dimension des Erinnerungs- und Schreibprozesses eine zentrale Thematik bildet.

> Ich muß erzählen! Ich werde erzählen. Es gibt nichts mehr, was mich in meiner Erinnerung stört. [...] Wenn meine Erinnerung aber nicht die gewöhnlichen Erinnerungen meinte, Zurückliegendes, Abgelebtes, Verlassenes, dann bin ich noch weit, sehr weit von der verschwiegenen Erinnerung, in der mich nichts mehr stören darf. (*Werke*, Bd.3, S.23)

Die Erinnerungsarbeit des Ichs in *Malina* ist radikal und strukturbildend für den Roman. Indem diese ins Präsens verlegt wird, ist die Vergangenheit in der Gegenwart als unerträglicher Schmerz omnipräsent. Das Erzählen der gewöhnlichen Erinnerungen, wie Zurückliegendes, Abgelebtes, Verlassenes wird nach einem knappen autobiographischen Rückblick im Prolog mit dem Einwand abgebrochen: 'Ich will nicht erzählen, es stört mich alles in der Erinnerung' (S.27). Erst in den Traumkapiteln 'Friedhof der ermordeten Töchter' wird die Schicht der verschwiegenen Erinnerung aufgedeckt, die als Dauerspur ins Unbewußte fest eingeschrieben ist. Diese Erinnerungsarbeit des Ichs spielt sich im Innern, im Imaginären, auf einer Gedankenbühne ab, wo die Einheit der Zeit aufgehoben ist, sind doch Träume 'überall und nirgends'. 'Die Zeit ist überhaupt nicht mehr, denn es könnte gestern gewesen sein, lange her gewesen sein, es kann wieder sein, immerzu sein, es wird einiges nie gewesen sein' (S.181). Auf der psychoanalytischen Textebene kann diese Erinnerungsarbeit als 'prähistorisierende' Arbeit im Sinne Lacans interpretiert werden. Auf Lacans 'symbolischen Vater' verweisen die übergroße, allmächtige Vaterfigur und Ingeborg Bachmanns Deutung dieser Figur als Mörder, der das ausübe, was die Gesellschaft ausübe.

Mit der Sprache des Traums und des Traumas hat sie eine Schreibweise entwickelt, durch die die Wiederkehr des Verdrängten in das Unbewußte erzählbar wurde.[41]

Mit der Veränderung der literarischen Methode, die vom Rückzug von der literarischen Szene begleitet war, nahm das Schreiben einen nahezu obsessiven Charakter an. 'Ich existiere nur, wenn ich schreibe, ich bin nichts, wenn ich nicht schreibe', steht in engem Zusammenhang mit ihrer Auffassung von der Sprache als Strafe, dem Schreiben als einsame, asoziale, ja, verdammte Lebensform, wie sie dies in ihrer letzten Preisrede anläßlich der zweiten österreichischen Auszeichnung feststellt[42] — den Großen Österreichischen Staatspreis hatte sie erst 1968 erhalten. Allerdings darf nicht übersehen werden, daß das Movens ihres Schreibens und ihrer Existenz auch während dieser Phase dem Prinzip Hoffnung verpflichtet blieb.[43]

Die Publikation von Adornos *Jargon der Eigentlichkeit* im Jahr 1964 signalisierte einen Umbesetzungsprozeß im kulturellen Wertesystem: existentialistische Erfahrungen wurden in den späten 60er Jahren als 'luxuriöser Subjektivismus und wohltönende Hohlheit'[44] abqualifiziert, Bachmanns Ablehnung der *littérature engagée* verurteilt, was sich an den Rezensionen zu ihrem Roman *Malina* ablesen lässt.[45] Während Kollegen aus der Gruppe 47, wie Grass, Walser, Johnson und Böll, epische Realpolitik betrieben, nämlich die erzählerische Erforschung der vorhandenen Gesellschaft, halte Bachmann dem Pathos der ersten Nachkriegszeit die Treue, der Wut wie der Trauer, schreibt ihr früherer Lektor Reinhard Baumgart.[46] Ingeborg Bachmanns lange unbeachtet gebliebene Äußerung in einem Interview von 1964 in bezug auf die politische Haltung der Gruppe 47 ist in diesem Kontext aufschlußreich:

> Mir ist höchstens aufgefallen, daß die deutschen Schriftsteller, die sich dem Verdacht aussetzen, radikale Ansichten zu vertreten, fast ausnahmslos derart gemäßigt denken, daß sie sich in einem anderen Land, etwa in Italien oder Frankreich, dem Verdacht aussetzen würden, zuwenig zu denken. Ich habe es darum schwer, werde darum immer Mühe haben, trotz des Verständnisses für die Lage, in der Berlin und die beiden deutschen Staaten sind, mich hier an einem politischen Gespräch zu beteiligen. (*Gu I*, S.51)

Erst posthum, ein Jahrzehnt später, nachdem sich im Laufe der siebziger Jahre eine neue Subjektivität als literarischer Trend etabliert hatte, fand auch ihr erzählerisches Werk durch die Zuschreibung zeitkritischer als auch zeitantizipatorischer Aspekte die gebührende Anerkennung.

Fußnoten

[1] S. Reinhard Lettau (Hrsg.), *Die Gruppe 47. Bericht, Kritik, Polemik. Ein Handbuch* (Neuwied und Berlin: Luchterhand, 1967). Weitere Hinweise auf diesen Band befinden sich im Text unter Lettau.

[2] Klaus Briegleb, 'Ingeborg Bachmann, Paul Celan. Ihr (Nicht-)Ort in der Gruppe 47 (1952-1964/65). Eine Skizze', in: Bernhard Böschenstein und Sigrid Weigel (Hrsg.), *Ingeborg Bachmann und Paul Celan. Poetische Korrespondenzen* (Frankfurt a. M.: Suhrkamp, 1997), S.29-81. Weitere Hinweise auf diesen Aufsatz befinden sich im Text unter Briegleb.

[3] Hans Werner Richter, *Im Etablissement der Schmetterlinge. Einundzwanzig Portraits aus der Gruppe 47* (München: Hanser, 1986), S.55.

[4] Auf den Aspekt der Selbstinszenierung hat auch Frauke Meyer-Gosau in 'Ecco un artista' hingewiesen: s. Heinz Ludwig Arnold (Hrsg.), *Ingeborg Bachmann*, (München: text + kritik, 1995), H.6, S.163-70; s. auch Ingeborg Bachmann, 'Homage à Maria Callas', *Werke*, hrsg. v. Christina Koschel, Inge von Weidenbaum, Clemens Münster (München, Zürich: Piper, 1978), Bd.4, S.342f. (Im folgenden zitiert als *Werke*.) Maria Gazetti weist auf ihre Diva-Eigenschaft hin: 'Eine italienische Lektüre', in: 'Ingeborg Bachmann. Das Lächeln der Sphinx', *du*, H.9 (1994), S.74.

[5] *Der Spiegel*, 34 /1954, S.26-29.

[6] Zitiert aus Kurt Bartsch, 'Früh kanonisiert und heftig umstritten', in: Wendelin Schmidt-Dengler, Johann Sonnleitner, Klaus Zeyringer (Hrsg.), *Die einen raus — die anderen rein. Kanon und Literatur. Vorüberlegungen zu einer Literaturgeschichte Österreichs* (Berlin: Schmidt, 1994), S.175.

[7] Peter Horst Neumann, 'Vier Gründe einer Befangenheit. Über Ingeborg Bachmann', *Merkur*, 32 (1978), 1130.

[8] Peter Beicken, *Ingeborg Bachmann* (München, Zürich: Piper, 1988).

[9] Ingeborg Bachmann, *Wir müssen wahre Sätze finden. Gespräche und Interviews*, hrsg. von Christine Koschel und Inge von Weidenbaum (München, Zürich: Piper, 1983), S.73. (Weitere Hinweise auf diesen Band befinden sich im Text unter *Gu.I*); [Rede zur Verleihung des Anton-Wildgans-Preises], *Werke*, Bd.4, S.296.

[10] Zitiert aus Ingrid Bachér, '...und die Frauen in der Gruppe 47?', in: Jürgen Schutte (Hrsg.), *Dichter und Richter. Die Gruppe 47 und die deutsche Nachkriegsliteratur. Ausstellungskatalog* (Berlin: Akademie der Künste, 1988), S.93.

[11] Richter, *Im Etablissement der Schmetterlinge*, S.58f.

[12] Walter Jens, *Deutsche Literatur der Gegenwart* (München: dtv, 1964), S.129f.

[13] Heimito von Doderer, 'Von der Unschuld im Indirekten', *Plan*, 2: 1 (1947), 2f.; vgl. auch Rüdiger Wischenbart, 'Zur Auseinandersetzung um die Moderne.

Literarischer "Nachholbedarf" — Auflösung der Literatur', in: Friedrich Aspetsberger, Norbert Frei, Hubert Lengauer (Hrsg.), *Literatur der Nachkriegszeit und der fünfziger Jahre in Österreich* (Wien: ÖBV, 1984), S.359.

[14] Richter, *Im Etablissement der Schmetterlinge*, S.15.

[15] Hans Weigel, *Die unvollendete Symphonie* (Graz,Wien, Köln: Styria,1992). Im Nachwort erwähnt Weigel, daß es sich um einen Schlüsselroman über die Bachmann und ihn handle. Hermann Hakel, 'Karriere und Gesichter der Ingeborg Bachmann', in: ders., *Dürre Äste — Welkes Gras. Begegnungen mit Literaten. Bemerkungen zur Literatur* (Wien: Lynkeus, 1991), S.195-214.

[16] Vgl. Georg Schmid, 'Die falschen "Füffziger"', in: Aspetsberger et al., *Literatur der Nachkriegszeit*, S.9-10. Weitere Hinweise auf diesen Aufsatz befinden sich im Text unter Schmid.

[17] Peter Rubel, 'Wir sind alle schuldig', *Plan*, 19 (1946), 781.

[18] Hans Lebert, *Die Wolfshaut* (Wien, Zürich: Europaverlag, 1960), S.389.

[19] Detaillierte Angaben liefert Georg Schmid (s. Anmerkung 16), S.14.

[20] Eine Zusammenstellung repräsentativer Titel bietet Heinz Lunzer, 'Der literarische Markt 1945-1955', in: Aspetsberger et al., *Literatur der Nachkriegszeit*, S.29-31. Weitere Hinweise auf diesen Aufsatz befinden sich im Text unter Lunzer.

[21] Friedrich Aspetsberger, *Literarisches Leben im Austrofaschismus. Der Staatspreis* (Königstein Ts.: Athenäum, 1980).

[22] Rückläufig waren die Übersetzungen aus dem Italienischen von 20 auf 4. Georg Schmid (s. Anmerkung 16), S.19.

[23] Diese Meinung vertritt Heinz Ludwig Arnold: '"...dann kann hier jemand nicht mehr kritisieren!". Kritik in der Gruppe 47 — Unsystematischer Versuch einer Annäherung', in: Schutte, *Dichter und Richter*, S.84.

[24] Sigrid Weigel, *Bilder des kulturellen Gedächtnisses. Beiträge zur Gegenwartsliteratur* (Dülmen-Hiddingsel: tende, 1994), S.143.

[25] Ingrid Bachér, (s. Anmerkung 10), S.92. Auf die dekorative Funktion von Frauen wird auch von Gabriele Wohmann in ihrem Resümee der Tagung in Princeton hingewiesen: 'Frau Richter und Frau Höllerer stellten andauernd fotografierend ihre dauernd wechselnden Kleider zur Schau, auch die übrigen weiblichen Teilnehmer, bis auf insgesamt drei Autorinnen, Gäste und Ehefrauen hatten ihre Kleiderschränke mitgenommen', *Darmstädter Echo*, 5.5.1966. Zitiert nach Irmela von der Lühe, 'Schriftstellerinnen in der Gruppe 47', in: Schutte, *Dichter und Richter*, S.94.

[26] 'Offener Brief in Sachen Unterschrift' von Hans Weigel, erschienen in *Forum*, 5 (1958). Aus Hans Höller (Hrsg.), *Der dunkle Schatten, dem ich seit Anfang folge. Ingeborg Bachmann. Vorschläge zu einer neuen Lektüre des Werks* (München: Löcker, 1982), S.168.

[27] Hans Schwab-Felisch, 'Gastprofessoren', *Frankfurter Allgemeine Zeitung*, 25.11.1959. Zitiert aus Holger Gehle, *NS-Zeit und literarische Gegenwart bei*

Ingeborg Bachmann (Wiesbaden: Deutscher Universitätsverlag, 1995), S.90. Gehle hat repräsentatives Pressematerial ausgewertet.

28 *Der Spiegel*, 17/1960, 52.

29 Vgl. auch Bernhard Böschenstein, 'Die Büchnerpreisreden von Paul Celan und Ingeborg Bachmann', in: Böschenstein, Weigel, *Ingeborg Bachmann und Paul Celan*, S.260-69.

30 Nachlaß 1638K/7976. [Deutschen]: deutschen T; [schlechter]: schoechter T. *Ingeborg Bachmann — Registratur des literarischen Nachlasses* (Wien, 1981).

31 Esther V. Schneider-Handschin, '"Die Wahrheit ist dem Menschen nämlich zumutbar" — Zum Wahrheitsbegriff bei Ingeborg Bachmann und Christa Wolf', Unpubl. Vorlesungsmanuskript, 1993.

32 Bachmann, Frankfurter Vorlesungen, *Werke*, Bd.4, S.185.

33 Bachmann, *Werke*, Bd.4, S.276. Robert Musil hat eine ähnliche Auffassung vertreten.

34 Bachmann, *Gu I*, S.19. Vgl. dazu Ludwig Wittgenstein, *Tractatus logico-philosophicus. Logisch-philosophische Abhandlung* (Frankfurt a. M.: Suhrkamp, 1963), T4.03: 'Ein Satz muß mit alten Ausdrücken einen neuen Sinn ausdrücken.'

35 Ingeborg Bachmann, 'Die Wahrheit ist dem Menschen nämlich zumutbar. Rede zur Verleihung des Hörspielpreises der Kriegsblinden', *Werke*, Bd.4, S.275f.

36 Ingeborg Bachmann, 'Die Welt Marcel Prousts — Einblicke in ein Pandämonium', *Werke*, Bd.4, S.255f. Vgl. über Ich-Variationen Sigrid Weigels Studie über die Intertextualität zwischen Roland Barthes und Ingeborg Bachmann, in: '"Ein Ende mit der Schrift. Ein anderer Anfang." Zur Entwicklung von Ingeborg Bachmanns Schreibweise', in: Hans Ludwig Arnold (Hrsg.), *Ingeborg Bachmann,* (München: text + kritik, 1984), S.69.

37 Christa Wolf, *Die Dimension des Autors* (Frankfurt a. M.: Luchterhand, 1990), Bd.1, S.86f.

38 Klaus Briegleb, 'Vergangenheit in der Gegenwart', in: *Gegenwartsliteratur nach 1968 =Hansers Sozialgeschichte der deutschen Literatur vom 16. Jahrhundert bis zur Gegenwart*, hrsg. von Rolf Grimminger, Bd.12, (München: Hanser, 1992), S.77.

39 Dan Diner (Hrsg.), *Zivilisationsbruch. Denken nach Auschwitz* (Frankfurt a. M.: Fischer, 1988), S.75. 'Auschwitz, das mangels einer allen umfassenden Grauens adäquaten Begrifflichkeit als Namen für den gesamten Vorgang der nationalsozialistischen Massenvernichtung steht.'

40 Ingeborg Bachmann, *Todesarten-Projekt*. Kritische Ausgabe, unter Leitung von Robert Pichl, hrsg. von Monika Albrecht und Dirk Göttsche (München, Zürich: Piper, 1995), Bd.1, S.619-21.

41 Sigrid Weigel, 'Zur Polyphonie des Anderen. Traumatisierung und Begehren in Ingeborg Bachmanns imaginärer Autobiographie "Malina"', in: *Bilder des kulturellen Gedächtnisses*, S.245f.

[42] Bachmann, [Rede zur Verteilung des Anton-Wildgans-Preises], *Werke*, Bd.4, S.294-97.

[43] 'Sie werden sich der Passagen in *Malina* erinnern. Die Ich-Person schreibt: Ein Tag wird kommen, an dem die Menschen [rotgoldene Augen haben, rotgoldenes Haar, und die Poesie ihres Geschlechts wird wiedererschaffen werden] [...] und diese Hoffnung des Menschen hört nicht auf, wird nie aufhören', äußert Ingeborg Bachmann in einem Interview aus dem Jahr 1973, *Gu I*, S.128.

[44] Peter von Matt, *Liebesverrat. Die Treulosen in der Literatur* (München: Hanser, 1991), S.265.

[45] Der Roman wurde mehrheitlich als 'radikal unzeitgemäß', 'antimodisch', als existentialphilosophische Ichbeschreibung ohne gesellschaftliche Relevanz etc. abgelehnt. S. Bartsch, (s. Anmerkung 6), S.179.

[46] Reinhard Baumgart, '"Ihr Menschen! Ihr Ungeheuer!" Eine Rede für Ingeborg Bachmann', *Die Zeit*, 4.7.86.

SABINE COFALLA

Elitewechsel im literarischen Feld nach 1945.
Eine soziologische Verortung der Gruppe 47

Die Gruppe 47 war durch einen besonderen Habitus gekennzeichnet, der sich deutlich von dem der literarischen Generation der Weimarer Republik und deren bildungs-bürgerlichen Selbstverständnis abgrenzte. Über diesen Habitus gelang es Hans Werner Richter, einen Wechsel innerhalb der literarischen Elite durchzusetzen. Sein Ziel war es, eine literarische Öffentlichkeit zu schaffen, welche die demokratische Entwicklung innerhalb der Bundesrepublik stützen sollte. Die Vertreter der Gruppe 47 verstanden sich selbst als nonkonformistisch; aus historischer Distanz kristalliert sich allerdings ihre Funktion als komplementäre Opposition zum System Adenauer heraus. Ende der sechziger Jahre, als sich ein neuerlicher Generationswechsel vollzog, brach diese Diskrepanz auf. Die Gruppe 47 wurde nun als Teil des bundesdeutschen Establishments betrachtet; sie hatte ihre Rolle in der Öffentlichkeit eingebüßt und löste sich auf.

Literarhistorische Periodisierungen sind dem Versuch geschuldet, unterschiedliche Schreibweisen, Poetologien und intellektuelle Stile auf einer Zeitleiste gegeneinander abzugrenzen. Linear erzählte Literatur-geschichte wird der Gleichzeitigkeit vielzähliger, auch disparater Strömungen abgetrotzt. Aus kultursoziologischer Perspektive betrieben, gewinnt Geschichtsschreibung hingegen an Komplexität; sie beschränkt sich nicht auf eine Chronologie ausgewählter Fakten, sondern hebt auf den *Prozeß* der Geschichte ab und hinterfragt die interpersonalen Beziehungen, die denselben konstituieren. Welcher Legitimations- und Durchsetzungsstrategien bedienen sich konkurrierende Akteure? Warum und wie setzt sich ein intellektueller Habitus[1] innerhalb eines sozialen Felds als repräsentativ durch? In welchen gesellschaftlichen Konstellationen finden bestimmte Schreibweisen besondere Anerkennung? Und wie vollzieht sich eine neuerliche Ablösung einer (Autoren-)Elite?

   Der Blick auf die literarische Entwicklung in den Westzonen resp. in der (alten) Bundesrepublik zeigt, daß zwischen 1945/49 und 1990 die Legitimation des jeweils dominanten Schriftstellerhabitus — trotz unterschiedlicher inhaltlicher Positionen — mit einer verblüffend ähnlichen Rhetorik transportiert wurde: So weist der 'Literaturstreit' der 90er Jahre[2] Parallelen zu den intellektuellen Auseinandersetzungen auf, über die sich Ende der 40er Jahre die 'junge Generation' positionierte,[3] und auch zu den Feuilletondebatten, die ab Mitte der 60er Jahre die Auflösung der Institution Gruppe 47 einleiteten.[4] Mit unterschiedlichem intellektuellem Gestus strebten die neuen Eliten ihre Distinktion von ihren Vorgängern, grenzten sich ab von der 'Kalligraphie' (Gustav René Hocke 1946) der 'Beschreibungs- literatur'(Peter Handke 1966), der 'Gesinnungsästhetik' (Ulrich Greiner 1990). 'Alte Schlacken' waren zu 'reinigen', der 'Muff unter den Talaren' zu lüften, ein als überkommen verstandener Autorenhabitus wurde abqualifiziert.

In solchen Feuilletondebatten manifestieren sich Kämpfe um die intellektuelle Einflußsphäre, um die verbindliche Definition der sozialen Wirklichkeit. In diesem Sinn sind sie nicht Teil des literarischen, sondern des politischen Diskurses; sie bilden Foren gesellschaftlicher Selbstverständigung. Das jeweils konstruierte Bild der Vergangenheit prägt dabei die Projektion gesellschaftlicher Zukunft; umgekehrt wirkt deren Entwurf linearisierend auf die Geschichtsschreibung zurück: 'Die Menschen rasen immer vorwärts und schleifen die Geschichte hinter sich her durch den Dreck. Wenn sie können, lassen sie sie fallen. Wenn sie sie wieder brauchen, erzählen sie sie neu.'[5] Nicht zuletzt vor diesem Hintergrund scheint es müßig, den Mythos Gruppe 47 'aufklären' zu wollen. Vielmehr möchte ich seiner Funktion für die Legitimation und Durchsetzung eines Elitewechsels im literarischen Feld nach 1945 nachspüren.[6]

Die Korrespondenz Hans Werner Richters[7] macht den Prozeß dieses Elitewechsels anschaulich. Als subjektive, zeitgenössische Dokumente erzählen die Briefe von der Konstitution, dem Aufstieg und der Auflösung der Gruppe 47. Die in ihnen fixierten Kommunikations- formen dokumentieren den politischen Standpunkt und den Habitus ihrer Autoren; darüber hinaus geben sie Aufschluß über die ideelle Basis und die interne Verfaßtheit dieser eigenwilligen Autorenassoziation.

Welche Bedeutung hatte der Brief als Medium für den locker assoziierten Kreis von Schriftstellern, Journalisten und Publizisten um Hans Werner Richter? Mitte der 60er Jahre kontrastierte Richter selbst die Formen seiner Korrespondenz der Nachkriegszeit mit der

Briefkultur der 20er Jahre: Während er in seiner Jugend in seitenlangen Briefen an Freunde literarische, politische und ökonomische Fragestellungen diskutiert hatte,[8] stellte er im Rückblick bedauernd fest, daß die soziale Basis eines solchen Briefwechsels mit dem Übergang zur modernen Industriegesellschaft, durch den Nationalsozialismus und durch den Krieg endgültig zerstört worden sei. Richter, 1965:

> Gewiss, ich trauere ihm nach — dem Brief als literarisches Ausdrucksmittel. Er gab mir die Möglichkeit zu sagen, was ich empfinde, was ich leide, denke, erlebe, und ich konnte es so subjektiv sagen, wie ich es wollte. [...] Würde ich heute versuchen, jenen Briefwechsel mit meinen Freunden aufzunehmen, ich würde mich nicht nur lächerlich machen. Ich bekäme nicht einmal eine Antwort, und der erste Brief würde schon der letzte sein.[9]

Der extensive und intime Austausch mit einer Person des Vertrauens entsprach nicht dem Selbstverständnis der 'jungen Generation', die sich die Distinktion von den etablierten bürgerlichen Schriftstellern zum Programm gemacht hatte. Geprägt von den Kriegserlebnissen und dem Wunsch, die eigene Geschichte im Nationalsozialismus zu verdrängen, mied die 'junge Generation' Introspektion und Selbsthinterfragung. So wirkt Richters Korrespondenz trotz des informellen Tons seltsam unpersönlich. Allein inhaltliche Brüche, Selbststilisierungen und formale Aspekte vermitteln, daß hinter der verschriftlichten noch eine private, verschwiegene Rede steht. Die meisten Schreiben Richters sind grundsätzlich keinem ästhetischen Anspruch verpflichtet, stilistisch stehen sie dem Alltagsgespräch nah. Poetologische Ausführungen finden sich nur selten, hingegen dienen sehr viele Briefe als Medium eines konkreten Projektmanagements.

Richter sah im kontinuierlichen und persönlichen Kontakt kritischer Intellektueller die Voraussetzung, um nach dem Nationalsozialismus eine demokratische Öffentlichkeit zu etablieren. Entsprechend widmete er der Kommunikation mit Schriftstellern, Journalisten und Politikern einen Großteil seiner Arbeitszeit. Kategorisierte Richter seine Jugendkorrespondenz noch in Reminiszenz an das 'große bürgerliche Jahrhundert' und dessen Bildungsideal, übernahm seine private Korrespondenz 1945 andere soziale Funktionen: Sie war Teil eines emanzipatorischen Programms, das allerdings kaum theoretisch fundiert war, sondern sich vielmehr aus Richters subjektiver politischer Erfahrungswelt ableitete. Der Leiter der Gruppe 47 war nicht im engeren Sinne 'intellektuell', seine Persönlichkeit zeichneten

Intuition, Pragmatismus, Humor und zupackende Entschiedenheit aus.
Als Richter 1963 versuchte, Ledig-Rowohlt für eine (finanzielle)
Unterstützung des politisch-literarischen Salons in Berlin zu gewinnen,
erläuterte er: 'Ich mache solche Sachen immer mehr intuitiv (Mangel an
intellektueller Intelligenz) bin aber auf diesem Weg mit der Gruppe 47
ganz gut aus dem Jahr 1947 in die Zukunft gefahren.'[10]   Wie
unmittelbar dieser Habitus in den ersten Nachkriegsjahren das
Lebensgefühl jüngerer, demokratisch orientierter Kriegsheimkehrer
traf, zeigt Hans Jürgen Krügers euphorische Stellungnahme zu Richters
Erfolgsroman *Die Geschlagenen*:

> Zunaechst: der Roman ist ausserordentlich. Es ist der gueltige Ausdruck fuer
> das, was geschah und hinter uns liegt und auch heute noch in uns wirkt. Jeder
> — der politisch gleich oder aehnlich oder verwandt empfindet — wird in
> diesem Roman, gerade seiner herben, phrasenlosen und realistischen
> Darstellung wegen, so etwas wie eine 'Offenbarung nach aussen' sehen. Er
> wird sagen: hier ist endlich gesagt *wie* es war! und er wird sich selbst darin
> wiedererkennen und wird es oft schmerzlich genug noch einmal erleben, was
> noch immer wie ein Schatten in ihm wirkt und was das persoenliche und
> allgemeine deutsche Schicksal bestimmte.[11]

Richters Schilderung der Kriegsjahre und seine Perspektive auf das
'allgemeine deutsche Schicksal' wurde von der 'jungen Generation' als
Identifikationsangebot wahrgenommen. Der Fischersohn, Antifaschist
und Autodidakt Richter stand für den Führungsanspruch einer neuen
Elite, die sich in Differenz zu traditionellen Mustern zu legitimieren
suchte.[12] Es gelang ihm, ein Wir-Gefühl zu schaffen, wo noch
weitgehende Unsicherheit herrschte. Instinktiv setzte er
Orientierungsmarken im zerstörten mentalen Raum.[13]

Unmittelbar nach der ersten Tagung schrieb Richter an Walter
Hilsbecher: 'Wir waren zwei Tage dort oben und es ist in diesen Tagen
viel vorgelesen und viel diskutiert worden. In diesen Gesprächen hat
sich der Kreis, der bisher in einem lockeren Zusammenhang stand, jetzt
fest konsolidiert.'[14] Und im Anschluß an das zweite Gruppentreffen im
November 1947 berichtete er Wolfdietrich Schnurre:

> Als wir spät nachts Ulm verliessen, hatte jeder von uns das Gefühl, dass
> nunmehr die Gruppe 47 völlig feste Konturen angenommen hat und dass sie
> in der deutschen Literarischen Öffentlichkeit sehr bald zu Wort kommen wird.
> Die nunmehr zusammengefassten literarischen Potenzen sind so
> ausserordentlich, dass der Erfolg nicht ausbleiben kann.[15]

Ungeachtet ihrer heterogenen Begabungen bezeichnete Richter die Tagungsbesucher als 'die stärksten Kräfte des jungen schreibenden Deutschland', er sah in ihnen 'das junge Deutschland' der Nachkriegszeit.[16] Und auch seine eigene Funktion als Gruppenleiter und -manager hatte Richter bereits klar vor Augen; am 27. August 1947 teilte er Fritz Drobilitsch mit: 'Die literarischen jungen Kräfte stehen mir im weitestem Ausmass zur Verfügung.' Richter agierte als Sprecher einer Autorengruppe, bevor sich diese selbst als solche verstand.

Doch was charakterisierte das 'junge Deutschland' Richters? Die Teilnehmer der ersten Tagungen fühlten sich vor allem durch die gemeinsame Erfahrung des Kriegs verbunden, weswegen ihnen auch pauschal die Mentalität von 'Obergefreiten' attestiert wurde.[17] Die soziale Herkunft der meisten war kleinbürgerlich geprägt.[18] Rolf Schroers skizzierte im Rückblick eine 'ganz unrepräsentative "Gruppe 47"', die nach dem Schweiß der Armut roch, die proletarisch grobschlächtig, gemütlich bösmäulig, ja, pubertär ungehobelt und derb war; und eine tiefe Verachtung für 'Bildung' — qua luxuriöse Geistigkeit — betonte.'[19] Ihr Habitus stand in Kontrast zu den bürgerlichen Schriftstellern, die nach 1945 den literarischen Markt weitgehend dominierten. Die 'junge Generation' definierte sich nicht über ihre Herkunft, stand nicht für ein spezifisches Bildungsniveau ein und formulierte auch kein ästhetisches Programm. Sie lehnte eine persönliche Verantwortung für den Nationalsozialismus ab, verknüpfte dies aber unmißverständlich mit dem Signal, die soziale und politische Zukunft des Landes mitgestalten zu wollen. Die selbstgewählte Bezeichnung 'junge Generation' wurde zum Kampfbegriff, der die Frontlinien gegenüber konkurrierenden Autorengruppierungen klarer abstecken sollte. Die Korrespondenz Richters dokumentiert, wie reelle Differenzen (so gegenüber Exilautoren) strategisch herausgearbeitet wurden bzw. eine relative Nähe (so zur 'inneren Emigration') rhetorisch negiert und überspielt wurde. Die Gruppe 47 sollte ein unverwechselbares und zukunftsweisendes Profil erhalten.[20] Entscheidend für die Legitimation der 'jungen Generation' war dabei die Verlagerung des Diskurses vom ästhetischen zum politischen Movens. Die Newcomer im literarischen Feld der Nachkriegszeit verstanden Literatur als politisch-pädagogisches Instrument.

Dieser Anspruch wurde mit dem ästhetischen Konzept eines 'wahren' Realismus verknüpft. Es galt nicht, für einen eingeweihten

Kreis Erlesenes zu produzieren, sondern über die Literatur Orientierungswissen bereitzustellen. Richter formulierte 1948: 'Der Mensch unserer Zeit ist der Mensch der Masse. Ihm hat der Schriftsteller zu dienen, [...]. Echt klar und wahr zu sein, das ist die Aufgabe, die dem Schriftsteller unserer Zeit gestellt werden muß.'[21] Die sprachlichen und formalen Konsequenzen dieser neuen, im Hinblick auf den Durchschnittsbürger konzipierten Poetologie wurde in verschiedenen Zeitungen und Zeitschriften kontrovers diskutiert,[22] wodurch die 'junge Generation' auch in der Öffentlichkeit eine Neubewertung der Gattungshierarchie beförderte. In den ersten Nachkriegsjahren wurden die ästhetischen Konzepte der klassischen Moderne, formale Experimente und hochverdichtete Lyrik als weltfremde 'Kalligraphie' kategorisiert.[23] Zum literarischen Maßstab avancierten die realistische Kurzgeschichte und ein karger journalistischer Stil, durch den sich die 'junge Generation' der Frontsoldaten von ihren bürgerlich gebildeten Vätern abgrenzte.[24]

Die Distanz vom humanistischen Bildungsideal und von artistischer Avantgarde korrespondierte — wie auch der informelle Umgang untereinander — mit der Konzentration der Gruppe 47 auf das 'Handwerk'. Es wurde keine Akademie gegründet, sondern eine Werkstatt eingerichtet. Es tagten keine vergeistigten, berufenen Dichter, sondern gesellschaftlich eingebundene Bürger. Das Schreiben folgte keiner Berufung, sondern war Teil eines Berufs. Die Selektion für den literarischen Betrieb erfolgte nicht über die 'feinen Unterschiede' (Pierre Bourdieu) Bildung und Herkunft, nicht über das Postulat der 'Berufung', sondern über eine von der Person des Autors (scheinbar) unabhängige 'literarische Qualität', die es im Tagungsdiskurs zu begründen galt.

Daß die 'junge Generation' ihr Selbstverständnis nicht an den dominanten ästhetischen und gesellschaftlichen Normen ausrichtete, sondern sich selbstbewußt von diesen distanzierte, war die Voraussetzung für die Ablösung der alten Elite. Die Gruppe 47 öffnete sich gegenüber neuen Leserschichten und kooperierte eng mit den expandierenden Medien. Sie bediente sich akademischer Autorität und publizistischer Einflußnahme und setzte sich an der Schnittstelle von Literatur und Politik durch. Im Rückblick stellt Nicolaus Sombart fest: 'Es war eine echte "Kulturrevolution"'.[25] Diese Verve entsprach der in den ersten Nachkriegsjahren verbreiteten Hoffnung auf einen 'Aufbau aus dem Nichts', provozierte jedoch auf seiten traditioneller Akteure erwartungsgemäß Skepsis und Abwehr. So bemerkte der Rowohlt-Lektor Ernst Wilhelm Geisenheyner am 20. November 1947 in einem Brief an Ernst Kreuder spitz:

> Was bei dieser ganzen Angelegenheit herauskommt und ob sich, was ja das wichtigste ist, in dieser Gruppe wirklich schöpferische junge Schriftsteller zusammengefunden haben, die in der Lage sind, etwas Neues zu gestalten, wird die Zukunft zeigen. Vorläufig scheint man im wesentlichen damit beschäftigt zu sein, Männer und Namen für sich in Anspruch zu nehmen, die bereits in der neuen Literatur einen gewissen Klang haben.[26]

1952 sprach die konservative Opposition der aufstrebenden Zeitgeisterscheinung Gruppe 47 die Befähigung zu 'kulturell wertvoller Arbeit' ab. Das neuartige Zeitschriftenprojekt *Die Literatur* wurde verrissen und auch nach einer verhältnismäßig kurzen Zeit eingestellt.[27] Die Redakteure und Autoren verfügten nicht über den Anfang der 50er Jahre noch verbindlichen (Spiel-)Einsatz für das literarische Feld:[28] die Bildung und den Habitus eines bürgerlichen Schriftstellers der Weimarer Republik.

Das Verhältnis zwischen der 'jungen Generation' und der literarischen Elite der zwanziger Jahre blieb hierarchisch geprägt, wie u.a. bei der Verleihung des René-Schickele-Preises an den Leiter der Gruppe 47 deutlich wurde. Sobald Richter die Nachricht erhielt, daß ihm dieser von Exilautoren gestiftete Preis für *Sie fielen aus Gottes Hand* zugesprochen worden war, schrieb er an Hans Georg Brenner, seinen engsten Mitarbeiter und Redakteur bei der Zeitschrift *Die Literatur*:

> Interne Mitteilung für Dich. Soeben kam die Nachricht, dass mir der René-Schickele-Preis zugesprochen worden ist. Ich fühle mich nicht ganz wohl dabei, aber Thomas Mann ist doch wohl unbestechlich. Was meinst Du? Natürlich wird es unserem Blatt gut tun, denn man will anscheinend einen grossen Rummel aufziehen. Und wir können Reklame gebrauchen.[29]

Die Antwort von Brenner ließ nicht lange auf sich warten. Er schrieb am 16. Januar 1952 zurück:

> Lieber Hans, hab herzlichen Dank für Deinen ausführlichen Schreibebrief und lass Dich von Herzen beglückwünschen. Du sollst Dich mit diesem Preis wohlfühlen, denn wenn nichts feststeht, so doch das Eine: dass Thomas Mann unbestechlich ist, vor allem, was Autoren in Deutschland anbelangt. Und es soll Dir auch wohl dabei sein, unserer Zeitschrift wegen und der

Gruppe wegen; beide werden in diesem Zusammenhang nicht wenig
profitieren.[30]

Thomas Mann war vielleicht nicht bestechlich, aber auch keineswegs
überzeugt von der getroffenen Wahl.[31] Nur schwer schloß er sich der
Einschätzung und den Vorschlägen der anderen Jurymitglieder an, unter
ihnen Hermann Kesten und Alfred Neumann. Am 13. Dezember 1951
schrieb er an Kesten:

> Ich will Ihnen sagen — *ich stimme*, nach langem Zögern, um ein Ende zu
> machen, *der Preiserteilung an Hans Werner Richters Roman zu*. Ich meine:
> falls nicht im letzten Augenblick sich noch etwas Besseres, nicht nur so sehr
> relativ, sondern absolut Preiswürdiges findet, was wohl unwahrscheinlich
> ist.[32]

Richter blieb die zögerliche Entscheidung Manns nicht verborgen. Am
8. April 1952 bedankte er sich bei Hermann Kesten

> recht herzlich für die Verleihung des Rene-Schickele-Preises [...]. Für mich
> war das eine grosse Freude und das stärkste Erlebnis dieser Nachkriegsjahre.
> Es war umso stärker, als es eben von den emigrierten deutschen
> Schriftstellern kam, denen ich so viel zu verdanken habe. Obwohl ich selbst
> glaube, dass mein zweites Buch diesen Preis noch nicht verdient hat (es ist
> noch zu unausgegoren, zu wenig durcharbeitet, hier und da geschludert),
> habe ich den Preis doch angenommen. Ich habe ihn angenommen, weil ich
> wohl weiss, dass bei dieser Verleihung auch literaturpolitische
> Gesichtspunkte mitgespielt haben und diese literaturpolitischen
> Gesichtspunkte sind in der augenblicklichen Situation Deutschlands für mich
> entscheidend. Diese Verleihung, so fassen es auch meine Freunde auf, war
> zugleich eine Auszeichnung der 'Gruppe 47', ihrer Mentalität, ihrer
> Bestrebungen und ihrer Arbeit. Haben wir es so richtig verstanden?[33]

Richter selbst hatte seinen Erfolg als einen kulturpolitischen erkannt. Er
war stellvertretend für die 'junge Generation' geehrt worden, deren
liberale, demokratische Auffassung den Exilautoren ein politischer
Garant für die Zukunft zu sein schien.

Wenngleich Richter nicht als besondere literarische oder
publizistische Begabung hervorstach, gelang es ihm, für seine
Generation einen verbindlichen mentalen Pol zu bestimmen. Sein
Verständnis von Literatur als indirekt politischer Einflußgröße traf
zentrale Bedürfnisse jüngerer Intellektueller. Unmittelbar nach 1945
war die Distanzierung vom Nationalsozialismus in den Westzonen mit
allgemeiner Skepsis gegenüber der politischen Sphäre verbunden.

Dieser 'totale Ideologieverdacht'[34] löste für das literarische Feld einen Autonomisierungsschub aus: Im Rekurs auf die Tradition der bürgerlichen Ethik und die Werte der französischen Revolution etablierte sich der Glaube an die bewußtseinsbildende, aufklärende Kraft der Literatur.[35]

Für Richter blieb es Zeit seines Lebens ein politisches Trauma, daß die Demokratie 1933 abgewählt worden war. Die bedrohliche Vorstellung einer Wiederholung der (nationalsozialistischen) Geschichte bildete die emotionale Basis seiner politischen Anschauungen, wobei er seine Erfahrungen aus den 20er und 30er Jahren unkritisch auf die Situation in der Bundesrepublik projizierte. Die Schriftsteller in der Bundesrepublik sollten stellvertretend und gleichsam nachholend für die Intellektuellen der Weimarer Republik agieren,[36] die in Richters Augen politisch versagt hatten. 1961 erläuterte er:

> Ich wollte nach dem Krieg einen anderen, weltzugewandten, politisch (nicht parteipolitisch) engagierten Schriftsteller. Ich sah damals das Unglück Deutschlands nicht nur in der politischen Entwicklung, sondern vor allen Dingen in seiner geistigen und damit auch literarischen. Das war der Grund warum ich meine eigene Arbeit immer wieder im Interesse der Gruppe und ihrer Entwicklung zurückgestellt habe. Praktisch war es immer eine pädagogische Arbeit. Deshalb bestimmte Formen der Kritik, des Ertragens der Kritik, und der immer geübten Achtung der Meinung und des Könnens des anderen. Das war eine harte aber mit viel Freude betriebene Arbeit von nunmehr fast fünfzehn Jahren. Manchmal frage ich mich heute, ob ich damit Erfolg gehabt habe oder nicht. Ich meine mit dieser Frage nicht das literarische Prestige der Gruppe. Das ist nur Abfallprodukt.[37]

Das Konzept der 'littérature engagée', das Sartre im literarischen, philosophischen und politischen Feld Frankreichs machtvoll umsetzte, wurde vielen westdeutschen Autoren zur Schablone ihres Selbstverständnisses. Richter suchte mit der Gruppe 47 eine gesellschaftspolitische Einflußgröße zu schaffen, die sich der Position Jean Paul Sartres in Frankreich annäherte.[38] Allerdings bildete sich in Deutschland im Gegensatz zu dem 'totalen Intellektuellen' Frankreichs — dem anerkannten Schriftsteller und Philosoph, dem Künstler und Kritiker in einer Person[39] — keine monolithische Autorität heraus. Vielmehr vernetzten sich die Autoren der 'jungen Generation' nach Maßgabe eines verbindlichen Habitus: des gesellschaftspolitisch engagierten, demokratischen Intellektuellen. Und im Unterschied zu der

zentralistisch ausgerichteten Kultur Frankreichs organisierten sie sich
— gewissermaßen dem Modell des bundesrepublikanischen
Föderalismus folgend — in einer dezentralisierten, ortsungebundenen
Form.

Mit dem internationalen Durchbruch der bundesdeutschen
Literatur, der sich 1959 in der Rede vom 'Literaturwunder'
manifestierte,[40] verankerte sich die Gruppe verstärkt im öffentlichen
Bewußtsein. Und auf der Grundlage der gesellschaftlichen Anerkennung
der Literatur, auf der Basis des symbolischen Kapitals, das ihr
zugemessen wurde, konnte Richter seine gesellschaftspolitischen Ziele
— Demokratisierung und Aufbau einer kritischen Öffentlichkeit —
vorantreiben.[41]

Daß dies gelang, war Richters geschicktem Positionieren der
Gruppe 47 an der strategischen Schnittstelle zwischen Öffentlichkeit und
Privatheit, zwischen Ästhetik und Politik geschuldet. Die Gruppe, die
keine Gruppe sein wollte, wurde von einem Mann gelenkt, der immer
mal wieder charmant zu zweifeln wußte, ob er denn selbst überhaupt
'dazu gehöre'.[42] Und ungeachtet ihres großen Einflusses auf das
literarische Leben hielt Hans Werner Richter daran fest, sie sei nichts
anderes als ein 'privater Freundeskreis'. Die Gruppe 47 — ein
Vexierspiel zwischen öffentlicher Privatheit und privater Öffentlichkeit,
das Richter sehr sensibel zu tarieren wußte. Es gelang ihm, die Gruppe
47 mit einer Aura zu umgeben und zu einem Ort mentalen Begehrens zu
machen, der beileibe nicht allen Interessierten frei zugänglich war.
Bemüht, sie als zivile informelle Einflußgröße im öffentlichen Raum zu
profilieren und zu bewahren, unterstützte er die Mystifizierung der
Gruppe 47 nach Kräften. Ein prägnantes Beispiel ist hierfür die Planung
der ersten Gruppendokumentation, des *Almanach*. Während Richter
sonst ständig unterstrich, es gebe keine Mitglieder der Gruppe 47, war
nun konkret zu klären, wer mit welchen Texten in dieser Publikation
vertreten sein sollte. Das warf Probleme auf. Richter meinte:

> in der Festlegung liegt für mich der Haken der ganzen Angelegenheit. Gerade
> das Nichtfestgelegte, nicht Vereinsmässige war ja das Wesen der Gruppe 47.
> Wenn man es jetzt so genau fixiert, geht etwas von dieser Atmosphäre der
> 'geheimnisvollen Loge' verloren. Ich weiß deshalb nicht recht, ob wir uns mit
> diesem Buch nicht selbst einen schlechten Dienst erweisen. [...] Wenn andere
> etwas in die Gruppe 47 hineininterpretieren, Doktoranden, Professoren,
> Literarhistoriker, ist das gut. Was wir aber selbst darstellen, hängt uns an.[43]

Die Stilisierungen und Verwischungen trugen dazu bei, die Gruppe 47 zu einer privaten Institution von größter öffentlicher Relevanz zu machen. Das strategische Spiel zwischen Privatheit und Öffentlichkeit entsprach der postulierten autonomen Stellung der Literatur gegenüber der Politik, die ausgehend von den ersten Nachkriegsjahren in der Bundesrepublik den literarischen Diskurs mehrere Jahrzehnte prägte: Die Literatur sollte das parlamentarische Kontrollinstrumentarium und die Medien als kritische politische Instanz ergänzen, 'Gewissen der Nation' sein.

Im gedanklichen Kontext der Ästhetik Adornos wurde in den 60er Jahren Literatur als a priori widerständiges Gesellschaftselement definiert, ausgezeichnet durch die 'Funktion der Funktionslosigkeit'. Enzensberger formulierte: 'Das Gedicht ist, in den Augen der Herrschaft, die außer ihr selber keine doxa anerkennen kann, anarchisch; unerträglich, weil sie darüber nicht verfügen kann; durch sein bloßes Dasein subversiv'[44] Entsprechend sahen viele hauptberufliche Schriftsteller den Schwerpunkt ihrer kritischen Tätigkeit in der literarischen Produktion, im Schreiben selbst. Hingegen bezeichnete Richter das 'literarische Prestige' der Gruppe 47 gern als 'Abfallprodukt' seiner pädagogisch-politischen Tätigkeit.[45] Zwischen den Gruppenautoren und ihrem Manager hatte sich eine Art Arbeitsteilung entwickelt: Richter arbeitete als Bankhalter mit dem symbolischen Kapital, das den Gruppenautoren zu eigen war. Er hielt die kommunikative Vernetzung aufrecht, trug die kulturpolitische Orientierung der Gruppe 47 nach außen und sicherte die Grundlage des Kapitaltransfers: die Abgrenzung der Literatur als kritisch-moralischem Prinzip von der politischen Macht.[46] Die Literatur im engeren Sinne schien ihm dabei manchmal etwas aus dem Blick zu gleiten. Fried mahnte 1966: 'Du weisst genau, unser politischer Einfluss hängt von unserm literarischen ab. Der literarische Einfluss darf nicht nur als Mittel zum Zweck des politischen Einflusses fortdauern, sondern nur, wenn wir glauben, dass es auch da noch Aufgaben gibt.'[47] Und doch bewährte sich die soziale Praxis an der Schnittstelle zwischen literarischem und politischem Feld. Anfang der 60er Jahre hatte sich der Habitus des gesellschaftspolitisch engagierten Schriftstellers durchgesetzt, für den die Gruppe als repräsentativ galt.

Doch welche politischen Inhalte vertrat die Gruppe 47? Wo positionierte sie sich im politischen Spektrum der Bundesrepublik?

Richters Korrespondenz zeigt, daß die wüsten Auseinandersetzungen zwischen 'rechts' und 'links', wie sie in den Feuilletons der 50er und 60er Jahre geführt wurden, nur historisch kontextualisiert zu verstehen sind. So sagt die vielfache Bezeichnung des Kreises um Richter als 'Sozialisten', Kommunisten', 'Linksintellektuellen' und 'Radikal-demokraten' zwar viel über die politischen Grabenkämpfe dieser Jahrzehnte aus, nicht aber über den eigentlichen politischen Standpunkt der Beteiligten.

Richters politische Vorstellungen waren keinesfalls 'radikal'. Er bezog nie 'zersetzend' Opposition, wie es etwa Heinrich Böll Ende der 60er Jahre forderte,[48] sondern agierte im Rahmen des breiten gesellschaftlichen Konsens der Nachkriegszeit, bemüht, diesen punktuell auszuweiten. Er war ein betont patriotischer Oppositioneller, dazu neigend:

> allzu scharfe Kritik, die ich hier im Inland äussere, im Ausland abzumildern, ja, den Glauben an die demokratische Entwicklung in Deutschland zu betonen. Das mag nicht immer richtig sein, scheint mir aber ein Gebot der Fairneß gegenüber dem eigenen Land.[49]

Es ging Richter weniger um die Umsetzung konkreter politischer Ziele, eher allgemeiner um die Förderung und Garantie eines lebendigen demokratischen Austauschs. In diesem Zusammenhang steht auch die Gründung des politisch-literarischen Salons; am 30. Dezember 1963 erläuterte er Thomas Dehler, FDP-Politiker und Vize-Präsident des Deutschen Bundestags:

> Ich habe die Absicht hier in Berlin so etwas wie einen literarisch-politischen 'Salon' einzurichten. Das ist natürlich zugleich ein 'Salon' der Gruppe 47. Hier sollen, abgesehen von den literarischen Abenden, vor allen Dingen Gespräche mit Politikern und anderen Personen des öffentlichen Lebens stattfinden. Um den Personenkreis zu umreißen: von Franz Josef Strauß bis zu Herbert Wehner, von Axel Cäsar Springer bis Döpfner oder Bengsch, ja, ich denke auch daran, Politiker, Literaten usw. (Ehrenburg, Fedin, Smirnov) aus dem Osten zu solchen Gesprächen einzuladen, auch, wenn es möglich ist, aus der 'DDR'. Gesprächspartner werden auf der anderen Seite Angehörige der Gruppe 47 sein [...]. Ich selbst werde als Gastgeber fungieren. [...] Worauf es mir dabei ankommt, ist nicht nur das private Gespräch, sondern auch die Herstellung 'legaler' Beziehungen zur Politik, mit anderen Worten, ich möchte das Gerede von den 'destruktiven' Intellektuellen, das ich für dumm und leider auch gefährlich halte, untergraben und zerstören.[50]

Richters strategischer Pragmatismus und sein Sinn für das Ausbalancieren heterogener Interessen paßten sich optimal in das zentrale mentale Paradigma der Bundesrepublik ein: Realpolitik und 'Vergangenheitspolitik'.[51] Und wie Richter hatte sich die 'junge Generation' im Staat Adenauers arrangiert. Die CDU-Politiker und die Gruppe 47 bildeten — sich in der Öffentlichkeit gegenseitig anfeindend — eine strategische Allianz, zuständig für die materielle bzw. die ideelle Stabilisierung der Demokratie. Die dabei auftretenden Reibungen sind nicht als unproduktive Störung einzuschätzen, sondern vielmehr als Rituale wechselseitiger Bestätigung. Das 'Gewissen der Nation' war ein konstitutiver Bestandteil des bundesrepublikanischen Nachkriegs-kollektivs.

Mitte der 60er Jahre hatte die Gruppe 47 die von Richter angestrebte dominante gesellschaftliche Position inne. Doch wo ihre Repräsentativität wuchs, verlor sie zunehmend ihre Glaubwürdigkeit als oppositionelle Kraft. Böll monierte: 'Die Gruppe ist pluralistisch geblieben, die Gesellschaft ist es geworden. [...] Es ergeht ihr mit ihrem Pluralismus wie der Gesellschaft, in der sie lebt und aus der sie sich rekrutiert; nach einer gewissen Zeit schlägt der Pluralismus in Promiskuität um'.[52] Der Habitus Hans Werner Richters, der zwei Jahrzehnte lang das Selbstverständnis vieler Schriftsteller in der Bundesrepublik repräsentierte, hatte an Kohäsionskraft eingebüßt. Parallel dazu entfalteten sich neue Distinktionsmuster, neue Schreibweisen und eine neue Dynamik im literarischen Feld. Das moralisch-demokratische Forum Gruppe 47 wurde zunehmend mit (partei-)politischen Inhalten konfrontiert. Durchaus zum Ärger Richters, der entrüstet gegen die 'Revolution der Neurotiker' wetterte.[53] Doch die Studentenbewegung gab sich mit konsensuellen Modellen zur Sicherung der formalen Grundlagen der Demokratie nicht mehr zufrieden:

> Die Jugend, die nach Vorbildern sucht, fühlt sich geneppt. [...] Die ältere Generation will ihre Ordnung auch der jungen Generation aufdrängen, die nicht weiß, was sie davon nehmen soll, weil alle Voraussetzungen mit Unwahrheiten und Rücksichtnahmen durchsetzt sind.[54]

Die APO schlug die Gruppe 47 unumwunden dem Establishment zu, gegen das diese selbst noch zu kämpfen glaubte.[55] Die Forderung nach einer Fundamentalopposition und einer konsequenten Auseinander-setzung mit dem Faschismus löste Richters pragmatisches Konzept strategischer Allianzen ab. Wie die 'junge Generation' in den ersten Nachkriegsjahren anderen Gruppierungen wie Exilautoren und 'inneren Emigranten' die politische Legitimität abgesprochen hatte, profilierte sich nun die APO in Negation ihrer 'nonkonformistischen' Vorgänger als die alternative gesellschaftliche Kraft der Bundesrepublik. Ein neuerlicher Wandel der intellektuellen Elite hatte sich vollzogen und die Gruppe 47 als Institution obsolet werden lassen. Dennoch bewies die mit ihr verbundene kulturpolitische Denkart weit über ihre reelle Existenz hinaus Beharrungsvermögen — bis sich der Literaturbetrieb mit der deutsch-deutschen Vereinigung endgültig von der Nachkriegszeit verabschiedete.

Der Rückblick bestätigt so auf gewisse Weise den von Richter jahrzehntelang konsequent verteidigten Anspruch, die Gruppe 47 sei keine Gruppe, sondern sie war Inbegriff eines intellektuellen *Selbstverständnisses*, das sich primär in einem politisch-moralischen, nicht in einem ästhetischen Rahmen situierte. Einem Selbstverständnis, das in Westeuropa nach dem Zweiten Weltkrieg Epoche machte.

Fußnoten

Vorbemerkung: Der Beitrag basiert auf Teil II der Dissertation der Verf., erschienen unter dem Titel: *Der "soziale Sinn" Hans Werner Richters. Zur Korrespondenz des Leiters der Gruppe 47* (Berlin: Weidler, 1997).

[1] Der Begriff 'Habitus' rekurriert auf die Kultursoziologie Pierre Bourdieus, die die methodische Basis meines Beitrags darstellt. Der Habitus manifestiert sich in für bestimmte gesellschaftliche Gruppen spezifischen Denk-, Wahrnehmungs- und Handlungsschemata und vermittelt als 'Leib gewordene Geschichte' zwischen den objektiv-materiellen Bedingungen des sozialen Felds und der konkreten sozialen Praxis der Akteure. Vgl. Pierre Bourdieu, *Zur Soziologie der symbolischen Formen*, übersetzt v. Wolfgang Fietkau (Frankfurt a. M.: Suhrkamp, 1974), S.40-41, S.125-58; Pierre Bourdieu, *Sozialer Sinn. Kritik der theoretischen Vernunft*, übersetzt von Günter Seibt. (Frankfurt a. M.: Suhrkamp, 1993), S.99-121; vgl. Cofalla, *Der 'soziale Sinn' Hans Werner Richters*, S.12-14.

[2] Vgl. zum 'Literaturstreit' 1990/91 die Dokumentation von Thomas Anz (Hrsg.), *"Es geht nicht um Christa Wolf". Der Literaturstreit im vereinten Deutschland* (München: Spangenberg, 1991).

[3] Vgl. dazu z. B. Alfred Andersch, 'Deutsche Literatur in der Entscheidung', *Volk und Zeit*, 2: 12 (1947), 369-73; Walter Kolbenhoff, 'Kunst und Künstler. Eine Antwort', *Horizont*, Berlin, 2: 5 (1947); ders., 'Gegen die Nebelrufer. Ein Brief an Wolfdietrich Schnurre', *Der Skorpion*, 1: 1 (1948), 42-43; Richter an Kolbenhoff, 11.6.1947, in: *HWRB* (s. Anmerkung 7), Nr. 47/2; Richter an Kolbenhoff, 4.7.1947, in: *HWRB*, Nr. 47/4; Wolfdietrich Schnurre, 'Kunst und Künstler. Unzeitgemäße Betrachtungen eines Außenseiters', *Horizont*, Berlin, 2: 1(1947), 23; ders., [erneute Stellungnahme zur Kolbenhoff-Debatte], *Horizont*, Berlin, 2: 11 (1947), 22-23, ders., 'Für die

Wahrhaftigkeit'. (Eine Antwort an Walter Kolbenhoff), *Der Skorpion*, 1: 1 (1948), 43-46; die Debatte zur Frage, 'Für wen schreiben die Schriftsteller?', *Frankfurter Rundschau*, 14.5.1949, 28.5.1949, 11.6.1949, 25.6.1949.

4 Vgl. zur Position der konservativen Opposition gegen die Gruppe 47 die Dokumentation des 'Züricher Literaturstreits' in: *Sprache im technischen Zeitalter*, 7: 22 (April/Juni 1967); zur Kritik progressiver Autoren an der gruppenspezifischen Verquickung von Literatur und Politik die Beiträge im *Kursbuch 15* (1968).

5 Nadja Klinger, 'Willkommen, Geschichte, recycelt!', *die tageszeitung*, 12.3.1997.

6 Als Elite definiere ich eine Gruppierung, deren Habitus und Selbstverständnis innerhalb einer spezifischen historischen Konstellation in einem spezifischen gesellschaftlichen Feld normbildend wirkt.

7 Vgl. Hans Werner Richter, *Briefe*, hrsg. v. Sabine Cofalla (München: Hanser, 1997) (abgekürzt als *HWRB*). Die Quellenangabe erfolgt mit dem Datum und ggf. der Briefnummer im Band *HWRB*. Wenn nicht anders angegeben, befinden sich die Originale im Hans Werner Richter-Archiv der Akademie der Künste Berlin-Brandenburg.

8 Vgl. Hans Werner Richter, 'Warum ich kein Tagebuch schreibe', in: *Das Tagebuch und der moderne Autor. Günther Anders u.a*, hrsg. v. Uwe Schultz (München: Hanser, 1965), S.95-109, hier, S.107-08.

9 Ebd., S.108; die Jugendbriefe Richters sind nicht erhalten.

10 Richter an Ledig-Rowohlt, 5.9.1963, in: *HWRB*, Nr. 63/22.

11 Krüger an Richter, 13.2.1949, in: *HWRB*, Nr. 49/1; Hervorhebungen im Brieftext sind in diesem Beitrag einheitlich kursiv gesetzt. — In seinem Bericht zur Tagung in Marktbreit 1949 stellte Horst Richard Münnich fest, 'Das, wovon man hier sprach, war man selbst' (Münnich, 'Tagung der Gruppe 47', in: *Süddeutsche Zeitung*, 7.5.1949).

12 Vgl. dazu auch die Beiträge von Jürgen Schutte, Wilfried van der Will und Rhys Williams in diesem Band.

13 Vgl. Friedrich an Richter, 30.10.1968, in: *HWRB*, Nr. 68/19.

14 Richter an Hilsbecher, 9.9.1947, in: *HWRB*, Nr. 47/14.

15 Richter an Schnurre, 14.11.1947, in: *HWRB*, Nr. 47/29.

16 Richter an Hilsbecher, 9.9.1947, in: *HWRB*, Nr. 47/14.

17 Vgl. Hans Schwab-Felisch, 'Die Literatur der Obergefreiten. Neue deutsche Kriegsromane und Kriegstagebücher', *Der Monat*, 4: 42 (1952), 644-51; Nicolaus Sombart, *Der unbekannte Obergefreite. Herrschaft und Gestalt* [unveröffentlichtes Manuskript]; vgl. ders., *Pariser Lehrjahre 1951-1954. Leçons de Sociologie*, 3. Aufl. (Hamburg: Hoffmann und Campe, 1995), S.254.

18 So war Richter Fischerssohn, der Vater von Grass war Tischler und Arbeiter, der Bölls Schreinermeister. Eine repräsentative Studie zur Herkunft und Familiengeschichte westdeutscher Autoren existiert meines Wissens nicht — wahrscheinlich ein Resultat der verbreiteten Distanz der deutschen Literaturwissenschaft gegenüber empirisch-

soziologischen Methoden. Aber auch ohne repräsentative Daten ist die Argumentation, die Gruppe 47 sei kleinbürgerlich geprägt gewesen, nicht hinfällig. Es gilt, den herrschenden Ton, die dominanten Wahrnehmungs-, Denk- und Handlungsschemata zu benennen. Und da ist festzuhalten: Die Gruppe 47 gab sich nicht elitär, sondern hemdsärmelig, man traf sich nicht zum Tee, sondern zum Bier, die Stimmung war weniger gediegen als zotig-verklemmt. Ähnliches gilt für die Frage der 'Akademisierung' der Gruppe 47: Trotz der vielzähligen Doktorentitel und niveauvoller Diskussionsbeiträge wurden die Tagungen nicht zu einer bildungspolitischen Veranstaltung, wurde der laxe Umgangston nicht von einem akademischen Diskurs abgelöst. Der dominante Habitus war kleinbürgerlich, aufstiegsorientiert und informell: Schreiben als Beruf.

[19] Rolf Schroers, 'Gruppe 47 und die deutsche Nachkriegsliteratur', *Merkur*, 19 (Mai 1965), 448-62. Das Zitat folgt dem Wiederabdruck in: Reinhard Lettau (Hrsg.), *Die Gruppe 47. Bericht, Kritik, Polemik. Ein Handbuch* (Neuwied und Berlin: Luchterhand, 1967), S.371-88, hier, S.376; vgl. auch Sombart, *Pariser Lehrjahre*, S.252-259. Thomas Mann charakterisierte das Benehmen der Gruppe als 'pöbelhaft' (Mann an Klaus Mampell, 17.5.1954, in: Thomas Mann, *Briefe 1948-1955 und Nachlese*, hrsg. v. Erika Mann (Frankfurt a. M.: Fischer, 1979), S.341).

[20] Vgl. dazu Cofalla, *Der 'soziale Sinn'*, S.16-33.

[21] Hans Werner Richter, [Leserbrief zur Debatte 'Für wen schreiben die Schriftsteller?'], *Frankfurter Rundschau*, 28.5.1949.

[22] Vgl. dazu oben Anmerkung 3.

[23] Vgl. Gustav René Hocke, 'Deutsche Kalligraphie oder: Glanz und Elend der modernen Literatur', *Der Ruf*, 1: 7 (15.11.46); auch in: Hans Schwab-Felisch (Hrsg.), *Der Ruf: Eine deutsche Nachkriegszeitschrift* (München: dtv, 1962), S.203-08.

[24] Pierre Bourdieu zeigt auf, daß eine außerordentliche Übereinstimmung zwischen der Hierarchie der gesellschaftlichen Positionen (bzw. der Genres und Stile) und der Hierarchie der sozialen Abstammungen (bzw. der Dispositionen) besteht. — Vgl. Pierre Bourdieu, *Die Intellektuellen und die Macht*, hrsg. v. Irene Dölling. Aus dem Französischen von Jürgen Bolder unter Mitarbeit von Ulrike Nordmann und Margareta Steinrücke (Hamburg: VSA-Verlag, 1991), S.122; vgl. ders., *Die feinen Unterschiede. Kritik der gesellschaftlichen Urteilskraft*, übersetzt von Bernd Schwibs und Achim Russer (Frankfurt a. M.: Suhrkamp, 1982).

[25] Sombart, *Pariser Lehrjahre*, S.259.

[26] Geisenheyner an Kreuder, 20.11.1947, Deutsches Literaturarchiv Marbach.

[27] Vgl. zur Kritik am mangelnden Niveau der 'Literatur' durch die etablierten Feuilletons: Holthusen an Richter, 19.3.1952, in: *HWRB*, Nr. 52/3; Richter an Schroers, 31.3.1952, in: *HWRB*, Nr. 52/4 und den Beitrag von Jürgen Schutte in diesem Band.

[28] Vgl. zum Begriff des 'enjeu', Pierre Bourdieu, *Les règles de l'art. Genèse et structure du champ littéraire* (Paris: Editions du Seuil, 1992), S.316-21.

[29] Richter an Brenner, 15.1.1952, vgl. dazu: *HWRB*, Nr. 52/2, Fußnote 3.

[30] Brenner an Richter, 16.1.1952, in: *HWRB*, Nr. 52/2.

31 Vgl. dazu die Lektüre von *Sie fielen aus Gottes Hand* von Klaus Briegleb aus der rekonstruiert-fiktiven Perspektive Thomas Manns: 'Literarische Nachverfolgung. Zu Hans Werner Richters "Sie fielen aus Gottes Hand" (1951)', in: Robert Weninger/Brigitte Rossbacher (Hrsg.), *Wendezeiten. Zeitenwenden. Positionsbestimmungen zur deutschsprachigen Literatur 1945-1995* (Tübingen: Stauffenburg Verlag, 1997), S.3-36.

32 Thomas Mann, *Briefe 1948-1955 und Nachlese*, S.235f.

33 Richter an Kesten, 8.4.1952, Monacensia Bibliothek und Literaturarchiv, in: *HWRB*, Nr. 52/5.

34 Vgl. Hans Mayer, *Zur deutschen Literatur der Zeit. Zusammenhänge, Schriftsteller, Bücher* (Reinbek bei Hamburg: Rowohlt, 1967), S.300-20.

35 Vgl. Hans Werner Richter, 'Wie entstand und was war die Gruppe 47?', in: Hans A. Neunzig (Hrsg.), *Hans Werner Richter und die Gruppe 47* (Berlin, Wien: Ullstein, 1981), S.27-110, hier S.49; vgl. Volker Wehdeking, *Anfänge westdeutscher Nachkriegsliteratur, Aufsätze, Interviews, Materialien.* (Aachen: Alano, 1989), S.15.

36 Vgl. Frank Trommler, 'Die nachgeholte Résistance. Politik und Gruppenethos im historischen Zusammenhang', in: Justus Fetscher, Eberhard Lämmert und Jürgen Schutte (Hrsg.), *Die Gruppe 47 in der Geschichte der Bundesrepublik* (Würzburg: Königshausen & Neumann, 1991), S.9-22.

37 Vgl. Richter an Leonhardt, 11.11.1961, in: *HWRB*, Nr. 61/29.

38 Wo genau die Differenzen und Gemeinsamkeiten im Selbstverständnis der gesellschaftspolitisch engagierten Autoren in Frankreich und Deutschland lagen, ist noch eigens zu untersuchen. Vgl. dazu Joseph Jurt, *Das literarische Feld. Das Konzept Pierre Bourdieus in Theorie und Praxis* (Darmstadt: Wissenschaftliche Buchgesellschaft, 1995); vgl. Mechtild Rahner, *'Tout est neuf ici, tout est à recommencer...'. Die Rezeption des französischen Existentialismus im kulturellen Feld Westdeutschlands (1945-1949)* (Würzburg: Könighausen & Neumann, 1993). Vgl. auch den Beitrag von Helmut Peitsch in diesem Band.

39 Vgl. dazu Pierre Bourdieu, 'Sartre', *London Review of Books*, 2 (20.11.-3.12.1980), 11-12; ders., 'Die Erfindung des totalen Intellektuellen', in: *Romanistische Zeitschrift für Literaturwissenschaft*, 5: 4 (1981), 385-92; ders., *Les règles de l'art*, S.293-97; vgl. Anna Boschetti, *Sartre et 'Les Temps modernes'. Une entreprise intellectuelle* (Paris: Edition de Minuit, 1985), S.14.

40 1959 wurden bei der Frankfurter Buchmesse die Romane *Die Blechtrommel* (Günter Grass), *Billard um halbzehn* (Heinrich Böll) und *Mutmaßungen über Jakob* (Uwe Johnson) vorgestellt. Auch andere Titel wie *Sansibar oder der letzte Grund* (Alfred Andersch, 1957), *Die Kunstfigur* (Heinz von Cramer, 1958) und *Halbzeit* (Martin Walser, 1960) waren international erfolgreich und trugen zum Renomee der bundesrepublikanischen Literatur bei. Der 'magische Realismus' war in den Hintergrund gerückt. Die Sprachkritik und die Reflexion über das Erzählen selbst hatte (wieder) Einzug in die Texte gefunden, wohingegen die 'Geschichte' häufig verfremdet, in ihrer Chronologie zersetzt erzählt wurde.

41 'Im Kampf um die Durchsetzung der legitimen Sicht von sozialer Welt, [...] besitzen die Akteure Macht jeweils proportional zum Umfang ihres symbolischen Kapitals, daß heißt proportional zum Maß ihrer Anerkennung durch eine Gruppe' (Pierre Bourdieu, *Zur Soziologie der symbolischen Formen*, S.22-23)

42 Vgl. das Gespräch Richters mit Horst Krüger, 12.4.1961, SWF Baden-Baden: 'Ein Kreis von lauter Einzelgängern. Zum 15-jährigen Bestehen der Gruppe 47'.

43 Richter an Mannzen, 18.2.1962.

44 Hans Magnus Enzensberger, 'Poesie und Politik' [1962], in: *Einzelheiten II. Poesie und Politik* (Frankfurt a. M.: Suhrkamp, 1964), S.113-37, hier S.136. Vgl. auch Alfred Andersch, 'Die Blindheit des Kunstwerks', in: ders., *Die Blindheit des Kunstwerks. Literarische Essays und Aufsätze* (Zürich: Diogenes, 1979), S.40-51; vgl. Heinrich Böll, 'Die Sprache als Hort der Freiheit', in: *Werke. Essayistische Schriften und Reden, I. 1952-1963*, hrsg. v. Bernd Balzer (Köln: Kiepenheuer und Witsch, 1978), S.301-05; vgl. Günter Eich, 'Rede zur Verleihung des Büchner-Preises' [1959], in: *Akzente. Zeitschrift für Dichtung*, 7 (1960), 35-47. Wenngleich diese Beiträge von Enzensberger, Andersch, Böll und Eich auf eigenständigen, durchaus von einander zu differenzierenden Poetologien beruhen, ist ihnen dennoch das Verständnis der Literatur als 'engagée' gemeinsam. Vgl. zum Begriff des Engagements in der Gruppe 47 den Beitrag von Helmut Peitsch in diesem Band.

45 Vgl. Richter an Leonhardt, 11.11.1961, in: *HWRB*, 61/29

46 Vgl. Richter an Leonhardt, 11.11.1961, in: *HWRB*, Nr. 61/29; Richter an Leonhardt, 29.1.1962, in: *HWRB*, Nr. 62/1.

47 Fried an Richter, 1.7.1966, in: *HWRB*, Nr. 66/14.

48 Vgl. dagegen Heinrich Böll, 'Nachtrag zum Notstand. zersetzen, zersetzen, zersetzen', in: *konkret*, H.10 (1968), S.38-40. — Böll war einer der vehementesten Kritiker der pragmatischen Anpassung Richters (und damit der Gruppe 47) an die Nachkriegsrealitäten. Vgl. dazu den Beitrag von Frank Finlay in diesem Band.

49 Hans Werner an Otto Richter, 9.12.1962, in: *HWRB*, Nr. 62/29.

50 Richter an Dehler, 30.12.1963, in: *HWRB*, Nr. 63/29.

51 Norbert Frei, *Vergangenheitspolitik. Die Anfänge der Bundesrepublik und die NS-Vergangenheit* (München: C. H. Beck, 1996).

52 Heinrich Böll, 'Angst vor der Gruppe 47?', *Merkur*, Stuttgart, 19, 2.Hj., August 1965, 75-83. Die Zitate folgen dem Wiederabdruck in: Lettau, *Handbuch*, S.389-400, hier S.391 und 395; vgl. auch Schroers, 'Gruppe 47 und die deutsche Nachkriegsliteratur', in: ebd., S.371-88.

53 Richter an Jens, 12.10.1968, in: *HWRB*, Nr. 68/18; vgl. auch Hans Werner Richter, *Briefe an einen jungen Sozialisten*. Vorwort von Leonard Reinisch. (Hamburg: Hoffmann und Campe, 1974).

54 Günter Herburger, 'Bankrott der Väter', *Der Monat*, 19: 226 (1967), 5-8.

55 Die kleine Demonstration von SDS-Vertretern bei der Tagung in der Pulvermühle (1967) erzürnte Richter nachhaltig; von Autoren, die sich mit den Studenten auch nur unterhalten hatten, fühlte er sich verraten (vgl. Lettau an Richter, 16.1.1968, in: *HWRB*, Nr. 68/1; Richter an Lettau, 31.3.1968, in: *HWRB*, Nr. 68/2).

JULIAN PREECE

What They Thought of Themselves and Each Other: The Gruppe 47 in Essay, Fiction, and Memoir

There is a large variety of literature relating to the self-image and self-presentation of the Gruppe 47 consisting of poems, portraits, satires and memoirs, not to mention the various newspaper reports. One of the most significant documents is Grass's laudatory prose work *Das Treffen in Telgte*, in which each incident relates to something that happened at a Group meeting. The Group's detractors were also not slow to put pen to paper, which in turn led to trenchant defences of its activities. Some reports about the Group, because of their their semi-fictional nature, were able to create an aura of myth, whilst differing accounts of the same incidents serve to emphasise the difficulties encountered by those trying to record events at which the spoken word dominated. However difficult it may be to arrive at the truth on the basis of the different accounts, this only adds to the fascination exercised by the Group.

The purpose of the Gruppe 47 was to exert influence on behalf of democratic thinking and practice, primarily by means of the printed word. In 1962 Hans Werner Richter preferred to describe those who attended the first meetings as 'Publizisten' rather than even 'Schriftsteller', and certainly not by the suspect appellation 'Dichter'.[1] Since its original purpose, which by 1962 Richter seems to think it had failed to achieve, was to get their point across to those who today would be known as 'opinion formers', the identity or image of the Group could never be incidental: 'anders als die praktischen Politiker wollten sie vorerst nicht die Massen zur Demokratie erziehen, sondern sich selbst, ihresgleichen, jene also, die fähig sind, mit dem Wort Einfluß zu gewinnen' (Richter, p.10). The Group's power to shape or change perceptions, probably recognised by its opponents more than by the Group itself, was, according to Heinrich Böll, 'strategisch' rather than 'taktisch'.[2] In other words, writers acting individually or collectively did not necessarily win single-issue campaigns, get laws changed, ministers dismissed, or controversial borders recognised, although they did some of these things too, but they affected the way people thought in the longer term: they formed others' opinions. Böll contended that they had been extremely successful.

The Gruppe 47 writers represented the new generation interested in a new beginning in a new republic, but they knew that the overwhelming majority of their fellow citizens, whether occupying the lowliest or the most exalted positions in society, continued to live mentally in the old world. Yet writing, publishing, and propagating literary texts might seem a strange way of setting about moulding public opinion or canvassing a new set of values. Two points can be made here. The first is that there was a programme of sorts explicit in the form the meetings took and the aesthetic assumptions which underpinned most of the works read. The whole ethos was one of a new beginning and a complete break with the past. The second point is that the Gruppe 47 was only ever one of several of Richter's projects, though by far the longest-lived. In the second half of the 1950s, he devoted more of his time and energy to more direct forms of political campaigning, first through the 'Grünwalder Kreis', then the 'Kampf dem Atomtod' movement. It was because of these new commitments that the Group ceased to meet twice a year from 1956. It emerges powerfully in his letters that he was a formidably busy man, for ever planning activities and organising others.

The first priority was to establish an identity for the Gruppe 47, a process which began more than 50 years ago, intensified from time to time when the Group was subject to attack, and which continues to the present, inasmuch as former 'members' continue to add to the literature. Each pamphlet or polemic, novel or play written by someone associated with the Gruppe 47 was somehow written by or for the Group, thus Grass's *Die Blechtrommel* is in some way seen as a Gruppe 47 novel and Weiss's *Die Verfolgung und Ermordung Jean Paul Marats dargestellt durch die Schauspielgruppe des Hospizes zu Charenton unter Anleitung des Herrn de Sade* similarly as a Gruppe 47 play. As most major post-war authors attended the meetings, valued them, became involved, liked Richter, and wanted to change or influence what went on, the literature on the Group is rich for reasons unrelated to the need to influence opinion, far richer than that on any other professional association — which the Gruppe 47 both was and was not — which evolved over the same time. This literature consists of poems and portraits, satires and memoirs, as well as thousands of newspaper articles and one medium-length literary prose text, the sole masterpiece of the genre, *Das Treffen in Telgte*, by Richter's most celebrated protégé, Günter Grass. Especially the 'Tagungsberichte' written by participants to finance their own expenses, according to Richter, have contributed to the succession of volumes on significant anniversaries, along with the argumentative newspaper articles, whether from supporters or critics.

In all of this literature there is much talk of legends and mythification. As the Group's identity was not fixed, as one could argue it existed only on days in the year during which the meetings were held, as it published nothing in its own name, and Richter himself was the sole constant factor, the rules and hastily established traditions associated with them assumed a disproportionate significance in establishing or explaining what the Group stood for. It occupied a semantic empty space; the term 'Gruppe 47' was a floating signifier attached to a specific signified which refused to be pinned down. None of the multitude of reports by participants, according to Christian Ferber in the *Almanach*, is worth calling 'eine wirklich zureichende Beschreibung einer Arbeitstagung'.[3] He believes 'Die GRUPPE 47 muß jedem Pressemann ein Ärgernis sein, weil sie so schwer in zwei klaren Sätzen unterzubringen ist' (p.38) and even the term '"Die GRUPPE 47" — das ist etwa so präzise wie "Der pazifische Tiefseefisch"' (p.39). A great many of the texts are consequently to do with definition of a somewhat elusive phenomenon.

Uwe Johnson, who did more than any other essayist or chronicler of the 'group that did not exist' to set the record straight in his Frankfurt Lectures of 1979, acknowledges the danger posed by the double-edged media sword. In the beginning Richter wanted press attention because all publicity meant an increase in the interest afforded to new German literature, which had to be a good thing. From 1947 the media set about generating a mythology because that is what the media do. While this was ultimately helpful, some of the interim results could be misleading, though the effects were not without their lighter side: 'Lustig ist es', writes Johnson, 'wie die öffentlichen Legenden den internen Betrieb verfehlen'.[4] The inaccuracies that arose were doubly unsurprising since impressions, images, anecdotes, and memories are the most convenient currency of representation, given that the Group had no constitution, no official membership, no finances, no written rules, and kept no written records. Journalists were not guided by press releases, let alone press spokesmen or 'spin doctors'.

Some of the legends were generated maliciously by outsiders, the so-called enemies of the Group, Günter Blöcker and Friedrich Sieburg, Hans Egon Holthusen and Rudolf Krämer-Badoni, most notoriously the CDU-Chairman, Hermann Josef Dufhues, all firmly in the conservative camp, either intellectually or politically, and on the whole a generation senior even to the Group's founding côterie. Krämer-Badoni was open in his criticism to Richter, his objections making it obvious that the Gruppe 47 was indeed constituted by like-minded liberals from the undogmatic, non-communist Left.[5] Invited to comment in *Die Zeit* after the fifteenth anniversary in 1962 Blöcker famously referred to it as 'die totale Clique, die das demokratische fair play durch Gruppenbeschlüsse außer Kraft setzen möchte', a 'demagogischer Clan' practising 'Meinungsterror'.[6] We may today be more inclined to forgive Blöcker his rhetorical exaggerations, since he was merely countering the Group's own polemical stance. Moreover, Blöcker *was* an opponent and in a democracy opponents engage in debate with each other. His epithets were nonetheless ineptly chosen in view of what the real practitioners of demagogy had achieved less than two decades previously. Attacks such as this called for responses, 'Aufklärungsarbeit', on the part of the participants; both the *Almanach* and the *Handbuch* fall into this category, belonging to a documentary mode which came into its own during the second decade of the Federal Republic. Books take a little time to produce, however, and Richter often needed 'instant rebuttals'. Alfred Andersch responded to Sieburg in 1952 and subsequently to Robert Neumann and Hans Erich Nossack in 1966 in the special issue of *Sprache im technischen Zeitalter*.[7] Marcel Reich-Ranicki had an easy time pointing out the inconsistencies, factual inaccuracies, and misquotations in Blöcker's article.[8] Johnson (admittedly sixteen years after the event) piles up facts to discredit both Blöcker and Dufhues in an avalanche of documentation and sarcasm. Hans Magnus Enzensberger takes on an earlier Blöcker onslaught too with a mixture of sarcasm and satire.[9] As we know now, these responses were co-ordinated, their impact calculated in advance. The Gruppe 47 won all of these debates conclusively. Richter and his acolytes had the better arguments, the better debaters (note how Andersch and Enzensberger are sent into the fray), and, though the students in 1967 might have found them frightfully middle-aged, the tide of history was on their side. A Berlin court made Dufhues climb down, though Böll and Johnson both felt that Richter could have pursued him further to create greater embarrassment. Richter believes that the rhetorical hostility — the battle for definitions fought out in the media and the courts — generally did them good.

If this is the terrain on which the Group fought, then image is indeed important. Impressions help as much as facts, perceptions even more than arguments. Looking back on the penultimate meeting in Princeton, Hans Mayer states 'wir sind an unserem Image gescheitert'.[10] Whoever lives by the media, the modern myth-making machine, risks perishing by it too. Princeton was an instance of the Group being unable to withstand its own publicity. The journalists, who had served it so well, wanted a row and they duly got one supplied by a twenty-four old poetic rebel, Peter Handke, intent on founding his own reputation and making his mark.[11] The image fitted, the story worked. The Gruppe 47 had weathered hostile criticism in the past, but not this sort; it had become the Establishment, having suddenly grown staid and fuddy-duddy, unable to respond to a new generation whose leading representative had to define himself in opposition to it. To argue over the merits of Handke's comments, as Mayer does, is to miss the point.

When it comes to precise definitions, more friendly accounts of the Group also contributed in their own way to the accretion of folklore, which generally served the Group's interests too. The Gruppe 47 has by and large controlled its own historiography because its erstwhile members have written it. As the great majority of writers quickly came to identify with the Group's procedures and rituals, the images transmitted by participants are overwhelmingly positive, deriving from personal experience, which, if the participant had been successful, coincided with the beginning of a career. The first meeting, which presupposed a first reading, became a rite of passage and consequently a topos in the literature; the invitation on its own signalled recognition and held out the promise of critical approval, a publishing contract, a radio or newspaper commission, even the fêted Prize, followed by fame and, if not riches, then the possibility of financial security. As Johnson was advised when he arrived in the Federal Republic: 'eine Einladung zu einer Tagung der Gruppe 47 sei unbesehen anzunehmen, als Bestandteil des schriftstellerischen Berufs in dieser

Gegend' (*Begleitumstände*, p.276). An amusing sub-genre within the
memoir literature is memories of each author's first meeting or advice
to an unnamed debutant.[12] The uninitiated are as overwhelmed by
anticipation, fear, ordeal, anti-climax, as if they are recalling their first
kiss. Richter who breaks in each of them might not ask them afterwards
'how was is it for you?', but he supplements these accounts with his own
memories of his first encounters with each of his 'butterflies'. He
follows something of a pattern here as he often makes out he cannot
recall inviting them or did not really want them to be there and was
persuaded at the last minute only to be pleasantly surprised and glad he
took the usually anonymous advice.

After the *Almanach* in 1962 semi-fictionalised accounts of
meetings, which were never of specific meetings, become more
numerous. These often owe more to the conventions of fiction than to
journalistic reportage and convert an originally oral tradition, upheld
by anyone who had ever attended a meeting, into literature. Events and
occasionally personalities are exaggerated, conflated with one another,
elaborated on, in short mythologised. Like Martin Walser in 'Brief an
einen ganz jungen Autor', Ruth Rehmann ('Was ist das für ein Verein?')
tries to explain to someone who knows nothing about the Group what it
does and whether he (maybe she) should go if an invitation should drop
through the letter box. Though she is witty and light-hearted she is
launching an assault on that empty semantic space covered over by the
term 'Gruppe 47'. By challenging some legends she reinforces others.[13]
Like Peter Rühmkorf, Rehmann is concerned with definitions and
correcting inaccurate perceptions, prejudicial views. In challenging
some legends she reinforces others. Both she and Rühmkorf notice that
the old-hands have been generating their legends and that the first
versions of history usually pass by word of mouth. Like many other
good things, the Gruppe 47 was never as good as it used to be, but the
news of its demise was always exaggerated until 1967. Helmut
Heißenbüttel also stresses that the Group lives on in the memory:

> Das offizielle Ende der Tagung besteht in dem von Hans Werner Richter
> gesprochenen Satz: Die Tagung der Gruppe 47 ist eine gewesene Tagung der
> Gruppe 47. Die gewesene Tagung der Gruppe 47 bedeutet eine Erinnerung an
> die Tagung der Gruppe 47. Die Erinnerung an die Tagung der Gruppe 47
> bedeutet eine Erinnerung an die Gruppe 47. (Anmerkung: die ausdrücklich
> weiterlebt.)[14]

Heißenbüttel summarises the procedural points and rituals, the unwritten rules and the rhythms of the three-day conferences, satirising the umpteen newspaper reports which each meeting generated, and defining the Group in terms of its rules and traditions and the roles played by the participants. Günter Grass refashions the same material in *Das Treffen in Telgte*.

The most obvious problem with written accounts is that the discussions were all conducted orally. The jump to the printed page, sometimes performed years after the event, always entails a transformation and a degree of distortion. Böll is not the only participant to see the lack of documentation to be the cause of the myth-making:

> Genaueres über die Gruppe 47 und ihre Probleme ließe sich sagen, lägen alle Tagungen, alle Lesungen, alle Gespräche, alles, was kritisch innerhalb und außerhalb der jeweiligen Aula gesagt wurde, im Protokoll vor; dazu gehören Gesichter, Geräusche, müßten Stimmungsbarometer und Meßgeräte für das, was man Tagungsgefälle nennen kann, aufgestellt gewesen.[15]

This point is echoed by others because everything that ever happened at a meeting became part of the history and thus part of the Group's identity. The incidents which have generated legends, versions and counter-versions, are legion: the animosity enflamed by a donated barrel of poor-quality wine at Marktbreit in 1949, Paul Celan's failure to make an impact at Niendorf in 1952, the police visit and the arrest of Rudolf Augstein in 1962, the ill-starred excursion to Princeton in 1966, or the student 'invasion' at the Pulvermühle the following year. In a surprisingly rare instance Walser subjects personalities to the same treatment in his portraits of the 'Big Five' critics, who came to dominate proceedings in the Group's last decade. They are larger than life literary characters. Walser speaks in general terms rather than about a specific occasion and we have to assume that the critics always spoke this way and could not do otherwise. Rehmann seems to agree on this subject:

> Es gibt Kritiker, die alte Garde, die sitzen immer in der gleichen Gegend, die haben ihre feste Hierarchie und Rollenverteilung, ihren Ritus, ihre kleinen Privatstreitigkeiten, die wissen, was man von ihnen erwartet und man weiß, was man von ihnen zu erwarten hat. Richter gibt den Einsatz, und sie spielen ihren Part, mit leichten Verschiebungen im Laufe der Jahre: diese werden toleranter, jene bissiger — das macht das Älterwerden. (Richter, p.431)

It is remarkable, however, how rarely writers have focused on individuals in their accounts of the Group. Walser's satire is an exception. It is impossible to match up the figures who appear at Telgte with their post-war counterparts. The Gruppe 47 was more than the sum of its members, a point which emerges perhaps in a comparison of Richter's two memoirs: whereas in the first he follows a chronological and thematic pattern, pausing only briefly to comment on individuals, in the second he portrays twenty-one leading members. As a result *Im Etablissement der Schmetterlinge* is not free of factual errors, not to mention gossip and personal point-scoring. It is a poorer book in all respects.

Most journalistic accounts were woefully deficient, according to Ferber, because reporters always leave out far too much by concentrating on the more conventional, formal activities. A proper description

> müßte vom Gehalt oder der Leere des Vorgelesenen ebenso künden wie vom Amüsement des Donnerstagnachmittags, wenn die Alten und die Neuen herbeitröpfeln, einander begrüßen oder auch nicht. Sie müßte weiter künden von den strapazierten Nerven der Vorleser (und bisweilen auch der Zuhörer), aber auch von neuen Freund- oder Feindschaften, von der dritten Morgenstunde mit dem Gespräch der letzten Zecher, vom schönen und vom bösen Klatsch, von triumphierenden oder weinenden Ehefrauen, vom gereizten Frühstück und Richters milder Bändigung der Wölfe und Schafe — man sieht: dies verlangt einen Schriftsteller und einen Journalisten von hohem Rang. (Richter, pp.38-39)

Apart from the fact that the Baroque writers who gathered between Münster and Osnabrück in 1647 wisely left their wives at home, this sounds like a summary of *Das Treffen in Telgte*. In homage to Richter, Grass makes a textual collage from familiar disputes, unplanned events, verbal exchanges fuelled by ambition or ideology, alcohol or sentiment. He inevitably distorts the record too. However brilliant the style and structure of *Das Treffen in Telgte*, however witty the asides and aperçus, and even though the little-known poets and grammarians are taught a harsh lesson, returning home convinced of their own insignificance and powerlessness, *Das Treffen in Telgte* is ultimately a self-congratulatory text. Even the writers' short-term failure — in the longer term they are guaranteed recognition which will be denied the ambassadors at the peace negotiations in Osnabrück and Münster — is disguised triumphalism since their overwhelming and undisputed moral superiority derives from their being on the losing side, which is clearly in every respect the better side. In 1979 when *Das Treffen in Telgte* was published, the Gruppe 47 writers had not failed, the SPD government many of them had helped get elected had been in power for ten years, and most of the values Richter had promoted for twenty years longer than that had shaped state policy. It had been the young Hans Jochen Vogel, future Parliamentary Chairman of the SPD and candidate for the chancellorship in 1983, who had founded the Grünwalder Kreis with Richter in 1956. The future Chancellor, Willy Brandt, sought contact with writers and attended the Gruppe 47 meeting in Berlin in 1965, in contrast to the Baroque political leaders who had not even heard of their literary contemporaries. Karl Schiller, Brandt's Minister of Finance and Economics, had corresponded with Richter at intervals from 1947 and had sought out the company and cooperation of writers in the 1960s in Berlin. Even Helmut Schmidt was prepared to discuss literature and politics with Richter, Grass, and their colleagues. Furthermore the insults hurled at Rolf Hochhuth and Grass by Chancellor Ludwig Erhard in the 1965 election campaign ultimately did him and his cause far more harm than they did the objects of his attack.[16]

As far as the historiography of the Group is concerned, the truth in Grass's birthday-present text to Richter is to be found in the detail and the thematic patterns rather than in the individual literary characters or in the pessimistic textual mood. Everything that happens at Telgte corresponds to something which occurred in reality. The reaction of the prudish protestant cleric, Paul Gerhardt, to Georg Greflinger's explicitly suggestive love lyrics, anticipates Wolfdietrich Schnurre walking out of a reading by Gisela Elsner from a story entitled 'Der Achte' on the grounds he found it pornographic.[17] The real hero of *Das Treffen in Telgte*, Christoffel Gelnhausen, for all is similarities with his creator, has similar ambitions to the unknown Walser when Richter encountered him in a radio van working for the Süddeutscher Rundfunk. Like Gelnhausen, Walser declared he was better than the established writers and would soon prove it.[18] On the final day at Telgte the poets dine on freshly caught pike, as Richter and his guests at the very first meeting had done in the idyllic surroundings on the Bannwaldsee courtesy of their hostess, Ilse Schneider-Lengyel, a latter-day Mother Courage, who also rustled up a black-market sack of potatoes. Grass records Libuschka's efforts on behalf of her guests no less prominently. According to Enzensberger, however, the refreshments and accommodation were generally nothing to write home about: 'Der Kaffee war dünn, die Betten waren spartanisch. War das ein Kulturleben? Es war kein Kulturleben' (Richter, p.23). Like the other contributors to the introductory section of the *Almanach*, Enzensberger, while denying Blöcker's description of 'demagogisches Managertum', is searching for a definition of his own. The Spartan beds and the weak coffee are an element in the Group's identity, just like Schneider-Lengyel's gratefully devoured fare in the days of universal shortages and rationing.

When it comes to proximity to history, the 1962 Berlin meeting, held at the height of the Cuba Missile Crisis and coinciding with the beginning of the '*Spiegel*-Affair', is the nearest the Group got to great events, unlike Simon Dach's guests. After the editor of *Der Spiegel*, due to attend the meeting, had been arrested and police had knocked on the door of the building where his colleagues had gathered, a letter was formulated. Looking back, Richter concluded: 'Unser Protest, der literarisch recht gut, politisch aber höchst ungeschickt formuliert ist, hilft zwar Rudolf Augstein nicht, trägt jedoch zur allgemeinen Aufregung bei',[19] although he might be erring on the side of modesty here. Dieter Wellershoff claimed that 'das öffentliche Protestschreiben der Gruppe, überall veröffentlicht und beachtet, entscheidend dazu beitrug, einen Angriff auf die Pressefreiheit abzuwehren'.[20] The '*Spiegel*-Affair', which resulted in a government climb-down and the resignation of Franz Josef Strauß the minister responsible, is usually thought to be a definitive event in the history of the Federal Republic. Grass, who refused to sign the Berlin statement after angry exchanges with Andersch and others, goes further than Richter by letting the Telgte manifesto disappear in the flames which engulf the Brückenhof at the end of the meeting: 'So blieb ungesagt, was doch nicht gehört worden wäre'.[21] This might have been a fair assessment in 1947 but it was emphatically not the case in 1962 or 1967 and is thus a spectacularly misleading comment on the Group's overall history.

The journey to the conference venue is another minor topos in writing about the Group. While Hans Mayer complains about Ernst Bloch's pipe smoke in the car taking them both to Saalgau in 1963 (Mayer, p.294), there are no accounts of participants being ambushed by highwaymen, as Schneuber and Moscherosch were in 1647. Travelling the length or breadth of Germany was not necessarily much less of an arduous undertaking in other respects, however, and required planning and finance. Heinz Friedrich and Richter devote whole paragraphs to the slow, uncomfortable progress they made to the first ever meeting on the Bannwaldsee, first in an overcrowded train, then, once the specially booked bus failed to materialise, in a 'Holzgas' lorry commandeered by Walter Guggenheimer.[22] By contrast, Guntram Vesper, describing his first invitation to what turned out to be the last meeting in 1967, takes it for granted that a poor student poet should have his own car, so far had literary Germany travelled in twenty years. In his excitement he seems to anticipate conquering more than the literary world: 'Ich durchmesse germanische und andere Kernlande, herbstliche Wälder, Spessart und was weiß ich; von hier ist mancher aufgebrochen: Ostland, Westmark, Nordmark, Tripolis, jetzt bin ich an der Reihe und am Drücker'.[23] His cross-country dash along the Autobahn is a journey through literary history to a rendez-vous with living legends: 'schnell schnell, es dämmert, und Grass ist vielleicht vor mir da [...], vorwärts vorwärts, Goethe war jedenfalls langsamer gen Italien' (p.25).

The three days, which were really two full working days and three nights, from Thursday evening to Sunday morning, give the meetings their special rhythm. According to Jürgen von Hollander, 'der erste Abend ist manchen alten 47ern der schönste der ganzen Tagung [...]. Am ersten Abend kann noch jeder mit jedem. Am letzten Abend können nur noch wenige mit wenigen'.[24] Grass exploits this temporal dimension to dazzling effect: the mood at Telgte, the feelings of the poets about themselves and each other evolve dramatically from the first morning to the second evening. It is a roller-coaster ride for all concerned. The meals register these shifts in mood most graphically, but the physical bio-rhythms of some participants are exposed to other pressures: after a night of erotic exertion or alcoholic elation come exhaustion or a hangover.

Whether at Telgte, Bad Dürkheim, or Großholzleute, finances are pressing: Böll was not the only Prize winner to need the money and Grass himself had to remind Richter to send him the cheque some two months afterwards.[25] Funding is the single greatest leitmotif in Richter's letters. The poets in Telgte were glad of any form of sponsorship and have to thank their publishers for compensating Libuschka when her premises are damaged. They then bask briefly in the reflected glow of their own importance when Gelnshausen tells them the rich fare he supplies has been donated by admiring politicians at the Peace Conference down the road in Münster, a comforting reassurance which turns out to be a complete lie. At Niendorf the electrical company Osram donated 500 light bulbs and Richter, grateful but baffled, decided to auction them to pay for the evening's party, the 'ausgelassene Nacht, die nun schon mit zu den Spielregeln gehört'.[26] Whether sponsored or not, these parties are as legendary as some of the readings and feature prominently in Heißenbüttel's definition:

> An den Nachtsitzungen nehmen nicht alle Teilnehmer teil. Es soll Teilnehmer geben, die die ganze Nacht schlafen. Nachtsitzungen fangen an und enden meist mit Splittergruppenverschwörungen. Die Anfänge zeichnen sich durch stummes Trinken und Wortkargheit aus: die Abschlüsse durch Gesangsdarbietungen und akrobatische Übungen. Es kann: soll aber nicht: zu Exzessen kommen. Im Mittelteil wird gelegentlich getanzt. (*Dichter*, p.41)

The least realistic element in *Das Treffen in Telgte* is the way Dach shoos the poets off to bed, thus forestalling the historically premature initiation of this particular tradition. The gossip at Telgte, however, is as compelling as at any of the 23 venues where the Group met three hundred years later, though Grass is arguably more even-handed than Richter in at least one incident. When Georg Weckherlin cries thief on discovering the disappearance of his purse, we assume, when it is discovered in Libuschka's room, that he has left it there himself on a secret nocturnal visit. When the staff at Elmau in 1959 inform Richter at the end of the meeting that they have found a nightdress in one of the rooms, he is careful to explain that it belonged to Ingeborg Bachmann — one of the chambermaids recognised it — and that it was not found in her own room. He tells them to send it on to her, but they refuse, wanting to keep it as 'ein Wunderding', 'eine Relique', 'um es vielleicht hinter Glas aufzubewahren'.[27] In which room the chambermaid found the nightdress, he does not specify.

The literature on the Gruppe 47 has followed either the anniversaries of the Group's founding, unsurprisingly since it took its name from a year half way between the end of the war and the beginning of the Federal Republic, or the birthdays of its founder. The *Almanach* appeared fifteen years after the first meeting in 1962; the

Handbuch in 1967 before anyone knew the last meeting would take place that year and mean in future that anniversaries of the Group's beginning would also commemorate its end. Henry Meyer-Brockmann's two collections of caricatures appeared concurrently in 1962 and 1967.[28] The next two anthologies are birthday presents to Richter: *Hans Werner Richter und die Gruppe 47* for his seventieth birthday in 1978, including a chapter from *Das Treffen in Telgte*; the *Lesebuch* for his seventy-fifth in 1983. The Akademie der Künste in Berlin staged its exhibition, publishing a catalogue containing more critical essays, memoirs and reminiscences, in 1988, coinciding with Richter's eightieth birthday; *Sprache im technischen Zeitalter* devoted its second special issue to the Group in that year too. The trend to mark anniversaries continued in 1997 with the publication of Richter's letters, which comprise by far the most informative history of the Group or indeed of post-war West German literature *tout court*, and a coffee-table book of portrait photographs by Toni Richter, interspersed with her own recollections and contributions by others.[29] There are some overlaps: Heinz Friedrich's 'Das Jahr 47' appears in the *Almanach* and the *Lesebuch*; Ruth Rehmann's 'Was ist das für ein Verein?' in the *Almanach* and the exhibition catalogue. Toni Richter plunders all the previous publications but has also coaxed original contributions from a handful of survivors.

In the midst of all these subjective textual variations re-establishing what really happened becomes a hasardous enterprise. Writers like to embellish, exaggerate, and experiment. Johnson's contribution stands out in this respect since he employs a rigorous moralism and documentary thoroughness to dismantle the most insulting myth of all, that peddled by Dufhues, on the back of a report by Blöcker in the *Frankfurter Allgemeine Zeitung* that the Group's influence resembled that of a 'geheime Reichsschrifttumskammer'. Johnson notes that Dufhues had been charged by his party to forge links with the intelligentsia 'nicht um der Union, sondern um des Wirkens für unser Volk willen' because, according to Dufhues, 'dieser auch getragen wird von seinen Dichtern, von den Künstlern, von den Publizisten' *Begleitumstände*, p.270). Heinrich von Brentano, the leader of the CDU in the Bundestag, 'der Fachmann' Johnson drily notes, had suggested the task and Blöcker had unwittingly supplied the material. Johnson takes the whole episode to pieces in order to examine the individual building blocks; he expects the same degree of rigour from Dufhues, a member of the Christian party, who has, unfortunately, simply not done his homework. Dufhues could have found out about the 1962 meeting, the occasion for Blöcker's critique. He could have informed himself of the role of the real *Reichsschrifttumskammer*. Johnson quotes from academic sources, unavailable it must be said in 1963, and concludes that Dufhues must think that Richter behaves in the same way as the Nazi functionaries. Who would then take the role of Joseph Goebbels? Why, none other than Brentano. Johnson then imagines informing Brentano about the Gruppe 47 in a letter much of which appeared in *Die Zeit* in October 1977. He explains that one of the rules of the Group is the ban on expressing either Stalinist or fascist opinions, he lists the statements issued and signed by members of the Group, and ends with an unfinished question: 'Wenn ich mir nunmehr erlauben darf, sehr geehrter Herr von Brentano, Sie hinzuweisen auf den Gegensatz zwischen einer solchen Praxis und der der Reichsschrifttumskammer [...]?' (p.282).

Johnson's hyper-sensitive moral strenuousness may be deeply unfashionable today, but then so are most things the Group became well-known for. When Hans Mayer looked back into history to search for antecedents he decided in 1962 that the Gruppe 47 was historically unique.[30] Von Hollander, on the other hand, identified the little-known 'Tunnel über der Spree' from the 1840s, which grouping included the young Theodor Fontane and evidently attracted Grass in his most recent literary exploration of German writers' history, *Ein weites Feld*. Whether 'gestern wird sein, was morgen gewesen ist' and similar groupings will emerge in the future, nobody can safely predict.[31] As long as there are German writers, however, they will be interested in the tradition of their calling and the Gruppe 47 will live on in literature.

Footnotes

[1] Hans Werner Richter, 'Fünfzehn Jahre', in: Richter, (ed.), *Almanach der Gruppe 47* (Reinbek bei Hamburg: Rowohlt, 1962), pp.8-14, here p.8. Further references to this volume are to be found in the text under Richter.

[2] Heinrich Böll, 'Angst vor der Gruppe 47?', in: Reinhard Lettau (ed.), *Die Gruppe 47. Bericht, Kritik, Polemik. Ein Handbuch* (Neuwied and Berlin: Luchterhand, 1967), pp.389-400, here pp.394f.

3 Christian Ferber, 'Die Gruppe 47 und die Presse', in: Richter, *Almanach* , pp.37-43, here p.38.

4 Uwe Johnson, *Begleitumstände. Frankfurter Vorlesungen* (Frankfurt a. M: Suhrkamp, 1980), p.278. Further references to this work are to be found in the text under *Begleitumstände*.

5 Letter to Richter, 22 May 1950, Hans Werner Richter, *Briefe* (=*HWRB*), ed. by Sabine Cofalla (Munich: Hanser, 1997), pp.115f.

6 Günter Blöcker, 'Die Gruppe 47 und ich', in: Lettau, *Handbuch*, pp.353-58, here p.357.

7 See Lettau, *Handbuch*, pp.336-52, esp. Alfred Andersch, 'Die Spaliere der Banalität', pp.340-46; and 'Zeilen schinden für die Gruppe', *Sprache im technischen Zeitalter*, 20 (1966), Sonderausgabe *Kunst und Elend der Schmährede. Zum Streit um die Gruppe 47*, pp.294-98.

8 Marcel Reich-Ranicki, 'Die Gruppe 47 und Er', in: Lettau, *Handbuch*, pp.359-67.

9 Hans Magnus Enzensberger, 'Die Clique', in: Richter, *Almanach der Gruppe 47*, pp.22-27.

10 Hans Mayer, *Ein Deutscher auf Widerruf. Erinnerungen*, vol.2 (Frankfurt a. M: Suhrkamp, 1984), p.307. Further references to this work are to be found in the text under Mayer.

11 See 'Wie Peter Handke Peter Handke wurde', in: Milo Dor, *Auf dem falschen Dampfer. Fragmente einer Autobiographie* (Vienna and Darmstadt: Paul Zsolnay, 1988), pp.19-38. See also the contribution by Sabine Cofalla in this volume.

12 Peter Rühmkorf, 'Zum ersten Mal bei der Gruppe 47', in: Richter, *Almanach*, pp.424-27; Guntram Vesper, 'Eingeladen meiner Hinrichtung beizuwohnen: Pulvermühle 1967', Hans A. Neunzig (ed.), *Lesebuch der Gruppe 47*, 2nd ed (Munich: dtv, 1997), pp.24-30.

13 Martin Walser, 'Brief an einen ganz jungen Autor', in: Richter, *Almanach*, pp.418-23; Ruth Rehmann, 'Was ist das fur ein Verein?', *Almanach*, pp.428-33.

14 Helmut Heißenbüttel, 'Bericht über eine Tagung der Gruppe 47', in: Jürgen Schutte (ed.), *Dichter und Richter. Die Gruppe 47 und die deutsche Nachkriegsliteratur. Ausstellungskatalog* (Berlin: Akademie der Künste, 1988), pp.40-41, here p.41. Further references to this volume are to be found in the text under *Dichter*.

15 Heinrich Böll, 'Angst vor der Gruppe 47?', in: Lettau, *Handbuch*, pp.389-400, here p.389.

16 His biographer calls the verbal onslaught in the 1965 election campaign 'das größte rhetorische Eigentor seiner Karriere'. Volker Hentschel, *Ludwig Erhard. Ein Politikerleben* (Munich and Landsberg am Lech: Günter Olzog, 1996), p.573.

17 'Wie entstand und was war die Gruppe 47?', in: Hans A. Neunzig (ed.), *Hans Werner Richter und die Gruppe 47* (Munich: nymphenburger, 1978), pp.41-176, here p.146.

[18] Hans Werner Richter, *Im Etablissement der Schmetterlinge. Einundzwanzig Portraits aus der Gruppe 47* (Munich: Carl Hanser, 1986), pp.249-50. See also the essay by Anthony Waine in this volume.

[19] Neunzig, *Hans Werner Richter und die Gruppe 47*, p.149.

[20] Dieter Wellershoff, 'Ein sozialer Raum ohne Entfremdung? Rückblick auf die Gruppe 47', *Sprache im technischen Zeitalter*, 26 (1988), 122-28, here 122.

[21] Günter Grass, *Werkausgabe*, ed. by Volker Neuhaus and Daniela Hermes, vol.9, *Das Treffen in Telgte*, ed. by Claudia Mayer-Iswandy (Göttingen: Steidl, 1997), p.173.

[22] Heinz Friedrich, 'Das Jahr 1947', in: Richter, *Almanach*, pp.15-21, here pp.19-20; Neunzig, *Hans Werner Richter und die Gruppe 47*, pp.78-79. One admires Walter Kolbenhoff's reticence here since to avoid further duplication he quotes Richter's version, Walter Kolbenhoff, *Schellingstraße 48. Erfahrungen mit Deutschland* (Frankfurt a. M.: Fischer, 1984), pp.232-36.

[23] Neunzig, *Lesebuch der Gruppe 47*, p.25.

[24] Jürgen von Hollander, 'Das Geheimnis der Gruppe 47', in: *Brockmanns gesammelte Siebenundvierziger. 100 Karikaturen literarischer Zeitgenossen* (Munich: dtv, 1967), pp.105-12, here p.105.

[25] Letter from Grass to Richter, 10 December 1958, in: *HWRB*, p.274.

[26] Neunzig, *Hans Werner Richter und die Gruppe 47*, p.97.

[27] Richter, *Im Etablissement der Schmetterlinge*, p.56.

[28] Henry Meyer-Brockmann, *Dichter und Richter. Die Gruppe 47 und ihre Gäste. 200 Porträtzeichnungen* (Munich: Rheinsberg Verlag, 1962).

[29] Toni Richter, *Die Gruppe 47 in Bildern und Texten* (Cologne: Kiepenheuer & Witsch, 1997).

[30] Hans Mayer, 'In Raum und Zeit', in: Richter, *Almanach der Gruppe 47*, pp.28-36.

[31] Grass, *Das Treffen in Telgte*, p.7.

HANS J. HAHN

'Literarische Gesinnungsnazis' oder spätbürgerliche Formalisten? Die Gruppe 47 als deutsches Problem

Obwohl die Gruppe 47 in ihrer Frühphase, vom *Ruf* herkommend, der entstehenden politisch-literarischen Öffentlichkeit Westdeutschlands kaum Neues zu bieten hatte, änderte sich dies zu Beginn der sechziger Jahre grundlegend: Die kritische Reaktion vieler ihrer Autoren auf die *Spiegel*-Affäre und den Skandal um den CDU-Politiker Dufhues sowie erste Auseinandersetzungen mit DDR-Funktionären trug zur Entstehung fundierter ethischer Grundhaltungen bei, die ihrerseits bei der Schaffung einer politisch-literarischen Öffentlichkeit in der Bundesrepublik entscheidend mitgewirkt haben. Da es sich bei der Genese von Öffentlichkeit allerdings um einen vielschichtigen Prozeß handelt, gab es auch eine rückläufige Bewegung, durch welche die Literatur der Gruppe selbst wieder von der öffentlichen Diskussion angeregt wurde. Die hier angesprochene Wechselwirkung von Literatur und Öffentlichkeit versteht sich daher auch als Beitrag zum Vorwurf einer 'Gesinnungsästhetik', wie er im Zusammenhang mit dem deutsch-deutschen Literaturstreit erhoben wurde.

Als letztem Redner der Jubiläumstagung kam mir die Rolle des Lumpensammlers zu. 'Lumpensammler', so nennt man den letzten Bus, der Arbeiter von der Spätschicht, Studenten von Parties oder Liebespärchen von Nachtfilmen nach Hause befördert. Wenn auch der Müdigkeit, Trunkenheit oder Verliebtheit halber die Fahrgäste im allgemeinen nicht gerade gesprächig sind, so verbindet sie doch ein gewisses Solidaritätsgefühl, und wehe dem Fahrer, der einem zu spät kommenden Fahrgast die Tür nicht doch noch öffnete. — Sie erkennen, worauf ich hinauswill: die Ähnlichkeiten zwischen dem Lumpensammlerbus und der sogenannten Gruppe 47 sind frappierend. In beiden Fällen sorgt eine an sich nicht besonders wichtige Begleiterscheinung dafür, daß ein bestimmtes Solidaritätsgefühl entsteht, welches die Basis abgeben kann für einen spezifischen Konsens. Sowohl Richter als auch Andersch waren Gefangene in Fort Kearney, *Der Ruf — Blätter für deutsche Kriegsgefangene* entstand in diesem Lager; *Der Ruf. Unabhängige Blätter für die junge Generation* und *Skorpion* waren mehr oder weniger Echos dieses 'Ur-*Rufs*'. Die Gruppe begann als eine Art Notgemeinschaft, eine weitere Parallele zum Lumpensammlerbus. Beide Gemeinschaften gebaren so etwas wie eine Gesinnung, im Bus die Gesinnung der 'Spätheimkehrer', bei der Gruppe diejenige einer Minderheit, die im Nachkriegsdeutschland einen neuen, demokratischen Anfang machen wollte. 'Gesinnung' wird hier verstanden als sittliche Grundhaltung, als Wertekodex, als Teil einer Ethik, die mit der Aufklärung und der Moderne verbunden ist,[1] und als eine Kategorie, die neuerdings, seit dem Literaturstreit, als der Ästhetik unbekömmlich in Verruf geraten ist.[2]

Wir wollen zunächst der 'Vorgruppenphase' der Gruppe 47 einige Gesinnungsproben entnehmen, um dann unsere Aufmerksamkeit auf den Winter 1962/63 zu lenken, als das geistige Klima der Republik in ein entscheidendes Stadium eingetreten war.[3] Wer in den Originalen des *Ruf* blättert, und zwar sowohl in denen des Ur-*Ruf* (1.3.1945 - 1.4.1946) wie auch in denen des in der US-Zone produzierten Münchener *Ruf* (15.8.1946 - 1.4.1947), den frappiert zunächst die Diversität der verschiedensten Stellungnahmen, die aber alle durch das Kriegserlebnis der Gefangenen zusammengehalten werden. Bereits in der Oktoberausgabe 1945 heißt es, man müsse 'einen dicken Strich unter die Vergangenheit ziehen',[4] ein gutes Jahr später wird behauptet, das deutsche Schuldkonto beginne sich allmählich zu schließen,[5] eine Abtretung deutscher Gebiete und die Vertreibung der Deutschen könnten nicht akzeptiert werden.[6] Die Polemiken gegen die Kollektivschuldthese und das amerikanische 're-education'-Programm sind bekannt,[7] weniger bekannt und von der Forschung direkt auch wohl kaum nachvollziehbar sind die Parallelen, die sich zwischen einer Ablehnung der Kollektivschuld und den Positionen Arendts und Jaspers ergeben.[8] Gerade hier aber enthüllt sich vielleicht doch ein gemeinsamer Nenner, der das geistige Milieu dieser Zwischenkriegsgeneration umspannen könnte und der in Anlehnung an den französischen Existentialimus entwickelt wurde. Die These von der Kollektivschuld wurde ja nicht aus nationalistischen oder opportunistischen Gründen abgelehnt, sondern entsprang einem tiefen Mißtrauen gegenüber jeder Art von Kollektiv, jedweder Form von Vermassung. Das persönliche Erlebnis, sowohl als Soldat an der Front wie auch als Abrechnung mit dem National-sozialismus und — bei ehemaligen Kommunisten wie Andersch, Kolbenhoff und Richter — auch mit dem Stalinismus, stand im

Vordergrund, jegliche ernsthafte Auseinandersetzung mit dem Holocaust verdeckend und verhindernd.

Der in der deutschen Tradition schon lange vorwaltende Drang zum Erlebnis, zu Ausdruck und Wandlung begegnet einem auch im *Ruf* in fast jeder Nummer, bisweilen als bizarrer logischer Salto: 'Die Wandlung als eigene Leistung' wird aus dem Existentialismus Sartres, Camus und de Beauvoirs abgeleitet, verstanden als 'religiöses Erlebnis, das die junge Generation aus dem Krieg mitbringt'.[9] Dieses Erlebnis manifestiert sich als 'Haltung', die ihrerseits den 'Brückenschlag zwischen den alliierten Soldaten, den Männern des europäischen Widerstandes und den deutschen Frontsoldaten, zwischen den politischen KZ-Häftlingen und den ehemaligen "Hitlerjungen"' herstellt, gleichzeitig aber Brücken abbricht zur älteren Generation, 'die in der Unverbindlichkeit ihres Toleranzbegriffs, ihrem Zurückschrecken vor dem letzten Einsatz, dem Unhold seinen Gang zur Macht erlaubte' (*Der Ruf*, 1: 1, 2). Dieser Leitartikel der ersten Nummer ist bestenfalls pubertäres Geschwafel: er bezweifelt, daß 'Erziehung, Bildung, Belehrung hier konkurrieren mit einer Erlebnissphäre, in der in jeder Stunde die ganze menschliche Existenz aufs Spiel gesetzt wurde'. Die Tatsache, daß etwas aufs Spiel gesetzt wird, gilt hier als maßgeblich, wofür diese Existenz eingesetzt wird, ist anscheinend nebensächlich. Angesichts dieser (pseudo)-existentialistischen Grundhaltung stößt die rationalistische Aufklärungsphilosophie der Amerikaner auf völliges Unverständnis; ein Demokratiekonzept, das auf schöpferische Kompromisse angelegt ist, erweckt bestenfalls Skepsis.[10] Politisierung wird mit Vermassung in Zusammenhang gebracht, Urteilskraft und Innerlichkeit des Einzelnen verdrängend.[11] Weitere Beispiele könnten erbracht werden. Zunächst schwer nachvollziehbar ist eine sich anbahnende Auffassung von Europa, von einem Europa, das auf den 'Grundpfeilern' von 'Antike und Christentum' ruht,[12] die die Völker Europas schicksalhaft miteinander verbindet und auch die Deutschen wieder in seinen Schoß aufnehmen soll.

Während der Hauptimpuls vom französischen Existentialismus ausging, spielten britische Beiträge von Arthur Koestler und Stephen Spender eine ebenfalls wichtige Rolle. Koestlers Synthese von Sozialismus und Humanismus sucht nach der Verwirklichung einer wahrhaft menschlichen Gesellschaft, sie verwirft jede Form von Nationalismus als falsche Wahrheit, kann aber auch die westliche

Demokratie nur als halbe Wahrheit anerkennen.[13] Spender ist pragmatischer, er versucht zu zeigen, daß eine Aussöhnung, gerade auch mit Frankreichs Elite, nicht von heute auf morgen möglich ist: 'Man sucht in Deutschland nach den Anzeichen einer grundlegenden geistigen Umkehr, stattdessen viele Ressentiments und keine Gesinnungsänderung.'[14]

Selbst Richters berühmter Essay 'Literatur im Interregnum',[15] der einem politisch-literarischen Manifest gleichkommt und auf Gruppen-Maximen der fünfziger Jahre vorausweist, versteht den Literaten als Suchenden, Irrenden, Verzweifelnden, der der bürgerlichen Welt den Rücken zugekehrt hat und auf eine 'sozialistisch-proletarische Welt von morgen' wartet. Die Sprache der älteren Generation wird abgelehnt, sie gebrauche 'Worte ohne Gehalt'. Obgleich Richter die Gefahr einer erneuten Verinnerlichung erkennt, sucht er nach einem Realismus, der denjenigen der Amerikaner sublimiert und ins Magische potenziert: 'Es ist das blutige Erlebnis unserer Zeit und unseres Lebens, es ist die Fragwürdigkeit unserer geistigen Existenz und es ist die Unsicherheit unserer seelischen Verwirrung, die ihn [den Realismus] aus der bloßen Wahrnehmung des Objektiven ins Magische erhebt.' Solche Maximen halten einer kritischen Analyse nicht stand, sie verachten den Intellekt und knüpfen an den Sturm-und-Drang-Rausch der Jugendbewegung und des Expressionismus an. Richters Suche nach neuen Ausdrucksmitteln ist ganz dem deutschen Irrationalismus verpflichtet: 'Das Erlebnis wird dem Nurwissen, das Leben der Reflexion, die Literatur der Literaturgeschichte gegenüberstehen.'

Gewiß ist das hier aus dem *Ruf* Zusammengetragene etwas einseitig überspitzt. Dennoch können wir als Ergebnis dieser Betrachtungen zur 'Vor-Gruppen-Phase' festhalten: die neuen politischen und literarischen Versuche tasteten weitgehend im dunkeln. Der Wille zu einem Bruch mit der Vergangenheit war zwar unüberhörbar, doch brach er sich an dem Unvermögen, intellektuelle Positionen kritisch zu erfassen. Die fast ganz auf dem Kriegserlebnis fußenden Ausflüsse reichten zu einer fundierten sittlichen Gesinnung nicht aus, und schon gar nicht zur Kreierung einer neuen politisch-literarischen Öffentlichkeit, welche die Grundlage zu einer der Demokratie verpflichteten politischen Kultur hätte abgeben können.[16]

Mittels unseres imaginären Zeitraffers wollen wir nun den Blick um fünfzehn Jahre vorausschicken, auf die Zeit von Oktober 1962 bis

März 1963.[17] Selbst die flüchtigste Analyse läßt erkennen: die Gruppe 47 war jetzt nicht nur gewillt, sondern auch fähig, klare ethische Grundhaltungen zu entwickeln und als Gewissen der neuen Republik zu fungieren. Eine 'öffentlich räsonierende Gesellschaft'[18] war entstanden, die ansprechbar geworden war und die auf politische und gesellschaftliche Herausforderungen reagieren konnte. Die Reaktion auf die *Spiegel*-Affäre ließ erkennen, daß es zu einer 'Interessensolidarisierung'[19] der jungen literarischen Intelligenz gekommen war, die maßvoll und zielsicher eine Korrektur der politischen Kultur anstrebte. Selbst der ansonsten eher pessimistische Jaspers bescheinigte den Intellektuellen 'Realitätssinn'.[20] Die von zahlreichen Schriftstellern der gerade in Berlin tagenden Gruppe unterschriebene Resolution war maßvoll, aber treffsicher und erstaunlich frei von emotionaler Aufgeregtheit.[21] Ganz bewußt wurde an Traditionen der Intellektuellen in der Weimarer Republik angeknüpft.[22] Die Feststellung, daß eine Aufklärung der Öffentlichkeit wichtiger sei als eine Bewahrung militärischer Geheimnisse, führte zu dem Skandal um Josef Hermann Dufhues, den Geschäftsführenden Vorsitzenden der CDU. Dieser hatte 'vor Journalisten seine [...] geheime Sorge über den Einfluß der Gruppe 47 nicht nur im kulturellen, sondern auch im politischen Bereich geäußert. Er nannte sie eine geheime Reichsschrifttumskammer'.[23] Das Echo auf Dufhues' Attacke ging weit über die literarische Öffentlichkeit hinaus. Bruno Friedrich beschuldigte Dufhues im *Vorwärts*, die Literaten zu 'literarischen Gesinnungsnazis' der deutschen Nachkriegsrepublik zu machen.[24] Dufhues versuchte die Affäre auszusitzen und veranlaßte, als Verwaltungsratsvorsitzender des WDR, die Entlassung Wolfdietrich Schnurres aus dieser Anstalt. Darüber hinaus inszenierte er hinterhältige Angriffe auf die Fernsehsendung *Panorama*.

Dufhues' böses Wort von der 'Reichsschrifttumskammer' richtete sich gegen ein 'kollektives Auftreten' von mit der 'Gruppe' assoziierten Schriftstellern, das zu einem 'regulierten und regulierenden Meinungsmonopol [...] führen kann.'[25] Das Zitat beweist, daß immerhin die Rechte eine gewisse Gruppendynamik zur Kenntnis nahm. Vorbereitet wurde diese Ansicht durch Polemiken rechter Literaturpäpste wie Friedrich Sieburg (1952), Günter Blöcker (1959) und Rudolf Krämer-Badoni (1961/2).[26] Letzterer bezichtigte die Gruppe nicht nur der 'Gesinnungsgemeinschaft', sondern verwies auch auf 'prinzipienlose Cliquenbildung' und ein 'rein kommerziell gerichtetes demagogisches

Managertum', dessen 'Helfer und Gefolgsleute [...] vielfach in den Redaktionen der Zeitungen und Rundfunkanstalten' sitzen (Lettau, S.292). Man sieht, auch hier verdankt eine literarische Gruppe ihre Eigendynamik vor allem ihren Opponenten; — der 'Gruppenchef' Richter hat sich stets geweigert, Gruppentage als mehr denn 'Redaktionssitzungen' zu bezeichnen, eingedenk der frühen Ängste vor dem Kollektiv.

Die Affäre Dufhues ist hinlänglich bekannt, sie gehört zu den zahlreichen Skandalen, in die sich der CDU-Staat Adenauers gegen seine Intellektuellen verwickelte. Lohnender ist ein Hinweis auf die Reaktion wichtiger Printmedien vom März 1963, als die Affäre ihrem Höhepunkt zusteuerte.[27] Eine solche Lektüre gibt Einblick in das politisch-geistige Klima jener Zeit und schafft — im hermeneutischen Sinn — einen Erfahrungshorizont, von dem aus der Öffentlichkeitscharakter der Gruppe beurteilt werden kann. Das kulturelle Klima war damals vom Kalten Krieg stark geprägt: die Kuba-Krise war soeben beendet worden, und linke Intellektuelle befanden sich in der Defensive. Eine Aufführung von Brechts *Furcht und Elend des Dritten Reiches* war abgesagt worden, die Fernsehaufführung des *Galilei* wurde als Skandal empfunden. Der Rezensent einer Taschenbuchausgabe der Briefe von Karl Marx schloß mit den Worten: 'Ablehnung und Unkenntnis des Werkes von Karl Marx hat die Bundesrepublik notdürftig getarnt als Ablehnung des Kommunismus, fast unverändert aus dem Erbe Hitlers übernommen'.[28] CSU-Innenminister Höcherl suchte die *Spiegel*-Affäre zu verharmlosen und blieb bei seinem Treuebekenntnis zu Strauß. Hochhuths *Stellvertreter* hatte soeben seine Premiere erfahren, und *Die Zeit* widmete dem Stück ein Dossier, in dem Kritiker verschiedenster Richtungen zu Wort kamen (15.3.1963, S.9f.). Die Stadt Wiesbaden aber lehnte die Benennung einer Straße nach Kurt Tucholsky ab.

Die Resonanz zum Dufhues-Skandal war groß: Dufhues' Briefwechsel mit Richter wurde abgedruckt (ebd. S.12), Gräfin Dönhoff veröffentlichte einen Leitartikel auf Seite eins, in dem sie die Presse und die Systemkritiker vor dem Vorwurf in Schutz nahm, das eigene Netz zu beschmutzen. Sie zitierte den Juristen Ludwig Raiser, Mitglied der Tübinger Acht, der den 'Zustand allgemeiner Unwahrhaftigkeit, Verflachung und Verspießerung' beklagte, in welchem der Geist nicht mehr angeregt werde. Sein Kollege Fabian von Schlabrenndorff schrieb einen Beitrag zum Thema 'Landesverrat', in welchem er sich schützend vor die Presse stellte, die in einer Demokratie 'den Bruch des Grundgesetzes oder der Verfassung eines Landes abwehrt'.[29] Das Thema 'Nestbeschmutzung' wurde auch vom Rat der Evangelischen Kirche diskutiert. Auf die in Frankfurt anstehenden Auschwitz-Prozesse wurde hingewiesen, die noch immer ausstehende Trauerarbeit müsse als Säuberung 'eines schwer beschmutzten Nestes' verstanden werden.[30]

Das neue Interesse an politischer Öffentlichkeit jener Jahre beweist auch die Habilitationsschrift von Jürgen Habermas, *Strukturwandel der Öffentlichkeit*, in der Öffentlichkeit allerdings als rein historische Kategorie verstanden wird, die ursächlich mit der europäischen Aufklärung in Verbindung stehe (S.7). Die heutige Forschung faßt den Begriff Öffentlichkeit etwas weiter als 'das unbewußte Bestreben von in einem Verband lebenden Menschen, zu einem gemeinsamen Urteil zu gelangen, zu einer Übereinstimmung, wie sie erforderlich ist, um handeln und wenn notwendig entscheiden zu können'.[31] Eine solche Definition basiert nicht auf feststehenden Normen, sondern auf ungeschriebenen Gesetzen, die sich mit der Zeit sehr wohl auch ändern können. Anders formuliert: Öffentlichkeit und Gesinnung sind wesensverwandt, sie wirken aufeinander ein und bestimmen sich gegenseitig. Die von Habermas proklamierte Suche nach 'der Kraft des besseren Arguments' (S.73) muß neu definiert werden: 'besser' ist kein feststehender Begriff mehr, sondern ist — im weitesten Sinne — der Mode unterworfen. Der Begriff Öffentlichkeit sollte auch nicht primär auf die Politik bezogen werden, noch sollte man der politischen eine literarische Öffentlichkeit entgegensetzen.[32] Und auch Politik ist ja ein Begriff, der sich nicht auf Regierungsgeschäfte einengen läßt, sondern der fast alle Dimensionen unseres Lebens berührt.

Es ist jetzt an der Zeit zu fragen, inwiefern die Gruppe an der Entwicklung einer bundesrepublikanischen Öffentlichkeit mitwirken konnte. Nicolaus Sombart glaubte bereits 1947, die Schaffung von Öffentlichkeit sei ein unabdingbares Ziel der neuen Literatur, nur so lasse sich schreibend die Gesellschaft verändern.[33] Sombart spricht auch für Richter selbst, der allerdings pessimistischer war und glaubte, die Intellektuellen hätten sich aus geistiger Ohnmacht in die Literatur abdrängen lassen, es sei ihnen nicht gelungen, politisch auf ihre Gesellschaft Einfluß zu nehmen.[34] Aus heutiger Sicht gesehen waren die Ambitionen von Sombart und Richter zu hoch angesetzt; es wäre vermessen zu glauben, eine Gruppe von Literaten könne von sich aus eine neue Öffentlichkeit schaffen. Stattdessen sollte man den langwierigen und vielschichtigen Prozeß der Wandlung von Öffentlichkeit als dialogischen Prozeß begreifen: erst in der kritischen Auseinandersetzung mit dem Adenauerstaat und der etablierten Mittelstandsgesellschaft konnte eine der Demokratie verpflichtete Öffentlichkeit entstehen. Die Literaten hatten daran zwar einen festen, gleichwohl aber doch bescheidenen Anteil. Dies bedeutet weder, daß man Günter Eichs pessimistische Auffassung teilen muß, der Dichtung als Gegnerschaft begriff, als Don Quichotterie und der sich 'auf verlorenem Posten' als 'Gegner der Macht aus Instinkt' sah.[35] Noch bedeutet es, daß man Johannes R. Becher und anderen DDR-Literaten zustimmen muß, die glaubten, die 'tragische Gegensätzlichkeit von Geist und Macht' gehe in ihrem Lande einer Lösung entgegen.[36] Kein Wunder, daß von dieser Warte aus gesehen die Literatur der Gruppe 47 als dekadent und modernistisch, das heißt als gesinnungslos gebrandmarkt wurde,[37] sodaß Alexander Abusch noch 1966 behaupten konnte, die nonkonformistischen Dichter Westdeutschlands wollten die 'Einheit von Geist und Macht' zerstören.[38]

Sowohl an der west- wie auch an der ostdeutschen Argumentation erkennen wir den Rückgriff in eine deutsche Vergangenheit, in der Geist und Macht als Antipoden verstanden wurden, besonders deutlich formuliert bei den Gebrüdern Mann.[39] Auch in den Äußerungen zum Dufhues-Skandal wird dieser Gegensatz angesprochen, so in Ralf Dahrendorfs *Zeit*-Artikel 'Der Intellektuelle und die Gesellschaft'.[40] Dahrendorf sieht den Intellektuellen in der Rolle des Hofnarren, ja, seine Aufgabe bestehe gerade darin, aus der Rolle zu fallen, er sei das 'unentbehrliche Korrektiv der Irrtümer absolutistischer Herren', die auch in demokratischen Gesellschaften ihre unentbehrliche Funktion hätten. Es entbehrt nicht einer gewissen Komik, daß sich Dahrendorf ausgerechnet auf Bismarck beruft, auch sonst verharrt er in einer vordemokratischen Position, vergleichbar derjenigen von Max Weber, wenn er meint, dem Intellektuellen fehle 'die gewichtige Ankerstelle der Verantwortung'. Auch heute feiert die 'Macht-Geist'-Antinomie wieder fröhliche Urständ, nicht nur im Zusammenhang mit dem zur Zeit der Vereinigung besonders heftigen deutsch-deutschen Literaturstreit, sondern auch in einer Rede von Walter Jens, dem Stammkritiker der Gruppe. Er geht ganz vom Geist aus und gibt der politischen Macht die Alleinschuld an Deutschlands Misere. Vergebens sucht er in der deutschen Geschichte das 'Kondominium von Politik und Poesie, von Sanssouci und Weimar', und er leitet aus diesem Fehlen Deutschlands Sonderstellung ab, eben jenes vielzitierte Defizit an Aufklärung.[41] Auch Hans Egon Holthusen hat der Gruppe ein falsches Verhältnis zur Macht vorgeworfen, das zu Nonkonformismus führe. Er vergleicht hier den Intellektuellen mit der Position einer 'Halbjungfrau in eroticis',[42] einer Position, die Holthusen als 'unappetitlich' empfindet. Man könnte dem hinzufügen, daß Appetit ja bekanntlich mit dem Essen kommt, dennoch macht sich Holthusen den Verdienst, darauf hinzuweisen, daß Geist nicht unbedingt gut und Macht nicht unbedingt schlecht zu sein braucht.

Es ließe sich zeigen, daß auch in Deutschland — zumindest in der Philosophie Hegels — eine Synthese von Geist und Macht möglich war und daß hierbei der Begriff 'Gesinnung', wenn auch negativ als das Unwirkliche, eine wichtige Rolle gespielt hat.[43] Dennoch empfiehlt es sich, die spezifisch deutsche Variante von Macht und Geist durch das Begriffspaar 'öffentlich' und 'privat' zu ersetzen und sich unter diesen Vorzeichen auf die Rolle der Literatur in der Öffentlichkeit zu besinnen. Daß Literatur und Literaten nicht immer öffentlich zu sein brauchen und daß die Freiheit der Ironie aus dem Privaten schöpft, hatte bereits Auden in seiner Zueignung zu Stephen Spender erkannt:

> Private faces in public places
>
> Are wiser and nicer
>
> Than public faces in private places.[44]

Richard Rorty hat kürzlich in einem *Zeit*-Interview Interessantes zu diesem Themenkreis verlauten lassen: in deutlicher Distanzierung zu post-modernen Positionen à la Foucault und Derrida rechtfertigt er den Versuch linker Intellektueller in den USA, Politik vor allem von einem kulturellen Blickwinkel aus zu treiben. Rorty versucht die Idee des Fortschritts von jener der Wahrheit abzukoppeln, dabei den Verlust intellektueller geistiger Souveränität hinnehmend. Obgleich er auf jeglichen Anspruch von universeller Wahrheit verzichtet, räumt er dennoch den Künsten ein eminent öffentliches Interesse ein. Gleichzeitig besteht er aber darauf, daß auch die Kunst eine private Sphäre braucht, eine Sphäre, die für rein politische Erwägungen irrelevant ist.[45] In letzterer Hinsicht könnte man Rorty vielleicht etwas korrigieren, vor allem, wenn man den Begriff 'Öffentlichkeit' etwas weiter faßt, als dies noch bei Habermas geschieht: Kunst, und insbesondere Literatur, kann auch abseits von Politik wesentlich zur Entwicklung einer demokratischen Öffentlichkeit beitragen.

Hiermit wollen wir ein letztes Mal zur Gruppe 47 zurückkehren, und zwar ganz spezifisch zu den späten fünfziger Jahren, als die Literaten sich scheinbar aus der Politik zurückgezogen hatten. Wenn man das politische Engagement betrachtet, welches Gruppenmitglieder seit der *Spiegel*-Affäre an den Tag gelegt haben, so scheint der von der Forschung auch heute noch vielfach erhobene Vorwurf politischer Nonkonformität revisionsbedürftig.[46] Wiederum mag Günter Eich als Beispiel gelten. Er behauptete, Gedichte zu schreiben, um sich 'in der Wirklichkeit zu orientieren'. Eich sucht ausdrücklich nach einer neuen Wirklichkeit, 'in der das Wort und das Ding zusammenfallen'. Nur so, durch eine adäquate Übersetzung der Dinge in Sprache, hofft er 'den höchsten Grad von Wirklichkeit' zu erreichen.[47] Mit diesem Ziel wendet sich Eich von der existentialistischen, auf dem persönlichen Erlebnis basierenden Position der Frühphase ab und sucht nach Bezugspunkten, er selbst spricht von 'trigonometrischen Punkten' (Ebd.), die als Voraussetzung für Kommunikation im weitesten Sinne begriffen werden und damit, wie indirekt auch immer, an einer Werteskala bauen, der sich auch die Politik nicht entziehen kann. Heinz Ludwig Arnold kommt daher auch zu dem Schluß, daß die Gruppe mittelbar, 'gerade durch die Beschränkung auf die genaue Darstellung dessen, was ist', das politische Klima in der Bundesrepublik verändert habe (Arnold, S.144).

Durch die Vermittlung einer genauen Sprache ergab sich auch eine genaue Sichtweise und eine erstmals wirklich ernst zu nehmende Trauerarbeit, wie sie dann am spektakulärsten in Günter Grass' *Blechtrommel* zum Vorschein kam, einem Buch, das vor allem durch sprachliche Genauigkeit und einen neuen Blickwinkel zur 'Ästhetisierung der Politik'[48] beigetragen hat. Durch ihr eigentliches Metier, die Schaffung von Wirklichkeit durch Sprache, haben die Schriftsteller im Umkreis der Gruppe an der Bildung einer öffentlichen Meinung maßgeblich mitgewirkt: sie haben Betroffenheit geschaffen und Unsicherheit insinuiert und haben dadurch die impenetrabel gewordenen Gefüge in Politik und Gesellschaft neu geöffnet, so daß jetzt auch weitere Teile der Öffentlichkeit Fragen stellen konnten, die den Sinn dieser Gesellschaft und ihrer Werteskala aufs Korn zu nehmen gewillt waren.

Die weitere Politisierung, sowohl der Öffentlichkeit als auch der Literatur, zu Ende der sechziger Jahre ist dann vielleicht auch mit schuld am Ende der Gruppe. Gewiß, keine literarische Gruppe, kein Salon, keine Sprachgesellschaft hat sich je über eine wesentlich längere Zeitspanne erhalten können; andererseits sind die Verlautbarungen, die zum Zeitpunkt des Endes der Gruppe grassierten, ein Indiz dafür, daß eine Aufgabe des Privaten und ein völliges Aufgehen im Öffentlichen zum Tod von Literatur beitragen können. Ich denke hier sowohl an Handkes Vorwurf der 'Beschreibungsimpotenz' wie auch, in einem weiteren Zusammenhang, an Enzensbergers Formel vom Tod der Literatur und an Leslie Fiedlers epochemachende Freiburger Rede.[49] Aber diese Überlegungen sprengen bereits unser Thema. Im Gegensatz zu der Lumpensammlergesellschaft ist es für Konferenzteilnehmer (und Leser!) wichtiger, daß man pünktlich zum Schluß kommt, ob man den Bestimmungsort erreicht hat oder nicht, ist dann eine andere Frage.

Fußnoten

[1] Vgl. Immanuel Kant, *Grundlagen zur Metaphysik der Sitten. I*, in: *Werke* (Berlin: Berliner Akademie der Wissenschaften, 1911), Bd.4, S.393.

[2] Hans Joachim Hahn, '"Es geht nicht um Literatur": Some Observations on the 1990 "Literaturstreit" and its Recent Anti-Intellectual Implications', *GLL*, 50 (1997), 65-81, insbesondere 75ff.

[3] Eberhard Lämmert, 'Einleitung', in: Justus Fechter, Eberhard Lämmert, Jürgen Schutte (Hrsg.), *Die Gruppe 47 in der Geschichte der BRD* (Würzburg: Könighausen & Neumann, 1991), S.4.

[4] L.W. Schoener, 'Geschichtsbetrachtung', *Der Ruf — Blätter für deutsche Kriegsgefangene*, 15.10.1945, 1.

[5] *Der Ruf*, 1: 8 (1. 12.1946), S1.

[6] *Der Ruf*, 1: 11 (15.1.1947), 1.

[7] Vgl. Heinz Ludwig Arnold (Hrsg.), *Die Gruppe 47. Ein kritischer Grundriß*, 2. Aufl. (München: text + kritik, 1987), 18 (Weitere Hinweise auf diesen Band befinden sich im Text unter Arnold); Hans Werner Richter, 'Wie entstand und was war die Gruppe 47?', in: Hans A. Neunzig (Hrsg.), *Hans Werner Richter und die Gruppe 47* (München: nymphenburger, 1979), S.41-74.

[8] Vgl. Hannah Arendt, 'Organisierte Schuld', *Die Wandlung*, 4 (1946), 337-44, erstmals veröffentlicht auf englisch als 'Organised Guilt", *Jewish Frontier*, 12 (Spring 1945). Als eine Art Antwort hierzu: Karl Jaspers, *Die Schuldfrage. Ein Beitrag zur deutschen Frage* (Zürich: Artemis, 1947).

[9] *Der Ruf*, 1: 1 (15.8.1946), S.1.

[10] Alfred Andersch, 'Jean Anouilhs Antigone, ein Drama der Jugend', *Der Ruf*, 1: 2, (1.9.1946), 13.

11 [Gustav René Hocke], 'Die inneren Mächte', *Der Ruf — Blätter für deutsche Kriegsgefangene*, 1.3.1945, 1.

12 [Hocke], 'Rettung des Abendlandes', *Der Ruf — Blätter für deutsche Kriegsgefangene*, 1.5.1945, 1.

13 Arthur Koestler, 'Die Gemeinschaft der Pessimisten', *Der Ruf*, 1: 1 (15.8.1946), 3.

14 Stephen Spender, 'Zerbrochene Brücken über den Rhein', *Der Ruf*, 1: 10 (1.1.1947), 6; auch in: Hans Schwab-Felisch (Hrsg.), *Der Ruf. Eine deutsche Nachkriegszeitschrift* (München: dtv, 1962), S.258-71.

15 Hans Werner Richter, 'Literatur im Interregnum", *Der Ruf*, 1: 15, (15.3.1947), 10f.

16 Gerade dies wurde aber von Richter, Arnold Bauer und anderen immer wieder betont, und auch Kritiker wie Arnold sind nicht frei davon. Vgl. Arnold, *Die Gruppe 47*, S.18. Außerdem: Friedhelm Kröll, *Die 'Gruppe 47'. Soziale Lage und gesellschaftliches Bewußtsein literarischer Intelligenz in der Bundesrepublik* (Stuttgart: Metzler, 1977).

17 Die Zeit zwischen 1958 und 1963 wird von Eberhard Falcke als 'Hochperiode' der Gruppe angesehen. ('Die Gruppe 47. Eine Agentur der literarischen Moderne', in: Rolf Grimminger, Jurij Murasov, Jörn Stückrath (Hrsg.), *Literarische Moderne. Europäische Literatur im 19. und 20. Jahrhundert* (Reinbek bei Hamburg: Rowohlt, 1995), S.565. Vgl. auch Arthur Nickel, *Hans Werner Richter — Ziehvater der Gruppe 47. Eine Analyse im Spiegel ausgewähler Zeitungs- und Zeitschriftenartikel* (Stuttgart: Heinz-Dieter Heinz, 1994), S.24.

18 Jürgen Habermas, *Strukturwandel der Öffentlichkeit*, 5. Aufl. (Neuwied und Berlin: Luchterhand, 1971), S.70. Weitere Hinweise auf dieses Werk befinden sich im Text unter Habermas.

19 Lämmert, 'Einleitung', in: Fetscher u.a., *Die Gruppe 47*, S.4.

20 Karl Jaspers, *Wohin treibt die Bundesrepublik?* (München und Zürich: Piper, 1988), S.181.

21 'Erklärung zur Spiegelaffäre', *Frankfurter Rundschau*, 29.10.1962, wiederabgedruckt in: Reinhard Lettau (Hrsg.), *Die Gruppe 47. Bericht, Kritik, Polemik. Ein Handbuch* (Neuwied und Berlin: Luchterhand, 1967), S.458f. Weitere Hinweise auf diesen Band befinden sich im Text unter Lettau.

22 Vor allem an Carl von Ossietzky, der im Weltbühnenprozeß wegen 'Verrat militärischer Geheimnisse' im März 1929 zu 18 Monaten Gefängnis verurteilt wurde.

23 *Frankfurter Allgemeine Zeitung*, 21,1.1963, zitiert nach Lettau, *Handbuch*, S.504.

24 Bruno Friedrich, 'Wie die Atmosphäre vergiftet werden kann', *Vorwärts*, 30.1.1963, zitiert nach Lettau, *Handbuch*, S.504.

25 Antwort Josef Hermann Dufhues' an Richter: 'Sie konnten zueinander nicht kommen', *Die Zeit*, 15.3.1963, S.12.

[26] Die Polemiken sind teilweise abgedruckt in: Lettau, *Handbuch,* und zwar zu Sieburg S.336, zu Krämer-Badoni und Blöcker S.292. Vgl. außerdem Sieburg, 'Kriechende Literatur', *Die Zeit,* 14.8.1952, S.3.

[27] Untersucht wurden *Die Zeit,* 10-13, 8.-29.3.1963, *Die Welt,* 14.2.1963, die *Süddeutsche Zeitung,* 17.2.1963 und die *Frankfurter Allgemeine Zeitung,* 21.1.1963.

[28] Walter Boehlich, 'Verteidigung des Wolfes gegen das Schaf', *Die Zeit,* 10/8.3.1963, S.17.

[29] Fabian von Schlabrenndorff, 'Kritik ist nicht Landesverrat. Die Normen unseres Strafrechts sind fragwürdig", *Die Zeit,* 22.3.1963, S.4.

[30] 'Die protestantische Kirche mahnt', *Die Zeit,* 22.3.1963, S.4.

[31] Elisabeth Noelle-Neumann, Winfried Schulz, Jürgen Wilke (Hrsg.), *Fischer Lexikon Publizistik, Massenkommunikation* (Frankfurt a. M.: Fischer, 1989), S.25.

[32] Habermas (*Strukurwandel,* S.69-76) unterscheidet zwischen literarischer und politischer Öffentlichkeit.

[33] Nicolaus Sombart, 'Publikation und Öffentlichkeit", *Der Skorpion,* 1:, 1 (1.1.1948), 16-18. Vgl. auch Hans Werner Richter, *Briefe an einen jungen Sozialisten* (Hamburg: Hoffmann & Campe, 1974), S.113. Zitiert nach Arnold, *Die Gruppe 47,* S.265.

[34] Hans Werner Richter (Hrsg.), *Almanach der Gruppe 47* (Reinbek bei Hamburg: Rowohlt, 1964), S.12.

[35] Günter Eich, 'Rede zur Verleihung des Georg Büchner Preises' [1959], in: *Gesammelte Werke,* hrsg v. H.F. Schlafroth (Frankfurt a. M.: Suhrkamp, 1973), Bd.4, S.455

[36] Zitiert nach Dennis Tate und Axel Goodbody (Hrsg.), *Geist und Macht. Writers and the State in the GDR, German Monitor 29* (Amsterdam and Atlanta GA.: Rodopi, 1992), preface.

[37] Einer der wenigen Angriffe auf die Gruppe von DDR-Ideologen kam von Kurt Hager anläßlich einer Rede an das Politbüro des Zentralkomitees und des Präsidiums des Ministerrats am 25. März 1963, abgedruckt in *Neues Deutschland,* 30.3.1963, in Auszügen wiederabgedruckt in: Elimar Schubbe (Hrsg.), *Dokumente zur Kunst-, Literatur- und Kulturpolitik der SED. Band 1 (1949-70)* (Stuttgart: Seewald, 1972), S.859-79, insbesondere S.875.

[38] Alexander Abusch, 'Der Sinn unserer Diskussion über Fragen der Kunst und Literatur' [24.3.1966], in: Schubbe, *Dokumente,* S.1187-96. Vgl auch Nickel, *Hans Werner Richter, Ziehvater,* S.220, der seit Dezember 1965 eine ablehnende Haltung unter Politikern und Ideologen der Gruppe gegenüber nachweist.

[39] Die antithetische Haltung von 'Geist und Macht' spiegelte sich bereits in einem der ersten Aufsatzfragmente bei Thomas Mann ('Geist und Kunst' [1910]), sie wurde ein zentrales Thema in der Auseinandersetzung mit Bruder Heinrich, ('Geist und Tat' (1910) und Zola (1914)), sie entwickelte sich weiter bis zum *Doktor Faustus* bzw. bei Heinrich bis zu dessen *Henri Quatre.*

[40] Ralf Dahrendorf, 'Der Intellektuelle und die Gesellschaft', *Die Zeit*, 29.3.1963, S.8.

[41] Walter Jens, 'Geist und Macht', in: W. Jens und W. Graf Vitzthum, *Dichter und Staat. Über Geist und Macht in Deutschland* (Berlin und New York: de Gruyter, 1991), S.69.

[42] Hans Egon Holthusen, 'Die literarische Opposition', *Süddeutsche Zeitung*, 26.11.1960, abgedruckt in: Lettau, *Handbuch*, S.489.

[43] G.W.F. Hegel, *Phänomenologie des Geistes*, 6. Aufl. (Hamburg: Felix Meiner, 1952), Bd.5, vor allem S.333 und S.336.

[44] W. H. Auden, *The Orators* (London: Faber and Faber, 1932), Zueignung an Stephen Spender. Das Zitat illustriert das Verhältnis des politisch weniger engagierten Auden zu dem weiter links und stark antifaschistisch eingestellten Spender.

[45] Richard Rorty, 'Zeitgespräch: Laßt uns das Thema wechseln. Der amerikanische Philosoph Richard Rorty über Wahrheit, Gerechtigkeit und die "kulturelle Linke"', *Die Zeit*, 30/18. Juli 1997, S.39f.

[46] Heinrich Böll erhob diesen Vorwurf bereits 1965 in dem Aufsatz 'Angst vor der Gruppe 47?', abgedruckt in: Lettau, *Handbuch*, S.389-400. Walter Hinderer erhob ähnliche Vorwürfe ('The Challenge of the Past: Turning Points in the Intellectual and Literary Reflections of West Germany, 1945-1985', in: Ernestine Schlant, J. Thomas Rimer (Hrsg.), *Legacies and Ambiguities. Postwar Fiction and Culture in West Germany and Japan* (Baltimore and London: Johns Hopkins U.P., 1988), S.83f. und S.88. Frank Trommler hingegen spricht von 'nachgeholter Résistance', er versteht gerade die politische Enthaltsamkeit der fünfziger Jahre als Ansatzpunkt zur Entwicklung einer paradigmatischen öffentlichen Funktion. ('Die nachgeholte Résistance. Politik und Gruppenethos im historischen Zusammenhang', in: Fetscher u.a., *Die Gruppe 47*, S.10-22.)

[47] Eich, 'Der Schriftsteller vor der Realität' [1956], *Gesammelte Werke*, Bd.4, S.441.

[48] Walter Benjamin, 'Das Kunstwerk im Zeitalter seiner Reproduzierbarkeit' in: Theodor W. Adorno, Gershom Scholem (Hrsg.), *Gesammelte Schriften*, Bd.1.2, hrsg v. Rolf Tiedemanns und Hermann Schweppenhäuser (Frankfurt a. M.: Suhrkamp, 1974), S.469.

[49] Zu Handkes Intervention auf dem Treffen in Princeton s.: Walter Höllerer, 'Fikten, Fakten oder über die Kunst, daneben zu treffen', *Sprache im technischen Zeitalter*, Oktober-Dezember 1966; Enzensberger, 'Gemeinplätze, die neueste Literatur betreffend', *Kursbuch* 15 (1968), S.187-97, vor allem S.193; Leslie A. Fiedler, 'Cross the Border — Close the Gap: Postmodernism', deutscher Text in: Uwe Wittstock, *Roman oder Leben. Postmoderne in der deutschen Literatur* (Leipzig: Reclam, 1994), S.14-40.

INDEX OF CONTRIBUTORS

Sabine Cofalla is a journalist currently working in publishing. Her research interests are post-1945 German literature and the history and development of media. She gained her doctorate for her edition of Hans Werner Richter's letters and for the volume *Der "soziale" Sinn Hans Werner Richters. Zur Korrespondenz des Leiters der Gruppe 47* (1997). She is also contributing to a volume that is due to appear to coincide with Richter's ninetieth birthday.

Clare Flanagan is Lecturer in German at the University of Bristol. Her research interests include cultural and political debate between 1945 and 1949 and writers and political theory since 1989. Her book *The Rethinking of Germany: political-cultural journals 1945-1949* is due to be published by the Mellen Press in 1999.

Frank Finlay is Senior Lecturer in German Studies at the University of Bradford. He is the author of a number of articles on German literature, culture and aesthetics. His work on Böll dates back to his time as a researcher in the Böll archives in Cologne and includes the monograph *On the Rationality of Poetry: Heinrich Böll's Aesthetic Thinking* (1996). He is co-editor of the new 27-volume edition of the writer's complete works.

Robert Gillett is Lecturer in German at Queen Mary and Westfield College, University of London. His eclectic research interests include East and West German, Austrian and Swiss authors of the nineteenth and twentieth centuries, as well as gender studies and film. He has recently published on Lilian Faschinger, Max Frisch and Hubert Fichte.

Hans Hahn is Head of the German Department at Oxford Brookes University. His research interests are nineteenth- and twentieth-century literature and thought, in particular the role of the intellectual, on which he has published widely. He is the author of *German Thought and Culture* (1995) and of *German Education and Society* (1998).

Katrin Kohl is Fellow and Tutor in German at Jesus College and Faculty Lecturer in German at the University of Oxford. Among her research interests are German poetry, particularly F. G. Klopstock, free verse, rhetoric and literature and the sublime. Recent publications include articles on Klopstock, Rilke, Bachmann and Lavant. She is co-editor of the series *Oxford Studies in Modern European Literature, Film and Culture*.

Stuart Parkes is Reader in German Literature and Society at the University of Sunderland. He is the co-editor of five volumes on contemporary Germany literature, most recently *Whose Story? — Continuities in Contemporary German-language Literature*. His most recent book is *Understanding Contemporary Germany* and he is a contributor to *Contemporary Germany*, which is due to appear in 1999.

Helmut Peitsch is Professor of European Studies at the University of Wales, Cardiff. He studied at the Free University of Berlin, writing his doctorate on Georg Forster and his *Habilitation* on West German autobiographical literature. His prolific publications cover the period of German literature from the late eighteenth century to the present day.

Julian Preece is Lecturer in German at the University of Kent, Canterbury. He has co-edited, with Stuart Parkes and Arthur Williams, two books on contemporary German literature, as well as publishing widely on a variety of East and West German writers. In 2000 he will be publishing *Günter Grass and the Germans: Literature, History and Politics*.

Esther V. Schneider-Handschin works in Adult Education in Basle and as a Research Associate of the University of Birmingham. Her main research interests include the literature of the Weimar Republic, Swiss literature and post-war literature. She is currently working on a study of the reception of Otto Weininger. She has published widely on numerous twentieth-century authors, including Robert Musil, Thomas Mann, Jakob Wassermann and Elfriede Jelinek.

Jürgen Schutte is Professor within the Fachbereich Germanistik at the Free University of Berlin. The main areas of his teaching and research include literary modernism, contemporary German literature and literary theory. Among his many publications are *Einführung in die*

Literaturinterpretation (1985) and *Dichter und Richter. Die Gruppe 47 und die deutsche Nachkriegsliteratur* (1988 as editor). He is currently working on an edition of the notebooks of Peter Weiss, about whom he published, with Gunilla Palmstierna-Weiss, *Peter Weiss. Leben und Werk* in 1991.

Johann Sonnleitner is Univ. Assistent at the Institut für Germanistik of the University of Vienna. His research interests encompass Austrian Literature from the eighteenth century to the present. In 1998 he published *Die Geschäfte des Herrn Robert Hohlbaum. Die Schriftstellerkarriere eines Österreichers in der Zwischenkriegszeit und im Dritten Reich.* He is editor and co-editor of five books on Austrian literature. He is currently working for his *Habilitation* on Viennese *Volkskomödie* between 1750 and 1850.

Stuart Taberner is Lecturer in German at the University of Bristol. His main research interests are Martin Walser, the New Right, Masculinity, post-1960 German cinema and the German novel. He has published articles on Grass, Walser and Johnson and is the author of *The Public and Private Faces of the Intellectual in the Work of Uwe Johnson, Günter Grass and Martin Walser 1965-1975* (1998).

Christina Ujma is Lecturer in German in the Department of European Studies at Loughborough University. Her major research interest is intellectual debates relating to Modernism and Marxism during the Weimar Republic. She has published on the works of Bloch and Benjamin, as well as on political zionism. She is the author of *Ernst Blochs Konstruktion der Moderne aus Messianismus und Marxismus* (1995).

Wilfried van der Will is Professor of Modern German Studies in the Department of German Studies at the University of Birmingham and Fellow in the Institute for German Studies at Birmingham. His research interests are modern German literature, culture, political culture and philosophy. His recent publications include contributions to *German Cultural Studies* (ed. Rob Burns, 1995) and he is the co-editor of *The Cambridge Companion to Modern German Studies* (1999).

Anthony Waine is Lecturer in German Studies at Lancaster University. His main research interests are the works of Rolf Dieter Brinkmann, Anna Seghers and Martin Walser, as well as the relationship between serious literature and popular culture. His recent publications include articles on Seghers and Walser, as well as on the dramas of Wolfgang Bauer.

John J. White is Professor of German and Comparative Literature at King's College, London. He is the author of *Mythology in the Modern Novel* (1971) and *Literary Futurism* (1990), and has co-edited volumes on Broch, Grass, Kafka, Mann, Musil, Stramm and Berlin in literature. He is currently writing a second monograph on Brecht and a critical survey of the German fiction of *Lebensraum*.

John Wieczorek is Lecturer in German Studies at the University of Reading. His major research interest is East German literature. His study of Johannes Bobrowski *Between Sarmatia and Socialism: the Life and Works of Johannes Bobrowski* is due to be published by Rodopi in 1999.

Rhys W. Williams is currently Professor of German and Pro-Vice-Chancellor at the University of Wales, Swansea. He has published on German Expressionism (Sternheim, Benn, Einstein, Kaiser and Toller) and on post-war literature (Andersch, Böll, Siegfried Lenz, Martin Walser). More recently he has been involved in editing the Contemporary German Writers series and has written articles for the volumes on Sarah Kirsch, Peter Schneider, Jurek Becker and Uwe Timm.

GÜNTER DE BRUYN
IN PERSPECTIVE

Ed. by Dennis Tate

Amsterdam/Atlanta, GA 1999. 234 pp.
(German Monitor 44)
ISBN: 90-420-0566-1   Bound Hfl. 120,-/US-$ 66.50
ISBN: 90-420-0556-4   Paper Hfl. 40,-/US-$ 22.-

Table of Contents: Dennis TATE: Changing Perspectives on Günter de Bruyn: An Introduction. Martin KANE: Ignore the Teller and read the Tale? A Fresh Look at Günter de Bruyn's *Der Hohlweg* in the Light of his Autobiographies. John J. WHITE: 'Denn rein psychologisch betrachtet (was allerdings immer gefährlich ist)...': Patterns of Self-Deception and Deceit in *Buridans Esel*. Nigel HARRIS: 'Noch im Untergang triumphiert die Liebe' - or does it? Günter de Bruyn's *Neuerzählung* of the Medieval Tristan Legend. York-Gothart MIX: Das Phantom der Wahrheit oder Was war und ist wirklich? Die Realität des Ministeriums für Staatssicherheit und die Erzählungen *Freiheitsberaubung* und *Märkische Forschungen*. Andy HOLLIS: Thirty Years of Anita Paschke: Günter de Bruyn's and Ulrich Plenzdorf's *Freiheitsberaubung*. Detlef GWOSC: Das raunende Unperfekt der Gesellschaft zur Sprache bringen: Günter de Bruyns Roman *Neue Herrlichkeit*. Lutz KUBE: *Mein Brandenburg*: Zur Konstruktion regionaler Identität in essayistischen Arbeiten Günter de Bruyns. J.H. REID: 'Das unerreichbare Vorbild': Günter de Bruyn und Heinrich Böll. Renate RECHTIEN: Gelebtes, erinnertes, erzähltes und erschriebenes Selbst: Günter de Bruyns *Zwischenbilanz* und Christa Wolfs *Kindheitsmuster*. Owen EVANS: 'Schlimmeres als geschah, hätte immer geschehen können': Günter de Bruyn and the GDR in *Vierzig Jahre*. Karin HIRDINA: Suchanzeige: Ironisches in der Autobiografie Günter de Bruyns. Chris LEWIS: Der verkaufte Schatten? Interview mit Günter de Bruyn am 27. September 1996. Notes on Contributors. Index.

Editions Rodopi B.V.

USA/Canada: 2015 South Park Place, Atlanta, GA 30339, Tel. (770) 933-0027, *Call toll-free* (U.S.only) 1-800-225-3998, Fax (770) 933-9644

All Other Countries: Tijnmuiden 7, 1046 AK Amsterdam, The Netherlands. Tel. + + 31 (0)20 6114821, Fax + + 31 (0)20 4472979
E-mail: orders-queries@rodopi.nl —— http://www.rodopi.nl

TRISTAN UND ISOLT IM SPÄTMITTELALTER

Vorträge eines interdisziplinären Symposiums vom 3. bis 8. Juni 1996 an der Justus-Liebig-Universität Gießen

Hrsg. von Xenja von Ertzdorff
unter redaktioneller Mitarbeit von Rudolf Schulz

Amsterdam/Atlanta, GA 1999. 590 pp.
(Chloe 29)
ISBN: 90-420-0605-6   Bound Hfl. 240,-/US-$ 133.-

Inhalt: Vorwort. Grußwort des Präsidenten der Justus-Liebig-Universität Gießen, Prof. Dr. Heinz Bauer. Norbert WERNER: Tristan-Darstellungen in der Kunst des Mittelalters. Jochem KÜPPERS: Zaubertränke, Liebe und Tod in der griechischen und römischen Literatur. Angelika HARTMANN: Das persische Epos *Wis und Ramin*. Rosemarie LÜHR: Tristan im Kymrischen. Xenja VON ERTZDORFF: Die Liebenden in den Romanen von Tristan und Isolt - Erzählstrukturen und literarische Individualität. Helmut BUSCH: Das Leiden an der Liebe in Gottfrieds Roman von Tristan und Isolt. Knut USENER: Verhinderte Liebschaft. Zur Ovidrezeption bei Gottfried von Straßburg. Lieselotte E. SAURMA-JELTSCH: Der Brüsseler *Tristan*: Ein mittelalterliches Haus- und Sachbuch. Klaus RIDDER: Liebestod und Selbstmord. Zur Sinnkonstitution im *Tristan*, im *Wilhelm von Orlens* und in *Partonopier und Meliur*. Rudolf VOSS: Die deutschen Tristan-Romane des Spätmittelalters - Variationen eines problematischen Themas. Ludger UDOLPH: Der alttschechische Roman von *Tristram a Izalda*. Geraldine BARNES: Tristan in late medieval Norse literature: saga and ballad. Heinz BERGNER: Die mittelenglischen Bearbeitungen des Tristanstoffes in *Sir Tristrem* und Sir Thomas Malorys *Morte Darthur*. Bart BESAMUSCA: Tristan und Isolt in den Niederlanden. Dietmar RIEGER: Tristans Wandlung. Zum altfranzösischen *Prosatristan* und seinen "auctores". Marie-José HEIJKANT: Tristan im Kampf mit dem Treulosen Ritter. Abenteuer, Gralssuche und Liebe in dem italienischen *Tristano Palatino*. Witold KOŚNY: Der weißrussische *Tristan*. Eliza MAŁEK: Why was the legend of Tristan and Isolde not translated in old Rus' and in Poland? Ulrich MÜLLER: Ein indischer Tristan: Der europäische Mythos von Tristan und Isolde im modernen anglo-indischen Roman: Raja Rao *The Serpent and the Rope* (1960). Helmut MARTIN: Der traditionelle Roman in China und Japan. Ansätze zu einem Vergleich mit dem Tristanroman Gottfrieds von Straßburg. Verzeichnis der Referentinnen und Referenten. Register: Verzeichnis der erwähnten Personen und Werke Zusammengestellt von Rudolf Schulz.

Editions Rodopi B.V.

USA/Canada: 2015 South Park Place, Atlanta, GA 30339, Tel. (770) 933-0027, *Call toll-free* (U.S.only) 1-800-225-3998, Fax (770) 933-9644

All Other Countries: Tijnmuiden 7, 1046 AK Amsterdam, The Netherlands. Tel. + + 31 (0)20 6114821, Fax + + 31 (0)20 4472979
E-mail: orders-queries@rodopi.nl —— http://www.rodopi.nl

TEXT AND VISUALITY: WORD & IMAGE INTERACTIONS III

Ed. by Martin Heusser, Michèle Hannoosh, Charlotte Schoell-

Glass and David Scott
Amsterdam/Atlanta, GA 1999. 321 pp.
(Textxet 22)
ISBN: 90-420-0736-2   Bound Hfl. 160,-/US-$ 88.50
ISBN: 90-420-0726-5   Paper Hfl. 50,-/US-$ 27.50

Table of Contents: THEORETICAL CONSIDERATIONS. Mieke BAL: Basic Instincts and Their Discontents. Hanjo BERRESSEM: One Surface Fits All: Texts, Images and the Topology of Hypermedia. Hugo CAVIOLA: The Rhetoric of Interdisciplinarity. Andrew ROTHWELL: Bernard Noël: Espace, Regard, Sens. Nigel SAINT: *Pour l'amour d'un plaisir sévère*: Following Louis Marin. Áron Kibédi VARGA: Entre le texte et l'image: une pragmatique des limites. Tamar YACOBI: The Ekphrastic Figure of Speech. PAINTINGS, PRINTS AND PHOTOGRAPHS. Leo H. HOEK: Le titre à l'oeuvre. Manet, modernisme et institutions. Shigemi INAGA: The Painter Who Disappeared in the Novel: Images of an Oriental Artist in European Literature. Debra KELLY: A Reading of the Structures of *La Guerre* (1916) by Pierre Albert-Birot. Laura MALOSETTI COSTA: Poetic Painting and Picturesque Poetry: Literature and Visual Arts in the Emergence of National Symbolic Repertoires in the River Plate Area. Jürgen MÜLLER: News from Plato's Cave: Jeff Wall's *A Sudden Gust of Wind* and *Dead Troops Talk*. Clara ORBAN: Bruised Words, Wounded Images, in Frida Kahlo. Véronique PLESCH: Pictorial *ars praedicandi* in Late Fifteenth-century Paintings. Ruth RENNIE: Visual Representations of Political Discourse: The Example of the French Communist Party Between the Wars. Charlotte SCHOELL-GLASS: *En grisaille* - Painting Difference. BOOKS, TYPOGRAPHY AND OTHER MEDIA. Francis EDELINE: Le Roi Arthur et la sémiotique visuelle. Eric T. HASKELL: IMAGINING the Text: Baudelaire's *Parfum Exotique*. Will HILL: The Digital Scriptorium. Towards a Pre-Gutenberg Perspective on Contemporary Typographic Practice. Renée RIESE HUBERT: From "Things as They Are" to What They Become: From Illustration to Bookwork. Yves JEANNERET: Matérialités de l'immatériel. Vers une sémiotique du multimédia. BEYOND MERE WORD AND IMAGE. Burratonie ABRIOUX: Ektopias: Two Landscapes of the Ideal. Penny FLORENCE: Touching Gender: The Word, the Image and the Tactile. Barbara Hepworth's "Stereognostic" Sculpture. Dario GAMBONI: Jasper Johns, Richard Hamilton et "le critique", 1959-1980. Kenneth G. HAY: Generic Specificity and the Problem of Translation in Galvano Della Volpe. John Dixon HUNT: Word & Image in the Garden.

Editions Rodopi B.V.

USA/Canada: 2015 South Park Place, Atlanta, GA 30339, Tel. (770) 933-0027, *Call toll-free* (U.S.only) 1-800-225-3998, Fax (770) 933-9644

All Other Countries: Tijnmuiden 7, 1046 AK Amsterdam, The Netherlands. Tel. + + 31 (0)20 6114821, Fax + + 31 (0)20 4472979
E-mail: orders-queries@rodopi.nl —— http://www.rodopi.nl

DEUTSCH UND ANDERE FREMDSPRACHEN - INTERNATIONAL

Länderberichte – Sprachenpolitische Analysen – Anregungen

Hrsg. von Albert Raasch

Amsterdam/Atlanta, GA 1999. 243 pp.
(Deutsch: Studien zum Sprachunterricht und zur interkulturellen Didaktik 3)
ISBN: 90-420-0445-2   Hfl. 75,-/US-$ 41.50

Sprachenpolitische Kenntnisse werden immer wichtiger: Welche Rolle spielen die Fremdsprachen heute in der Welt? Warum werden Fremdsprachen gelernt? In welcher Reihenfolge werden sie angeboten, welche werden überhaupt angeboten? Und welchen Status hat das Deutsche (als Fremdsprache) in dem Konzert der Sprachen? Bleibt neben Englisch noch Raum für andere Sprachen? Wie kann man Mehrsprachigkeit sicherstellen und Multikulturalität verwirklichen?
Sprachenpolitische Kenntnisse sind Voraussetzung für notwendiges sprachenpolitisches Handeln aller Spracheninteressierten.
Der vorliegende Band vermittelt Kenntnisse über die Situation in zahlreichen Ländern, von China über Tartarstan und Luxemburg bis Argentinien ("Länderberichte"); ein besonderen Schwerpunkt liegt auf der neuen Freihandelszone "Mercosur/Mercosul", die ähnlich wie das zusammenwachsende Europa spezifische sprachenpolitische Aspekte aufweist. Damit ergänzt diese Publikation den Band "Spachenpolitik Deutsch als Fremdsprache", der mit zahlreichen Länderberichten anläßlich der Internationalen Deutschlehrertagung in Amsterdam 1997 erschienen ist. "Deutsch und andere Fremdsprachen – international" ist aus den Beiträgen der Sektion 1 ("Sprachenpolitik") des Amsterdamer Kongresses hervorgegangen. Neben den Länderberichten enthält die vorliegende Veröffentlichung grundsätzliche Thesen zur Sprachenpolitik, die von anerkannten Experten zur Diskussion gestellt werden. Beide Bände zusammen bieten einen umfassenden aktuellen Überblick über die Sprachenpolitik in mehr als 40 Ländern aller Kontinente unter besonderer Berücksichtigung des Deutschen als Fremdsprache.

Editions Rodopi B.V.

USA/Canada: 2015 South Park Place, Atlanta, GA 30339, Tel. (770) 933-0027, *Call toll-free* (U.S.only) 1-800-225-3998, Fax (770) 933-9644

All Other Countries: Tijnmuiden 7, 1046 AK Amsterdam, The Netherlands. Tel. ++ 31 (0)20 6114821, Fax ++ 31 (0)20 4472979
E-mail: orders-queries@rodopi.nl —— http://www.rodopi.nl

WENDEZEICHEN?
NEUE SICHTWEISEN
AUF DIE LITERATUR DER DDR

Hrsg. von Roswitha Skare und Rainer B. Hoppe

Amsterdam/Atlanta, GA 1999. 243 pp. (Amsterdamer Beiträge zur neueren Germanistik 46)
ISBN: 90-420-0655-2   Bound Hfl. 110,-/US-$ 61.-
ISBN: 90-420-0645-5   Paper Hfl. 35,-/US-$ 19.-

Die Beiträger dieses Sammelbandes wollen die nach 1989 offensichtliche Verunsicherung des Forschungsfeldes DDR-Literatur produktiv überwinden. Vier Beiträge befassen sich mit Umgang, Stellenwert und zukünftiger Rolle von DDR-Literatur (Literaturgeschichtsschreibung und methodisch-theoretische Fragestellungen). Neben zwei fachübergreifenden Beiträgen zur DDR-Geschichtsschreibung und zum russischen Autor Wladimir Dudinzew suchen mehrere Beiträge Texten 'typischer' und 'untypischer' DDR-Autoren neue Sichtweisen abzugewinnen. Brigitte Reimanns *Franziska Linkerhand*, aber auch ihre frühen und eher vergessenen Texte, Johannes Bobrowskis Lyrik, Bertolt Brechts *Der kaukasische Kreidekreis*, Christoph Heins *Horns Ende* und Volker Brauns *Das Nichtgelebte* sind Gegenstand dieser Beiträge - auf das neues Leben blühe aus den Ruinen.

Editions Rodopi B.V.

USA/Canada: 2015 South Park Place, Atlanta, GA 30339, Tel. (770) 933-0027, *Call toll-free* (U.S.only) 1-800-225-3998, Fax (770) 933-9644

All Other Countries: Tijnmuiden 7, 1046 AK Amsterdam, The Netherlands. Tel. + + 31 (0)20 6114821, Fax + + 31 (0)20 4472979 *E-mail:* orders-queries@rodopi.nl —— http://www.rodopi.nl

KARL JASPERS -
Philosophy on the Way to "World Philosophy". Philosophie auf dem Weg zur "Weltphilosophie"

Eds./Hg. Leonard H. Ehrlich and Richard Wisser

Amsterdam/Atlanta, GA, Würzburg 1998. 366 pp.
ISBN: 90-420-0492-4   Hfl. 75,-/US-$ 41.50

Contents/Inhalt: Preface. Vorwort. Abbreviations/Siglen. I. Jaspers on World Philosophy and World History of Philosophy/Jaspers über Weltphilosophie und Weltgeschichte der Philosophie. II. Introduction/Einleitung. III. Legacy and Task. Vermächtnis und Aufgabe. IV. Dimensions of Communication/Räume der Kommunikation. V. Communicative World History of Philosophy/Kommunikative Weltgeschichte der Philosophie. VI. Communicative World Philosophy: East and West/Kommunikative Weltphilosophie: Ost und West. VII. Communicative World Philosophy: Freedom and Tolerance/Kommunikative Weltphilosophie: Freiheit und Toleranz. Appendix/Anhang.

Editions Rodopi B.V.
USA/Canada: 2015 South Park Place, Atlanta, GA 30339, Tel. (770) 933-0027, *Call toll-free* (U.S.only) 1-800-225-3998, Fax (770) 933-9644

All Other Countries: Tijnmuiden 7, 1046 AK Amsterdam, The Netherlands. Tel. ++ 31 (0)20 6114821, Fax ++ 31 (0)20 4472979
E-mail: orders-queries@rodopi.nl ---- http://www.rodopi.nl

EXPANDING EUROPEAN UNITY - CENTRAL AND EASTERN EUROPE

Ed. by László Marácz

Amsterdam/Atlanta, GA 1999. XVI,171 pp.
(Yearbook of European Studies/Annuaire d'Etudes
Europeennes 11)
ISBN: 90-420-0455-X   Hfl. 60,-/US-$ 33.-

Since the fall of the Berlin wall in 1989 the former Communist
countries of Central and Eastern Europe have been pushing for
a quick 'return to Europe'. The project of 'expanding
European unity' is in full progress, however, so far none of the
former Soviet bloc countries have been able to join the
European Union. Technical problems, related to financial
management and administrative matters, still have to be
overcome, but more fundamental issues are also at stake: what
are the borders of Central and Eastern Europe? And will the
eastward expansion of the European Union be conducted on
the basis of western images and stereotypes of 'the East'? This
volume examines the state of affairs after ten years of attempts
to further enlarge the Union. Written by authors from 'the
East' as well as 'the West' some of the articles focus on the
general issue of how to distinguish between Western, Central
and Eastern Europe, while others discuss the specific situation
of the countries that are closest to joining the European Union:
Poland, the Czech Republic and Hungary.

Editions Rodopi B.V.

USA/Canada: 2015 South Park Place, Atlanta, GA 30339, Tel. (770)
933-0027, *Call toll-free* (U.S.only) 1-800-225-3998, Fax (770) 933-9644

All Other Countries: Tijnmuiden 7, 1046 AK Amsterdam, The
Netherlands. Tel. + + 31 (0)20 6114821, Fax + + 31 (0)20 4472979
E-mail: orders-queries@rodopi.nl —— http://www.rodopi.nl

VIVAT HELVETIA
Die Herausforderung einer nationalen Identität

Hrsg. von Jattie Enklaar und Hans Ester

Amsterdam/Atlanta, GA 1998. 250 pp.
(Duitse Kroniek 48)
ISBN: 90-420-0674-9   Hfl. 75,-/US-$ 41.50

Die Frage nach der *nationalen Identität* bedeutet ein Nachdenken über geschichtliche Entstehungsbedingungen einer Nation und eine Neuorientierung in einer immer komplexer werdenden Gesellschaft der Gegenwart. Der Schutz, der eine "nationale Identität" — oft geprägt von Mythen — dem Kollektiv der Individuen, das wir "Staat" nennen, bietet, legt die Möglichkeiten einer Zukunft fest und kann sie einschränken. Auf der anderen Seite gibt es das Anti-Modell eines aufklärerischen Internationalismus, ein oft modisches Konzept, das die Nation als die Erfindung des Nationalismus definiert; es kann als realistische Alternative betrachtet, aber auch als Utopie in Frage gestellt werden.
Anlässlich des 150jährigen Bestehens der schweizerischen Bundesverfassung beschäftigen sich die Beiträge in diesem Band mit Fragen zu Kunst- und Kulturpolitik, Politik und Staatswesen, Geschichte, Sprache und Religion sowie mit der Darstellung der schweizerischen Wirklichkeit in literarischen Texten, mit dem Zweck, im Gedenkjahr 1998 ein Bild der heutigen Schweiz zu vermitteln, wobei besondere Aufmerksamkeit dem Übergang zu einem überstaatlichen Föderalismus gilt, der sich vor der Frage gestellt sieht, alte Mythen zu ersetzen oder umzudeuten. Dieser Prozess, der heutzutage in der Schweiz stattfindet und tief in die Geschichte des Staates zurückreicht, dankt seinen Erfolg der inneren Selbstbestimmung, deren Bedeutung für die Herausforderung einer eigenen Identität hier in thematisch unterschiedlichen Beiträgen dargelegt wird.

Editions Rodopi B.V.

USA/Canada: 2015 South Park Place, Atlanta, GA 30339, Tel. (770) 933-0027, *Call toll-free* (U.S.only) 1-800-225-3998, Fax (770) 933-9644

All Other Countries: Tijnmuiden 7, 1046 AK Amsterdam, The Netherlands. Tel. + + 31 (0)20 6114821, Fax + + 31 (0)20 4472979
E-mail: orders-queries@rodopi.nl —— http://www.rodopi.nl